Advance Praise

Look no further for a comprehensive account of Bangladesh's rapid structural transformation against 'the odds' from a disaster-prone agrarian nation wrecked by conflict, exploited and dominated by outside interests, to an industrializing and exceptional 'flying goose' whose poverty has dramatically declined. Responding to the singularity of previous attempts to explain this remarkable trajectory, *The Odds Revisited* develops a holistic method in political economy grounded in transformations to the rural material base, their repercussions, and their spatial and sectoral multipliers. In so doing, it covers a range of theoretical arguments, debates and contentions in social science, mobilizes rich empirical detail, spans a wide range of institutions and does not flinch from tackling the international relations of development or domestic authoritarianism and corruption. Dr Murshid's fine history of the present is an essential text, one relevant not just to economists of Bangladesh but also to scholars, whatever their parent discipline and their regional focus, concerned with the surmounting of rooted and intransigent development problems from the past and the prospects for resolving present and future ones.

– **Barbara Harriss-White**, University of Oxford

Bangladesh is widely seen as a success story in economic and social development, making significant progress both in increasing the living standards of its citizens and in social outcomes such as in family planning, health, primary education and women's empowerment. What explains these remarkable achievements, given the large disadvantages that Bangladesh faced at independence in 1971? K. A. S. Murshid provides an insightful account of the factors that contributed to Bangladesh's success, weaving a historical reading of the country's experience, with in-depth data analysis. The book is a must-read for scholars and practitioners interested in understanding how a poor developing country could surmount the numerous challenges it faced at the beginning of its development path.

– **Kunal Sen**, University of Manchester

Captures the development puzzle of Bangladesh through a comprehensive, jargon-free account of its political economy over the last 50 years of its liberation from a near standing start in 1971. While acknowledging ongoing problems of governance, democracy and inequality, it tracks a broadly supportive state facilitating both agricultural and industrial growth, especially in the garments sector, alongside remittances from overseas. It compares this dynamically changing country favorably with its South Asian neighbours, while looking to inspiration from East Asian trajectories. Not only an insightful 'must-read' about Bangladesh but also a model for analyzing lower middle-income societies needing to move their economies to the next level in pursuit of human and social needs. A well-evidenced, authoritative, interdisciplinary triumph which celebrates the agency of his people.

— **Geof Wood**, University of Bath

The Odds Revisited is an attempt to unravel Bangladesh's complex development story. The breadth, scope and analytical depth of the book provide the reader with an engaging, comprehensive treatment of a difficult journey. The book begins with the premise that interventions in food and family planning laid the foundation for future development, initially in social outcomes which subsequently prepared Bangladesh to tap into global opportunities in the form of export-led growth and remittance earnings. Where the book breaks new ground is in its reassessment of the social sector, as well as a fresh analysis of Bangladesh's industrialization experience that goes well beyond the RMG. The other important addition is its treatment of Dhaka's mega transformation. This is a comprehensive book to have on hand for occasional browsing, or serious diving into the subject, for development scholars and for anyone interested in Bangladesh and South Asia.

— **Muhammad Yunus**, founder, Grameen Bank

The Odds Revisited

This book looks at Bangladesh at and beyond its 50 years since its formation in 1971. A comprehensive, holistic narrative is constructed to track key development dynamics at the sectoral, sub-sectoral and macro levels. This much-needed exercise dispels the notion that the 'Bangladesh surprise' can be reduced to singular dimensions such as the trauma of the 1971 war or women's empowerment and micro-credit. The mixture of economic history, political economy, and institutional and actor analysis provide fresh insights to the themes addressed.

A well-argued case to view emerging Bangladesh as the newest member of the Flying Geese club, *The Odds Revisited* provides a detailed review of macro and sectoral developments over the last 50 years and provides new material and insights into the rise of Bangladesh's capitalist class, a socio-economic perspective of the role of Dhaka-based urbanization and the rise of a new middle class.

K. A. S. Murshid is a Bangladeshi development economist with a distinguished career in academia and research leadership. He has made seminal contributions to development literature, particularly on agrarian markets and rural development, and published extensively in development journals. He retired as the director general of the Bangladesh Institute of Development Studies in early 2021. He has conducted policy research on diverse subjects, including rural electrification, solar homes, informal finance, mobile financial systems, cross-border trade and transit, food policy, adolescent violence and youth unemployment.

SOUTH ASIA IN THE SOCIAL SCIENCES

South Asia has become a laboratory for devising new institutions and practices of modern social life. Forms of capitalist enterprise, providing welfare and social services, the public role of religion, the management of ethnic conflict, popular culture and mass democracy in the countries of the region have shown a marked divergence from known patterns in other parts of the world. South Asia is now being studied for its relevance to the general theoretical understanding of modernity itself.

South Asia in the Social Sciences will feature books that offer innovative research on contemporary South Asia. It will focus on the place of the region in the various global disciplines of the social sciences and highlight research that uses unconventional sources of information and novel research methods. While recognising that most current research is focused on the larger countries, the series will attempt to showcase research on the smaller countries of the region.

General Editor
Partha Chatterjee
Columbia University

Editorial Board
Pranab Bardhan
University of California at Berkeley

Stuart Corbridge
Durham University

Satish Deshpande
University of Delhi

Christophe Jaffrelot
Centre d'etudes et de recherches internationales, Paris

Nivedita Menon
Jawaharlal Nehru University

Other books in the series:

Government as Practice: Democratic Left in a Transforming India
Dwaipayan Bhattacharyya

Courting the People: Public Interest Litigation in Post-Emergency India
Anuj Bhuwania

Development after Statism: Industrial Firms and the Political Economy of South Asia
Adnan Naseemullah

Politics of the Poor: Negotiating Democracy in Contemporary India
Indrajit Roy

South Asian Governmentalities: Michel Foucault and the Question of Postcolonial Orderings
Stephen Legg and Deana Heath (eds.)

Nationalism, Development and Ethnic Conflict in Sri Lanka
Rajesh Venugopal

Adivasis and the State: Subalternity and Citizenship in India's Bhil Heartland
Alf Gunvald Nilsen

Maoist People's War and the Revolution of Everyday Life in Nepal
Ina Zharkevich

New Perspectives on Pakistan's Political Economy: State, Class and Social Change
Matthew McCartney and S. Akbar Zaidi (eds.)

Crafty Oligarchs, Savvy Voters: Democracy under Inequality in Rural Pakistan
Shandana Khan Mohmand

Dynamics of Caste and Law: Dalits, Oppression and Constitutional Democracy in India
Dag-Erik Berg

Simultaneous Identities: Language, Education and the Nepali Nation
Uma Pradhan

Deceptive Majority: Dalits, Hinduism, and Underground Religion
Joel Lee

Colossus: The Anatomy of Delhi
Sanjoy Chakravorty and Neelanjan Sircar (eds.)

When Ideas Matter: Democracy and Corruption in India
Bilal A. Baloch

In Search of Home: Citizenship, Law and the Politics of the Poor
Kaveri Haritas

Bureaucratic Archaeology: State, Science, and Past in Postcolonial India
Ashish Avikunthak

The Odds Revisited

Political Economy of the Development of Bangladesh

K. A. S. Murshid

CAMBRIDGE
UNIVERSITY PRESS

CAMBRIDGE
UNIVERSITY PRESS

University Printing House, Cambridge CB2 8BS, United Kingdom

One Liberty Plaza, 20th Floor, New York, NY 10006, USA

477 Williamstown Road, Port Melbourne, vic 3207, Australia

314 to 321, 3rd Floor, Plot No.3, Splendor Forum, Jasola District Centre, New Delhi 110025, India

103 Penang Road, #05–06/07, Visioncrest Commercial, Singapore 238467

Cambridge University Press is part of the University of Cambridge.

It furthers the University's mission by disseminating knowledge in the pursuit of education, learning and research at the highest international levels of excellence.

www.cambridge.org
Information on this title: www.cambridge.org/9781009123136

© K. A. S. Murshid 2022

This publication is in copyright. Subject to statutory exception and to the provisions of relevant collective licensing agreements, no reproduction of any part may take place without the written permission of Cambridge University Press.

First published 2022

Printed in India by Avantika Printers Pvt. Ltd.

A catalogue record for this publication is available from the British Library

ISBN 978-1-009-12313-6 Hardback

Cambridge University Press has no responsibility for the persistence or accuracy of URLs for external or third-party internet websites referred to in this publication, and does not guarantee that any content on such websites is, or will remain, accurate or appropriate.

To Amma, Abba and Shabab

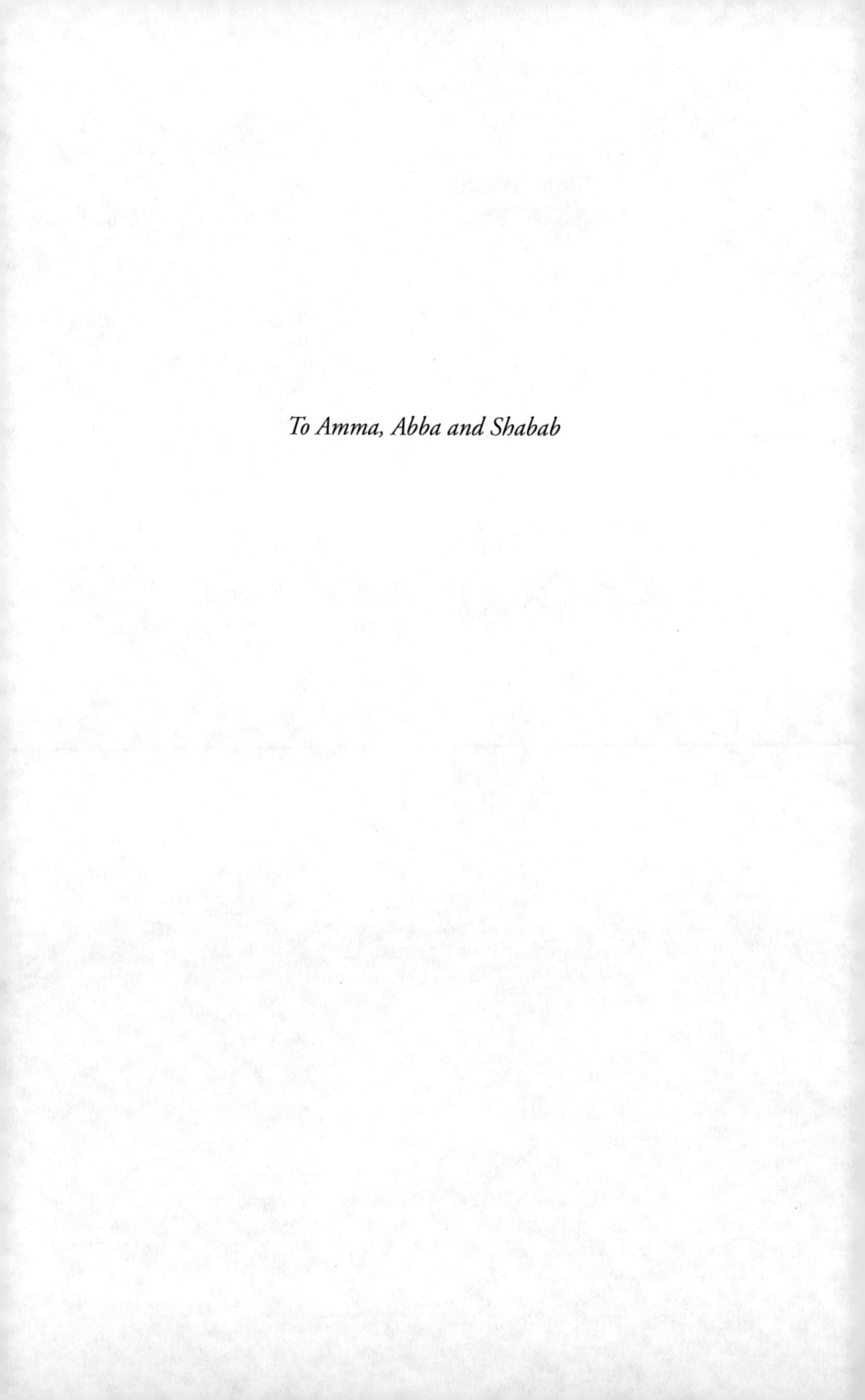

Contents

List of Tables and Figures	xiii
Acknowledgements	xvii
List of Abbreviations	xix
Introduction	1
1. A Bird's-Eye View of the Bangladesh Economy: 1971–2020	8
2. Initial Conditions: The Odds Revisited	37
3. The Food Security Challenge	48
4. Exploring Transition and Change in the Rice Market	58
5. International Migration	78
6. The Rural Non-farm (RNF) Sector	84
7. Industrialization and the Rise of RMG	99
8. Industrialization: Other Stories	114
9. The Social Sector Puzzle	143
10. Dhaka: Capital Formation—Urbanization, Competition and the Rise of a Business Class	171
Conclusion	217
Notes	233
Glossary	255
References	257
Index	305

Tables and Figures

Tables

1.1	Selected balance of payments data	14
1.2	Bangladesh: Sectoral shares of GDP	15
1.3	Share of services in GDP and total employment	21
1.4	Availability of doctors, nurses and other technical staff	24
1.5	Access to health services	25
1.6	Bangladesh nutrition data	27
1.7	Bangladesh: School enrolment trends	29
1.8	Bangladesh: Trends in dropout rates	30
1.9	Student–teacher ratios over time	31
1.10	Women empowerment indicators	31
1.11	Trends in rural poverty	34
1.12	Trends in moderate and extreme poverty	34
1.13	Trends in inequality	35
2.1	Sectoral shares of GDP	41
2.2	Sectoral growth rates	42
2.3	Coup and counter-coup	45
3.1	Agricultural input market reforms	54
4.1	Characterization of market sites	62
4.2	Socio-economic profile of traders	65
4.3	Types of financial relations in backward area paddy market	68
4.4	Changes in *dhaner upore* rate	69
5.1	Out-migration of workers from Bangladesh	79

5.2	Remittance of exports and GDP	79
5.3	Chronology of major government interventions	80
6.1	Rural employment by agriculture and non-agriculture	87
6.2	Employment in RNF by components	87
6.3	Structure of farm and non-farm employment	88
6.4	Growth rate in rural incomes and consumption	89
6.5	Sources of rural income	90
6.6	Changes in household income by agriculture and non-agriculture	91
6.7	Rural employment in the new millennium	92
6.8	Structure and size of rural employment	93
6.9	Growth trends in fisheries output	97
7.1	RMG export trends	101
7.2	Changes in structure of production of RMG	103
7.3	Back-to-back LC and master LC	106
7.4	De facto classification of Bangladesh's exchange rate regime	110
8.1	Summary table of potential non-RMG sectors	122
8.2	The electronic brand landscape	123
8.3	Profits and losses, manufacturing SOEs	133
8.4	Selected countries at Bangladesh's level	136
8.5	Export structure	137
9.1	Prevalence of morbidity	164
10.1	Population and area size of Dhaka city	173
10.2	Population of Dhaka city	181
10.3	White-collar occupations	203
10.4	Dhaka: Profile of the middle class	204
10.5	Number of shanties and their population in Dhaka	208

Figures

1.1	Per capita GDP in constant 2010 USD prices	9
1.2	Consumption	10
1.3	Revenue	11
1.4	Private and public investment	11
1.5	Total reserves in months of imports	13
1.6	China: Industry and services as share of GDP	17
1.7	China: Share of employment	17
1.8	Republic of Korea: Services and industry in GDP	19
1.9	Republic of Korea: Employment in services and industry	19
1.10	Bangladesh and India: Share of industry and services in GDP	20
1.11	Bangladesh and India: Employment shares	21
1.12	Fertility rate, total	22
1.13	Infant mortality rate	23
1.14	Maternal mortality ratio	24
2.1	GDP growth rates	39
4.1	The paddy circuit	64
8.1	International arrivals	119

Acknowledgements

The economy of Bangladesh has emerged from a poor, agrarian economy to a vibrant industrializing one that has attracted the attention of the global development community. Bangladesh has notched up an impressive development record led by strong, sustained growth that was widely shared and driven by agriculture, industry and services. There were also parallel changes in rural institutions for which Bangladesh became famous, ushering in transformative change across a number of fronts, from the Green Revolution and the rural non-farm economy to micro-credit for the poor, women's empowerment, girls' education and fertility decline. These changes were accompanied by a strong macro-economic position that was sustained by ready-made garments (RMG) exports, international migrant remittances and good policy. Thus, as the country approached 50 years of its journey in 2021 as an independent country, the need to take stock and review the road traversed gained traction.

The Bangladesh development literature is rich, covering all major development debates. A component of this literature is also addressed to what has variously been described as the Bangladesh surprise, paradox or miracle. While interesting insights have emerged, these studies have tended to be too narrowly focused. In other words, a thorough, more comprehensive, well-integrated analysis of Bangladesh's development story remains to be told. I was determined to try and fill this gap as best as I could.

I began to work on this manuscript in mid-2016. Not much progress was made until 2019, although, by this time, I knew in what direction my story would need to go. It was really under the prolonged lockdown and stay-at-home mandates beginning in March 2020 that gave a big push to this study. In fact, the first draft was completed within a year of the pandemic, which under normal circumstances would not have been possible.

I was also fortunate that as a freedom fighter and a member of one of Bangladesh's leading intellectual-political families, I was well acquainted with the principal political, social and economic actors of my time, thus allowing for a rare and invaluable development perspective from a close range. It is my earnest hope that readers will enjoy reading this book, which I have felt compelled to write as the personal reflections of a Bangladeshi economist and a living witness to its unique, complex journey.

My interest in Bangladesh's development is attributable to a life-long desire to be relevant to a country that has seen more than its fair share of tragedy and turbulence. This desire has been instilled in me by my parents, my friends, and contemporaries in academia and outside.

As I began writing this book, I realized that I owe an intellectual debt to many whose ideas, works and conversations have shaped my perspective on Bangladesh's development. I must especially mention Sir Austin Robinson, my supervisor at Cambridge, who quietly directed me towards the area of food security, which at the time was Bangladesh's pre-eminent priority. Other stalwarts include W. B. Reddaway, Suzy Paine, Ben Crow and Barbara Harris-White.

Prominent Bangladeshi scholars to whom I am indebted are Rehman Sobhan, Abu Abdullah, Mahabub Hossain, Wahiduddin Mahmud, Siddiqur Rahman Osmani and Shahid Khandker. Other names that come to mind are Thomas Reardon, Paul Dorosh and Santosh Mehrotra. My many colleagues at Bangladesh Institute of Development Studies (BIDS) have been a source of great strength and wisdom. They include researchers like Quazi Shahabuddin, Simeen Mahmud, Nuimuddin Choudhury, Atiq Rahman, Atiur Rahman, Hossain Z. Rahman, Md. Asaduzzaman, Binayak Sen, Kazi Ali Toufique, Anwara Begum, Raisul Islam Mahmood, Monzur Hossain, Asad Islam, Minhaj Mahmud, Kazi Iqbal, Md. Yunus, Nazneen Ahmed and S. M. Zulfiqar Ali, to name a few.

I would particularly like to thank Willem van der Geest for painstakingly going through several chapters of my manuscript and providing invaluable comments.

I am indebted to Musa Miah for providing access to rare newspaper reports from the *Daily Bonik Barta*. I am also grateful to the *International Journal of Agrarian Studies* for permitting me to reproduce one of my articles.

I have greatly benefited from talking to industry leaders, prominent businessmen and bankers in Dhaka, including Salman F. Rahman, Ajmal Kabir, Matin Choudhury, Tapan Choudhury, Anis A. Khan and Shams Mahmud, all of whom liberally shared their views and insights on Bangladesh's development with me.

I would also like to acknowledge the assistance received from junior colleagues at BIDS, including Tanvir Mahmud, Nahian Azad Shashi and Mahir Rahman. I am grateful to my research assistants, Farhana Kabir, Samanta Sharmin Laskar, Selvia Arshad and Nabila Akter, for their excellent work under tight deadlines.

I would especially like to thank Anwesha Rana at Cambridge University Press, without whose encouragement this book could not have materialized. I have benefited hugely from discussing various ideas with my daughters Nadine S. Murshid and Navine Murshid – I thank them for their support and for believing in me. Finally, I thank my wife Shameem Subrana for her patience and understanding.

This book is dedicated to the memory of my parents and my son Shabab, whose faith in Bangladesh never wavered.

Abbreviations

ACCORD	Accord on Fire and Building Safety in Bangladesh
ADB	Asian Development Bank
ADP	Annual Development Programme
AL	Awami League
API	active pharmaceutical ingredients
ASA	Association for Social Advancement
ASEAN	Association of Southeast Asian Nations
BADC	Bangladesh Agricultural Development Corporation
BAIRA	Bangladesh Association of International Recruiting Agencies
BANBEIS	Bangladesh Bureau of Educational Information and Statistics
BBS	Bangladesh Bureau of Statistics
BCIC	Bangladesh Chemical Industries Corporation
BCPS	Bangladesh Contraceptive Prevalence Survey
BDHS	Bangladesh Demographic and Health Surveys
BDT/Tk.	Bangladesh currency (Taka)
BEPZA	Bangladesh Export Processing Zones Authority
BEZA	Bangladesh Economic Zones Authority
BFIC	Bangladesh Forest Industries Development Corporation
BGMEA	Bangladesh Garments Manufacturers and Exporters Association
BIDS	Bangladesh Institute of Development Studies
BIHS	Bangladesh Integrated Household Survey
BINP	Bangladesh Integrated Nutrition Project
BJMC	Bangladesh Jute Mills Corporation
BMET	Bureau of Manpower Export and Training
BNP	Bangladesh Nationalist Party
BOESL	Bangladesh Overseas Employment Services Limited
BOP	balance of payments
BPDB	Bangladesh Power Development Board
BRAC	Bangladesh Rural Advancement Committee
BRDB	Bangladesh Rural Development Board

BSFIC	Bangladesh Sugar and Food Industries Corporation
BSCIC	Bangladesh Small and Cottage Industries Corporation
BSEC	Bangladesh Steel and Engineering Corporation
BSRS	Bangladesh Shilpa Rin Sangstha
BTMA	Bangladesh Textile Manufacturers Association
BTMC	Bangladesh Textile Mills Corporation
BWDB	Bangladesh Water Development Board
CAGR	compound annual growth rate
CAP	corrective action plan
CBN	cost of basic needs
CBO	community-based organization
CCT	conditional cash transfer
CDC	Centres for Disease Control and Prevention
CDF	Credit and Development Forum
CM	Crow and Murshid/Comilla Model
CMLA	chief martial law administrator
CO	contracting out
CPD	Centre for Policy Dialogue
CPI	Corruption Perception Index
CPR	contraceptive prevalence rate
CPS	contraceptive prevalence survey
DAC	Development Assistance Committee
DCI	direct calorie intake
DFI	development financial institution
DFID	Department of Foreign and International Development
DGHS	Directorate General of Health Services
DGNM	Directorate General of Nursing and Midwifery
DHS	Demographic and Health Survey
DPE	Directorate of Primary Education
DTW	deep tube well
EBA	Everything but Arms
EPZ	export processing zone
ERD	Economic Relations Division
ETDZ	economic and technological development zone
e-TIN	electronic tax identification numbers
EU	European Union
FAD	food availability decline
FBCCI	Federation of Bangladesh Chambers of Commerce and Industries
FDI	foreign direct investment
FEI	food energy intake

FFE	Food for Education
FFW	Food for Work
FGP	flying geese paradigm
FM	frequency modulation
FSSAP	Female Secondary School Assistance Project
FWC	family welfare centre
FY	fiscal year
G2G	government-to-government
GDI	Gender Development Index
GDP	gross domestic product
GII	Gender Inequality Index
GNI	gross national income
GO	government organization
GR	Green Revolution
GSM	Global System for Mobile Communication
GSP	generalized system of preferences
HDI	Human Development Index
HES	household expenditure survey
HH	household
HIES	household income–expenditure survey
HMP	higher than market price
HSC	Higher Secondary Certificate
HYV	high-yielding variety
ICDDRB	International Centre for Diarrhoeal Diseases Research, Bangladesh
ICT	information and communications technology
IFI	international financial institution
IFPRI	International Food Policy Research Institute
ILO	International Labour Office
IMF	International Monetary Fund
IMR	infant mortality rate
InM	Institute of Microfinance
IPRSP	Interim Poverty Reduction Strategy Paper
IR-8	high-yielding semi-dwarf rice variety
IRRI	International Rice Research Institute
IR-TES	Information Revolution and Information Technology Enabled Services
ISI	import substitution for industrialization
ITC	International Trade Centre

IUD	intrauterine device
JI	Jamat-i-Islami
JICA	Japan International Cooperation Agency
JP	Jatiya Party
KPI	key performance indicator
LB	line balancing
LC	letter of credit
LDC	least developed country
LFS	labour force survey
LGED	Local Government Engineering Department
LGRDC	Local Government, Rural Development and Cooperatives
LP	labour productivity
LPG	liquefied petroleum gas
MAC	middle and affluent class
MCH-FP	mother and child health and family planning
MDG	millennium development goal
MFA	Multi-fibre Arrangement
MFI	microfinance institution
MFS	mobile financial services
MIEZ	Meghna Industrial Economic Zone
MIS	management information system
MNC	multinational corporation
MOHFW	Ministry of Health and Family Welfare
MOP	Ministry of Planning
MOU	memorandum of understanding
MRA	Microfinance Regulatory Authority
MUAC	mid-upper arm circumference
NBR	National Board of Revenue
NER	nominal exchange rate
NGO	non-governmental organization
NNP	net national product/National Nutritional Programme
NPR	National Public Radio
NSAPR	National Strategy for Augmented Poverty Reduction
ODA	overseas development assistance
OECD	Organization of Economic Cooperation and Development
OMS	open market sale
ORT	oral rehydration therapy
PESP	Primary Education Stipend Programme

Abbreviations

PFDS	Public Food Distribution System
PHC	primary healthcare
PKB	Probashi Kalyan Bank
PL	poverty line
POW	prisoner of war
PPE	personal protective equipment
PPP	purchasing power parity/public–private partnership
PRC	People's Republic of China
PTS	primary textiles sector
R&D	research and development
RCT	randomized control trial
RDRS	Rangpur–Dinajpur Rural Service
REER	real effective exchange rate
RMB	Chinese currency (Yuan)
RMG	ready-made garments
RMMRU	Refugee and Migratory Movements Research Unit
RNF	rural non-farm
RNFE	rural non-farm employment
ROO	rules of origin
SARC	South Asian Association for Regional Cooperation
SBW	special bonded warehouse
SDG	sustainable development goal
SEDP	Secondary Education Development Programme
SEZ	special economic zone
SME	small and medium enterprises
SOE	state-owned enterprise
SOI	state-owned industry
SSC	Secondary School Certificate
STW	shallow tube well
T&C	textile and clothing
TBA	traditional birth attendant
TCB	Trading Corporation of Bangladesh
TCCA	Thana Central Cooperative Association
TFR	total fertility rate
THC	*thana* health complex
TRIPS	Trade-Related Aspects of Intellectual Property Rights
TSER	Transforming Secondary Education Results
TTDC	Thana Training and Development Centre
TV	television

UAE	United Arab Emirates
UMIC	upper middle-income country
UN	United Nations
UNESCO	United Nations Education Social and Cultural Organization
UNHCR	United Nations High Commissioner for Refugees
UNICEF	United Nations Children's Fund
UNROD	United Nations Relief Operations in Dhaka
UPHCP	Urban Primary Health Care Project
USAID	United States Agency for International Development
USD	United States currency (US dollar)
UXO	unexploded ordnance
V-AID	Village Agricultural and Industrial Programme
VAT	value-added tax
VGD	vulnerable group development
VO	village organization
WASH	Water, Sanitation and Hygiene
WB	World Bank
WES	Wage Earners' Scheme
WEWF	Wage Earners' Welfare Fund
WGI	World Governance Index
WHO	World Health Organization
WIP	work in process
WITS	World Integrated Trade Solution
WTO	World Trade Organization
EPZ	export processing zone

Introduction

The story of Bangladesh is an extraordinary tale of struggle against immense odds. It is the story of a nation state that broke into the world stage dramatically after an armed struggle against what became viewed as an occupation army attempting to remain in power through massive repression and large-scale killings that sent over 10 million people into India to seek shelter and refuge.[1] Before these events, Bangladesh was an unremarkable part of Pakistan (East Pakistan) whose main value for the ruling elite was its jute exports that enabled the country to earn valuable foreign exchange – much of which was appropriated for investment in West Pakistan, especially in the emerging industrial sector there. Bangladesh was overwhelmingly rural and agricultural with a high population density and massive illiteracy, malnutrition and poverty. This is where it was stuck: as the rural backwaters located in the biggest delta in the world periodically visited by violent storms and floods, and debilitating epidemics. This state of affairs continued, largely unchanged over 24 years since gaining independence from Britain in 1947, until the country broke away from West Pakistan and became Bangladesh in 1971.

While the economy remained stagnant as part of Pakistan, the same cannot be said of its politics. A nascent but vocal middle class emerged, consisting of students, teachers, lawyers, journalists and government officers. This group was strengthened by an emerging industrial working class – all largely drawn from the ranks of the peasantry, including surplus peasants. This served to challenge the traditional political power structure, which was dominated by feudal elements under the banner of the Muslim League – the party that was instrumental in the creation of Pakistan (Jalal 1994; Naqvi 1986). This newly emerged middle class became the logical political base of the Awami League (AL) formed from a breakaway group of the Muslim League. The AL adopted a distinctly more democratic, secular and 'progressive' stance compared to the Muslim League and quickly drew a large following from the new, aspiring middle classes.

It was therefore only a matter of time when the disparity and inequality between the two 'wings' of Pakistan would become apparent, which, combined by the reluctance of the ruling military–bureaucratic–feudal elite based in the west to share power with the east, did not bode well. The story of the emergence of Bangladesh from the ashes of Pakistan has been extensively written on (Choudhury 1972; Islam 1978; Owen 1972; Thorp 1987). In this book we address ourselves to a different question. The journey of Bangladesh from hopelessness to hope, from extreme forms of aid dependence to relative economic independence, from abject, widespread poverty to relative prosperity would appear to be nothing short of a miracle. The Bangladesh experience has been commented upon – most compellingly by Amartya Sen (2013) and Drèze and Sen (2012) but also by the London-based *Economist* magazine as well as by a number of Bangladeshi and international scholars, as seen in their contributions to the prestigious British medical journal *Lancet*[2] and others.[3] So, what was so unusual about Bangladesh's development journey? How did the 'test case' turn into a paradox or puzzle, thrusting the country into a new development trajectory that attracted considerable attention at home and abroad? The politicians were of course quick to claim credit, profusely singing praise and apportioning accolades at having transformed the country. Some even referred to it as a 'role model'.[4] While one may debate the extent of progress made at various levels while at the same time pointing awkwardly to adverse indicators related to corruption, governance, institutional weaknesses and poor implementation of development projects, the numbers do add up. There is little doubt that a new set of powerful dynamics have been set in motion, not unlike similar dynamics that have been observed elsewhere, especially in Southeast Asia or East Asia. This came as a shock to local and foreign observers, who completely failed to predict these outcomes, and therefore had to resort to phrases like 'puzzle' and 'paradox' to make up for it. Thus, while the 'what' questions have received attention, the same cannot be said of the 'how' or 'why' questions.

These questions have not been adequately confronted in the literature, although a development narrative has emerged within mainstream official thinking that probably errs on the side of overstatement. First, it is important to critically revisit this narrative to clearly articulate what have been the country's major achievements. This needs to be a detailed exposition that is carefully and credibly conducted based on the best available data.

Naomi Hossain (2017) made a brave attempt to grapple with some of the issues raised in this book but in my view became entrapped in a restrictive framework and an inability to comprehensively address Bangladesh's complex development dynamics. I find some of her basic assumptions somewhat problematic but nevertheless commend her work for extending our appreciation of Bangladesh's development history.[5]

Introduction

This book provides an analytical–descriptive narrative of the Bangladesh journey by trying to forge a comprehensive, integrated story that is holistic but at the same time able to track key development dynamics at the sectoral, sub-sectoral and macro levels. This is a much-needed exercise to dispel the notion that the 'Bangladesh surprise' can be reduced to certain singular dimensions, such as the trauma of 1971 or 1974, low-cost health solutions, ready-made garments (RMG) and remittances, or women's empowerment and micro-credit. What has been attempted here is to develop an integrated story that places such piecemeal explanations within a broader, integrated and coherent appreciation. It is hoped that this book would be able to make a small contribution towards filling this large gap in the story.

However, it is important, given the nature of this book, to begin at the beginning, with an introduction to the 'initial conditions' the country faced after secession from Pakistan in 1971. Bangladesh was the original development 'basket case', the demeaning term used in Henry Kissinger's state department for countries that would always depend on aid. The Nixon government in the United States (US) went out of its way to be hostile to the Bangladesh movement, which was seeking to secede from Pakistan in 1971. Nixon's position was overwhelmingly influenced by one overriding factor – his intense desire to enter into a dialogue with China and to open up diplomatic relations with that country. His channel to China was through Pakistan, a country that was close to China, and in particular through its president General Yahya Khan, with whom Nixon established a close personal rapport (Bass 2013; Jahan 2013). Therefore, despite the dire reports emanating from East Pakistan (as Bangladesh was then known) and the frantic memos sent to Washington by the US Consulate in Dhaka describing in graphic detail the lead up to the military crackdown in Bangladesh on 25 March 1971 and the subsequent atrocities reaching genocidal proportions, Nixon and Kissinger remained unmoved and unrelenting, and did nothing to reign in the Pakistanis. The subsequent violence, with some 3 million people officially thought to have died, led to an outpouring of refugees on a scale not witnessed before in Bangladesh, perhaps even globally. This presented India with a huge administrative, financial and security burden – a burden that was not sustainable. By and large, the international community kept aloof, and it became clear to India that the only way to end the violence was through military intervention. Fortunately, the Soviet Union and the Eastern Bloc supported India and provided the necessary diplomatic cover (and implied military threat) to make this happen. Bangladesh was finally rid of the Pakistan Army on 16 December 1971 after a brief but bloody war launched jointly by Indian and Bangladeshi forces, taking more than 94,000 Pakistani prisoners of war (POWs).

The government in exile was able to return to Dhaka to take over the reins of power in the fractured state with the declaration of victory by the Joint Forces.

A Bengali-led government finally assumed power after some 770 years from the collapse of the Sena dynasty in Eastern Bengal following the Turkish invasion of 1203 led by Bakhtiyar Khilji and the fall of the Sena capital of Nabadwip (modern-day Nadia, now in West Bengal, adjoining Bangladesh). The Sena rule continued in Eastern Bengal, based in Vikrampur near Dhaka until 1230 (Sarkar 1927; Islam 2011).

For much of recorded history, Bengal, especially Eastern Bengal, remained splintered, loosely governed and frequently ruled by local chieftains. It came under more centralized rule sporadically under the Mauryas, Guptas, Maghadhians, Palas and Senas, and later under the Turks and the Moghuls, and, of course, the British. Forests, rivers and lowlands combined with difficult logistics made this area very difficult to govern. It was only with more modern infrastructure and communications (especially the railways) under the British that the scale of exploitation of Bengal took on astronomical proportions. During British rule, as many as seven famines were recorded by historians (1770, 1783, 1866, 1873, 1892, 1897, 1943–44).[6] Records of famines in the pre-British period are almost non-existent.

The birth of Bangladesh therefore is a historical anomaly – no other South Asian nation or subnation or ethnic group has acquired an independent status. Bengalis have their own country for the first time in recorded history or at least since the emergence of a separate Bengali identity based on a language that took root around 1,000 years ago, flowing from Sanskrit, Pali and Prakrit (Banglapedia 2015a).

The emergence of Bangladesh is also unique from another perspective. This is the first country in South Asia that was able to free itself not only politically but also from the deeply entrenched power structures sanctified by caste, class and religion – the former stemming from the dominance of caste elites among Hindus that remains a huge challenge in India even today but which has greatly diminished in modern Bangladesh, especially with the out-migration of caste Hindus since 1947, when the subcontinent was partitioned along religious lines.

Even when Hindu dominance ended, there was a second form of dominance to contend with. This was the dominance of non-Bengali-speaking Muslims who drew their authority from supposed or actual lineage from Muslim immigrants of the Sultanate period or later, freshly aligned with their co-linguists among the Pakistani ruling elites after 1947. The chief political vehicle used by this group was the Muslim League, whose popularity steadily declined from 1947 to 1971 as it was unable to keep in step with growing Bengali nationalism and the demands for a greater share of the national economic wealth. The liberation of

Bangladesh dealt the final blow to Muslim League aspirations, creating the much-needed economic and political space that Bengalis could aspire to fill. Thus, for the first time, the people of this region were able to rid themselves of the deeply embedded, structurally sanctified systems of exploitation carried out by Hindu and Muslim elites over the ages – a true subaltern revolution that appears to have gone largely unnoticed and deserves deeper analysis.

The Main Building Blocks

Bangladesh has achieved remarkable successes in a number of areas. One of the most important developments has been rapid urbanization, and the rise of an entrepreneurial class based mainly in Dhaka, encouraged by a policy that allowed primitive capital accumulation through access to bank credit (and subsequent default), project financing by donor-fuelled, state-sponsored financial institutions, over- and under-invoicing overlooked by the state, and patronage enjoyed by people with connections to politics, the military and the bureaucracy. It would also be true to say that there was significant 'old' capital as well, dating back to the 1950s, 1960s and 1970s, which flourished in independent Bangladesh. This class could even be described as 'semi-independent' in the sense that its origin was not 'comprador' in nature, meaning that its rise was not principally linked to agency, commission or middlemen services provided to foreign businesses but was essentially an indigenous phenomenon.[7] The emergence of the indigenous capitalist class in Bangladesh is of great significance in the pursuit of private-sector-led, public-sector-supported growth. This is discussed in Chapter 10 in the context of the rise of Dhaka Megacity.

Several other momentous milestones were initiated within the first two decades of Liberation. The most well known of these was the micro-credit revolution that swept Bangladesh, pioneered by Professor Muhammad Yunus, the founder of Grameen Bank. The direct and indirect effects of micro-credit were profound, although its role in poverty eradication and development is not without controversy.

Almost of equal significance was the phenomenal rise of local non-governmental organizations (NGOs) led by pioneers like the Bangladesh Rural Advancement Committee (BRAC) and Rangpur–Dinajpur Rural Service (RDRS) along with Grameen, the Association for Social Advancement (ASA) and Proshika.[8] These pioneers, especially BRAC and Grameen, experimented with and developed grassroots development models that subsequently set the pace, tone and even content of the nature and form of rural development interventions adopted by the NGO movement as a whole and even by relevant government bodies like the Bangladesh Rural Development Board (BRDB) (Chapter 9).

The third factor, which in some ways may be considered the most important factor of all, was the initiation of the Green Revolution in rice in the country. The key here was irrigation and the availability of high-yielding seeds and chemical fertilizers, which posed a considerable challenge to policymakers. By the 1990s, these challenges were largely resolved, laying the basis for the eventual realization of a long-term national obsession, namely self-sufficiency in rice production. This in turn enabled broad-based growth and exceptional outcomes in nutrition and growth of the rural non-farm (RNF) sector (Chapters 3, 6 and 9). A crucial factor not often discussed in the food security literature is the supportive role of the rice market, which is taken up for detailed analysis in Chapter 4.

Family planning and fertility decline is an area that registered one of the earliest successes. While the factors behind the decline were intensely debated, the outcomes surfaced even when various Malthusian controversies were still raging. Falling fertility and the success with the Green Revolution transformed rural Bangladesh from its traditional slumber (Chapter 9).

Reference must also be made to industrialization and RMG exports and remittances whose origins can also be traced back to the early years. These were the two most important sources of foreign exchange, employment and growth to have emerged, displacing the long dominance of jute exports and external aid in Bangladesh's economy and ultimately allowing it some space in its macro-management capacity (Chapters 5 and 7). While Bangladesh's industrialization narrative remains confined to the emergence of RMG, Chapter 8 brings out 'other stories' that point to promise and potential that becomes apparent on closer scrutiny.

An area in which Bangladesh's achievements have been spectacular is its social sector outcomes, including health, education and women's empowerment – outcomes that appear not to have been associated with high levels of public expenditure. Various attempts have been made to explain this phenomenon by, among others, Sen (2013) and Asadullah, Savoia and Mahmud (2014). Chapter 9 provides a different historical–analytical perspective to the debate.

On the back of the Green Revolution, rise of RMG and international remittances, we also witnessed the rising contribution of the RNF sector that underwent structural change and expansion. The RNF sector's contribution in terms of wages, employment, poverty reduction and growth soon outpaced that of the farm sector and created a more productive economic space within the rural economy (Chapter 6).

In other words, changes took place across a number of crucial sectors in the decades following the liberation of Bangladesh in 1971. This was a time when the basic foundations were introduced and gradually took root that would serve the country well in the years ahead. All these beginnings took place against the backdrop of severe political instability, authoritarian rule and a restive, impatient populace. At the same time, the country moved steadily away from its socialistic aspirations to a market-led development model underpinned by trade liberalization and market reforms.

Thus, clues to the later successes lie in key developments that took place during this volatile but fascinating formative period. However, the bulk of scholarly attention has in fact gone towards exploring developments since 1991, and especially in the new millennium and beyond, because that is when outcomes related to growth and various social and health indicators began to be noticed. The ready temptation to lay all this at the altar of World Bank–IMF (International Monetary Fund) reforms by some observers is at best naïve and perhaps even opportunistic.[9] A true, much more nuanced understanding of the story of Bangladesh can only emerge if we adopt a far more fundamental, disaggregated stance, where we look for key turning points in our development history, even attempting a brick-by-brick reconstruction in the manner, perhaps, of an economic historian, while at the same time exploring reforms, policy changes, technology and institutional innovations, and altering political–economic tensions – in other words, factors that unleashed positive processes and changed outcomes as well as beneficiaries.

1

A Bird's-Eye View of the Bangladesh Economy

1971–2020

The traditional image of Bangladesh as a woefully poor, overpopulated nation plagued by food shortages, natural disasters, massive malnutrition, illiteracy and under-employment has finally receded into the background. The country has now begun to attract attention from the world for its economic performance and potential business opportunities rather than for its poverty and misery. The growth rate for 2018–19 was a record 8.15 per cent. This came down to an estimated 5.24 per cent in 2019–20 as against earlier projections by the government of 8.19 per cent – purportedly due to economic shutdown in the wake of COVID-19. If the official figures are proven correct, the growth rate achieved in 2018–19 is the highest on record for the country and one of the highest in the world.

In terms of per capita income, Bangladesh became a lower-middle-income country in 2015 and is on track to graduate out of the least developed country (LDC) status by 2024, after all three indicators for crossing the initial threshold were met in 2018 – the only LDC in Asia–Pacific to have done so (Murshid 2019).[1] Per capita income in 2019 was USD 1856, and the country has set ambitious targets to become an upper-middle-income country and a developed country by 2031 and 2041.[2] That the country can dream to become a high-income country by 2041 itself speaks volumes about its confidence and 'can-do' mindset – a far cry from the hand-to-mouth existence of the early years when foreign aid was the only way to make ends meet.

Growth

In general, the growth rate has steadily climbed, displaying quite a lot of variability in the 1970s, with a great deal of year-to-year fluctuation. The instability is clear from Figure 1.1, where we see that it persisted into 1981–82 before entering into a long, unbroken period of stable growth. Growth in the 1980s was low, hovering around the 3.5–4.0 per cent mark but gradually crawling up to reach just over 5 per cent on average during 1995–2000. By 2005, another 0.5 percentage point was added, with the trend continuing to top 6 and then 7 per cent in 2005 and 2015. Bangladesh's growth performance appears remarkably stable,

■ GDP per capita (constant 2010 US$) —— GDP per capita annual growth rate in constant prices

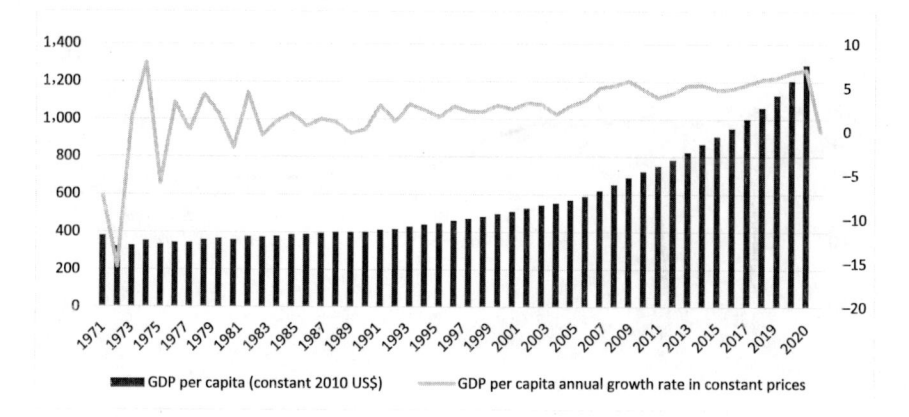

Figure 1.1 Per capita GDP in constant 2010 USD prices, and annual growth rates of Bangladesh (1972–2020)

Sources: 'GDP per Capita Growth', World Bank Databank, https://data.worldbank.org/indicator/NY.GDP.PCAP.KD.ZG?locations=BD (accessed 11 November 2021); Bangladesh Bank provisional estimate for 2020.

especially after 2003 – a feature that is also borne out in comparison with that of neighbouring countries.[3]

Consumption, Savings and Investment

In the early days almost all of the gross domestic product (GDP) went into consumption, leaving just a tiny amount for savings and investment. For much of the 1980s, the consumption–GDP ratio remained above 95 per cent. From 1990, it began a steady decline to reach 81 per cent in 2000. Thereafter, the decline continued but at a more moderate rate, reaching 77 per cent in 2016 and around 75 per cent in 2020. In other words, domestic savings grew from around 2 per cent in 1980 to 15 per cent in 1990, 20 per cent in 2000 and over 25 per cent in 2020, while national savings rose from 8 per cent in 1980 to 35.6 per cent in 2020.[4]

The data series from 1991 onwards is quite well behaved, declining gradually and smoothly with few disturbances. However, complete records for the period preceding 1990 are missing, with several breaks in the data series. In terms of public and private consumption, the trend is distinctly for public consumption to rise and private consumption to fall as a proportion of GDP, indicating corresponding changes in savings and investment (Figure 1.2).

Total investment in the economy is at 31–32 per cent of GDP (over 2017–20) – an achievement that could only be dreamt of in earlier decades.[5]

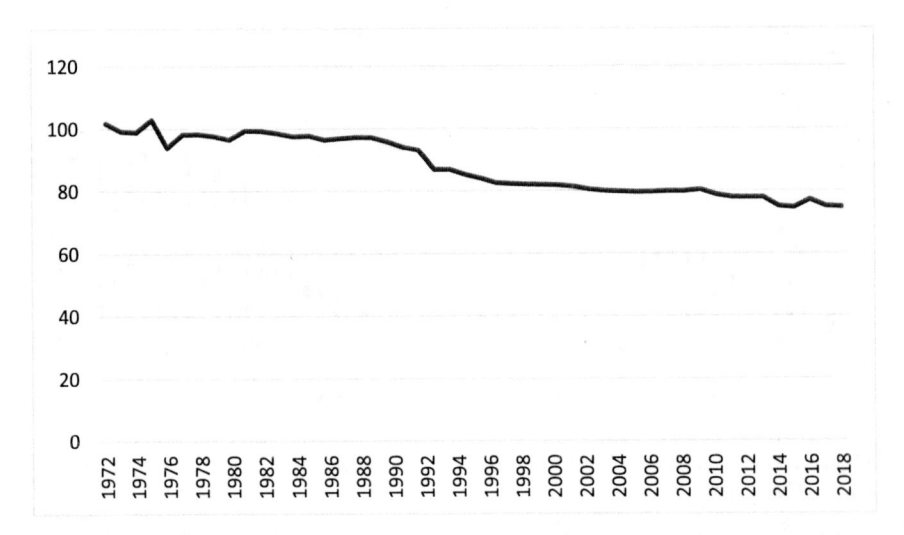

Figure 1.2 Consumption (per cent of GDP)

Sources: Bangladesh Bureau of Statistics: (*a*) Twenty Years of National Accounting of Bangladesh, 1972–73 to 1991–92; (*b*) *Bangladesh Economic Review* (Government of Bangladesh 2005, 2011, 2020).

In the early 1980s, it was 10–12 per cent, reaching the 20 per cent mark only in the mid-1990s and 25–26 per cent by 2005–06. Much of the investment was of course by the private sector, whose share grew steadily. In fact, until about 1990, public investment was either greater or at about the same level as private investment. It was only after 1990 that private investment shot up and the gap between private and public investment (as a percentage of GDP) steadily widened as the private sector grew and matured.

Financing Growth

There was a time when the development literature talked about the two-gap theory in the context of development financing, namely the savings gap and the foreign exchange gap. If savings rates are too low, resource mobilization falters and investments suffer. On the other hand, even when domestic savings are adequate, it is important to have sufficient access to foreign exchange resources in order to be able to undertake the necessary imports, including food and energy imports, as well as imports of machinery, capital and intermediate goods. Theoretically, if there is a foreign exchange shortage, it could act as an independent brake on growth.

Although savings and investment have picked up, there still remains considerable scope to improve domestic resource mobilization given an extremely narrow tax base and one of the lowest tax–GDP ratios in the world (Figure 1.4).

A Bird's-Eye View of the Bangladesh Economy

It has, however, been difficult to reform the tax collection machinery to enable the potential to be exploited. The country's ambition to expand the growth rate at a sustainable 8 per cent a year will depend on whether this challenge can be met. Tax evasion has gone hand in hand with systemic corruption throughout

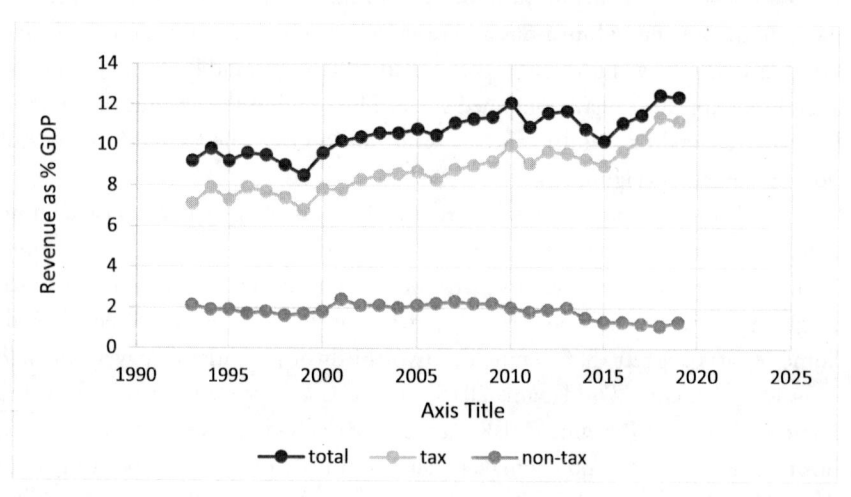

Figure 1.3 Revenue (per cent of GDP)

Source: *Bangladesh Economic Review* (Government of Bangladesh 2005, 2011, 2020) published by Bangladesh Bureau of Statistics.

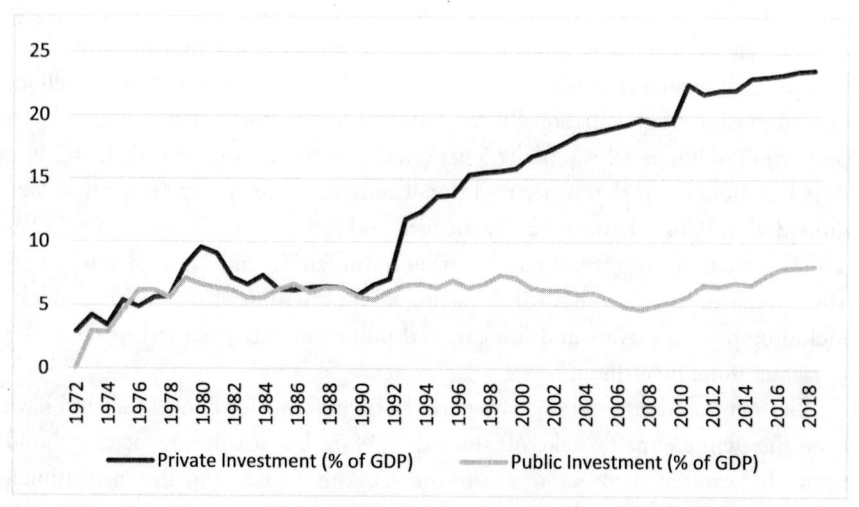

Figure 1.4 Private and public investment (per cent of GDP), 1972–2020

Sources: Bangladesh Bureau of Statistics: (*a*) Twenty Years of National Accounting of Bangladesh, 1972–73 to 1991–92; (*b*) *Bangladesh Economic Review* (Government of Bangladesh 2005, 2011, 2020).

the revenue collection system. However, given that until a decade ago there were just 1.4 million taxpayers in a population of 160 million, the scope for improving performance was large. Although various efforts have now led to 4.4 million people being registered with electronic tax identification numbers (e-TIN) in 2019 and there are plans to raise this to 10 million by 2024, actual progress in terms of income tax submissions and revenue generation remains poor. The tax–GDP ratio has moved up from 6 per cent in 2001 to around 8–9 per cent now – a level that appears to have remained stuck. The trend in the revenue–GDP ratio basically reflects the trend in the tax–GDP ratio given the flat performance of non-tax revenues (Figure 1.3).

In addition to being low, the tax structure is regressive, given the overwhelming dependence on indirect taxes, mainly value-added tax (VAT). Tax evasion, a complex tax collection system made worse by multiple rates and a reluctance to give up discretionary powers enjoyed by top tax officials are often blamed. Some reports suggest that as much as two-thirds of potential taxpayers are able to evade payment (World Bank 2015). There is an urgent need to reform the National Board of Revenue (NBR), a view that is widely shared by economists, businessmen and even policy makers, although little progress has been made to date. This does not bode well for Bangladesh's ambitious plans and points to deep-seated opposition to change from within.

The foreign exchange constraint has traditionally been a much stronger problem, leading to extreme aid dependence for the country. Exports, led by RMG and labour remittances from abroad have dramatically altered the scenario, relegating aid dependence to a relatively small area of economic activity. Although net overseas development assistance (ODA) received by Bangladesh is still over USD 3 billion, as a proportion of gross national income (GNI) this is around 1 per cent and as a proportion of imports this is under 5 per cent (Government of Bangladesh 2020).

One should add that other traditional sources of foreign exchange have not done well in Bangladesh, especially tourism and foreign direct investment (FDI). The approach of the government has been to initiate an ambitious plan to set up 100 special economic zones (SEZs) using a combination of ownership models, including public, private and foreign, and public–private partnerships, in order to attract more investment.[6]

Garments and remittances have played a pivotal role for Bangladesh and have been the twin engine for take-off since the 1980s, but it will now need to build upon these initial successes to create the economic space and the institutional structures that can lead the country into the next higher stages along the path of economic development. In particular, diversification has become crucial for Bangladesh – in agriculture, in exports and in industry.

Balance of Payments: A Positive Current Account?

The balance of trade was around –10.8 per cent of GDP in 1980, but over the next few decades it registered a steady rise to –3.8 per cent in 2000. In other words, the gap between exports and imports, while still negative, was narrowed considerably. After 2000, we observe rising trade deficits again, reaching –8.6 and –1.4 per cent in 2010 and 2020–21 (Figure 1.1). This has now begun to recede since, highlighting the existence of various sources of instability on the external account, including need for sudden food imports, spurt in imports linked to mega projects like the Rooppur Nuclear Power Plant and the metro rail project for Dhaka, in the face of temporary impediments to export and remittance growth (Haroon 2018; World Bank 2019b). Despite such fluctuations, Bangladesh's external front remains satisfactory – a status that it has been able to carry into the pandemic as well. Despite COVID-19, Bangladesh's remittance earnings continued to flow in unabated and its crucial RMG exports are on the way to recovery. Initial economic worries for the economy have receded, although the COVID-19 gauntlet remains alive and well. Thus, Bangladesh's foreign exchange reserves have continued to climb, crossing the USD 40 billion mark in October 2020. This is in part due to larger remittance flows but also because of slower imports due to COVID-19. As of July 2020, reserves were equivalent to 10.3 months of imports. To put it in perspective, for most of Bangladesh's history until about 2010, reserves were generally equivalent to just two–three months of imports, occasionally hitting five months (Figure 1.5).

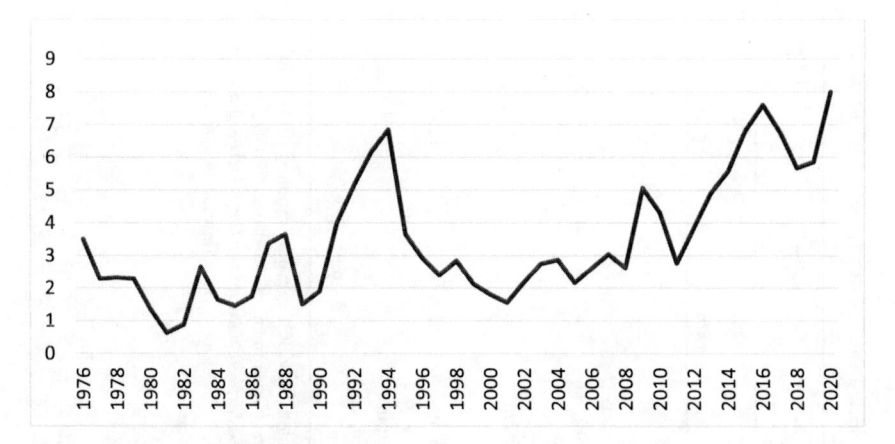

Figure 1.5 Total reserves in months of imports, 1976–2020 (Bangladesh)

Source: 'Total Reserves in Months of Imports', World Bank Databank, https://data.worldbank.org/indicator/FI.RES.TOTL.MO?locations=BD&view=chart (accessed 14 November 2021).

Table 1.1 Selected balance of payments (BOP) data (1973–2020)

Indicators	1973–74 USD (mn)	1973–74 GDP (%)	1980 USD (mn)	1980 GDP (%)	1990 USD (mn)	1990 GDP (%)	2000 USD (mn)	2000 GDP (%)	2010 USD (mn)	2010 GDP (%)	2020–21(p) July–November USD (mn)	2020–21(p) July–November GDP (%)
Trade balance	−521.2	−5.48	−1,957.6	−10.79	−1,801	−5.82	−2,011	−3.76	−9,935	−8.61	−4,715	−1.43
Current transfers (includes workers' remittances)	−76.7	−0.81	402.5	2.22	846	2.73	2,171	4.07	12,315	10.68	11,104	3.36
Current account balance	−597.9	−6.29	−1,539.4	−8.49	−981	−3.17	−1,098	−2.06	−1,686	−1.46	4,109	1.24
Capital account	−115.74	−1.22	1,346.64	7.42	1,087	3.51	432	0.81	642	0.55	59	0.02
Financial account	–	–	136.2	0.75	–	–	682	1.27	651	0.56	949	0.29
Overall balance	80.09	0.84	−160.96	−0.88	313	−1.01	−281	−0.53	−656	−0.57	5,068	1.54

Sources: Bangladesh Bank BOP data publication of 1974–75 for 1973–74 data converted from *taka* (BDT). Bangladesh Economic Survey (1981–82, 1992–93); *Bangladesh Economic Review* (Government of Bangladesh 2005) of Bangladesh Bureau of Statistics and World Bank for 1980–2010 data ('BOP (% of GDP)—Bangladesh', World Bank Databank, https://data.worldbank.org/ [accessed 10 January 2021]). Bangladesh Bank Provisional BOP data and *Bangladesh Economic Review* (Government of Bangladesh 2019); Bangladesh Bank (https://www.bb.org.bd/econdata/bop.php [accessed 10 January 2021]) for 2020–21 data converted from BDT using Bangladesh Bank exchange rates.

Bangladesh has made tremendous progress in its balance of payments (BOP) position, beginning from a precarious, aid-dependent regime in the 1970s and 1980s to one of manageable deficits and even periodic surpluses, supported by strong export performance, remittance flows and satisfactory reserves (Table 1.1). Aid dependence is no longer an issue while efforts are underway to try and encourage FDI – an area where progress has been difficult – as the country is poised to graduate out of LDC status in 2024.[7]

Structural Change

Changes in the BOP, exports and growth were accompanied by profound structural changes whereby the economy was transformed from a primarily agricultural country based on traditional subsistence agriculture to one much more heavily dependent on modern industry and services (Table 1.2). In the process, rural–urban wages have converged to a large extent, although low-productivity employment still dominates the rural sector.

In the 1970s and 1980s, agriculture, especially rice cultivation, dominated the economy while jute was the largest cash crop and the dominant source of export earnings. Agriculture accounted for over 50 per cent of GDP then, declining to around 13 per cent in 2017. At the same time, the share of industry rose from 15 per cent to over 30 per cent. The service sector also expanded but at a lower rate.

The major driver of industrial growth was the rapid rise of the RMG industry and textiles sector, beginning in the mid-1980s and finally emerging as the second-largest RMG exporter today after China, accounting for some 6.8 per cent of the global share (in 2020) and over 80 per cent of Bangladesh's total exports.

Table 1.2 Bangladesh: Sectoral shares of GDP (1972–2020)

Indicator	1972	1980	1990	2000	2010	2020(p)
Agriculture	60.1	44.23	37.6	25.03	15.89	13.13
Industry	6.6	15.57	17.16	26.2	27.86	31.13
Service	32.8	40.2	45.24	48.77	56.25	55.86

Sources: Bangladesh Bureau of Statistics (1993); Bangladesh Bureau of Statistics, Gross Domestic Product (GDP) of Bangladesh 2013–2014 and 2017–18 from http://www.bbs.gov.bd/site/page/dc2bc6ce-7080-48b3-9a04-73cec782d0df/Gross-Domestic-Product-(GDP) (accessed 14 November 2021); *Bangladesh Economic Review* (Government of Bangladesh 2005: chap. 1); Bangladesh Bank (http://bbs.portal.gov.bd/sites/default/files/files/bbs.portal.gov.bd/page/057b0f3b_a9e8_4fde_b3a6_6daec3853586/2020-08-10-14-49-94b60708240f454c1036d64090cf38ec.pdf [accessed 14 November 2021]) for 2019–20 (GDP provisional estimates).

Within agriculture, too, the changes were momentous. Rice production trebled, allowing the country to become self-sufficient in staples – a long-time national dream. There was a lot of diversification as well, especially with quite dramatic expansion in fisheries and poultry farming, as well as a host of rural non-farm activities. In other words, Bangladesh's industrialization did not leave agriculture behind – in fact, agriculture supplied food at low, stable prices to urban workers, releasing cheap labour, male and female, for industry. The underlying rural transformation was influenced by the role of NGOs, microcredit, grassroots organizations and large inflows of remittances from abroad, from workers to their families back home.

Role of Services

Services include both modern and traditional forms. In terms of share of GDP, the dominant service sub-sectors are trade, transport, storage, communications, repair services and purchase of personal and household goods – accounting for 26 per cent of the sector (2018–19). Other significant components are 'community, social and personal' services (around 10 per cent), public administration, health and education (7.5 per cent), and real estate (7 per cent). Financial intermediation is also growing in importance (over 3 per cent). The structure of services suggests that the modern component is decisively in the ascendant.

Generally, during the initial stages of industrialization, the share of agricultural GDP declines and that of industry and services increases. At some point along the development path, the industrial share of GDP stagnates while that of services continues to rise. However, this 'classical' pattern can vary. In other words, while both industrial and service sectors grow, these do so at different rates at different periods of a country's development journey, and no two countries will necessarily display the exact same pattern of structural change – at least going by the recent development history of East Asia.

The share of employment generated in industry and services broadly follows the pattern of its contribution to GDP, although once again considerable variation may be seen in terms of rates of employment by sectors or sub-sectors. Here, we briefly examine the experience of some countries in the Asia region to help put Bangladesh's experience in perspective.

China, People's Republic of China (PRC)

In PRC, GDP has been mostly led by industry almost throughout the entire period, only dipping below services after 2010. On the other hand, in terms of employment, services took the lead from 1993 onwards, gradually widening the gap with industry share over time (Figures 1.6–1.7).

A Bird's-Eye View of the Bangladesh Economy 17

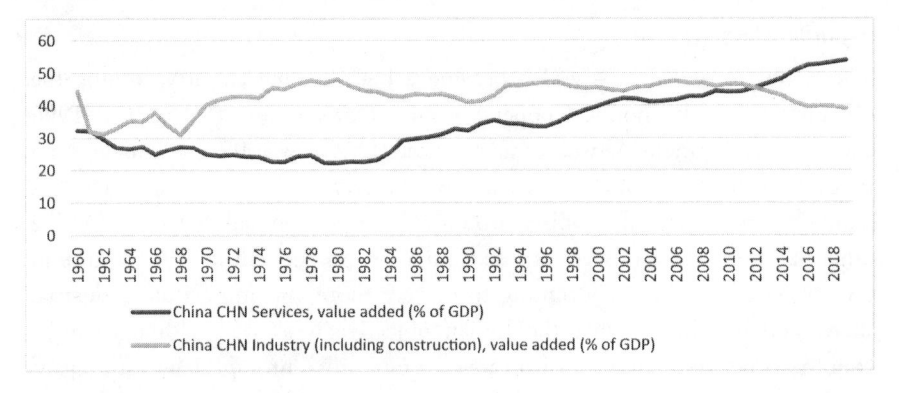

Figure 1.6 China: Industry and services as share of GDP

Sources: 'Services - China', World Bank Databank, https://data.worldbank.org/indicator/NV.SRV.TOTL.ZS?locations=CN&view=chart (accessed 14 November 2021); 'Industry (Including Construction) - China', World Bank Databank, https://data.worldbank.org/indicator/NV.IND.TOTL.ZS?locations=CN (accessed 14 November 2021).

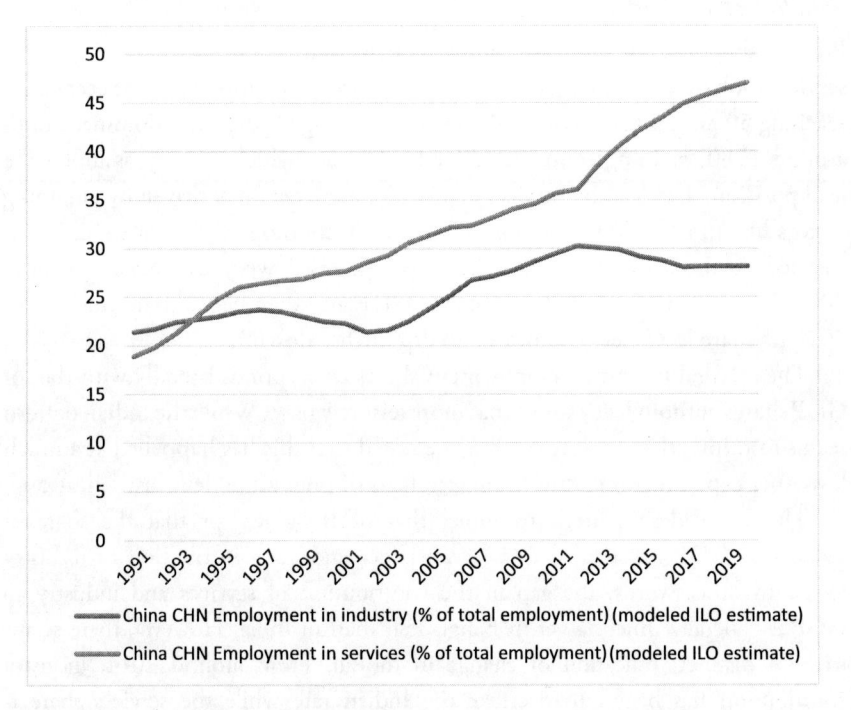

Figure 1.7 China: Share of employment

Sources: 'Employment in Services - China', World Bank Databank, https://data.worldbank.org/indicator/SL.SRV.EMPL.ZS?locations=CN (accessed 14 November 2021); 'Employment in Industry - China', World Bank Databank, https://data.worldbank.org/indicator/SL.IND.EMPL.ZS?locations=CN (accessed 14 November 2021).

Republic of Korea

The Republic of Korea – which became a high-income country, joining the Organization of Economic Cooperation and Development (OECD) in 1996 and the Development Assistance Committee (DAC) in 2009 – is known as an innovation-driven economy. The share of industry in GDP peaked in 1991 at around 38 per cent and stabilized around 32–34 per cent subsequently. On the other hand, the share of services rose from a low 30 per cent in 1963 to around 58 per cent in 2019 – continuing to diverge more and more from industrial share. Perhaps this is what the Indian objective is as well, although initial conditions between India and Korea were quite different, especially with regard to education. It may also be noted that in terms of contribution to employment, the gap between services and industry widened from around 12 per cent in the early 1990s to a whopping 40 per cent today (Figures 1.8 and 1.9). Thus, PRC and Korea display quite different trajectories of structural change.

Bangladesh and India

Prior to the 1980s, GDP was dominated by agriculture in India. Subsequently, services took over as the largest sector and its share has continued to rise ever since, reaching 50 per cent in 2019. In Bangladesh, too, agriculture was dominant until around 1980, yielding soon thereafter to services, which quickly assumed the lead position. The lead by services kept widening over time, driven by emerging sectors like information and communications technology (ICT) in which India excelled. At the same time, industrial output shares slowed, reaching a plateau in 2007–08, when it reached 30 per cent of GDP, and then began to decline – as of 2020 its share is 25 per cent and set to dip further down.[8]

The sectoral pattern of employment shares corresponds broadly with that of GDP shares, although at a somewhat more leisurely pace. While the Indian pattern seems to mimic that of Korea, it may be noted that this has happened at a much lower per capita income, thus leading to fears of premature deindustrialization.[9]

The Bangladesh pattern resembles that of India, except that the share of services in GDP has tended to be even larger and the contribution of industry lower. In other words, the gap in the contribution of services and industry to GDP is generally much larger in Bangladesh than in India. However, there seems to be a distinct indication of change in the air. From around 2014, industry contribution has begun to overtake the Indian rate while the services share is declining and tending to converge to the Indian rate – and may soon dip below it. This could signal that after having followed a similar path for decades, the two neighbouring economies are now all set to diverge – India hopes to emerge as an innovation-centred, service economy, perhaps like Korea, while Bangladesh is staying with the more conventional, time-tested industry-led approach (Figure 1.10).

A Bird's-Eye View of the Bangladesh Economy

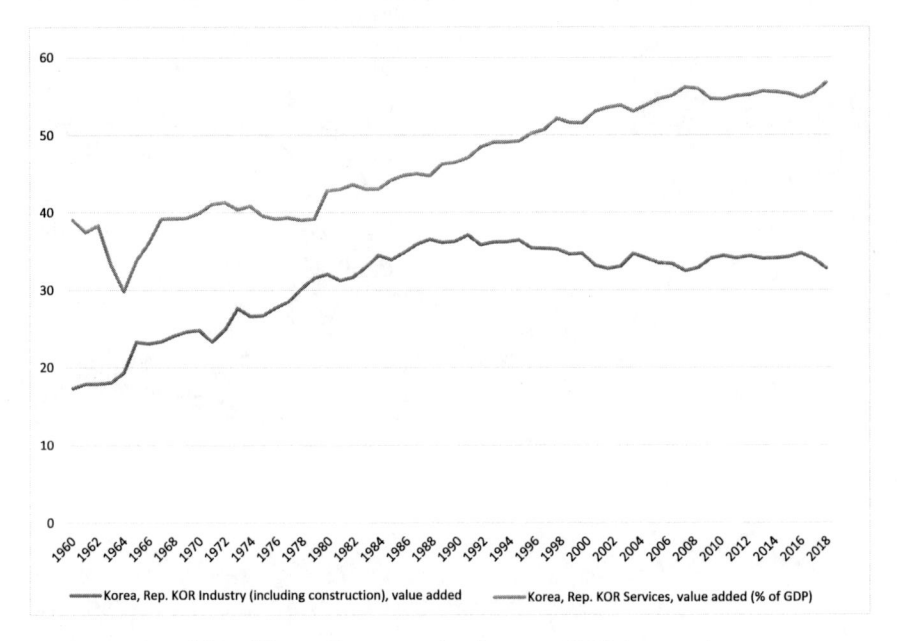

Figure 1.8 Republic of Korea: Services and industry in GDP (per cent)

Sources: 'Services - Korea, Rep.', World Bank Databank, https://data.worldbank.org/indicator/NV.SRV.TOTL.ZS?locations=KR (accessed 14 November 2021); 'Industry (Including Construction) - Korea, Rep.', World Bank Databank, https://data.worldbank.org/indicator/NV.IND.TOTL.ZS?locations=KR (accessed 14 November 2021).

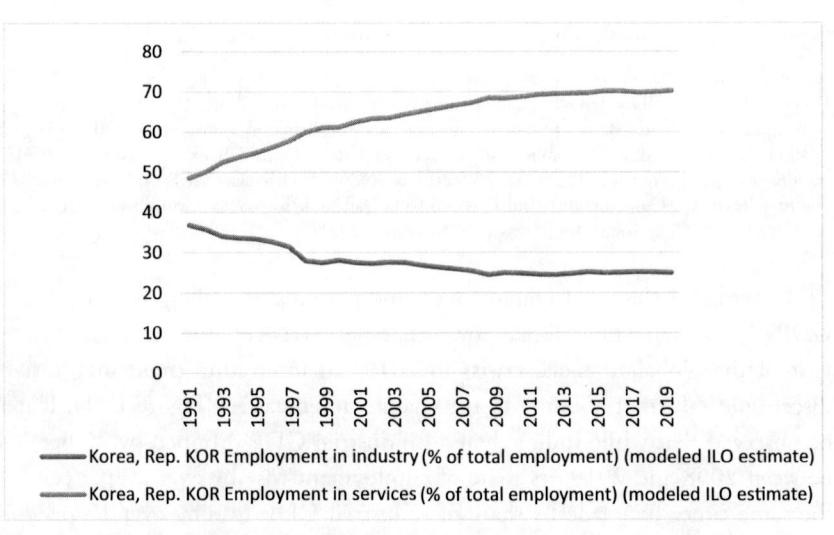

Figure 1.9 Republic of Korea: Employment in services and industry (per cent)

Sources: 'Employment in Services - Korea, Rep.', World Bank Databank, https://data.worldbank.org/indicator/SL.SRV.EMPL.ZS?locations=KR (accessed 14 November 2021); 'Employment in Industry - Korea, Rep.', World Bank Databank, https://data.worldbank.org/indicator/SL.IND.EMPL.ZS?locations=KR&view=chart (accessed 14 November 2021).

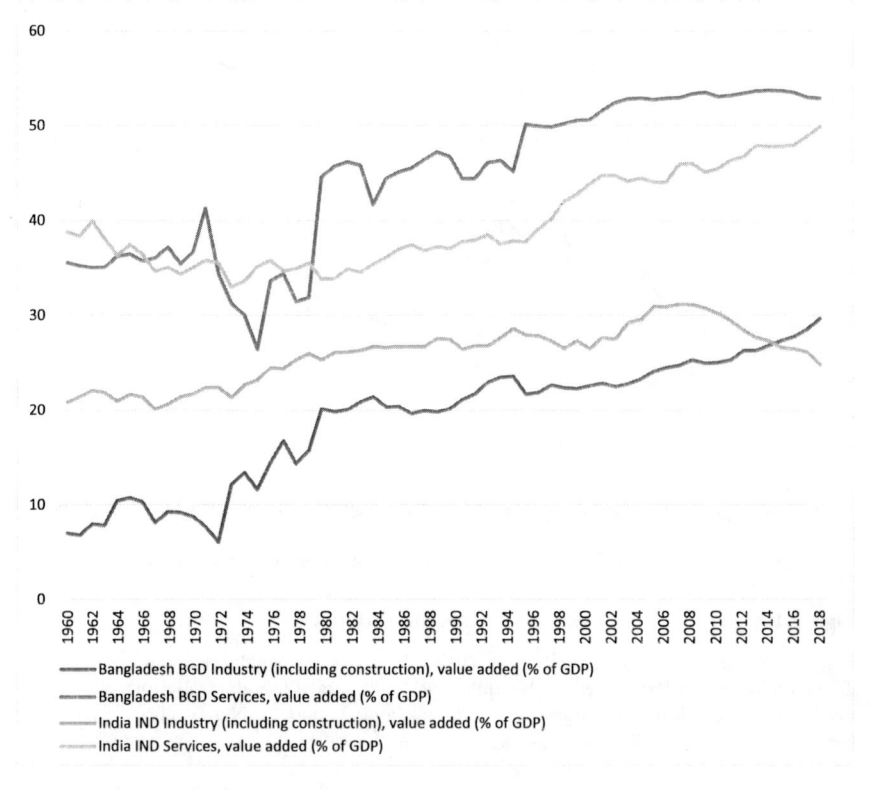

Figure 1.10 Bangladesh and India: Share of industry and services in GDP

Sources: 'Services - Bangladesh', World Bank Databank, https://data.worldbank.org/indicator/NV.SRV.TOTL.ZS?locations=BD&view=chart (accessed 14 November 2021); 'Industry (Including Construction) - Bangladesh', World Bank Databank, https://data.worldbank.org/indicator/NV.IND.TOTL.ZS?locations=BD (accessed 14 November 2021); 'Services - India', World Bank Databank, https://data.worldbank.org/indicator/NV.SRV.TOTL.ZS?locations=IN&view=chart (accessed 14 November 2021); 'Industry (Including Construction) - India', World Bank Databank, https://data.worldbank.org/indicator/NV.IND.TOTL.ZS?locations=IN (accessed 14 November 2021).

In terms of shares of employment, the patterns essentially reflect those of GDP shares. On closer look, however, especially over the period 2008 (the year of the global financial crisis) to 2019, an interesting trend may just be discernible – further alluding to the change noted earlier (Figure 1.11). It may be observed that while India's share of industrial GDP dropped by 21 per cent between 2008 and 2019, its share of employment rose by over 22 per cent! At the same time, Bangladesh's share of industrial GDP rose by over 19 per cent while the corresponding increase in employment share was around 37 per cent. In the case of services in GDP, India registered a rise of around 9 per cent while

A Bird's-Eye View of the Bangladesh Economy

[Line chart showing employment shares in Bangladesh and India, 1991–2020]

— Bangladesh BGD Employment in services (% of total employment) (modeled ILO estimate)
— Bangladesh BGD Employment in industry (% of total employment) (modeled ILO estimate)
— India IND Employment in services (% of total employment) (modeled ILO estimate)
— India IND Employment in industry (% of total employment) (modeled ILO estimate)

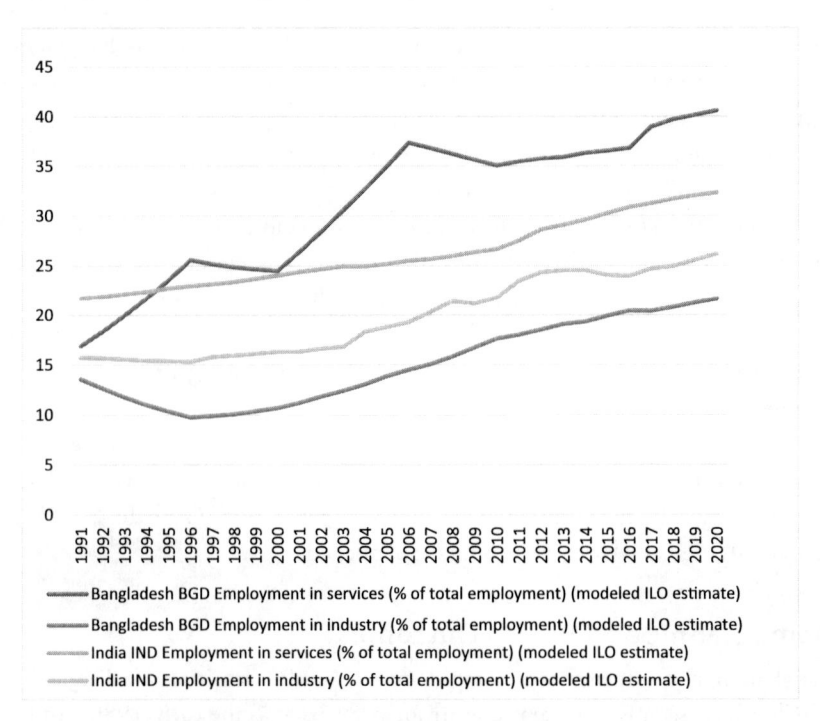

Figure 1.11 Bangladesh and India: Employment shares

Sources: 'Employment in Services - Bangladesh', World Bank Databank, https://data.worldbank.org/indicator/SL.SRV.EMPL.ZS?locations=BD&view=chart (accessed 14 November 2021); 'Employment in Industry - Bangladesh', World Bank Databank, https://data.worldbank.org/indicator/SL.IND.EMPL.ZS?locations=BD (accessed 14 November 2021); 'Employment in Services - India', World Bank Databank, https://data.worldbank.org/indicator/SL.SRV.EMPL.ZS?locations=IN&view=chart (accessed 14 November 2021); 'Employment in Industry - India', World Bank Databank, https://data.worldbank.org/indicator/SL.IND.EMPL.ZS?locations=IN (accessed 14 November 2021).

Table 1.3 Share of services in GDP and total employment: India and Bangladesh, 2008–19 (per cent)

Sector	Share of GDP 2008	Share of GDP 2019	Per Cent Change	Employment 2008	Employment 2019	Per Cent Change
Industry						
India	31.1	24.7	−21	21.4	26.2	22.4
Bangladesh	24.9	29.7	19.3	15.8	21.6	36.7
Services						
India	45.9	49.9	8.7	26.0	32.3	24.2
Bangladesh	52.9	52.8	–	35.1	40.6	15.7

Source: Based on data from World Bank Databank (https://data.worldbank.org/indicator/ [accessed 14 November 2021]).

the corresponding share of employment rose by 24 per cent. In Bangladesh, services share in GDP stagnated, although its employment share still rose – by almost 16 per cent (Table 1.3).

This is also reflected in agriculture – or more precisely, in its decline. In 2010, over 47 per cent of employment in Bangladesh was still being accounted for by agriculture (when its GDP share was considerably smaller, at 17 per cent). By 2020, employment derived from services overtook agriculture; agriculture's share declined further to under 38 per cent while service sector employment rose from 35 per cent to almost 41 per cent. In other words, for the first time in history, services became the largest employer, ousting agriculture from the premier position.

Could this be the moment when the economy enters a new phase as it is propelled forward by expanding industrialization? Could this also lead to a bigger relative role for industry in employment generation? Over the last decade (2010–20), that is what appears to have happened.

Demographic and Health Outcomes

Bangladesh also experienced a rapid demographic transition, indications of which can be seen in the data series from as far back as the early 1980s. In fact, one observes a steep decline in the fertility rate from well over 5 children per woman in 1980 to 2.5 by the late 1990s. After that, the rate of decline eases off

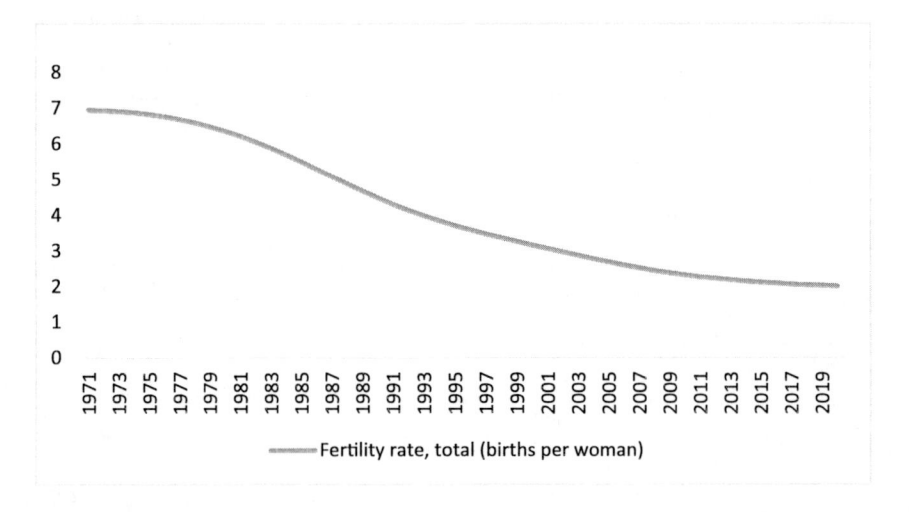

Figure 1.12 Fertility rate, total (births per woman, ages 15–49), Bangladesh, 1972–2020

Source: 'Fertility Rate - Bangladesh', World Bank Databank, https://data.worldbank.org/indicator/SP.DYN.TFRT.IN?locations=BD&view=chart (accessed 14 November 2021).

A Bird's-Eye View of the Bangladesh Economy 23

but reaches 2.3 before levelling off by 2009 (Figure 1.12). If we think back to the Malthusian debates of the 1970s and 1980s, this is a far cry from that era and a clear indication that while population remains a concern for Bangladesh in the context of scarce arable land, it cannot be considered a nightmare anymore. The challenge is in fact to exploit the demographic dividend that has emerged, according to some, a bit too early relative to its economic transition.

Of course, the fertility rate is one aspect of the 'population problem'. The other thing to note is the progress made in reducing infant, child and maternal mortality. The decline in infant mortality was actually steeper and longer than in the fertility rate (Figure 1.13). The decline in maternal mortality, while striking, was slower than the decline in fertility (Figure 1.14). Basically, the various health-demographic indicators moved broadly together, resulting in life expectancy rising from under 50 in the 1970s to over 71 years in 2020 – higher than in India – and the emergence of the 'demographic dividend', which if properly used can result in a once-in-a-lifetime big push forward for the economy. It is interesting to note that the declining trend began quite early, from the early 1980s, and was sustained for at least three decades before stabilizing. This also finds reflection in the health infrastructure that evolved and ultimately in life expectancy. Indicators on access to health services show a steady expansion in the availability of medical personnel, including doctors, nurses and technicians in both the public and private sectors (Tables 1.4 and 1.5). While quantitative gains seem significant, the inability of the health infrastructure to deal with anything beyond basic health services remains poor, as mercilessly exposed by COVID-19.[10]

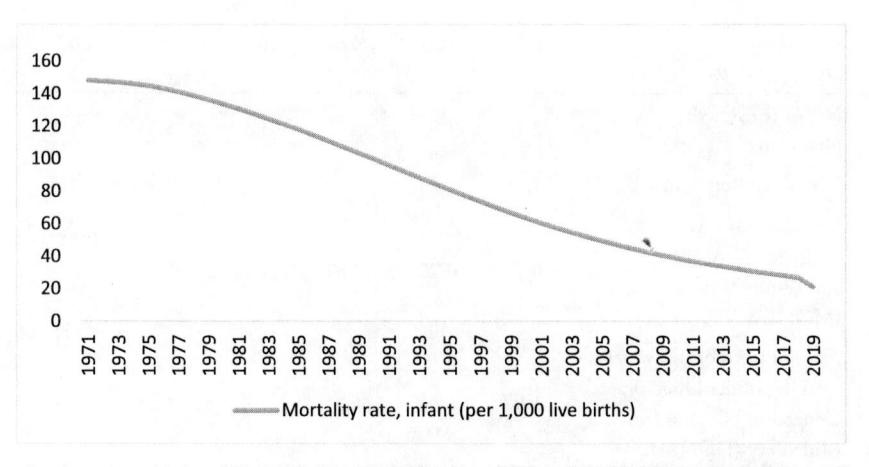

Figure 1.13 Infant mortality rate (per 1,000 live births), Bangladesh, 1972–2020

Source: 'Mortality Rate, Infant - Bangladesh', World Bank Databank, https://data.worldbank.org/indicator/SP.DYN.IMRT.IN?locations=BD (accessed 14 November 2021).

[Chart showing maternal mortality ratio declining from ~1,329 in 1980 to ~200 by 2017, with steepest decline between 1980-1995]

— Maternal mortality ratio (modeled estimate, per 100,000 live births)

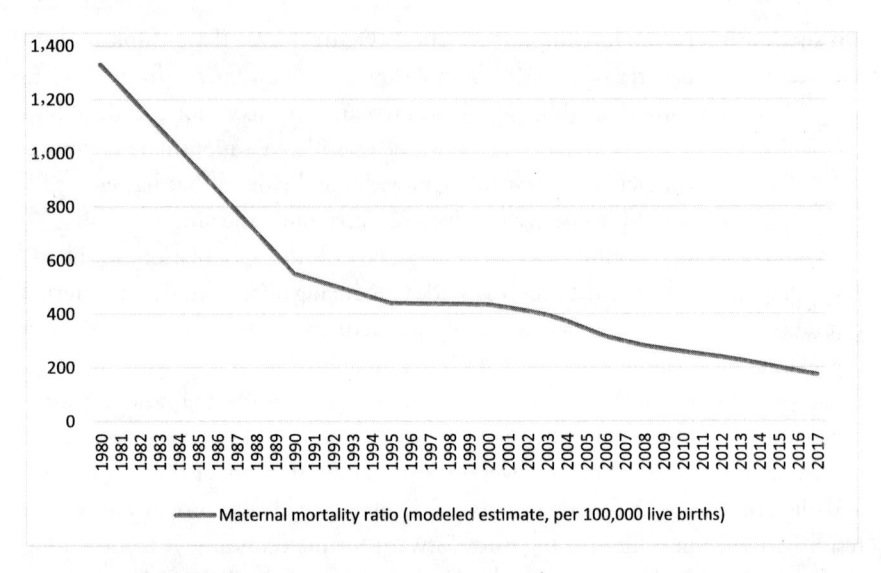

Figure 1.14 Maternal mortality ratio (modelled estimate, per 100,000 live births)

Sources: Data point (1,329.4) of 1980 was from http://ghdx.healthdata.org/record/ihme-data/maternal-mortality-estimates-country-1980-2008 (accessed 15 November 2021); Data points for 1990 and 1995 taken from WHO, https://www.who.int/pmnch/knowledge/publications/bangladesh.pdf (accessed 15 November 2021); Data points for 2000–19 were taken from World Bank Databank, https://data.worldbank.org/indicator/SH.STA.MMRT?locations=BD (accessed 15 November 2021). All remaining points were extrapolated.

Table 1.4 Availability of doctors, nurses and other technical staff in government health services occupations

Indicators (Per 10,000 Population)	1997	2005	2010	2014	2016	2019
No. of registered physicians	2.15	3.3	3.42	3.8	5.34	6.73
No. of registered nurses	1.24	1.04	1.64	1.15	2.996	–
No. of doctors working under Ministry of Health and Family Welfare (MOHFW)	0.7	0.72	0.81	1.37	1.29	1.55
No. of nurses or midwives working under Directorate General of Nursing and Midwifery (DGNM)	1.07	1.35	1.54	–	1.71	–

(*Contd.*)

Table 1.4 (*Contd.*)

Indicators (Per 10,000 Population)	1997	2005	2010	2014	2016	2019
No. of medical technologists working under Directorate General of Health Services (DGHS)	0.11	0.13	–	0.38	0.33	0.6
No. of community and domiciliary health workers working under MOHFW	1.69	1.46	–	3.92	2.15	2.26
No. of beds in DGHS-run public hospitals	2.43	2.48	2.59	2.91 (2015)	2.89	3.30
Total no. of beds in the DGHS-run hospitals and registered private hospitals	3.35	3.75	5.36	7.6 (2015)	8.4	5.53
Life expectancy	59.6	65.1	67.7	71.8	72.49	72

Source: 'Real Time Health Information Dashboard', Directorate General of Health Services (DGHS), https://www.dghs.gov.bd/index.php/en/publications/health-bulletin/dghs-health-bulletin (accessed 15 November 2021).

Table 1.5 Access to health services

Indicators (Per 10,000 Population)	1997	2005	2010	2014	2016	2019
No. of registered physicians	2.15	3.3	3.42	3.8	5.34	6.73
No. of registered nurses	1.24	1.04	1.64	1.15	2.996	–
No. of doctors working under Ministry of Health and Family Welfare (MOHFW)	0.7	0.72	0.81	1.37	1.29	1.55
No. of nurses or midwives working under Directorate General of Nursing and Midwifery (DGNM)	1.07	1.35	1.54	–	1.71	–
No. of medical technologists working under Directorate General of Health Services (DGHS)	0.11	0.13	–	0.38	0.33	0.6
No. of community and domiciliary health workers working under MOHFW	1.69	1.46	–	3.92	2.15	2.26
No. of beds in DGHS–run public hospitals	2.43	2.48	2.59	2.91 (2015)	2.89	3.30

(*Contd.*)

Table 1.5 (*Contd.*)

Indicators (Per 10,000 Population)	1997	2005	2010	2014	2016	2019
Total no. of beds in the DGHS-run hospitals and registered private hospitals	3.35	3.75	5.36	7.6 (2015)	8.4	5.53
Life expectancy		59.6	65.1	67.7	71.8	72.49	72

Source: 'Real Time Health Information Dashboard', Directorate General of Health Services (DGHS), https://www.dghs.gov.bd/index.php/en/publications/health-bulletin/dghs-health-bulletin (accessed 15 November 2021).

Food and Nutrition

Progress in food consumption and nutritional outcomes in terms of calories, undernutrition, wasting and stunting, especially of children, is particularly noteworthy. This aspect has two separate dimensions: (*a*) the first-generation issue of basic 'food' security – which for most of Bangladesh's history meant having enough rice to eat, and (*b*) nutritional status in terms of ensuring availability and access to a balanced diet. Bangladesh has declared victory over the first food security challenge, while the challenge of nutrition has now come to the fore. Nevertheless, Bangladesh has made significant advances in tackling nutrition,[11] although a considerable distance remains to be travelled before victory can be announced on this complex front.

Thus, food and calorie availability and intake steadily increased over the years, accompanying the success of the Green Revolution (GR) in rice in the 1980s and 1990s, resulting in the achievement of national food 'self-sufficiency', low food prices, higher rural wages and large declines in the poverty rate.[12] This was Bangladesh's single biggest breakthrough, paving the way for subsequent developments in many other fields, including rural incomes, rural poverty, child and maternal nutrition, health and education. In fact, given the dominant role that the food economy traditionally played in Bangladesh, the breakthrough in rice production and yields would inevitably have large micro- or household-level impacts for rural households as well as economy-wide impacts, via a number of pathways, including food import decline and BOP effects, lower inflation and higher overall growth (K. A. S. Murshid 1985a).

Advances in nutritional indicators followed suit. Thus, in terms of 'height for age' (stunting), an improvement of nearly 50 per cent was recorded for children under 5 between 1985 and 2014. The estimates were based on multiple rounds of consistently measured, comparable data from the Bangladesh Demographic and Health Surveys (BDHS) (UNICEF 1990; Black et al. 2013). A number of other indicators are also shown in Table 1.6, including nutrition, height and

Table 1.6 Bangladesh nutrition data

Indicators (in Per Cent)	1985	1990	1996	2000	2004	2007	2011	2014	2018
Prevalence of stunting among children under 5 years (0–59 months)	70.9	63.4	60	51	51	43	41	36	31
Prevalence of underweight among children under 5 years (0–59 months)	66.8	61.5	54	42.2	42.8	41	36	33	22
Prevalence of wasting among children under 5 years (0–59 months)	17.3	17.5	15.5	12.5	14.6	17.5	16	14	8
Prevalence of anaemia among children (6–59 months)	–	72.5	67.3	62.2	49	52.7	51	51	40.26 (2016)
Prevalence of anaemia among women of reproductive age (15–49 years)	–	55.3	51.0	48.1	45.5	43.5	40.8	39.7	39.89 (2016)
Prevalence of children (0–5 months) exclusively breastfed	–	46 (1993)	45.2	46	36.2	43	64	55	65
Prevalence of low birthweight (less than 2.5 kilograms) (of children whose birthweights are known)	–	–	–	–	43	41	36	23	27.8 (2015)
Trends in nutritional status of women (15–49 years) (underweight)	–	–	52	45.4	34	30	24	19	–
Trends in nutritional status of women (15–49 years) (short stature)	–	–	17.3	15.9	16	15	13	13	–
Trends in nutritional status of women (15–49 years) (overweight or obese)	–	–	2.9	–	9	12	17	24	–

Sources: Save the Children calculation based on the Demographic and Health Survey (DHS); Real-time health information dashboard Directorate General of Health Services (DGHS), USAID: Bangladesh: Nutrition Profile 2018; Bangladesh DHS (2018, 2011, 2014, 1996, 1999) (see Mitra and Associates, various years); UNICEF data warehouse.

weight status, anaemia in women, and low birthweight of babies – all of which demonstrate considerable progress.

Nisbett et al. (2017) note the strong nutritional performance of Bangladesh in addressing basic as well as underlying factors, for example, assets, paternal and maternal education, mother's weight, incidence of open defecation and availability of piped water or safe water. These have in fact led to nutritional gains for Bangladesh that is considered to have been one of the highest in the world. Headey and Hoddinot (2016) also explored various explanatory variables underlying alternative nutritional outcomes and found a strong, primal impact of rising rural incomes. It can be argued with some conviction that rural incomes improved largely because of GR in rice in the 1980s and 1990s through higher yields and rising wages. The trend was strengthened by rising labour demand in industry and abroad, and growth of the non-farm sector.

Educational Outcomes and Gender

Bangladesh has made striking progress in education, gender equality and women's empowerment, which in turn generated gender outcomes that are much better than that of many of its neighbours, resulting in larger participation of women in the labour market and a more productive labour force. One needs to dwell on the full implications of this outcome for just a moment.

The conventional view of Bangladesh was that it was a poor, Muslim-majority country where women are particularly disadvantaged in terms of access to education and health services, are unable to move outside their homes for work or entertainment, are victims of the patriarchy that leaves them with little control over their destinies and with very little say in key decision-making roles (see Chapter 9). Thus, for example, no one in their wildest imagination could predict that one day Bangladesh would outperform (non-Muslim) India in participation of women in the labour market or experience better gender scores in terms of gender development or inequality indicators. It is perhaps another matter that the initial 'Muslim' diagnosis of Bangladesh may have been incorrect, led by Eurocentric scholars who failed to understand that Bangladeshi Islam was different and that Bengali society was far more open and accepting to new opportunities and influences than they were given credit for. The fact that Bengalis in Bangladesh 'silently' converted, first to Buddhism and then to Islam, should have alerted us. Similarly, Bengalis in Bangladesh quickly accepted the new development mantras brought in first by NGOs and then pressed home by the government and later by the private sector, which suddenly found themselves in need of large numbers of women workers for the RMG industry. The path of these women workers was facilitated by the hordes of women staff working for NGOs as paramedics, motivators, organizers, field officers and teachers whose presence in rural Bangladesh, riding around in their bikes in the 1970s and 1980s, was not only ubiquitous but also revolutionary.[13] There was some pushback from religious forces but that was contained. The rural folks thus became increasingly used to the idea of seeing women working outside the homestead. Today, village women are working as maids in the Middle East, Malaysia and Singapore.

School Enrolment

Primary school enrolment rose from around 70 per cent (gross – which includes children who are over or under the official age for this group) in 1980 to 111 per cent in 2018 – the increase being slightly higher for girls. In the case of secondary schools, gross enrolment rose from 18 to 67 per cent over the same period. Girls' enrolment in 1980 was 9 per cent – lower than that of boys, but by 2017 it rose to 73 per cent, which is a full 10 per cent higher than for boys! Tertiary enrolment made significant strides, although the numbers are modest, rising from 3 per cent to 13 per cent over the period. The male–female gap narrowed considerably here as well but was not eliminated (Table 1.7).

The dropout rate figures are also extremely interesting. Girls dropping out of primary schools was rampant in 1981 – 44.7 per cent compared to less than

Table 1.7 Bangladesh: School enrolment trends

Year	Primary (% gross)	Male (% gross)	Female (% gross)	Secondary* (% gross)	Male (% gross)	Female (% gross)	Tertiary (% gross)	Male (% gross)	Female (% gross)
1970	56.27	36.78	75.01	20.76	30.49	10.73	2.13	3.76	0.43
1975	79.98	103.41	55.55	17.82	26.33	8.91	2.79	4.84	0.71
1980	70.61	86.97	53.45	18.46	27.73	8.96	3.19	5.43	0.9
1990	81.05	87.82	74.01	20.40	26.84	13.69	4.09	6.78	1.32
2000	–	–	–	48.11	47.44	48.81	5.45	7.27	3.57
2005	98.66	96.46	100.95	45.52	44.10	47.00	6.24	8.15	4.25
2010	102.66	99.58	105.86	50.12	47.27	53.08	13.28	15.66	10.86
2015	120.43	115.96	125.09	63.52	59.80	67.42	13.44	15.43	11.39
2020	109.49	106.15	113.20	72.56	67.01	78.28	24.02	27.87	20.02

Sources: (a) 'Bangladesh', World Bank Databank https://data.worldbank.org/country/bangladesh?view=chart (accessed 15 November 2021); (b) Annual Primary School Census (DPE 2019).

Note: *Figures for 1970 and 1975 refer to 1973 and 1976.

half of that for boys. By 2017, the dropout rate for boys declined to 8 per cent, but for girls it declined to less than 2 per cent. This is nothing short of a miracle in a country where girls were supposedly more undervalued compared to boys.

While not as dramatic, secondary school dropouts reflect similar trends – significant reduction over time, with the reduction rate being much sharper for girls (Table 1.8). The trends in the student–teacher ratio show a decline for primary schools but a modest rise in both secondary and tertiary education, reflecting an attempt to keep the ratio manageable – clearly, this is very unfavourable by regional and international standards (Table 1.9).

The considerable narrowing of the gender gap in schools appears to have had a pronounced effect on various women's empowerment indicators. Thus, the Gender Development Index (GDI) rose from 0.698 in 1995 (not available for earlier years) to 0.881 in 2017. Similarly, the Gender Inequality Index (GII) declined from 0.71 to 0.54 over the same period.[14] Other indicators like the male and female Human Development Index (HDI) also tell a similar tale (Table 1.10).

It would be misleading to end the discussion on gender without putting up some serious flags relating to areas of growing concern. One such area is the issue of child marriage that persists, with nearly 59 per cent of girls aged 20–24 who reported getting married before the age of 18 (UNICEF 2021).

Table 1.8 Bangladesh: Trends in dropout rates

	Children out of School (% of Primary School Age)			Adolescents out of School (% of Lower Secondary School Age)		
Year	Total	Male	Female	Total	Male	Female
1981	32.38	20.65	44.69	–	–	–
1990	27.54	21.91	33.38	–	–	–
2005	4.63	7.27	1.88	32.29	35.85	28.33
2010	5.07	9.92	0.02	28.063	31.43	24.26
2015	–	–	–	20.57	28.13	12.69
2017	4.85	7.85	1.72	10.27	–	–

Sources: United Nations Educational, Scientific, and Cultural Organization (UNESCO) Institute for Statistics; 'Children out of School – Bangladesh', World Bank Databank, https://data.worldbank.org/indicator/SE.PRM.UNER.ZS?locations=BD (accessed 15 November 2021); 'Bangladesh – Out-of-school rate for Children of Lower Secondary School Age', Knoema, https://knoema.com/atlas/Bangladesh/topics/Education/Secondary-Education/Out-of-school-rate-for-children-of-lower-secondary-school-age (accessed 15 November 2021).

Note: This data is based on World Bank data but does not appear to match the data currently available in the World Bank data website. The updated Bank data seems to be from a new series thus creating a problem with interpreting change, and hence not used.

A Bird's-Eye View of the Bangladesh Economy

Table 1.9 Student–teacher ratios over time

Year	Primary	Secondary	Tertiary
1980	53.56	23.76	19.33
1990	63	27.44	19.35
2000	–	38.43	19.75
2005	47.04	23.92	17.43
2010	42.97	28.33	25.96 (2011)
2015	36.13	35.2 (2013)	22.87 (2014)
2017	30.01	33.98	30.34

Sources: United Nations Educational, Scientific, and Cultural Organization (UNESCO, n.d.) Institute for Statistics, World Bank; 'Pupil–Teacher Ratio, Primary', World Bank Databank, https://data.worldbank.org/indicator/SE.PRM.ENRL.TC.ZS?locations=BD (accessed 15 November 2021); 'Pupil–Teacher Ratio, Secondary', World Bank Databank, https://data.worldbank.org/indicator/SE.SEC.ENRL.TC.ZS?locations=BD (accessed 15 November 2021); 'Pupil–Teacher Ratio, Tertiary', World Bank Databank, https://data.worldbank.org/indicator/SE.TER.ENRL.TC.ZS?locations=BD (accessed 15 November 2021).

Table 1.10 Women empowerment indicators

Indicator	1995	2000	2005	2010	2015	2017
Gender Development Index (GDI)	0.698	0.753	0.791	0.843	0.879	0.881
Gender Inequality Index (GII)	0.710	0.680	0.634	0.586	0.547	0.542
Human Development Index (HDI), female	0.335	0.388	0.431	0.488	0.554	0.567

Sources: For GDI, see http://hdr.undp.org/en/indicators/137906 (accessed 15 November 2021); for GII, see http://hdr.undp.org/en/indicators/68606 (accessed 15 November 2021); for HDI (female), see http://hdr.undp.org/en/indicators/136906 (accessed 15 November 2021).

Other concerns relate to violence against women, which appears to have increased (or perhaps become more visible) as women began to assert themselves in the workplace, in schools and at home (Murshid and Murshid 2019). There is a growing imbalance in literacy rates as well: while on average literacy rates are still higher for males compared to females, this seems set to change. For youth aged 15–24, literacy rates are significantly higher for girls (94.9 per cent) compared to boys (91.8 per cent). How these kinds of reversed inequalities might affect sociocultural norms and gender relations should give us pause.

Poverty and Inequality
Poverty
Perhaps no other topic has attracted more attention in the Bangladesh development literature than poverty and the related issue of food insecurity throughout much of the past 50 years. Interspersed with this discussion, observers also kept an eye out for inequality trends, although the scholarly preoccupation was almost entirely with poverty studies. The same could also be said about development partners, multilateral development agencies and NGOs that have engaged closely with Bangladesh. This consensus among all key actors about the need to focus on poverty was certainly commendable. While the question of inequality inevitably arose, it was generally assumed that it would eventually diminish after a certain point in the development cycle had been reached (à la Kuznets) and that indeed 'all boats would rise with the tide'. In the meantime, the best option was to pursue the growth and poverty reduction agenda energetically. Given the increasingly louder criticism against trickle-down,[15] a compromise approach was advocated: for social groups unable to enter mainstream economic activity in a growth-led, dynamic market, the answer temporarily would have to be to establish well-targeted safety net programmes. This was essentially the route that was adopted in Bangladesh; in other words, the question of inequality remained largely ignored by policymakers.

There was another kind of engagement that generated considerable hope – that the numerous donor-supported NGOs involved in grassroots-level development work and experimenting with numerous, heterogeneous micro-interventions in the area of education, health, awareness building, basic technical skills for poultry and homestead agriculture or family planning, water sanitation and, of course, microcredit would successfully evolve a battery of tested, effective, anti-poverty tools that would have some impact at the margin and, taken together, a powerful anti-poverty role.

One could go even further to say that both policies and interventions generally proved effective. Despite all the strenuous debates, especially in the 1970s and 1980s, arguing for or against a particular policy position in Bangladesh, for example, on the impact of the GR, the solution to the population problem, aid effectiveness or effectiveness of targeted, micro-interventions (including microcredit), impact of rural infrastructure (rural roads, rural energy, water sanitation), as well as of macro policies like structural adjustment and trade liberalization – all these policy interventions and innovations actually did deliver, although these seem to have found limited, piecemeal expression in the literature.[16] However, let us go back to poverty and inequality outcomes and trends over the past 50 years.

Much research effort has been directed to the definition and estimation of poverty, to understand its nature, extent, dimensions, location, correlates and trends. Quite apart from the conventional approach to measurement of static poverty, efforts have also been expended to assess poverty dynamics and to distinguish between chronic and transient poverty based on panel data. Fortunately, panel data sets generated by research institutes proved invaluable in taking such exercises forward. While calorie, income or expenditure-based measures have dominated, some observers have also experimented with asset-based measures or even multidimensional measures of poverty, including estimating an HDI, which incorporates poverty with other measures of deprivation.

In the context of Bangladesh, the staple database for poverty analyses is the household expenditure surveys (HES) of the early years (prior to 1995), subsequently expanded to include income data and renamed as household income–expenditure surveys (HIES). These are produced every five years by the Bangladesh Bureau of Statistics (BBS). In addition, the panel datasets also allowed researchers to provide an independent assessment of change.

The longest panel is the Bangladesh Institute of Development Studies (BIDS) dataset in 2000, 2003–04 and 2007 (Hossain and Nargis 2009). Additional panels have also been generated by InM (Institute of Microfinance) and World Bank–BIDS. These collectively take us up to 2010 (Khandker and Samad 2014; Osmani and Latif 2013). After 2010, we have one round of HIES available (BBS 2016), while another InM–BIDS panel is currently being processed.

It should be mentioned briefly that the official poverty line moved out of the 'direct calorie intake' (DCI) and 'food-energy intake' (FEI) measures in 1995 when these were replaced by the more reliable 'cost of basic needs' (CBN) measure.[17] CBN is constructed by estimating income or expenditure required for a minimum consumption bundle that is sufficient to meet calorie needs as well as covering additional essential expenditures. The measure reflects ability rather than actual consumption and has been widely adopted.

According to the latest official estimates available, one in four people were poor in 2016 (24.3 per cent), with urban poverty at 18.3 per cent and rural poverty at 26.4 per cent. Poverty has been steadily declining since the early 1980s, decelerating more quickly in the 1990s and the first decade of 2000. The decline appears to have slowed down somewhat after 2010.[18]

This trend is corroborated by studies based on panel data as well.[19] In addition, World Bank estimates based on the international poverty line of USD 1.90 per capita (in 2011, purchasing power parity [PPP]) also show impressive gains for the period 1991–92 to 2016.

The best estimates of rural poverty for the 1970–90 period are from Hossain and Sen (1992). As noted earlier, these were estimated using BBS (HES) data using a standard methodology similar to CBN, which was also adopted by BBS from HIES (1995–96) onwards.[20] The poverty estimates presented later show a decline in the headcount index steadily over the period, reaching around 40 per cent in 1988–89.

These figures are not strictly comparable with the BBS estimates shown in Table 1.11, although the broad trend indicated would seem valid. This trend has continued into the 1990s and beyond, marking a dramatic shift in urban and rural poverty as well as moderate and extreme poverty (Table 1.12). In particular, the relatively sharp decline in extreme poverty is especially noteworthy given the widespread notion that it was deeply entrenched and difficult to eradicate.

While Bangladesh's poverty eradication record is excellent, aided by broad-based growth that involved both urban and rural areas and supported by inclusive finance, remittances from workers abroad, the GR and family planning, there is still some way to go before victory can be declared. The growth–poverty relationship may be weakening, for one. In addition, in terms of international

Table 1.11 Trends in rural poverty (1973–74 to 1988–89)

1973–74	1976–77	1977–78	1981–82	1983–84	1985–86	1988–89
71.3	–	–	65.3	50	41.3	43.8
			(60.8)	(42.8)	(38.9)	(38.7)

Source: Hossain and Sen (1992: 6–7). Based on BBS data.
Note: Figures in brackets are based on income rather than expenditure.

Table 1.12 Trends in moderate and extreme poverty (1991–92 to 2016)

	Moderate Poverty			Extreme Poverty		
	Rural	Urban	National	Rural	Urban	National
1991–92	58.7	42.7	56.6	43.7	23.6	41.0
1995–96	54.5	27.8	50.1	39.4	13.7	35.1
2000	52.3	35.2	48.9	37.9	20.0	34.3
2005	43.8	28.4	40.0	28.6	14.6	25.1
2010	35.2	21.3	31.5	21.1	7.7	17.6
2016	26.7	19.3	24.5	15.0	8.0	13.0

Sources: World Bank (2013); World Bank (2008); Murgai and Zaidi (2004); World Bank (2019a). Extreme poverty as defined in CBN method (Ahmed et al. 2019).

comparisons using the World Bank USD 1.90 a day poverty line, many countries in the region remain ahead of Bangladesh as far as poverty rates are concerned (Roome, Gapihan and Lee 2019).

Economic Inequality

Given Bangladesh's performance in accelerating GDP growth, it is not surprising that inequality, especially in incomes, has been rising to levels that many observers find 'alarming' (Osmani and Sen 2011; A. R. Khan 2005). This appears to be an urgent area of concern, although policy responses to tackle this have been weak. The role of fiscal policies is limited due to its poor coverage and the vast size of the informal sector. However, there is one feature of the inequality aspect that is particularly interesting: while income distribution has been worsening rapidly, the same is not true for the distribution of consumption expenditure. Over time, the gap between the two distributions has widened: consumption expenditure data (generally considered more reliable) depict a relatively egalitarian picture in terms of the standard of living enjoyed, suggesting that conspicuous consumption by the rich was not stark. Growing inequality in income distribution, on the other hand, implies that the level of resources accumulating with the richer classes was taking place at a relatively fast rate, and the rich therefore were very likely to be saving or -investing at a high rate as well – a situation that is perhaps not as alarming as it might initially appear and seems favourable for continued growth and poverty reduction (Table 1.13).[21]

Table 1.13 Trends in inequality (income and consumption Gini coefficients)

Period	*Income Gini*	*Consumption Gini*	*Gap (Income–Consumption)*
1973–74	0.36	–	–
1981–82	0.39	–	–
1991–92	0.39	0.26	0.13
1995–96	0.43	0.31	0.12
2000	0.45	0.33	0.12
2005	0.47	0.33	0.14
2010	0.46	0.32	0.14
2016	0.48	0.32	0.16

Source: BBS data (HES and HIES, various years).

Conclusion

It is relatively easy to tell the story of Bangladesh in descriptive terms. Many authors have done that to conclude that the outcomes were unexpected – a development surprise, a paradox, a miracle or even a quiet transformation![22] The extent of surprise is related directly to the initial conditions that existed at birth. Given the high aid dependence, widespread poverty and few resources, the outlook for Bangladesh in the 1970s was dim. Thus, even modest development would evoke a sense of surprise, especially to observers who were privy to the realities of those early times.

The notion of 'paradox' was put forward in at least two senses. First, there was the reference to 'governance' and corruption. There is little doubt that governance was acutely poor while the country regularly clocked in as 'one of the most corrupt' in the world as ranked by Transparency International. However, despite the poor governance, Bangladesh still managed to achieve decent progress, especially in the social indicators – hence a paradox.

There was another sense in which the word was used: Bangladesh's investment in the social sectors like health and education was less than spectacular – in fact, as a per cent of GDP it was lower than most of its neighbours. The outcomes, however, were much better – so how did this happen? In other words, Bangladesh was an 'outlier', a paradox. Some overenthusiastic observers went even further by invoking the 'miracle' claim (Sawada, Mahmud and Kitano 2018). Again, this notion alludes to the stark, hopeless conditions of the 1970s when everyone agreed that only a miracle could get Bangladesh out of its woes.

The rest of this book is devoted to understanding the processes underlying these outcomes, rather than the outcomes themselves. These processes relate to transformation of real sectors, markets, institutions, policies, innovations, and technology driven by the complex interplay of government, NGOs, donor partners and the private sector. First, however, it is important to re-examine Bangladesh's initial conditions.

It is perhaps best to flag early on, however, that while this book has explored various facets of micro-governance in relevant chapters, it has deliberately stayed away from the broader question of poor macro-governance and its relationship with shifts in political dynamics and concerns of growing authoritarianism amidst a shrinking democratic space. Bangladesh's poor record on governance does not appear to be reflected in its economic development performance. As far as the rise of authoritarianism and growing 'democratic deficiency' is concerned, I would argue that these deserve separate treatment as dependent variables in their own right and are best left to scholars trained in political science (Riaz 2019, 2021; Devine et al. 2017).

2

Initial Conditions

The Odds Revisited

Overview

The conditions at the time of its birth in 1971 could not have been less auspicious for Bangladesh. The country was overwhelmingly agricultural and rural at the time with much of agriculture dominated by just one crop, namely rice, which was grown in the vast flood plains under risky, rain-fed conditions. The other important crop was jute – the main foreign exchange earner for the country. As it happened, floods and poor successive rice harvests combined with a much-weakened administration which, along with depleted food reserves, empty coffers and an infrastructure in tatters, ushered in famine in 1974 that not only took a heavy toll in terms of human lives but also succeeded in branding Bangladesh as a poor, famine-prone and crisis-prone country that would heavily need to depend on foreign aid for a very long time – an abiding image that is only now beginning to be shed.[1]

The infrastructure, rudimentary to begin with, was in shambles with bridges blown up, roads in poor shape and even the country's ports at Chittagong and Mongla rendered inoperative – both experiencing massive damage and destruction. The Chittagong Port suffered the greatest damage from the operations of Bengali Naval Commandos during the 1971 war who used limpet mines to blow up ships anchored in Chittagong. This disrupted shipping while at the same time sending a stark message to the enemy. It was a Russian naval contingent under Rear Admiral Sergey Pavlovich Zuenko who took up the challenge of clearing the port of all obstacles, including innumerable mines and sunken ships, to make it ready for normal operations – a process that was declared complete on 30 June 1974.[2] It took less time to clear out the Mongla Port, which too suffered heavy damage during the war, mainly from aerial bombing.[3]

In addition, there was the need to resettle and rehabilitate 10 million refugees who were now returning from camps in India where they had taken shelter during the hostilities, placing a huge administrative and fiscal burden on the country.[4] There were shortages all around – for construction material, essential raw materials, clothes, food and medicine.

Widespread shortages of essential commodities led to rapid inflation, putting the new administration under immense pressure to bring back stability and normalcy. This in turn prompted the central bank to print more money, adding further to inflationary pressures. Thus, Bose (1973: 266) observes:

> Our analysis has clearly indicated that the major factors behind the rise in prices during the post-liberation period are (a) a substantial decline in output and availability of goods and (b) a very large increase in money supply. An increase of 80 percent in money supply during a year in which domestic commodity output declined by 20 percent and overall availability of goods declined by 19 percent has resulted in over 100 percent increase in the general price level.

On top of an already volatile price situation by the end of 1973, Bangladesh experienced a famine in 1974 during which food prices skyrocketed, agricultural wages slumped and the government was sorely challenged to procure food and stabilize prices. Apart from an expectation of a poor rice harvest, the famine was preceded by at least three consecutive rice crop failures that left both the government and rural farm households bereft of food reserves to tide them over the grave situation. The immediate impact, as detailed in Ravallion (1982), was on the widening gap between wages and prices that hit the poor hard.[5]

The economic cost of the war was clearly large, although no formal attempts were made at the time to make a thorough assessment of what it was. Mascarenhas (1986: 21) talked about a large chart in the office of Dr Viktor Umbricht, who was head of the United Nations Relief Operations in Dhaka (UNROD), from which he gleaned the following information: '1.5 million houses had to be rebuilt; $78 million were needed for food and housing in early 1972; $80 million needed for additional food imports; another $15 million for railway repairs; $13 million for riverine transport; $200 million for industrial and agricultural equipment, inputs, and so on.'

Faaland and Parkinson (1976: 12) refer to a United Nations Relief Operation document that estimates the war's material damages at USD 1200 million. There is no information available as to how the figure was arrived at. Choudhry and Basher (2002) point out that total UN assistance to Bangladesh reached USD 1200 million by the end of 1972, and at around the same time UNROD came out with its 'Survey of Damages and Repairs' – which curiously also assessed war damages at USD 1,200 million – implying that UN assistance had made up for war damages suffered within just two years.

As if these troubles were not enough, the country was soon plunged into a period of political turmoil following the assassination of the Father of the Nation, Bangabandhu Sheikh Mujibur Rahman, giving rise to power struggles

Initial Conditions

and prolonged political instability that have waxed and waned but never quite gone away. This was symptomatic of the times – a period when institutions were still weak and had not recovered from the war, when the chain of command both within the military and the bureaucracy was tenuous, with senior officers trying hard to re-establish order and discipline.

The generic, almost formulaic narrative of the era is captured in the following quote:

> The decade of the 1970s was on the whole a very difficult period for the new nation of Bangladesh. In some respects, these years witnessed a net deterioration in the welfare of the people, as indicated for instance by worsening per capita nutrition levels, particularly among the rural population. This reflected the lag in the growth of domestic food production vis-à-vis the rapid growth in population and occurred despite large and growing volumes of aid-financed food imports. (World Bank Group 1980: 1)

The period of the 1970s was marked by great economic challenges as well. The macro-economic conditions were precarious as the economy that was dominated by agriculture went through a series of weather-related shocks due to floods and drought, compounded by world food and oil price hikes, as well as political turbulence, resulting in high rates of inflation, serious shortages and a constant crisis-like atmosphere, especially revolving around food production and availability. As a result, the growth rate was volatile as borne out by Figure 2.1. The government struggled to provide basic food and other essentials in the face of

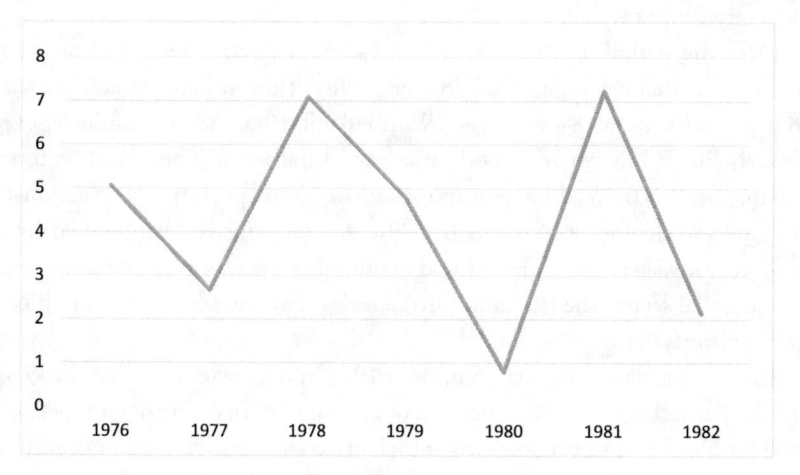

Figure 2.1 GDP growth rates (1976–82)

Source: 'GDP Growth - Bangladesh', World Bank Databank, https://data.worldbank.org/indicator/NY.GDP.MKTP.KD.ZG?locations=BD&view=chart (accessed 16 November 2021).

a severe foreign exchange constraint on the one hand, and extremely low revenues on the other. This basically meant that the economy had to be shored up by a healthy dose of foreign assistance in all three forms: food aid, commodity aid and project aid. The main challenge was how to manage these diverse resources that were not entirely predictable in terms of levels, flows or timing, in combination with the meagre domestic resources available, to inject a modicum of stability and growth in the economy. By any standards, this was clever jugglery.[6]

However, some positive indications were already visible by the end of the decade, leading the World Bank to term these developments as 'encouraging', although noting that progress made in the two most critical areas, namely family planning and agriculture, '[has] been far from satisfactory' (World Bank Group 1980: 1).[7] There is also some early indication of gradual structural changes with agricultural value added in decline and manufacturing and services increasing their shares (Tables 2.1 and 2.2).

However, basic socio-economic indicators provided little grounds for optimism. The population was growing at 2.7–2.8 per cent per annum and had already reached 89.1 million in a country of 144,000 square kilometres, much of it low-lying, deltaic flood plains. The adult literacy rate was a paltry 22 per cent and primary school enrolment was 73 per cent. The situation in terms of health and sanitation was abysmal. Government revenues had improved but still remained small, at 10.3 per cent of GDP, while exchange reserves in 1980 were enough to finance less than three months' worth of imports – underscoring the critical dependence of external finance for both imports and budgetary support.

Over the period 1966–67 to 1973–74, rural poverty remained at around the same, extremely high, level (83 per cent) while urban poverty increased from 76 per cent to 81 per cent (World Bank 1980: 199). Extreme poverty ('poverty line II') increased in both urban and rural areas.[8] The poverty estimates available for 1976–77 show continued worsening of poverty – a situation that continued to deteriorate for much of the decade. This is corroborated by the trend in real wages, particularly for agricultural workers. Given the small size of the industrial sector, the rise in industrial real wages was not of great significance for the poverty status.

However, it was perhaps the famine of 1974 in Bangladesh that left the longest and the deepest scar on the country. Policymakers were determined to solve the 'food problem' and to become 'self-sufficient' in food production, and until that was achieved, it was important to ensure that another famine did not occur. This formed the cornerstone of government policy aimed at rice production as well as building up buffer stocks and reserves of rice and wheat from food

Table 2.1 Sectoral shares of GDP (per cent) in Bangladesh in the 1970s

	1972–73	1973–74	1974–75	1975–76	1976–77	1977–78	1978–79	1979–80	1980–81
Agriculture	49.57	51.03	59.26	49.81	45.91	47.48	44.79	41.22	40.96
Crops	39.10	42.04	51.83	40.69	36.34	37.75	35.49	32.20	33.05
Forestry	2.28	2.09	1.70	1.74	1.67	2.57	2.51	2.27	2.32
Livestock	3.28	3.04	2.44	2.88	2.84	3.09	3.41	3.70	3.00
Fisheries	4.91	3.85	3.28	4.49	5.07	4.07	3.38	3.05	2.59
Industry	12.30	12.51	10.35	13.11	15.15	14.26	15.42	15.98	16.51
Manufacturing	7.91	8.95	7.19	9.29	10.62	10.08	9.87	1.23	10.88
Large	2.41	4.54	3.20	4.02	5.17	4.91	5.27	6.01	5.40
Small	5.50	4.41	4.01	5.28	5.45	5.17	4.60	5.21	5.49
Construction	4.39	3.56	3.16	3.82	4.52	4.17	5.55	4.75	5.62
Mining and quarrying	0.00	0.00	0.00	0.00	0.01	0.01	0.01	0.00	0.00
Services	38.12	36.46	30.39	37.08	38.94	38.27	39.79	42.80	42.53
Trade	7.97	9.63	8.95	9.14	8.54	9.53	9.09	9.78	8.71
Transport	10.52	9.41	7.30	9.34	9.99	10.12	11.41	11.55	12.39
Housing	9.41	7.75	6.33	8.35	9.02	8.18	8.14	8.96	8.60
Others	10.23	9.67	7.81	10.26	11.40	10.43	11.14	12.51	12.83

Source: BBS (1993).

Table 2.2 Sectoral growth rates (1974–80)

Sector	Annual Growth Rates %	
	1974–78	1978–80
Agriculture (rice)	3.7	0.1
Manufacturing	–0.3	3.3
Construction	7.8	9.1
Power and gas	22.3	3.0
Housing	3.6	8.5
Trade, transport and services	5.6	9.7
GDP	4.0	3.9
GDP per capita	1.1	1.2

Source: Based on BBS (1993).

aid, domestic procurement and even cash imports for subsidized distribution to various target groups, referred to as 'statutory rationing'. The ration system existed for long in South Asia, carried over from the colonial period with the noble idea of providing cheap food to the general public. Remnants of the system have survived to varying degrees.

The effect of 1974 reverberates even today in the statements of policymakers and their continued hypersensitivity to rice price increases despite the fact that Bangladesh in the meantime moved far away from the shadows of famine and widespread hunger (Ahmed, Haggblade and Choudhury 2000; Ravallion 1985).

The Social Sectors: Putting the Infrastructure in Place

Population and Family Planning

The 1970s were also a time of the population scare when dire Malthusian outcomes were freely aired. The *First Five-Year Plan of Bangladesh* (1973–78) underscored 'the necessity of immediate adoption of drastic steps to slow down the population growth' and reiterated that 'no civilized measure would be too drastic to keep the population of Bangladesh on the smaller side of fifteen crore [that is, 150 million] for sheer ecological viability of the nation' (Government of Bangladesh 1994: 7).[9]

By 1981, the population had reached 87.1 million (from 75 million in 1971) and grew at a rate of 2.8 per cent per annum.[10] The marital fertility rate for 1979 was estimated at 6.19. From that vantage point, the unfolding demographics looked daunting, even alarming.

The population problem began to gain policy momentum from the mid-1970s, promoted by robust donor support. Thus, between 1975 and 1980 there was an eightfold increase in financial resources to the family planning sector. During this time, an 'elaborate organization capable of implementing a substantial' programme was put in place (World Bank 1982: 43). The service delivery system went through substantial expansion, including coverage of *thana* health complexes (THCs)[11] (84.3 per cent), while mother and child health and family planning (MCH-FP) units were functional in all *thana*s, both rural and urban, staffed by family welfare visitors. Capacity even below the *thana* at the union level was being expanded, with family welfare centres set up in some 2,000 unions out of some 4,350 by 1980. In addition, 25,000 trained 'traditional birth attendants' were fielded by the voluntary sector by 1982 – one per village. With this infrastructure in place, health and family planning activities were easily integrated at the local level, with good capacity to take on the task of non-clinical family planning services (World Bank 1982; Robinson and Ross 2007).

The facilities for clinical contraceptive services also expanded. At the end of the decade, sterilization was being performed in 200 THCs, 93 Maternal and Child Welfare Centres, all sub-divisional, district and medical college hospitals, and another 84 clinics and hospitals in other sectors. Mobile units were also operating in 20 districts, while intrauterine devices (IUDs) were available in all union-level centres. In fact, a wide network of distribution services for contraceptive devices covered the countryside complemented by a private-sector commercial distribution system under the Social Marketing Project, consisting of 70,000 outlets in urban and rural areas (Government of Bangladesh 1981, 1983; Mitra and Kamal 1984; M. R. Khan 1984).

Staffing also grew dramatically: the number of female paramedics grew from 1 for 90,000 to 1 for 30,000 from 1976 to 1981. Apart from staff capacity training, a comprehensive media and promotional mass campaign was launched aimed at creating awareness, generating knowledge and changing attitudes in favour of smaller families (Mitra and Kamal 1984).

The 1979 Bangladesh Contraceptive Prevalence Survey (BCPS) revealed that almost every woman had a basic awareness of contraception and relevant methods (Government of Bangladesh 1981). Despite these major strides, contraceptive prevalence remained low, although registering significant growth.[12] The achievements fell short of various government targets for 1981, for example, for sterilization (62 per cent), IUDs (43 per cent), condoms (70 per cent), oral pills (40 per cent) and other methods (73 per cent). Some institutional steps were also adopted to inject a monitoring and evaluation or management information system (MIS) capacity for these activities (Government of Bangladesh 1981).

Mother and Child Health

Policymakers were aware of the close link between mother and child health (MCH) and family planning (FP), and recognized the need to achieve a balanced delivery of services between the two. A high infant and child mortality rate seemed to favour the desire for larger families. Cross-country experience suggested that when the infant mortality rate (IMR) reaches around 45–50 per thousand, fertility begins to decline. The IMR in the late 1970s was between 120 and 140 per thousand (Mitra 1979; Mitra and Associates 2003).

About 20 per cent of all children born did not live beyond the age of five, and 30 per cent of all deaths occurred during infancy (0–11 months) and another 25 per cent during early childhood (1–4 years). The main factors underlying these adverse rates were high incidence of diarrhoea, tetanus and respiratory infections – almost 50 per cent of all infant and child deaths were accounted for by these three types of illnesses (Chen et al. 1983).

Bangladesh took on the challenge by addressing three simple measures that promised quick results: (*a*) oral rehydration therapy, (*b*) tetanus toxoid immunization for pregnant women and (*c*) training traditional birth attendants in simple and safe delivery methods – these initiatives were launched through three separate programmes. In other words, these low-cost, labour-intensive solutions ultimately proved to be highly effective in reining in infant mortality (Larson and Mitra 1992; Greenspan 1992).

Political Instability

Following the assassination of Father of the Nation Bangabandhu Sheikh Mujibur Rahman in August 1975, the country entered into a dangerous phase of intense and bloody power struggles carried out by different factions within the military.[13] In the months that followed, state power changed hands a number of times, and in the process key leaders of the Awami League (AL) as well as influential pro-AL senior military officers got eliminated, leading to the emergence of a new power bloc composed of a section of freedom-fighter military officers in the Army who were opposed to the AL, combined with a wide array of anti-AL forces both on the left and on the right, including the pro-Pakistan/anti-liberation forces that had been dormant since 1971. This ushered in a period of military rule initially under various proxy arrangements until April 1977, when General Ziaur Rahman directly assumed the post of president and chief martial law administrator (S. S. Islam 1984). The general was himself killed in 1981 by members of the military (Table 2.3), paving the way to the capture of power by yet another general: General H. M. Ershad. General Ershad was a repatriated

Initial Conditions

Table 2.3 Coup and counter coup in the 1970s

Date	Event	Comment
September–October 1974	Famine	Widespread criticism of the way the crisis was handled
14 August 1975	Assassination of Sheikh Mujibur Rahman, 'Father of the Nation'	Became elected in 1973 and assumed power as prime minister; declared one-party rule in 1975 and assumed the post of president of the country; widespread criticism of one-party rule; bitter criticism of influential family members of the president for supposed corruption and high-handed behaviour; moment chosen by disgruntled young officers who appear to have been blessed by key senior figures in the military and politics.
August–November 1975	Mushtaq Ahmed, senior AL politician who took over control of the government at the behest of the killers of Mujib	Mushtaq Ahmed may have been involved with the conspirators from the start or he may have been co-opted later – but what is not in doubt was his unhappiness with Mujib as well as his close family ties with at least one key conspirator.
3 November 1975	Four prominent AL leaders who gave leadership in 1975 were assassinated	The killers appear to belong to the same faction that was responsible for Mujib's assassination.
6 November 1975	Failed coup attempt by General Khaled Musharraf, generally considered pro-AL	Section of soldiers ('sepoys' or other ranks) was led by Colonel Taher to thwart General Musharraf. Taher billed himself as a revolutionary-socialist and considered Mujib too far right. In this turn of events, Musharraf was killed and General Ziaur Rahman emerged victorious (with support from Taher) but installed a 'puppet' (Justice Sayem) as head of a military-backed government.
April 1977	General Zia took over direct power and made himself president and chief martial law administrator (CMLA)	Islam was adopted as the 'state religion'.

(*Contd.*)

Table 2.3 (*Contd.*)

Date	Event	Comment
1979	Martial Law lifted and elections held	General Zia was elected prime minister.
1981	General Zia assassinated	Zia's rule marked a period that was characterized by 19 coup attempts and the subsequent execution of numerous military officers for their reported involvement.

Sources: Maniruzzaman (1980, 1976); S. S. Islam (1984); Jahan (1976).

Notes: The term 'pro-liberation' began to be increasingly used to signify pro-AL forces or, more widely, those who supported the Liberation War in 1971 as opposed to those who were against it. While such a neat dichotomy may have been useful during the war, it became more and more blurred over time as other unresolved issues came up, including the role of Islam and the notion of secularism, and the role of 'socialism' (both secularism and socialism were 'pillars' of the 1972 constitution).

army officer from Pakistan and not a freedom fighter, that is someone from across a sensitive fault line of the time.

Despite the turbulence, there was a brief period of relative stability under Zia, especially between 1979 and 1981 when the economy was beginning to respond to the higher aid flows and improved development expenditures. This was also a period of a degree of social experimentation and non-government initiatives never seen before. Amidst all the uncertainties and vicissitudes in both the polity and the economy (or perhaps because of it), dedicated individuals entered into the development arena, supported by aid money, and undertook grassroots-level recovery, reconstruction and innovative development work – in the process hoping to make a dent in the widespread poverty, hunger, poor health, illiteracy and deprivation. These social entrepreneurs included the likes of Mohammed Yunus, founder of the Grameen Bank; Fazle Hassan Abed, founder of BRAC; Zafrullah Chowdhury, founder of Gonosasthya Kendro; Qazi Faruque Ahmed of Proshika; and Shafiqual Haque Choudhury of ASA. The NGOs of Bangladesh have played a remarkable role in the country's development – and for the most part their journey began in the 1970s.

Even though General Zia's rule was abruptly terminated, he nevertheless left behind his centre-right political party (the Bangladesh Nationalist Party or BNP) that was distinctly less secular, thought widely to be anti-Indian – and therefore pro-Pakistani – and was more favourably disposed towards pro-Islamic political parties and politicians.

In fact, one of the most controversial actions attributed to Zia was the rehabilitation of politicians who were tainted for 'collaboration' with the Pakistani

Army during the 1971 war and allowing 'Islamic' parties like the Jamaat-i-Islami to re-enter mainstream electoral politics.[14] That such fundamental policy reversals could occur so soon after independence was itself remarkable, and that this shift in the body politic became permanent remains a matter of grave concern for more progressive elements in Bangladesh. This therefore has remained a basic unresolved issue in Bangladesh's often vicious politics – one that continues to cast a long shadow over the sociopolitical life of the country.

The donor community seemed more comfortable with Zia. It is possible that the AL's public posture in favour of 'socialism' as a core objective of the liberation struggle made (Western) donors wary, even though the AL position was more rhetorical in nature rather than a reflection of a genuine commitment to socialist ideals. Thus, one thing that Zia and his BNP did was *not* talk about socialism, instead making an early commitment to market-led, private sector-led development as against AL's indecisive position between socialism, a mixed economy and free markets. Despite subsequent political changes, the debate over socialism seemed to quietly fade away into the distance.

Thus, even though the period 1972–80 was the most difficult for Bangladesh, it was, nevertheless, also a time of moving from reconstruction and rehabilitation to development, a time for consolidation and putting in place the basic requisites of growth in the form of physical and social infrastructure, energy access, better technology and policy reforms. Above all, the period will be remembered for its intense social experimentation led by a dynamic NGO sector as well as the infrastructure built up to tackle FP or MCH – both elements, of course, were supported and nurtured by the donor community.

In short, this was a period marked by both political and economic turbulence, poor governance and extreme weather shocks. It was also a time of intense debate, controversy and struggle. Thus, despite all these hazards, there existed a space for civil society, for NGOs, for academia, development partners and indeed policymakers to discuss, disagree with or criticize government or donor policy or positions – in short, to grow and evolve. Thus, despite the formal absence of (electoral) democracy, the nature of the state remained soft enough to allow a degree of dissent, generally remaining unfazed by the quite bitter criticism levelled against the government and leadership, both by opposition politicians and by civil society and the media. Another way of looking at it would be that the state institutions, either of coercion or of persuasion, had not matured sufficiently to clamp down on dissent, and thus the default position (of being relatively free as well as being open to donor advice) remained in force. The recent experience of the Liberation War itself played a role: it was viewed as being pro-democratic, secular and liberal, which continued as goals to aspire to, although thought to be temporarily 'on hold'.

3

The Food Security Challenge

Rice is the staple food of the more than 165 million people of Bangladesh, with rice production continuing to dominate the country's agriculture. The share of agriculture in national GDP has been steadily declining over the years. In 2018–19 its contribution to GDP was 13.7 per cent, with crops accounting for slightly over 7 per cent and rice production dominating crop production (Government of Bangladesh 2020: 287). Rice accounts for two-thirds of calories, half of the protein intake and a similar share of the household budget of rural Bangladeshis. In terms of production, it accounts for almost 80 per cent of the cropped area (World Bank 2013). Thus, rice is crucial to Bangladesh's food security, with self-sufficiency in rice having been a major policy goal of the government for the last five decades.

Today, Bangladesh is self-sufficient on average, even managing to produce a surplus from time to time, a feat underscored by the fact that the population of the country more than doubled since 1972. Total rice production increased at a rate of about 3 per cent per year over the period 1972–73 to 2007–08, of which *boro* rice (the dominant rice crop) registered the highest growth of over 6.0 per cent per year. This was possible because of the GR technology of the 1970s and 1980s combined with market reforms and structural adjustments of the 1990s, and attention to the availability, quality and distribution of key inputs like diesel, fertilizers and seeds in more recent years (N. Ahmed et al. 2007; R. Ahmed et al. 2000).

This is a far cry from the early years when the Bangladesh economy was overwhelmingly rural and agricultural, with 90 per cent of the population living in rural areas and only 10 per cent in the towns, concentrated mainly in Dhaka and Chittagong. Agriculture's share of GDP was 60 per cent, and rice was the main crop grown in subsistence mode under traditional, rain-fed conditions. Jute was the main cash crop and the main foreign exchange earner accounting for 90 per cent of commodity exports. Industry was skeletal, mainly in the public domain, and run so badly that it was a constant drain on meagre public resources instead of making a contribution to the exchequer. Given the high population density and the low land–man ratio – one of the most adverse in the world – the biggest, immediate challenge facing Bangladesh was that of attaining 'food self-sufficiency', defined rather simply as ensuring that people had enough rice to eat.[1] The 1974 famine highlighted this urgency further, and thus the call for self-sufficiency remained a core clarion call until its achievement in the late 1990s. Indeed, rice-related sensitivity still remains in the national psyche, as reflected in the high degree of political sensitivity with regard to rice prices.

It is difficult, sitting in 2020, to explain to modern readers how crucial the food (rice) problem was for Bangladesh. Rice cultivation dominated agriculture and rural farm incomes. It affected all economic activities directly and indirectly: inflation, market demand, trade and transport, household consumption as well as consumption of non-rice food and non-food items, wages, fiscal policy, and even the BOP and foreign exchange reserves via the trade and food-aid channels.

The twin problems of low productivity and strong seasonal production patterns, which were further affected by weather shocks, imparted a high degree of uncertainty and risk to rice yields. Thus, while the rice economy was central to the smooth functioning of the overall economy, it was also highly susceptible to weather shocks. There was a strong sense of economic instability for much of the early decades, at least until the late 1990s, requiring large public food reserves (food stocks), food aid, cash-food imports and the need to maintain sufficient foreign exchange reserves should sudden imports become necessary. Substantial government capacity and resources were tied up with food management and food policy.

Thus, it was commonly observed that the food problem was a critical aspect of Bangladesh's struggle for economic development: it was a production problem because of lagging production relative to population growth, compounded by issues of unemployment and low incomes of the poor, and sluggish growth of the non-agricultural sector (World Bank 1979).

At the household level, rice accounted for 60 per cent of average expenditures and 85 per cent of calories. Majority of rural households had a calorie intake per capita that was lower than the norm (2,120 calories), while 25 per cent of children were severely undernourished and another 50 per cent were moderately undernourished.

The central task for policymakers and planners was to address the food problem. In the short term, food production and consumption needed to be stabilized but the longer-term solution lay in addressing low productivity in agriculture. In other words, national food security was seen to lie in expanded rice production and ensuring availability of sufficient food for consumption and market stability. The problem of 'access' was acknowledged but was treated (rightly) as a second-order problem, left largely to NGOs and specialized public sector development agencies like BRDB (Lewis 2019).

The GR had already transformed various parts of the rural-agricultural world – in Mexico, Philippines, Punjab (in India and Pakistan) – but seemed concentrated on wheat rather than rice, although the Philippines experienced large rice productivity increases with a particular 'dwarf' rice variety developed by the International Rice Research Institute (IRRI), designated as IR-8. So, by the late 1960s, dramatic successes were in evidence and seemed to be the way ahead for impoverished rice-growing areas, especially in South Asia. Bangladesh, which was overwhelmingly dependent on rice, seemed an excellent choice.

Introduction of the new technology involved putting the infrastructure and logistics in place (irrigation networks and distribution systems for chemical fertilizers, high-yielding seed varieties or HYV and pesticides), field-level dissemination of the new technology through demonstration and extension work, and encouraging adoption, often by providing subsidies on water and fertilizers. In other words, the initial thrust came from the public sector backed by considerable donor support.

Actually there was some limited experience with the new technology even in the 1960s when it was tried out under the 'Comilla Model' (Bose 1974). In fact, Bose had predicted that given the success of the new technology in the Comilla Model experimental areas in terms of raising rice productivity and distribution of benefits, one could expect that results could be widely replicated in other areas of the country. That did happen eventually but not before another decade and a half.

The new rice technology came as a package consisting of irrigation water, new seed varieties, pesticides and chemical fertilizers – all of which had to be made available to the farmers at the right time and location. This may sound simple enough but for traditional farmers, using their own rice seeds saved from the preceding harvest and dependent mainly on rainwater for irrigation with little or no familiarity with chemical fertilizers, this was anything but. For the government, the challenge was to put in place the irrigation infrastructure – water control is central not only to the GR but also in arranging for the distribution of the complementary inputs required. The initial instinct was obviously going to be to get the public sector to try and do this on its own. The public sector agency of choice for the job was the Bangladesh Agricultural Development Corporation (BADC), a parastatal mandated with numerous tasks related to agricultural promotion, including seed and fertilizer distribution and installation of pumps and deep tube wells (DTWs) for irrigation.

The Irrigation Revolution: From Surface Systems to Groundwater Mining

The image of Bangladesh is of a country criss-crossed by hundreds of rivers which frequently burst their banks and caused widespread flooding, especially after the heavy seasonal downpours during the monsoons. In reality, Bangladesh's hydrological system faces extreme seasonal variation. The Bengal delta contains one of the largest river systems in the world. It drains on average 100,000–140,000 cubic metres per second into the Bay of Bengal. It also displays acute seasonality in water flows with over 80 per cent of the total water flow concentrated in just four months (June–September) (S. N. Islam 2016). This sharp seasonal fluctuation is further accentuated by the massive diversion of water from the upper reaches of the rivers by India during the dry season, contributing to the increased seasonal water stress experienced. The hydrological regime is characterized by extremes – excessive water during the monsoons and acute scarcity in the dry, winter months.

Irrigation using traditional techniques has been prevalent in Bangladesh for long, especially during the dry season for *boro* rice cultivation and cultivation of winter vegetables. These were mostly manual techniques with the ability to irrigate tiny plots of land and used in areas located close to surface water sources. The bulk of the *boro* rice was cultivated on low or very low land that is normally flooded but retains some residual moisture in the dry season to permit *boro* cultivation.

The introduction of modern irrigation began with large-scale, surface water, gravity-flow systems like the Ganges–Kobadak Irrigation Project, the Pabna Irrigation and Drainage Project, the Meghna–Dhonagoda Project and the Chandpur Irrigation Project, mostly operated by the Bangladesh Water Development Board (BWDB) – a public sector parastatal. These use pumps to divert river water into a network of irrigation channels that distribute water to large numbers of farms using gravity flow. These large-scale projects proved wasteful, inefficient and costly, mainly due to governance issues that required the participation of thousands of farmers. It was also increasingly clear that there was not enough surface water available, requiring large amounts of silt deposits to be dredged from the rivers every year, adding to the already high costs.

With increasing attention to groundwater-based irrigation following the realization that Bangladesh had large groundwater reserves at reasonably low depths which were seasonally recharged, public agencies like BADC and BWDB began experimenting with 'deep tube wells' – pumps attached to wells that could lift water up from depths of 300 feet below or more. These pumps could lift sufficient water to irrigate around 100 acres of rice. Given that these projects were much smaller than the large, surface water-based systems that have commanding areas of thousands of hectares, the hope was that these would entail far less governance problems. However, even these smaller projects required the cooperation of a large number of farmers, whose landholdings were typically less than 2.5 acres. Thus, DTWs also proved operationally difficult and prone to elite capture despite the formation of user groups and irrigation committees. The technology was not appropriate given Bangladesh's land ownership structure and the difficulty of getting numerous farmers to cooperate over water charges, fuel costs and water distribution. The system required excessive subsidies and gave rise to numerous debilitating conflicts over water distribution and collection of charges, and inevitably operated at a fraction of the potential command areas (K. A. S. Murshid 1985; Kundu 2002). The mainly donor-funded DTW projects, in other words, were colossal failures, just like the large-scale irrigation and drainage systems such as the Ganges–Kobadak Project. The percentage of land irrigated remained small and without expansion of irrigation coverage, the GR would remain elusive.

The GR also required adequate supply of modern inputs, including modern high-yielding seeds, chemical fertilizers and pesticides, along with the knowledge of how best to use these inputs in combination with water for optimal impact. Timing was critical so that all these inputs needed to be available at the right time and place to be effective. This was the challenge, which with hindsight sounds simple enough but at the time led to agonizing debates around adoption behaviour of farmers, farmer rationality, profitability and, of course, distributional consequences. There was a large literature that dwelt on the inequality that the GR would usher in, since only the large farmers were expected to adopt the new technology (Asaduzzaman 1979; M. Hossain 1988a; Alauddin and Tisdell 1991a, 1991b; Pingali 2012; Orr 2012). The input supply–distribution system also came in for much scrutiny given the huge effort expended by organizations like BADC to develop an effective distribution system to reach farmers with the vital inputs. This struggle proved formidable, and it took many years to come to the conclusion that it would be best to leave such things to the market.

However, let us return to the irrigation story. Even smaller-scale technologies began to be introduced with the support of donors, especially the World Bank. The most important of these was the shallow tube well (STW) along with surface water pumps. STWs had small command areas and could be easily installed or even moved around to tap groundwater at shallow depths. In other words, this technique was ideal for much of Bangladesh both in terms of water availability and divisibility of technology – a feature that was of crucial importance for the small farm size situation in the country. It was also much more affordable and even led to the emergence of irrigation entrepreneurs who would install these STWs on rent, leading to the emergence of a rental market. For much of the 1980s and 1990s, the major source of irrigation expansion was in fact through STWs, further accelerating in the face of import liberalization and lifting of regulations surrounding installation. The reforms resulted in a dramatic fall in the price of irrigation equipment and far better availability of spares. Thus, out of a total potential irrigable area of 7.56 million hectares, 20 per cent was actually irrigated in 1982, of which almost 60 per cent was irrigated by surface water systems (DTWs and large-scale systems mainly). By 1992, the percentage of area under irrigation moved up to 36 per cent, with surface water systems accounting for 29.3 per cent of the area. In other words, the bulk of the irrigation focus shifted to groundwater, mainly STWs and DTWs, each accounting for 16–17 per cent of the irrigated area. Today, the irrigation percentage is around 56 per cent – this figure, however, fails to convey the magnitude of the achievement.

This essentially means that virtually all the cultivable land in the dry *boro* season is actually irrigated by modern techniques. However, irrigation is not required during the wet *aman* season when cultivation takes place under rain-fed conditions, while some supplementary irrigation is used during the minor third season, *aus*, so that the percentage of area under irrigation in *aus* and *aman* is tiny. In other words, the irrigation thrust was centred upon *boro*, allowing Bangladesh's farmers to grow an additional rice crop in a year, which in fact has emerged as the largest crop. This was Bangladesh's GR.

Although in the new millennium other interesting techniques were introduced, mainly with a view to reduce costs and improve efficiency, notably solar pumps for STWs and DTWs, rubber dams in some rivers, the main thrust of irrigation came from STWs creating the preconditions for the GR. DTWs remained useful in certain areas where water is available only at greater depths, while donors like the Asian Development Bank (ADB) continued with their efforts to improve large-scale public systems by experimenting with new management and governance techniques (ADB 2020).

Input Distribution, Subsidies and Reforms

It is well known that the GR requires an effective distribution system of inputs: water, high-yielding seeds, chemical fertilizers, pesticides, fuel to operate pumps and, of course, the necessary know-how. Once again an appropriate model was needed, initially spearheaded by the public sector but which eventually gave way to market-based solutions. This was a tortuous journey. It was initiated and continued with donor insistence, backed by research findings from local and international scholars that ultimately brought about important shifts starting from a state monopoly to gradual introduction of market forces and private sector involvement. In other words, a series of reforms were enacted with regard to the import, distribution and marketing of inputs, especially irrigation equipment, fertilizers, pesticides and seeds.

Thus, the policy to begin handover of state control to the private sector was evident as early as 1982 (World Bank 1982). This is evident from the following quote describing the policy stance of the government: '... handing over responsibility for the procurement, marketing, servicing and management of minor irrigation equipment to the private sector, direct sale of pumps and tubewells to farmers and cooperatives, phasing out of seasonal equipment rentals, moving towards full-cost pricing for agricultural production, assets and inputs, and vigorous extension training ...' (World Bank 1982: 5).

Indeed, the reforms consisted mainly of subsidy reductions, lifting restrictions on imports and trade generally, and moving away from a long history of administered prices, particularly in the 1980s and 1990s. A chronology of the major reforms undertaken at this time is shown in Table 3.1. It needs to be borne in mind that these reforms have had a profound impact on Bangladesh's success with the GR.

In 1981, subsidies on fertilizers totalled some BDT 1.2 billion, which was equivalent to 15 per cent of tax revenues. Another BDT 600 million accrued to subsidies for minor irrigation systems. The gradual elimination of subsidies thus meant that over 1972–73 and 1983–84, nominal fertilizer prices rose fifteen times, with the fertilizer–paddy price ratio rising from 0.74 to 2.03 (Osmani and Quasem 1990). However, the reforms also introduced competition and greatly improved access to farmers.

On the other hand, trade liberalization and other reforms, backed by credit support (see Table 3.1), resulted in a sharp reduction in the price of irrigation equipment, power tillers, tractors and spares. This led to a huge boost in farm mechanization and productivity.

Table 3.1 Agricultural input market reforms in 1980s and 1990s

Item	Policy Action	Period	Remarks
	Fertilizer		
1	BADC withdrew from retail and wholesale markets at *thana** level	1978–83	
2	Licencing requirement to sell fertilizer abolished	1982–83	
3	Deregulation of fertilizer price	1982–84	Real competition introduced

(Contd.)

Table 3.1 (*Contd.*)

Item	Policy Action	Period	Remarks
4	Private traders allowed to purchase directly from factory gate or port	1987	Strong response
5	Direct fertilizer imports opened up to private traders	1992	Good response
6	Suffered fertilizer supply crisis causing partial reversal of some policies	1994–95	
	Irrigation Equipment		
1	BADC started sales of irrigation machines to individual and groups backed by credit support	1980–85	Good response
2	Import liberalization for irrigation equipment and standardization restrictions	1987–88	Drastic price reduction
	Other: Power Tillers, Pesticides, Seeds		
1	Import and standardization restrictions on power tillers lifted	1989	Modest response
2	Imports of power tillers or tractors made duty free and backed by credit support	1995	Vigorous response
3	Pesticide restrictions to specific brands removed and imports opened up	1989	Modest response
4	Private sector allowed to import certified hybrid seeds	1998–99	

Source: Based on R. Ahmed (2001: Table 3.1).
Note: *Lowest level administrative unit.

The Rice Market

Given the importance of rice in the national and household economy, the performance of the rice market was of crucial importance for everyone: producers, consumers, traders, millers and the government. In particular, a major policy challenge was to keep the rice market stable, actually meaning low, 'affordable' prices for consumers and 'fair' prices for producers. This dual challenge formed the cornerstone for much of rice price and distribution policy of the government, which embarked on a complex set of policies in pursuit of multiple objectives: price stabilization, producer price support, consumer price stability, subsidized food grain distribution for the poor in rural and urban areas and various other 'special' categories (N. Chowdhury 1986, 1987; Alwang 1991; Adams Jr 1998; Dorosh and Shahabuddin 1999; A. U. Ahmed et al. 2010). In other words, the food grain market was clearly segmented into a vast private market, which to all purposes operated unfettered, was highly competitive and performed efficiently (Ravallion 1985; Goletti, Ahmed and Farid 1995; Dawson and Dey 2002; Murshid et al. 2013; K. A. S. Murshid 2014),[2] and a small Public Food Distribution System (PFDS) tasked with the complex roles indicated earlier. Evolution and change in Bangladesh's crucial rice market are explored in Chapter 4.

The main policy challenge therefore was how to treat the PFDS in the face of conflicting demands and tight budgetary constraints. Bangladesh moved away from a generalized food distribution system that was broadly targeted, covering both rural and urban areas, to one that was narrowed down considerably, focusing much more on poor, vulnerable groups in rural areas.[3] Again, persistent donor-funded technical and policy work ultimately managed to persuade the government to undertake reforms of the food distribution system from the late 1980s and early 1990s (for example, see Shawkat Ali et al. 2008). Thus, the ration component consisting of distribution of subsidized rice and other food was dismantled and considerably narrowed to target the poor. Rural and urban rationing were abolished in 1992–93 and food grain imports (rice and wheat) were liberalized, allowing the private sector to make direct imports at will, a sphere that was previously a government monopoly.

The PFDS retained a number of politically important roles: (*a*) price stabilization through open market sales when needed, (*b*) holding food reserves to feed its (streamlined) distribution channels, (*c*) conducting safety net operations and (*d*) undertaking domestic procurement of food grains from farmers and millers after harvest as a means to support prices or replenish reserves. The first three roles are generally considered to have been effective, while the last not very. PFDS reforms not only created a better-functioning public food system, it also significantly reduced wastage and losses, thereby having a healthy impact on the government budget as well.

Conclusion

The GR aided by reforms in both input and output markets, and trade liberalization backed by massive investment in infrastructure, particularly irrigation, transformed Bangladesh's food security regime – a goal that at one stage seemed so distant. This, along with fertility declines, was Bangladesh's main achievement of the 1980s and 1990s, and one that was central to its development journey. The impact of the GR was immense: on rural wages, on food prices and consumption, on poverty, and on the government budget and BOP – the last resulting from a much-reduced need to make large food imports. This was perhaps the much-needed basis on which Bangladesh's industrialization, which was sputtering in fits and starts, could actually take off. There were other concomitant factors that coalesced around this time imparting further stimuli to a journey that had already started. The GR and population control also constitute two core areas for which the government can take much of the credit for success.

The role of the donor community should also be duly acknowledged. Irrigation, flood control and drainage were financed mostly by donors, especially the World Bank and ADB, but also bilateral donors like the United States Agency for International Development (USAID), the Department of Foreign and International Development (DFID) and the Japan International Cooperation Agency (JICA). Technical assistance from these agencies was important in terms of taking the reform agenda forward in Bangladesh in general and supporting the quest for food self-sufficiency.

A direct consequence of the success in agriculture was the expansion of the RNF sector, which, aided by the influx of remittances sent from the Middle East by expatriate workers, provided a major boost to employment, wages and productivity. Chapter 6 is devoted to an examination of the contribution of RNF to Bangladesh's economic performance.

4

Exploring Transition and Change in the Rice Market

This chapter explores the question of how the large, complex paddy-rice market in Bangladesh was able to transform itself and evolve in the face of changing risks and incentives into a better-functioning market system. It notes significant but opposing trends over two decades in different areas, particularly in terms of market structure, trade circuits and exchange relations. Evidence of a sharp decline in tied transactions points to the growing importance of impersonal exchange. Underlying causes of these changes are explored with particular reference to microfinance, remittances, rural roads, mobile telephony and mobile financial services (MFS).[1]

Much has changed in the rural economy in recent decades: the micro-credit revolution has matured, remittances have grown enormously, mobile phones have brought on an information revolution in the country and there have been major transformative changes in health, education, especially girls' education, and physical infrastructure.

We explore the Bangladesh paddy-rice market, which has tended to be described variously as traditional, backward, complex, hierarchical, interlocked and exploitative,[2] on the one hand, and well integrated, competitive and efficient on the other (Ravallion 1986, 1987; Baulch et al. 1998; Dawson and Dey 2002; Goletti, Ahmed and Farid 1995). In actual practice, the rice market displays elements of both aspects, with some backward areas associated with complex forms of tied exchange á la Crow and Murshid (CM henceforth) (1994), while other more advanced areas display a much more competitive outcome based on increasingly less personalized transactions.

The central message of this chapter is that the huge paddy-rice market is not static but is constantly changing, adapting and evolving into a better-functioning market system. In particular, the backward forms that have been well noted are in recession, and over the course of the last several decades various forms of tied finance have been dramatically reduced. It is suggested that the improvements in agricultural performance – especially in rice production and, broadly, in the rural socio-economic regime marked by exogenous developments in infrastructure, mobile telephony and MFS, and rural finance – have played a significant role in transforming rural markets.

While the overall impact on employment and livelihoods in the sector is expected to be positive, adverse effects on the poor and other vulnerable actors in the trade circuit cannot be ruled out. The role of endogenous traditional market institutions, however, remains essentially unaltered or even in decline and therefore cannot be held responsible for the changes described.

The study draws heavily on the definitive work of CM, which lays the analytical–descriptive basis of the rice market as it existed in two contrasting areas of Bangladesh in the late 1980s. This provided the comparative basis for the fieldwork conducted by the author in 2008 (with a selective follow up in 2010) in the same CM areas.

Conceptualizing Market Dynamics

The 'ideal' market is best thought to be approached by impersonal markets frequently associated with those in advanced economies.[3] North (1990, 1998) argues that the rise and sustainability of impersonal exchange in advanced economies are based on both internal and external institutions (rules, norms, values) where the legal framework and a constant threat of enforcement are seen to be critical. In addition, internally generated social and market values (honesty, fairness, reliability) play a critical role. These values-based approaches provide private, internal institutions more cheaply compared to externally imposed solutions (Goodenough and Cheney 2008). Thus, one way of looking at transformation and change in market systems would be to focus on the nature of exchange relations in the expectation that these will entail a shift towards impersonal exchange as institutions, both internal and external, mature and strengthen.

Building Trust and Norms

Trust-enhancing institutions generally evolve over time through the efforts of participants in long-term, repeated market-exchange environments. These allow traders an opportunity to establish a reputation of reliability, making transactions less costly and more stable than would be the case otherwise. Thus, in a game of 'Snatch', where traders face a choice between 'snatch' and trade given a one-off exchange (for example, buy now and pay later), the result, almost always, is snatch (that is, never pay), preventing a market from developing (Schwab and Ostrom 2008). Once some simple norms are introduced, exchange is enabled as people are found to trust one another more frequently than theoretically predicted (Camerer 2003; Ostrom and Walker 2003).

Various modifications of the 'Snatch' game have been demonstrated to show that different (more desirable) equilibria are possible. One possibility is that players adopt norms that lead them to derive utility from self-consciously avoiding snatch. Crawford and Ostrom (2005) model this as a delta (δ) parameter ('warm glow'), which, if large enough, can offset the utility from snatch, leading to a new Nash equilibrium that supports exchange (Clark 1994; Chalfin 2004).

A second possibility is that players develop a reputation for fair play over time. There is enough evidence to show that reputation effects play a critical role in decisions regarding with whom to trade (Colson 1974; Sally 2002). It is believed, however, that for reputation to lead to trust, institutions are needed that can verify and disseminate information on reputation quickly, reliably and cheaply in the market. Reputation, trust and reciprocity provide a strong interactive concoction that can sustain exchange and make snatching costly (Schwab and Ostrom 2008) and could even lead to norms supporting 'generalised morality' (or multilateral trust that supports impersonal exchange) in the longer run (Platteau 1994a; 1994b).

External Incentives

Contract law provides an external incentive to behave correctly providing additional assurance that the risks of trading will be small. This happens in three ways: (*a*) through remedy for breach of promise, (*b*) through flexibility of contract law to allow parties to structure provisions to reflect specific concerns (for example, with regard to grades or standards) and (*c*) through support to existing norms (O'Hara 2008).

In traditional markets, endogenously created trader associations often play this role (Lyon and Porter 2007), while in advanced markets this is the role of the formal legal system. However, passing and enforcing rules, especially formal ones, involve large costs, thus reiterating the importance of endogenous solutions in less developed contexts. Hence, any functioning system has evolved its own rules and norms that are intended to generate trust. The role of external interventions should be to complement not substitute these processes, as ill-considered moves to realign incentives have been widely accused of having adverse, unintended effects (Schwab and Ostrom 2008). For example, it is likely that state interventions in policy or infrastructure (especially rural roads), microfinance or telecommunications could play such a vital, supportive role.

The Applied Literature

Analyses of agricultural markets and institutions have tended to focus on food grains and commodity markets where the major concerns have been with efficiency and equity. The initial phase of this research consisted of 'mapping' market structures and identifying the role of marketing agents and market conditions along the supply chain (prices, margins) and was rooted in at least two broader strands: (*a*) the structure–conduct–performance literature (Bain 1959; Farruk 1970; Baulch et al. 1998), and (*b*) the literature on transactions cost economics, coordination and institutions (Arrow 1969; Williamson 1975; North 1981). There was a third strand invoking social capital, trust, norms and reputation as a determinant of traditional market performance (Abbot 1962; van der Laan 1975; Lyon and Porter 2009). This work combined with the transactions cost approach gave rise to renewed interest in field-based analysis of traditional market performance in the 1990s, for example, the work on contracts, transactions costs and social capital in African markets (Fafchamps 2004; Reardon and Timmer 2005).

The findings from the applied literature yield two contrasting views. One strand suggests that traditional market intermediaries were efficient, with little evidence of exploitative monopsony. In peasant markets they were not earning super profits and the high trader margins reported reflected various constraints and costs of trade (Bauer 1957), which were later to be referred to as 'transactions costs'. This stream of thought later gave rise to the work on transactions costs in trade circuits, such as the work of Fafchamps (2004), Kopicki et al. (2004) and Escobal (2005).

The other strand presented evidence of 'structural and institutional features of intermediation' (Reardon and Timmer 2005: 15) that tended to generate monopsony or oligopsony, resulting in depressed prices for producers or high consumer prices. Studies representing this school of thought include the works of Wharton Jr (1962), Mears (1957), Harriss (1979), CM (1994), with the last generally emphasizing 'complexity' in describing exchange relations and institutional arrangements arising from the difficulty of reducing what appears to be numerous exchange relationships between a large number of diverse market actors offering and receiving a wide range of exchange terms, frequently involving various tying conditions or interlocking markets (Olsen 1999; Crow 2001; Harriss-White 1997, 1999, 2008). While this literature has advanced our understanding of the institutional underpinnings of agricultural markets in a complex development context, the conclusions remained weak, generally reinforcing the notion of the rich landlord or large trader controlling prices and terms of exchange locally, at the expense of poor producers or traders, providing little policy insight on how this could be changed.

Methodological Note

Rich case study materials were generated by the author with a particular focus on market institutions and transactions, from a number of markets previously studied in 1989 by CM in the districts of Bogra and Noakhali, and in the capital, Dhaka. Bogra is located in the GR belt ('advanced area'), much of Noakhali consists of low-lying, mono-cropped, *char* areas ('backward area') and Dhaka markets cater to the demand of a densely populated metropolis (Table 4.1).

The field evidence was collected based on detailed, semi-structured, open-ended interviews involving different categories of market participants, including *aratdar*s, traders and millers. A total of almost 200 in-depth interviews were conducted, repeated during a second round. The first round was conducted in May–June 2008, coinciding with the harvest period of the main *boro* rice crop. The second round was conducted in the lean agricultural season of August–September 2008. A third round of more structured interviews was conducted in June–July 2010 on a sub-sample of 35 traders each, from Bogra and Noakhali, especially focusing on transactions and trading relations.

Issues explicitly discussed with traders include entry history of the firm, changes in trading partners over time, how trading linkages were established, communications and use of mobile phones, changes in sale and purchase patterns, use of cash, credit and bank transactions, whether trading partners are fixed, use

Table 4.1 Characterization of market sites

Sites	Hinterland Type	Food Surplus/ Deficit	Growth	Change 1989–2010
Dhaka	Large, urban centre; large, rapidly growing population	Deficit, consuming area	Rapid growth in demand	From one central market to many decentralized ones
Bogra	GR 'advanced area'	Surplus food production area	Rapid increase in food production, mainly hybrid rice	Rapid increase in modern milling; need to broaden procurement area of paddy
Noakhali	Mono-cropped, 'backward area'	Deficit area	Change to hybrid rice production – some growth	Local oligopoly no longer seen; rise of automatic mills; distress sale by growers reduced

Source: Based on CM (1994) and author's field survey.

of *dadon*, or tied credit, quality and weight issues, problem of risk and default, and transport arrangements.

Sampling Technique

Fixed premise traders and millers were selected on the basis of consultations with *samiti* officials who also served to introduce the researchers to the respondents. The officials were told that the CM markets were being revisited after 20 years to look at what changes had taken place. Their advice to respondents (requested to include both large and small firms as locally understood) was accepted.

Itinerant traders were selected arbitrarily on the basis of their availability at the time of the field visits. No attempt was made to be statistically representative due to the difficulty of putting together a sample frame for any meaningful level of aggregation (for example, district or region).

Resources for data collection are generally constrained, and there is a well-known trade-off between coverage and depth. This study, however, had the advantage of being able to build on CM's work and thus was able to cover a somewhat larger sample using the 'greater understanding of what to look for' that is already provided by their detailed investigation (Crow 1999: 125).

Changing Contrasts, 1989–2008

Market Structure, Intermediaries and Their Socio-Economic Profiles

The market for agricultural produce can be thought of as comprising two kinds of circuits: a simple, local circuit catering to localized demand and a more complex long-distance circuit that connects local supplies to distant markets. Trade basically revolves around spatial arbitrage, although some degree of temporal arbitrage also exists, especially when commodities are storable.

Typically, the market consists of a number of essential intermediation roles carried out by numerous specialized agents. It is important to bear in mind that while different names are used to denote different agents and their functions, there are a number of overlapping functions carried out by the same agent as well as the use of different local names to refer to the same or similar functions that can lead to confusion. Figure 4.1 shows a generic representation of the paddy-rice trade circuit in Bangladesh.

The most common types of intermediaries referred to in the vernacular are *faria*, *bepari*, *aratdar* and *paikar*. In addition, there are various local names in different regions of the country like *cycle bepari*, *kanda bepari*, and *bharkiwala* and *lai faria*. Complications arise because of the changing roles of some

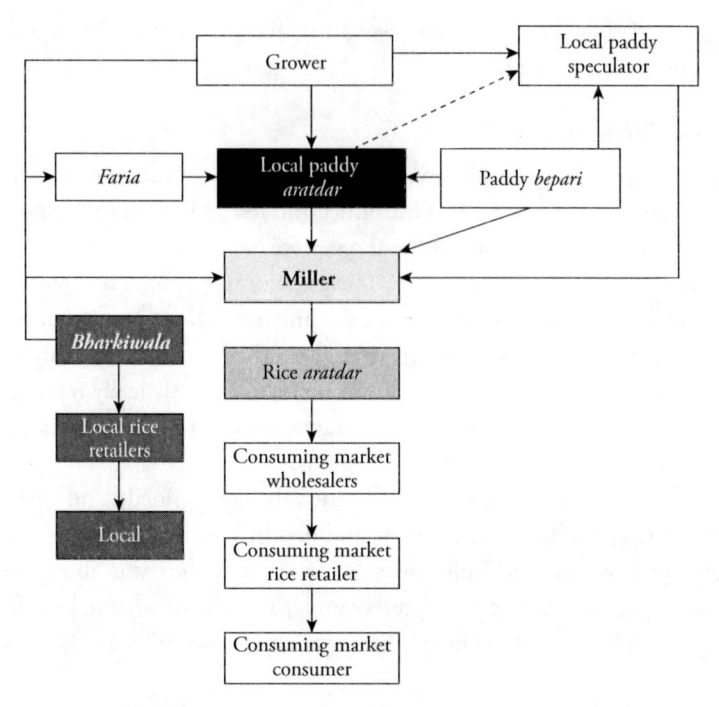

Figure 4.1 The paddy circuit

Source: Author's field survey (2008).

Note: Shaded boxes pinpoint changes over time: the decline in traditional milling (dark grey), the rise of modern milling (light grey), the ebb-flow of paddy *aratdars* (re-emergence in Bogra and decline in Noakhali) – black, and the growing importance of rice *aratdars* (medium grey).

intermediaries with time even though their nomenclature remains unchanged. The various types of intermediaries and their socio-economic status are described ahead. Table 4.2 describes their socio-economic characteristics and changing roles over time.

Faria

Itinerant trader operating in local village markets procuring supplies from growers and selling to *bepari*s locally. The *faria* are literally at the bottom of the pile along with 'microprocessors' (see later), plying their trade locally at the level of the village and the village market. They have very few assets and only manage to eke out an existence using their own or family labour.

Bepari

Also an itinerant trader who trades long distance collecting from *faria*s and growers, carrying out some sorting, grading and bulking, and connecting to an *aratdar*.

Table 4.2 Socio-economic profile of traders

Trader	Socio-economic Category	Socio-economic Characteristics	Dynamics
Farial Cycle Bepari/ Microprocessor	Poor/Very poor	Low amount of capital; use of own and family labour; indebted to higher-order trader; no fixed premises	In decline
Bepari	Poor to medium	Variable capital with large ones investing substantial amounts; relies on own labour; no fixed premises	Continues to play a key role; tied-*bepari* numbers greatly reduced
Aratdar	Medium to rich	Fixed premises; hires salaried staff and labour; has access to formal finance	Paddy *aratdar*s in decline in backward areas but re-emergence in advanced areas; rice *aratdar*s ascendant and plays key facilitating role in trade
Millers	Medium to very rich	Deploys substantial fixed and working capital; has access to formal finance	Decline of traditional milling and rise of automatic and semi-automatic rice mills

Source: CM (1994).

Aratdar

A broker or commission agent operating from fixed premises who links *bepari*s with buyers (other *bepari*s, millers or processors, *paikar*s or even retailers). While the pure function of the *aratdar* is that of a commission-based broker, he is also known to wear other hats as well, sometimes combining brokerage with direct trading.

Paikar

A wholesale buyer purchasing directly from an *aratdar* or using a *bepari* to buy on his behalf.

Retailer

Procures supplies from a *bepari* or a *paikar*.

Processors

In addition to modern semi-automatic and automatic mills, there are traditional, small-scale paddy processors (for example, *bharkiwala*) who procure paddy from growers and use family labour to dry and parboil the paddy before milling.

The local paddy circuit is shown on the left (Figure 4.1), where the main actor is the traditional microprocessor (*bharkiwala*). The top right-hand corner shows the paddy speculator: people with some surplus funds undertaking speculative seasonal trading. The other segments of the market are self-explanatory, involving milling, the role of paddy and rice *aratdar*s, and retailing.

Trade Circuits: Changing Contrasts
The Paddy Circuit

It would be interesting to explore if trade circuits and market structure have changed over time, and if this in turn is related to changing incentives facing market actors. The paddy *aratdar* (black box in Figure 4.1) was not even reported from the advanced area (Bogra) by CM as it played a minor role then. Millers procured paddy directly from growers often as kind loans to be paid later in cash at 'higher than market price' (HMP). Today, the main flow of paddy to the millers is through paddy *aratdar*s and *beparis*, accounting for 80–90 per cent of supplies.

Competition has increased manifold among millers in Bogra. In 1990 there were 100 semi-automatic mills, rising to 550 in 2009, including 7 automatic mills, generating considerable demand for paddy. Paddy has to be sourced now from a much wider area, from distant production centres. This was the perfect setting for the paddy *aratdar* to re-emerge in Bogra, in the face of changing costs imposed by distance and risk. In fact, the advanced area paddy circuit has increasingly come to resemble that of the backward area chain of 20 years ago.

In contrast, the backward area paddy *aratdar*s have declined, prompting one of the few who are left to observe: 'No new traders enter the paddy *aratdari* business – rather, most have left because millers buy directly from growers and *beparis*'.[4]

Twenty years ago, the paddy *aratdar*s in Noakhali were charged with the job of procuring supplies either from outside districts or from the *char*s. While in terms of distance, the *char*s were not far from the market town, access was difficult due to poor roads. Moreover, these were often newly settled areas with loosely organized communities, representing greater risks in exchange, especially when it came to trade with outside entities. It was under these circumstances that paddy *aratdari* proliferated at the time. These conditions have now changed with better infrastructure, communications and the advent of large automatic mills deep inside the *char*s.

The Milling Sector

Major changes have occurred in the milling sector in both areas, with virtually the entire traditional milling system consisting of a host of microprocessors dramatically reduced (medium grey boxes in Figure 4.1). Older technology in the shape of husking mills, boiler-operated mills and shallow-engine-operated mills are in decline with fully automatic mills rapidly taking over. These changes have been particularly sharp in Noakhali where a total of 20 large mills (including 3 in the *char*s) now account for over 90 per cent of the market. In Bogra, the milling capacity is more evenly spread across different technologies.

The introduction of automatic mills has altered incentives for traders in a number of important ways. Weighing and bagging are done using modern techniques. The quality of the grain produced is standardized and does not vary with the weather as drying is automatic. Important concerns with colour, quality and weight of rice have become largely irrelevant. This also means that price negotiations can be conducted under a better information regime.

The Rice Circuit

The rice part of the circuit remains unchanged over time with the role of the rice *aratdar* becoming even more important. The rapid expansion of milling capacity has resulted in intense competition among millers to sell, and this has strengthened the role of the rice *aratdar*, whose numbers failed to grow in the same proportion given strong entry constraints. There are signs of vertical integration of rice *aratdar*s in the Bogra market where 20 out of the 30 rice *aratdar*s have also become automatic mill owners, fully equipped with rice-sorting machines and even trucks and transport vehicles.

Decline in Tied Transactions

Twenty years ago, larger farmers were able to obtain a 'free' (untied) market price for their produce in open, face-to-face transactions but small and marginal farmers were often tied into credit-based relations requiring them to surrender a part of the produce at a significantly lower price than prevalent in the market. Poorer growers were often found to accept cash advances from traders, millers or their agents which had to be repaid after harvest at a low price. At the same time, surplus farmers were known to provide credit in kind to traders or millers which had to be repaid in cash at the end of the season, at the highest price of the season. The former was widespread, especially in the (backward rice-deficit) *char*s of Noakhali, while the latter was well known in (rice surplus) Bogra.

Various types of tied transactions have been well documented in the literature on paddy-rice markets but are certainly not restricted to that market alone (CM 1994; Olsen 1999). The objective of tying loans is to improve the returns of one party (the dominant or lending party) at the expense of the other, or to transfer risk, in the context of a given transaction. The main forms of these tying loans are given ahead:

- *Dhaner upore*, where cash is advanced to peasants by trading intermediaries before harvest, to be repaid partly in cash (usually the principal) and in kind (interest) at harvest at an agreed (higher than market) rate
- Trader *dadon*, where working capital is advanced in cash by higher-order traders to a subordinate trader (typically by an *aratdar* to a *bepari*) on the condition that the subordinate trader must trade exclusively with the higher-order trader until such time as the advance is repaid
- Credit in kind advanced by surplus peasants to traders, processors or other peasants to be repaid in cash at the highest price of the season
- Short-term *paikari baki* (trade credit) among traders that serves to promote client loyalty or signal trustworthiness
- Loans in kind from shopkeepers, millers or rich peasants to poor peasants and repaid in kind or cash

With the exception of *paikari baki*, a rate of interest is implicitly charged in all tying transactions (Tables 4.3 and 4.4).

Table 4.3 Different types of financial relations in the backward area paddy market

Type	Parties	Amount (BDT)	Terms (Implicit Interest Rate)
Dhaner upore ('money on paddy')	Sub-trader to poor peasant	Usually 1,000–3,000	Cash for paddy at harvest (100–180 per cent); in recent years, changed to repayment in cash (for principal) and kind (for interest)
Dadon	Big trader to small	15,000–100,000	All the small trader's procurement promised to the big
Advance purchase	Trader to peasant	1,000–3,000	Cash loan for paddy at harvest (very high)
Paddy loans	Big grower to trader	1,000–50,000	Paddy loan repaid in cash at above market price

Source: Based on CM (1994) and updated by author. These financial relations were reported 20 years ago by CM and have since declined dramatically.

Table 4.4 Changes in the *dhaner upore* rate over time

Year	Implicit DU Price (BDT/maund)	Market Price (BDT/maund)	% Loss to Grower
2008	417	600	30
2000	182	215	15
1989	143	200	29
1975	83	115	28
1972	20	67	70
1953	10	13	23

Source: Based on CM (1994) and updated by author.

Tied exchanges allow the dominant party to bypass the market and derive superior terms. However, tied exchanges are also risky as there is an incentive for borrowers to renege if possible.

The risk can be addressed in two ways: (*a*) through better information on borrower characteristics and (*b*) countervailing power at the local level to ensure repayment. Thus, for exchanges like *dhaner upore* to be credibly conducted, the distant lender must engage an influential local agent who is better informed and can ensure repayment.

The question then is what binds the local agent to the higher-order trader or lender? This relationship is similar to *dadon*, which binds subordinate traders to superior ones. The main glue is trust borne out of a history of successful repeat transactions bolstered by an element of threat: there is a clear market norm that *a subordinate must trade only with his principal as long as he remains indebted to him*. No other trader in a given market area will engage in any exchange with a tied trader. Clearly, the relevant information relating to different traders in a market and their tied subordinates or agents becomes public knowledge quite quickly. Under the circumstances, agents have little choice than to play by the rules.

A majority of peasants in the backward area were reported by CM to be tied to moneylenders in the past. This is no longer the case, although it still persists, especially in more distant *char*s. Hitherto subordinate traders and agents have now emerged as small, independent financiers at the local level. The ties with big traders and moneylenders have become weakened in the face of a much-improved situation with respect to availability of credit and finance (due to micro-credit NGOs and remittances) and the demise of monopoly power of big traders–moneylenders reported earlier by CM. *Char* area *beparis* and paddy *aratdars* have also reported increased risk in lending to growers who often find excuses to delay payment or even renege, pointing to a changing balance of power in the area.

In keeping with the general decline in tied exchange, trader *dadon*, which used to be widespread in commodity markets across Bangladesh, is no longer seen. Subordinate traders are no longer tied (for example, to millers or *aratdar*s) but engage in voluntary trade with their principals. This leads us to ask how the dominant forms of trade ('free exchange') are structured and sustained given the fact that *dadon* used to be such a key mechanism adopted by major market actors to ensure supply at a low price.

Transactions in the Paddy-Rice Market
Growers' Transactions

The grower engages in transactions primarily with the paddy *bepari*s and *faria*s. Transactions are in cash and at the farm gate. Unlike in the past when growers would go to the village market to sell, they are now able to sell directly from the farm gate. There is strong competition among collecting traders; growers are able to verify the market price easily with the help of mobile phones. In Bogra, growers used to sell on credit to millers but this practice is now rare as demand is high and the risk of credit default is significant. In Noakhali, the story is similar: cash sale at the farm gate is the norm and the practice of advance sale, or *dhaner upore*, is rarely seen. The use of weighing balances rather than the traditional basket has also gone in the growers' favour. Increased competition, better information (due to mobile phones) and easier access to microcredit from NGOs, and for Noakhali remittances from abroad, have translated into better terms for growers.

Paddy Aratdar

In Noakhali, local paddy *aratdar*s have declined, having lost out to *bepari*s for local supply and to distant *aratdar*s for out-of-district supplies. In Bogra, paddy *aratdar*s have re-emerged with the need to source supplies increasingly from further afield. In the former, transactions are in cash with no commission sales, while in the latter commission sales dominate. They do not get an advance from millers; indeed, they are more likely to sell on credit. Some advance payments to *bepari*s have also been reported from Noakhali (but not from Bogra) serving to tie in supplies, but this accounts for no more than 25 per cent of volume. Payments are made in cash and through banks. Thus, in Bogra the paddy *aratdar* combines a bulking function with a brokerage function, while in Noakhali the brokerage function has given way completely to the bulking function in the face of rapid transformation and expansion of the milling sector.

Rice Miller

Millers buy paddy and sell rice both in cash and on credit. Most of the transaction is done on credit, especially when business agents live in distant areas. Cash transaction is 10 per cent, transaction through banks is 60 per cent and transaction on credit is 30 per cent. If transactions are in cash, a discount of BDT 5–10 is given to the buyer per *maund* (40 kilograms). Transactions made on credit are settled within seven days, a facility given to *aratdar*s who are regular clients. Problems of exchange that remain include supply of low-quality paddy, delay in repayment, loss due to default by agents and so forth. Rice (unlike paddy) is always sold through *aratdar*s, who bear the entire risk of transaction between millers and distant wholesalers–retailers.

Rice Aratdars

The rice *aratdar* in Bogra is able to procure milled rice on credit as competition to sell is intense. Around 75–80 per cent of supplies are from semi-automatic and automatic mills, and orders are usually placed by mobile phone. At least 50 per cent of payments are made by bank transfers or online banking. It is likely that by 2020 this has been replaced by MFS. Sales are made to non-local rice *bepari*s and wholesalers in the network (75 per cent) and non-network members (25 per cent) – the latter are not granted credit. In case of credit, two–seven days are required to settle dues. Commission is BDT 4–5 per *maund*.

In Noakhali, *aratdar*s buy from automatic mills with 30–40 per cent of traded volumes taken on credit from regular suppliers. Purchases are paid for through bank transfers or online banking as well as cash, while sales are in cash, mainly to local retailers (75 per cent).[5] Since sales are local, no networks are used unlike in the past when 25–30 per cent of sales went to fixed retailers in the *char*s with credit playing a big role. Twenty years ago, transactions with millers were on commission basis; this is no longer practised.

The *aratdar* is mainly interested in turnover, especially when operating on commission. This requires a trusted client base of suppliers and buyers. As part of his business strategy, trader *dadon* used to be rampant 20 years ago but has now reduced to a trickle in all major markets in Bangladesh. Verbal contracts are now entered into with free (untied) traders who have the option of going elsewhere with their business if there is lack of trust. Thus, rice *aratdar*s have to compete on the basis of the total quality of service provided to clients (including short-term credit, timely deliver and quality). In practice, trading partnerships once established remain loyal, even if there are minor breaches in contract as it is difficult and time-consuming to build new ones.

Rice Wholesalers

Wholesalers are based in main consumption centres, procuring rice supplies from *aratdar*s and sometimes directly from millers. There are no tied agents with the main strength of the business resting on reputation: suppliers of rice look for wholesalers who have a good reputation for regular payment and good price. It was common 20 years ago to keep a representative permanently posted in the supply region to ensure that the verbal contract was honoured. This practice has disappeared because of the easing of the supply situation, reduced concern with quality and weight, and the ability to maintain close contact with suppliers over mobile phones. Risks for wholesalers have declined, although not disappeared.

More than 80 per cent of the surveyed wholesalers in Dhaka have reported incurring losses due to default. Retailers sometimes do not make payment on time; sometimes, they leave the business without making repayment and cannot be traced.

Rice Retailers

There are no tying arrangements, but generally each retailer purchases from a few fixed wholesalers, whom they trust and from whom they can purchase on credit. In Dhaka, business transaction is entirely on credit for purchase of rice from regular wholesalers living in or around the retail market. However, when rice is purchased from distant wholesalers, only 30–40 per cent can be purchased on credit, underscoring the increased problem of monitoring and risk associated with long-distance trading.

Retail markets are more likely to see one-off transactions between unknown agents, opening up the possibility of 'snatch'. However, for a staple like rice this is likely to be less problematic given widely available information and consumer familiarity.

Generally, the retail trade was yet to develop into a large, modern operation where branding or reputation effects could come into play, for example, due to the rise of supermarkets and transformation of commodities into products (Reardon and Timmer 2005).

Today, the scenario is likely to have changed quite a bit. Modern retail and agro-processing industries have evolved considerably. At the same time, automatic rice millers have also gone into branding and packaging so that the retail market in 2020 has undergone considerable change, especially in urban areas. Urban middle-class consumers today are far more likely to buy rice from modern retail outlets or even online, while the poorer classes still depend on less reliable wet markets.

Supporting Market Transformation

Market-wide norms, culture, rules and institutions support credible, low-cost exchange. These relate to social capital, mechanisms for grievance resolution, security of transactions, information dissemination, the legal regime, and dealing with the police and 'authorities' – all designed to limit default and lower transaction costs (Reardon et al. 2014). These factors have not undergone any qualitative change over time and cannot really explain the very significant transformation of the market system reported earlier. For an explanation, it is important to focus on a number of key exogenous factors that are likely to have eliminated various constraints to 'free' trade: rural financial markets (micro-credit, remittance inflows), physical infrastructure (mainly rural roads) and mobile telephony. In addition, state policy reforms may also have facilitated the observed changes in market performance.

Rural Finance and Remittances

Major changes have taken place in financial markets. On the supply side, there has been a proliferation of microcredit organizations, branches of both public and private sector banks, and large inflows of remittances. In Noakhali, for example, almost every family has a member working abroad and sending back money periodically. This has meant that producers no longer depend as much on distress borrowing or sales, and if credit is needed, it can be obtained locally. Similarly, traders and millers have much better access to trade credit from the formal banking sector with the proliferation of bank branches and much superior liquidity disposition. In addition, long-distance or large transactions are invariably now done through bank transfers to minimize risk, often using online banking facilities or mobile banking platforms.

It can be said that although micro-credit or microfinance was introduced experimentally in the 1970s in Bangladesh, it was not until the early 1990s that it really took off, registering phenomenal growth in microfinance institutions (MFIs), a trend that continued into the 2000s (S. Ahmed, n.d.).

By the mid-1990s, 'second-generation' products were launched with the objective of better targeting of the poorest as well as covering non-poor micro and small entrepreneurs (Hulme and Moore 2006). By 2001–02, more diversified financial products emerged addressing agriculture, housing, education, and various types of small enterprises.

Thus, by June 1998 the revolving loan fund for micro-credit stood at USD 328.7 million, rising to around USD 644 million by 2002 and further climbing to a massive figure exceeding USD 3 billion by 2008 (InM and CDF 2011). This has further risen to USD 4 billion in 2014 and USD 9 billion in 2018 (MRA 2018).

In parallel to developments in rural finance, Bangladesh has seen a massive increase in remittance earnings sent home by around 10 million workers abroad, mostly to rural areas. Total remittances grew dramatically to over USD 13 billion in 2012 (*Economist* 2012) from around USD 1.2 billion in 1995 and 4.8 billion in 2005 (Government of Bangladesh 2007) – a figure that is many times the volume of micro-credit. Remittances have kept climbing steadily, reaching USD 20 billion in 2020 and rising 18 per cent year on year in the context of a 14 per cent decline in global remittance flows (S. Islam 2021). The knock-on effects of this kind of inflow are large, creating demand, employment and stimulating rural wages (*Economist* 2012).

Rural Roads

A major factor holding back the 'backward' area was its remote location and difficulty of access from the nearest market town in Noakhali in the late 1980s. Since then, all-weather roads have improved physical communication enormously, leading to investments in rice mills and establishment of bank branches deep inside the *char*s.

Generally, there have been massive investments in rural roads in Bangladesh over the last two decades implemented by the Local Government Engineering Department (LGED). Thus, over the period 1991–2006, LGED constructed around 65,000 kilometres of dirt roads, 43,000 kilometres of paved roads and over 500,000 metre bridges and culverts in rural Bangladesh. Between 2000 and 2006 alone, rural road lengths tripled and local bridges doubled in number. In addition, LGED also developed around 2,000 new rural growth centres and markets (Government of Bangladesh 2007). The momentum in expansion of rural infrastructure has not abated. Over the Seventh Plan period (2016–20), 116,419 kilometres of paved roads, 236,913 kilometres of earthen roads and 152,346 metres of bridges and culverts were added to the stock (*Seventh Five-Year Plan* 2020). Thus, today 83.5 per cent of all villagers live within 2 kilometres of a road, although the percentage is still low for access to all-weather roads (under 50 per cent) (Ovi 2020).

Mobile Phones and New Technology

The spread of cellular mobile phone access revolutionized markets since its introduction in Bangladesh in 1993. At the time, high tariffs and monopoly rents severely restricted the market, which responded very favourably with the introduction of three GSM licences in 1996 and a total investment of around USD 4 billion in 2008. Teledensity rapidly increased from 0.4 per cent in 1997 to 31 per cent in 2008 (CIA 2012). By 2020, the digital scenario has become further transformed. Mobile phone connections have jumped to 99 per cent (79 per cent in India), 41 per cent have an internet connection (45 per cent in India) and 22 per cent are connected to social media (32.3 per cent in India).

The other technological advance of note is the rapid spread of MFS, which is likely to have further benefited market transactions. The major MFS operator (bKash) started operations in 2011. Between 2015 and 2019, total transactions expanded from USD 1.7 billion to USD 3.8 billion and the number of clients increased from 30 million to 70 million (Murshid et al. 2020).

The impact on the rice market was immense: 90 per cent of traders interviewed in 2008 already had access to mobile phones, enabling millers, traders and growers to talk to clients readily, and were able to place orders over the phone, reducing the need for face-to-face exchange. Quality, grades and weight issues were of lesser concern due to technological changes in milling. Better communications quickly resulted in opening up backward markets and reducing information asymmetry and transactions costs, stimulating more direct trade.

Technological change took place on a number of other fronts as well: (*a*) milling – the rise of automatic rice mills that set new standards and new tastes (uniform quality and grades, automated weighing and bagging) and (*b*) paddy production – shift to hybrid paddy which is well suited to automatic and semi-automatic mills (displacing husking mills and *bharkiwalas*).

State Policy Reforms

The policy regime went through a sharp change in orientation in the mid-1990s from a focus almost entirely on agricultural, particularly rice, production through support to irrigation and distribution of modern inputs and HYV of seeds, to a broadened policy shift to include a programme of trade liberalization and structural adjustment involving dismantling of the massive, inefficient PFDS, abolition of the state monopoly on rice imports, permission for cross-border trade of rice with India (enabling rapid access to India's massive grain reserves in times of need) and quite dramatic changes in the subsidy regime.[6]

The objective of the state was to impart additional stimuli to growth through realignment of market incentives to raise efficiency and productivity. Generally, these market-friendly reforms were warmly applauded and appeared to have been successful (N. Ahmed et al. 2007). The 'losers' were to be compensated through expanded social safety nets like the Vulnerable Group Development (VGD) and

Food-for-Work (FFW) programmes, bolstered by the open market sale (OMS) of rice and wheat, to stabilize prices and consumption.

However, state policy was never explicitly adopted to address the problem of backward forms of exchange that used to be rampant in Bangladesh, although indirectly there may have been some impact in the wake of better market opportunities that presented themselves.

Conclusion

This chapter presents evidence to show that far-reaching changes have been taking place in the Bangladesh rice market. Backward areas were found to be associated with complex forms of tied exchange á la CM, while other more advanced areas displayed much more competitive outcomes based on less personalized transactions. The evidence shows a sharp decline in the backward forms over the course of two decades revealing that the huge paddy-rice market is not static but is constantly changing and adapting and evolving into a better functioning market system.

It is suggested that the improvements in agricultural performance, especially in rice production and broadly in the rural socio-economic regime marked by exogenous developments in roads and infrastructure, mobile telephony, rural finance and remittances, are likely to have played a significant role in transforming rural markets by reducing risk, improving information flows and reducing transactions costs. The role of endogenous traditional market institutions remains essentially unaltered and therefore cannot be held responsible for the changes described.

The notion of backwardness with which tied exchange is closely related arises from lack of access in a number of senses: physical, financial and informational. In backward areas, powerful merchant–trader–landlord groups are able to exercise considerable control over access (CM 1994) to introduce and sustain tied exchange with subordinate traders and poor peasants. Roads and infrastructure development in rural Bangladesh effectively solved the problem of physical access, while microcredit and remittances transformed rural financial markets to provide access even to poor peasants and traders. The third element – mobile telephony – spread rapidly to loosen the final constraint, namely informational access, thereby ushering in rapid transformation of agricultural markets. Future empirical work could seek to further explore and assess the relative importance of these transformative factors. There is little doubt that MFS that have gained momentum over the last decade have further facilitated market transformation.

The impact on employment, livelihoods and vulnerability is an area of particular concern. It is likely that the returns to traders across the value chain have improved as backward forms of exchange were replaced. However, at the lowest rung of the circuit occupied by small processors and traders, the outcome is less clear. One possibility is that they too were able to access better terms and cheaper finance and became transformed into independent small-scale traders. It is almost certain that some would find themselves faced with serious livelihood challenges. This is another area that requires further empirical investigation.

Going forward, the traditional market will have to confront the challenge of the rise of a growing supermarket segment in the country. The crucial question is whether the traditional market will survive by adapting and meeting the demands of this emerging segment or ultimately take a back seat to a more dynamic, efficient supply chain that overtakes it. This is an important area of both empirical and analytical research with far-reaching policy implications. For the moment, it seems modern retail has not affected traditional market chains to a great extent, but as per capita incomes rise, some degree of polarization already in evidence will certainly deepen.

5

International Migration

At the same time that Bangladesh was struggling with the GR, a silent process of migration was already afoot – a beginning which would eventually gather steam and take off. In 1976, only 6,000 workers left for the Middle East for work but by 1981 this rose to around 56,000. Other countries in Asia, including Pakistan, India, Sri Lanka, Nepal, Thailand and Philippines, were able to respond more quickly to the dramatic opening up of labour markets in the oil-rich Middle East following the lifting of the oil embargo in 1973 and a surge in the petrodollar economies of the Gulf and Saudi Arabia. Thus, the number of Indians sent out in 1976 was around 4,000 but this figure grew to over 275,000 in 1981. In the case of Pakistan, the figure for 1976 was less than 42,000, which went up to over 168,000 in 1981 (Arnold and Shah 1986).

The slower initial response rate from Bangladesh may have been due to labour market preferences or more likely due to the poor institutional arrangements and high migration costs in Bangladesh compared to competing countries.[1] Bangladesh in the mid-1970s was a country that was still struggling with the aftermath of war and famine. Migration rates, nevertheless, picked up quickly but spiked in 1991–95 and 2006–10, the latter including the global financial crisis period. In fact, only during 2011–15 we observe a 12 per cent drop in outmigration, which appears to be related to the 8 per cent decline in remittance growth in the subsequent period (Table 5.1).[2]

Migrant remittances continue to play a big role in a number of Asian countries including Bangladesh, helping to strengthen the BOP and shore up foreign exchange reserves while also having an impact on rural households in terms of income, consumption, savings and investment. A related impact of remittances, historically, has been its timing – gaining ascendance at a time when donor fatigue was setting in, putting aid-dependent countries like Bangladesh at considerable risk (Rodríguez 2020). For example, for Bangladesh, remittance earnings comprised 40 per cent of exports and 5.7 per cent of GDP in 2018. In fact, the comparative figures for a number of countries like Nepal, Sri Lanka, Pakistan and Philippines are higher (Table 5.2).

Table 5.1 Out-migration of workers from Bangladesh (1976–2018)

	Workers/Annum '000	USD Million	Per Cent Change Workers	Per Cent Change USD
1976–80	24.4	178	–	–
1981–85	65.8	543.8	169.7	205.5
1986–90	85.8	745.4	30.4	37.1
1991–95	199.2	1,059.8	132.2	42.2
1996–00	240.4	1,707.4	20.7	61.1
2001–05	252.8	3,517	5.2	105.9
2006–10	612.2	9,243.8	142.2	162.8
2011–15	537.6	14,356	-12.2	55.3
2016–18	780.7	13,206.7	45.2	-8

Source: Calculated from Government of Bangladesh (2019).

Table 5.2 Remittance as per cent of exports and GDP: Selected Asian countries

	Per Cent of GDP 1980	Per Cent of GDP 2018	Per Cent of Exports 1980	Per Cent of Exports 2018
Bangladesh	1.86	5.65	3.0	39.6
Nepal	1.50 (1993)	28.0	107.7	233.3
Sri Lanka	3.80	8.40	11.6	39.2
India	1.48	2.88	24.8	16.1
Pakistan	8.64	6.73	61.9	69.8
Philippines	1.92	10.21	8.72	37.9
Thailand	1.18	1.48	4.79	2.2

Sources: 'Personal Remittances Received', World Bank Databank, https://data.worldbank.org/indicator/BX.TRF.PWKR.DT.GD.ZS (accessed 16 October 2020); 'Exports of Goods and Services', World Bank Databank, https://data.worldbank.org/indicator/BX.GSR.GNFS.CD?view=chart (accessed 16 October 2020).

In the 1980s there was a lot of speculation on whether the demand for migrant workers would be sustained over time. Demands have sustained and grown, and new destinations have emerged. These include Malaysia, Singapore, Lebanon and South Korea, and, more recently, Japan, Maldives and Mauritius. Increasingly, however, the demand is for skilled workers, especially as robotics began to displace humans from tedious, repetitive occupations. Today, more than 10 million Bangladeshi workers are thought to be abroad and there is no sign that the numbers will decline anytime soon.

Migrant work opportunities have played a major role in the development of Bangladesh by stabilizing the macro-economy, including the exchange rate, building up foreign exchange reserves, enabling imports of capital and intermediate goods, and transferring incomes to the rural economy where the majority of the people and the poor live. While the economic impact is well researched and documented, the socio-economic impact is less well understood, although there is enough anecdotal evidence and some studies to indicate that the reverse side of the coin can be dismal (T. Siddiqui 2001, 2006, 2008); R. Roy 2017). One important aspect has to do with abuse and loss of freedom and rights in receiving countries, for both male and female migrants but especially for the latter. The other relates to the cost of migration, the incidence of violation of contracts, prevalence of dubious methods of recruitment and cheating of would-be migrants of their savings or borrowings. Thus, the 'success' of the migration-remittance phenomenon is not unequivocal but comes at considerable cost – costs that are well known but which policymakers often turn a blind eye to.

While Bangladesh has tried to create institutions that would regulate, monitor and provide oversight to the entire process of recruitment, migration and sending–receiving remittances through official channels, the entire system remains exposed to a lot of abuse and weaknesses even today. The government has over the years set up various agencies to make the process more efficient and less costly. It has also instituted policies to encourage remittances while also negotiating with countries like Saudi Arabia and Malaysia to recruit more labour from Bangladesh. The chronology of major policy measures adopted is indicated in Table 5.3.

Table 5.3 Chronology of major government interventions

Period	Intervention
1974	Introduction of the Wage Earners' Scheme (WES, premium on the exchange rate for remittances)
1976	Setting up of the Bureau of Manpower Export and Training (BMET)
1982	Promulgation of the New Emigration Ordinance to replace the Emigration Act, 1922
1984	Formation of Bangladesh Association of International Recruiting Agencies (BAIRA) – currently has 1100+ agents working under it
1984	BOESL (Bangladesh Overseas Employment Services Limited) – only state-owned recruiting company
1990	Wage Earners' Welfare Fund (WEWF) set up

(*Contd.*)

International Migration 81

Table 5.3 (*Contd.*)

Period	Intervention
1998	Signed the UN International Convention on Protection of Rights of Workers and Families (no receiving country has ratified the convention)
2002	Introduced the official licencing system for recruiting agencies
2003	Government relaxes restrictions on female labour migration
2010	Migrant Welfare Bank or Probashi Kalyan Bank (PKB)
2011	Migration and Overseas Employment Act
2012	Memorandum of understanding (MOU) signed with Malaysia for G2G arrangements for sending workers
2013	Enacted the Overseas Employment and Migration Act, 2013 (more focus on women and safe migration; accountability of recruiting agents)

Sources: Based on Mallick and Etzold (2015); 'Institutional Assessment of Migration Systems in Bangladesh', http://documents1.worldbank.org/curated/en/446181539106128109/pdf/Institutional-assessment-of-Bangladesh-migration-system.pdf (accessed 19 November 2021).

The government recognized the remittance potential quite early on, responding way back in 1974 – well before the migrant market blossomed – by introducing the Wage Earners' Scheme (WES), quickly followed by setting up the Bureau of Manpower Export and Training (BMET) – the public agency intended to oversee all aspects of the worker migration process. In the context of an administered and fixed exchange rate regime, the WES was an important mechanism to provide quasi-market benefits to remitters. BMET has struggled since inception to cope with the complex tasks that it was mandated to perform. It was only in 2015 that a comprehensive review of BMET was conducted, in an attempt to identify key areas of intervention (ILO 2015).

The initial spurt in migration occurred in 1981–85, growing by 170 per cent over the preceding five-year period (Table 5.3). Although a big percentage jump, this was from a low base. The most important policy intervention during this period was the setting up of BAIRA, the Bangladesh Association of International Recruiting Agencies, and BOESL (Bangladesh Overseas Services Limited), the lone public-sector recruiting agency, both at the fag end of the period in 1984. In other words, the growth spurt in 1981–85 cannot be attributed to any specific policy intervention but more likely a result of independent, private-sector responses.

The growth spurt of 1991–95 of 132 per cent and that of 2006–10 were large and occurred from a fairly high base level. These spurts contributed immensely to the current position of Bangladesh as a major remittance-receiving nation.

In response to this rapidly growing market, a large number of recruitment agencies were set up by people wanting to cash in on this boom.[3]

The basic organization for the migration of workers has been private sector dominated from the very early days. The sourcing, hiring and placement of workers from sending countries to receiving countries has been described as a large transnational industry in which influential interests have become involved on both sides. There are scouting agents who will scour the countryside, essentially connecting potential migrants to private recruiting agencies who are licenced by BAIRA. These companies will then negotiate with agencies operating in the receiving countries. In the process, multiple nodes have developed from the potential migrant to the ultimate employer, pushing up transaction costs at each node: one estimate suggests that 60 per cent of the cost of migration is accounted for by 'agents' (T. Siddiqui 2011; Barkat, Osman and Sen Gupta 2014). As if this was not enough, the poor migrants, in addition, have to constantly contend with spurious documents (including visas and contracts) that often lead to their becoming undocumented workers overnight once they have arrived in a host country to discover that the job or the employer that they were promised does not exist. These risks, although widely reported, have not deterred supply of workers given the high social status they enjoy at home once they start sending money back.

The global labour market demand for Bangladeshi workers has fluctuated considerably over time as older markets closed and new ones emerged. This has happened in the case of Saudi Arabia and the UAE which at one stage stopped recruiting from Bangladesh, although this was later offset by greater demand from Qatar and Oman, and the emergence of newer markets in Southeast and East Asia (Murata 2018).

In the present context of the Bangladesh story that we are trying to unravel, the role of remittances has not only been entirely positive and complementary but indeed critical to the various other development efforts initiated by the government (food, family planning and infrastructure), the non-government (education, health, grassroots institutions, micro-credit) and the private sector. The immediate impact of remittances was to ensure a significant, more predictable flow of scarce foreign exchange to complement meagre export earnings and unpredictable aid, thereby having a huge impact on the balance of payments and reserves, paving the way towards macro-economic stability.

At the household level, remittances increased savings and investment, and generally had a positive impact on livelihoods. Chami, Fullenkamp and Jahjah (2003), World Bank (2008) and Raihan et al. (2009) suggest that remittances had a positive impact on reducing poverty, improving food security, education of wards and empowerment of women recipients, and improved health sanitation. While it was frequently observed that remittances were not being 'productively' used, the increased household spending that resulted, nevertheless, helped stimulate the local economy through increased demand as well as some diversification of agriculture into cash crops and aquaculture (M. M. Rahman 2013; World Bank 2012; Siddiqui and Mahmood 2014).

At the root of the success of migrant remittances is the generation of strong demand in the international market set off by the oil price boom of the 1970s coupled with surplus, low-wage labour supplies available in countries like Bangladesh. Despite Bangladesh's slow start, it did not take long for it to catch up because of its ability to compete with low wages in that market segment. In fact, this combination of market access and low wages was also crucial for the RMG story of Bangladesh. Similarly, the flow of substantial remittances to rural areas resulted in a much more vigorous rural economy and expansion of the RNF sector.

Luckily for Bangladesh, the flow of remittances sustained a robust growth over decades even in the face of grave uncertainties and dire predictions. This counter-cyclical behaviour of the Bangladesh economy appears to have become a normal, even routine feature. Thus, we saw how remittances were scarcely affected by the Global Financial Crisis of 2007–09, unlike many countries that were reeling under its influence (Murshid et al. 2009). More recently, the prediction from the World Bank (2021) of a large likely fall in global remittances had to be revised when the fall turned out to be quite muted, and in the case of Bangladesh robust remittance growth continued to buck the trend. Similar patterns have been noted from other countries in South Asia.

While various plausible explanations have been floated, these remain speculative and require empirical validation. These include travel restrictions that prevented migrants from returning home (and bringing in cash directly), shift from informal to formal channels because of stricter monitoring, a more favourable exchange rate policy for official remitters making the traditional *hawala* system less attractive, a tendency to send out savings in larger amounts because of an uncertain climate, the greater-than-usual demand from families back at home for assistance due to COVID-related unemployment or ill health and, finally, the hefty stimulus packages deployed for the recovery of host-country economies.

6

The Rural Non-farm (RNF) Sector

Introduction

Traditionally, the RNF sector consisted of an assortment of rural households dependent on a variety of service sector livelihoods comprising artisans, barbers, petty food processors and vendors, craftsmen, milkmen, potters, tinkers, tailors and carpenters. They depended on the custom of the vast farming population whose demands they tried to cater to. However, given low productivity and low rural incomes, the demand for the services of these non-farm groups was low and unstable (mirroring unstable farm incomes), making their livelihoods quite precarious. This was the state of RNF in the 1960s and 1970s, before the advent of the GR.

The more recent development history of East and Southeast Asia and parts of South Asia suggests that rural industry and commerce expand in parallel with agricultural production, as linkages between the two deepen (Ranis and Stewart 1993; Yusuf and Kumar 1996; Bhattacharya 1996). Typically, RNF is viewed as having two distinct components: (*a*) a high labour productivity segment and (*b*) a low productivity segment. The former is associated with higher incomes, while the latter operates more as a residual. In the process of rural development, RNF is expected to gradually lose its residual character, giving way to more productive, better-paying activities.

In the context of poverty alleviation, it has been noted that non-farm earnings led to an absolute improvement in incomes of the poor, suggesting that a dynamic RNF sector will have a strong anti-poverty impact (Lanjouw and Lanjouw 1999; Lanjouw 1999; B. Sen 1996; Haggblade and Hazell 1989; Haggblade, Hazell and Brown 1989). In the context of the Indian literature, Lanjouw (2007) and Haggblade, Hazell and Reardon (2010) have argued that the impact is not automatic and in fact appears to be muted with a tendency to bypass the extreme poor. Experience from Bangladesh, however, paints a much more positive picture (Pitt and Khandker 1998; Khandker 2005; Khandker, Khalily and Samad 2016a).

Over a 20-year period (1991–92 to 2010–11), moderate poverty headcount declined from 78 per cent to 27.5 per cent, while extreme poverty declined from 64.8 per cent to 14 per cent. RNF adopters experienced a faster growth of income and a faster decline in poverty. RNF incomes grew 29 per cent faster than farm incomes, while the decline in poverty for RNF was 8 per cent faster (Khandker, Khalily and Samad 2016b). During the same period, it was further observed that the growth in RNF was led by the farm sector: a 10 per cent income in farm incomes increased RNF incomes by 6 per cent, and within RNF the role of the enterprise sector was most important. The reason for the 'better performance' of Bangladesh may be the targeted interventions via micro-credit and skills training that went mainly to the non-farm poor which were not as prevalent in India. In addition, social stratification and institutional discrimination may be a bigger problem in India than in Bangladesh.[1]

Thus, since the GR, RNF began to diversify and expand, giving rise to new activities, new livelihoods and new earning opportunities in the wake of the introduction of new rice varieties that require modern irrigation and water control and the use of complementary seed-fertilizer inputs.[2]

At the same time, rural Bangladesh began to experience resource inflows via international remittances and microcredit from NGOs that boosted rural demand for goods and services. The rural areas also experienced investment in a range of areas like aquaculture and poultry, as well as in irrigation equipment and agricultural machinery.

Growing urbanization and industrialization also encouraged RNF, especially in areas that were well connected to major urban centres (Deichmann, Shilpi and Vakis 2009). As the urban-industrial labour force expanded, rural areas forged even closer linkages with urban areas. Domestic remittances expanded quickly as urban-industrial workers sent back much of their savings home to families in the villages, in much the same way as wage earners working abroad. In other words, the rural areas witnessed an unprecedented inflow of resources into the economy which stimulated investment, employment and wages. Rural Bangladesh today has, thus, become significantly transformed with the growth in rural industry and enterprises (for example, automatic rice mills, cold stores, repair shops, modern food processing enterprises) and spectacular expansion of non-crop sectors. The contribution of RNF, however, rarely figures in the development narratives that are currently popular.[3] This chapter, therefore, attempts to understand the historical role of RNF with reference to structure, employment, wages and incomes, especially of the poor and women.

There are a number of national-level databases that researchers have used in the past: (*a*) the periodic labour force surveys (LFSs) which are conducted by

BBS every 2–3 years, starting from 1983 to 1984 (Varma and Kumar 1996); (*b*) census data that are available every decade (W. Mahmud 1996); (*c*) HIES data generated every five years exploited by Khandker, Khaliliy and Samad (2016b); (*d*) panel data on a representative sample of rural households for 1987–88 and 2000 (M. Hossain 2004); (*e*) the nationally representative (rural) panel data from the International Food Policy Research Institute (IFPRI) called the Bangladesh Integrated Household Survey (BIHS) pertaining to 2011–12 and 2015 (A. Ahmed 2016); and finally, (*f*) World Bank panel data exploited by Khandker, Khalily and Samad (2016a) covering the 20-year period between 1990 and 2010.

Employment in RNF

During the 1980s and 1990s, RNF was growing slowly, registering a growth of just 3.2 per cent between 1983–84 and 1990–91 (Varma and Kumar 1996). Nevertheless, its contribution to employment was large. For example, a micro study from two villages in Manikganj in 1981–82 shows that non-agricultural households consisted of around 33 per cent of all rural households (Rahman and Islam 1985). However, both farm and non-farm households performed agricultural and non-agricultural work, although at different rates. Land-owning farm households were mostly self-employed, while non-farm households combined self-employment with a lot of wage work. Thus, in the early 1980s, self-employment was widespread for all rural households (over 70 per cent), while wage-based work was limited mostly to the landless and to non-farm households (W. Mahmud 1996; Rahman and Islam 1985).

National level data confirms the importance of RNF. According to a BIDS–IRRI study, the employment share of RNF was 34.5 per cent in 1987–88 (M. Hossain 2004), while estimates based on census data put this figure at 32.6 per cent in 1981, and 37.9 per cent in 1991. LFS-based estimates are similar, at 34.3 per cent for 1983–84 and 38.6 per cent for 1990–91 (W. Mahmud 1996).

Thus, from the late 1980s, non-farm employment began to rise, reaching almost 45 per cent by the mid-1990s (BIDS–IRRI household surveys – see M. Hossain [2004]). Estimates based on LFS reveal a similar trend, although the proportions given are somewhat lower (34 per cent in 1984–85 and almost 40 per cent in 1995–96). The structure of non-farm employment, however, remained broadly unchanged, although 'other non-agriculture' grew at a slightly higher rate (Table 6.1).

The data shown in Table 6.1 is quite interesting: first, employment in crop agriculture declined over the period (1987–88 to 1994–95), while it increased in non-agriculture; second, employment in 'other agriculture' actually registered the highest growth – at over 10 per cent over the period. This was driven by poultry, dairy and fisheries in which there was a boom; third, in 'non-agriculture', the most growth was seen in 'other non-agriculture' – basically rural industry, especially handlooms.

In fact, Table 6.2 provides further details about the composition of RNF in the late 1980s. Trade and services are large, as expected. What really stands out, however, is the importance of handlooms whose contribution at 25 per cent is higher than that of trade. Of course, in a decade, as we shall see, this will have completely changed with the virtual extinction of handlooms, despite the temporary relief brought about by converting the handlooms into more efficient power looms.

Table 6.1 Rural employment by agriculture and non-agriculture

Sector	1987–88 Survey No. of Workers	Per Cent	1994–95 Survey No. of Workers	Per Cent	Per Cent Change
Agriculture	1,271	65.5	1,235	55.3	−0.4
Crops	832	42.9	826	37.0	−0.1
Wage labour in agriculture	424	21.9	375	16.8	−1.7
Other agriculture	15	0.8	34	1.5	10.5
Non-agriculture	668	34.5	997	44.7	5.9
Trade	178	9.2	262	11.7	5.7
Services	315	16.2	457	20.5	5.5
Other non-agriculture	175	9.0	278	12.5	6.8
Economically active members	1,939	100	2,232	100	2.0

Source: BIDS–IRRI surveys cited by M. Hossain (2004).

Table 6.2 Employment in RNF by components (1989–90)

Sector	In Millions	Per Cent
Manufacturing	0.16	4.0
Trade	0.84	21.0
Services	1.4	35.0
HH manufactures	0.34	8.5
HH trade-services	0.26	6.5
Handloom	1.0	25.0
Total	4.0	100

Sources: BBS (1991); BBS (1992) cited in Varma and Kumar (1996).

Table 6.3 Structure of farm and non-farm employment (per cent)

Sector	1995	2000	2005	2010
Farm Employment	60.36	63.12	56.76	55.16
Crop	54.63	55.19	52.90	49.24
Non-crop	5.73	7.93	3.86	5.92
Non-farm Employment	39.64	36.88	43.24	44.84
Total	100	100	100	100

Source: HIES, different years.

After 1995, the trend in further expansion of non-farm employment continued (Table 6.3). By 2010, the contribution of farm employment declined to 55 per cent from over 60 per cent in 1995. Much of this was attributable to the crop sub-sector, while the non-crop agricultural sector managed to retain its share of the labour market. However, it is the non-farm sector that expanded its share of employment by more than five percentage points.

The trend has continued – indeed it has intensified somewhat in subsequent years. The LFS (2016–17) conducted by BBS estimates that farm employment ('agriculture, forestry and fisheries') constituted 41.2 per cent of total rural employment. In the case of women, this was 63 per cent. This means that RNF in 2016–17 was 58.8 per cent, a huge increase from the 2010 level by around 13 percentage points, making the contribution of rural non-farm employment (RNFE) significantly greater than agricultural employment.

In other words, the preponderance of agriculture-dependent employment has decisively now shifted away into non-agricultural work in rural areas. This speaks of a structural change in the rural labour market that likely reflects a realignment of livelihoods and economic activities. The question is what is driving these changes and, indeed, whether this is 'good' or 'bad'. If this is leading to increased employment and higher wages or incomes, then that is likely to be related to higher productivity. The alternative would be that RNFE is a residual sector characterized by low productivity and wages where people struggle to eke out an existence. This tendency is also likely to indicate a move away from land as a source of livelihoods in rural areas and its diminishing importance, indicating perhaps a potential development journey that does not have to depend as much on access to land.

Rural Incomes and RNF

In one study, rural incomes were divided into agricultural, non-agricultural and 'wages and salaries' – the last consisting of incomes derived from both agriculture and non-agriculture sectors (B. Sen 1996). This study shows that total rural income or consumption registered a negative growth rate for the period 1983–91. Agricultural income, wages and salaries posted negative growth rates of –1.2 to –2.8 per cent per annum in this period. Non-agricultural income, on the other hand, posted a growth rate of 2.8 per cent per annum at the same time.

Thus, we see that per capita agricultural income fell from BDT 1,661 to 1,511, while wages fell from BDT 972 to 777, over 1983–91. Per capita non-agricultural income rose from BDT 1,149 to 1,438, considerably narrowing the income differential between agricultural and non-agricultural incomes (Table 6.4).

In the early to mid-1980s, agricultural income was 43 per cent, non-agricultural income was 31 per cent and wages and salaries consisted of 25–26 per cent of total rural income. At the beginning of the 1990s, the share of agricultural income rose slightly (40 per cent); however, there was a sharp increase in the share of non-agricultural income (39 per cent) and a corresponding fall in 'wages and salaries' (21 per cent). This is clearly an interesting shift.

The shift is particularly pronounced for the poor whose dependence on non-agricultural income rose quite sharply (from 26 per cent to 35 per cent between 1983–84 and 1991–92), while the share of agricultural income remained unchanged. In other words, their share of 'salaries and wages' declined significantly. For the non-poor, non-agricultural income also recorded a significant increase.

These trends suggest that rural non-farm activities were expanding quickly, affecting all groups but particularly the poor. One is tempted to think that this

Table 6.4 Growth rate in rural incomes and consumption (1983–91)

Sources	1983–84	1985–86	1988–89	1991–92	Annual Growth Rate 1983–91 (%)
Agricultural income (excluding agricultural wages)	1,661	1,712	1,524	1,511	–1.2
Wages and salaries (agricultural and non-agricultural)	972	957	1,053	777	–2.8
Non-agricultural income	1,149	1,186	1,288	1,438	2.8
Total income	3,782	3,855	3,865	3,726	–0.2
Total consumption	3,418	3,814	3,448	3,242	–0.7

Source: B. Sen (1996).

might be a result of micro-credit (for the poor) and international remittances (for the non-poor) that were driving these shifts in rural Bangladesh. This also signals a tendency of declining labour supply, which would tend to firm up wages (Table 6.5).

M. Hossain et al. (2000) uses BIDS panel data from 'The Analysis of Poverty Trends' Project to trace the changes in agricultural and non-agricultural income between 1987–88 and 1994–95. He estimates that at 1995 prices, the annual growth rate of per capita rural income was 4.2 per cent, while that in average household income was 4.0 per cent. For agriculture, income per household grew at only 1 per cent per annum, while non-agricultural income grew at 7.2 per cent. Within non-agriculture, income from services grew the most rapidly, at 13 per cent per annum.

Overall rural household income (constant 1995 prices) rose from BDT 39,917 to 52,767 (1987–95) and per capita income rose from BDT 6,630 to 8,883. In other words, the earlier trend seen in the data from B. Sen (1996) further intensified, ushering in a clearly hyperactive non-farm–non-agricultural sector by 1995. This led to a rising share of non-agricultural incomes, especially services, as earlier noted. Thus, the late 1980s to the early 1990s seem to be the period characterizing a turning point for the rural economy of Bangladesh away from agriculture (Table 6.6).

In the late 1990s onwards, some important changes occurred in the labour market. The migration of labour picked up momentum, initially affecting mainly

Table 6.5 Sources of rural income: All and poor households

	1983–84	1985–86	1988–89	1991–92
Rural (all)				
Agricultural income	43.1	43.8	38.9	40.1
Non-agricultural income	30.8	31.1	33.6	38.9
Wages and salaries	26.1	25.1	27.5	21.0
Total (all)	100	100	100	100
Rural (poor)				
Agricultural income	37.1	36.5	35.2	36.9
Non-agricultural income	26.3	24.6	29.0	34.6
Wages and salaries	36.6	38.9	35.8	28.5
Total (poor)	100	100	100	100

Source: B. Sen (1996).

Note: *Wages and salaries include both agricultural and non-agricultural salaries. Agricultural/non-agricultural income excludes salaries.

The Rural Non-farm (RNF) Sector

Table 6.6 Changes in household income by agriculture and non-agriculture (1987–88 to 1994–95)

Income Source	Household Income 1987–88 (%)	Household Income 1994–95 (%)	Annual Rate of Growth 1987–95 (%)
Agriculture	62.9	54.3	1.9
Crops	36.5	34.3	3.1
Other agriculture	14.3	14.4	4.2
Agricultural wage	12.1	5.5	−7.1
Non-agricultural sector	37.1	45.7	5.5
Trade and business	18.2	16.1	3.7
Industry, trade, construction	6.5	7.4	5.8
Services	12.4	22.3	13.0
Household income (in 1995 prices)	39,917	52,767	4.0
Per capita income (BDT/Annum)	6,630	8,883	4.2

Source: M. Hossain (2004).

young men from rural areas. Increasingly, young women began to migrate as well resulting in much wider participation in both urban and rural labour markets.

Let us first examine the data from the various LFS, namely those available for LFS 2002–03 (data relates to 1999–2000), 2005–06, 2010 and 2016 (related to 2013 data), and the corresponding HIES data on occupational status of household heads (Table 6.7).

What we see are two alternative series on RNF per cent, both upward trending but one showing a much higher proportion than the other. Conceptually, LFS figures are superior as these relate directly to persons employed rather than occupation of heads of households used in HIES. These suggest that while RNF has been rising, it has happened slowly over 1999–2013 and does not appear to be much higher than in the 1990s – in fact, if compared to various panel data, there has been a decline.

If we look at the HIES estimates then RNF has continued to accelerate swiftly, from 36.9 per cent to over 50 per cent over 1999–2013 – taking RNF to a higher level than agriculture. The LFS depict a much more modest picture, one of gradual rise but remaining under 40 per cent of rural employment.[4]

In other words, while alternative data sources provide different figures for the share of RNF workers or employment, there is a consensus that these figures have risen quite significantly over time. This leads to the next question:

Table 6.7 Rural employment in the new millennium, based on alternative sources (figures in millions)

Data Source	Rural Employment	Farm/Agricultural Employment	Rural Non-farm	RNF (%)
LFS 2002–03 (1999–2000)	33.6	22.8	10.8	32.14
HIES 2000		21.20	12.4	36.90
LFS 2005–06	36.1	23.00	13.1	36.28
HIES 2005		20.49	15.6	43.20
LFS 2010	41.7	25.70	16.0	38.37
HIES 2010		23.00	18.7	44.84
LFS 2016	41.9	26.20	15.7	37.47
HIES 2016		20.5	21.4	51.07

Sources: HIES (1995, 2000, 2005, 1010, 2019); LFS (2002, 2004, 2007, 2011, 2018).

Note: HIES reports the per cent of rural household heads reporting agriculture as their main occupation. This proportion was used to break down the total rural employment numbers from LFS to estimate farm/non-farm employment, from HIES.

what has been the nature of these changes? Was this a result of growing work opportunities associated with higher productivity and rising incomes, or does this merely reflect a crowding-in effect to a residual sector marked by low productivity and earnings?

The literature cites the initial role of the GR in expanding RNF accompanied by rising productivity (Shilpi and Emran 2016), while others have examined microcredit or infrastructure as a factor along with a fast-growing remittance economy based on resource flows from urban-industrial workers as well as international migrants into rural areas (Khandker, Samad and Khan 1998; Khandker and Koolwal 2010).[5] Proximity to urban areas and rural infrastructure have also come in for a closer look and generally found to have had a positive impact (Deichmann, Shilpi and Vakis 2009). Sen et al. (2018) also point to the growing importance of salary-based earnings in rural areas – a dramatic and very positive development in a sector that has been characterized by self-employment and low productivity for many decades. These certainly point to vast changes in RNF – mostly positive, concentrated in rural manufacturing and construction and almost certainly assisted by better education and health of the rural population. RNF does not represent a residual sector for rural employment anymore, as in the past (Table 6.8).

The Rural Non-farm (RNF) Sector

Table 6.8 Structure and size of rural employment (1995 and 2010)

	1995		2010	
	Million	*Per Cent*	*Million*	*Per Cent*
Agriculture	13.73	59.3	14.8	53.7
Manufacturing	1.46	6.3	3.83	13.9
Construction	0.85	3.7	1.29	4.7
Other industry	0.28	1.2	0.17	0.6
Services	6.83	29.5	7.48	27.1
Total	**23.16**	**100**	**27.58**	**100**
(Per cent change in employment, 1995–2010)	19.08			

Source: HIES quoted in Sen et al. (2018).

Thus, there have been important demographic shifts, industrialization, the availability of cheap food, rising rural incomes due to both GR and resource flows, including microcredit – all of which served to raise rural demand for goods and services. Currently, RNF provides nearly as much employment as agriculture, higher earnings and, more importantly, more stable earnings compared to agriculture. Bangladesh's development story would not be complete without paying due respect to this sector.

As rural manufacturing and services expanded, some traditional activities dwindled. The starkest example is the handloom sector, which was the dominant non-farm activity in Bangladesh for hundreds of years. The handloom sector still exists but just barely. The RNF sector has undergone restructuring and transformation.

We can see that the most significant change has been in manufacturing – which also points to the reason why salary incomes have risen so much. Until 2010, the services sector did not represent a bigger share, while construction shows a mild expansion. If we now focus on the income data from HIES 2016–17, the story of structural change is easy to spot. This points to changes by sectors in terms of income shares received with agriculture rising to as much as 30 per cent in 2010 but then falling sharply to around 18 per cent. This is the period when non-crop agriculture grew very rapidly, in particular fisheries and poultry (HIES 2019).

The share of 'business and commerce' – which historically has grown quickly in the 1980s and 1990s – began to taper off subsequently, reaching less than 12 per cent in 2016 from 13 per cent in 1987 and 22 per cent in 2000.[6] The biggest jump in shares is seen in 'professional wages and salaries', which grew to over

48 per cent from 28 per cent over 2000–16. The rise in wages and salaries is a relatively recent phenomenon and almost certainly reflects growing formalization of the rural labour market, especially the non-farm labour market. In the absence of specific evidence underlying this change, we would speculate that many types of rural services related to banking and finance, MFS, as well as factory-based work related to food processing, especially rice processing, have expanded significantly. These new sectors of growth will require further exploration and may be attempted when data is available.

As the rise in salaried income would suggest, there has been a sharp growth in rural enterprises, which in fact have grown at a higher rate than urban enterprises in recent years, mainly concentrated in transport and storage sub-sectors (Iqbal 2019). Murshid et al. (2020), based on nationally representative data, report that 82 per cent of rural household incomes originate in RNF, with the remittance share at 15 per cent. In terms of per capita or per household income, RNF households do significantly better than agriculture.[7]

The Decline of Handlooms

After agriculture, Bangladesh's biggest sector was handlooms, which produced traditional clothes and fabric for the population. The sector mainly employed a large number of family-based workers. There was consistent growth of the handloom industry during 1946–90 and decline thereafter. The number of looms increased from 134,000 in 1946 to 437,000 in 1990 and then declined to 362,000 in 2003. This trend is clearly reflected in employment as well, increasing from 407,000 workers in 1951 to 947,000 in 1990 and falling to 798,000 in 2003. In terms of output, cloth production increased from 286 million metres in 1955–56 to 704 million metres in 1989–90, falling subsequently to 520 million metres in 2003–04. Output grew at a faster rate than the number of looms due to higher productivity resulting from technological change (Latif 2019).

Neither the number of looms nor employment or output figures are available for the period after 2003. Nevertheless, the figure for the number of handloom establishments is available for the three census years, namely 1990, 2003 and 2018. This shows a long-term decline of the industry over the period 1990–2018 with the number of establishments declining from 212,421 in 1990 to 183,512 in 2003, and further to 116,006 in 2018 (BBS 2018).

The factors behind the long-term growth of the handloom industry during 1947–1990 may be summarized as follows: a favourable government policy towards protecting handlooms against competition from mills and imports, and expansion of surplus yarn production by textile mills to provide handlooms with an adequate yarn supply needed to produce handloom clothes.

Mills were confident that handlooms would survive and grow, and consumer demand would stay strong, especially for *lungi* and *sari*. There were also the economic factors: handlooms were produced in homesteads using cheap family labour for pre-weaving processes.

The long-term decline of the handloom industry during 1990–2013 was due to new technology – displacement by cheap reconditioned power looms from China, as well as by locally fabricated power looms, including the conversion of 'Chittaranjan handlooms' into power looms.[8]

Another big shift occurred on the demand side, namely change in women's dress preferences, away from handloom *saris* towards the three-piece *salwar-qameez-dupatta* woven on power looms and finished in dyeing factories. Latif (2019) thinks this quiet shift was spurred on by a continuous propaganda in rural areas carried out by Islamic groups who argued that the *sari* was a Hindu dress and women should adopt the more Islamic *salwar-qameez* instead, along with appropriate head cover.[9] These items cannot be made by handlooms.

The survival and growth of the traditional throw-shuttle handlooms is due to its ability to produce high-value, artistically designed material – especially the famous Jamdani and Banarasi *saris*, constituting a growing niche market, much in demand from richer, more sophisticated urban consumers.

Similarly, for the other widely used traditional technology, the fly-shuttle, the process of replacement was not completed by 2003. This loom is well suited for the production of Tangail silk *saris* and certain varieties of fabrics woven with coarse yarn. These include fabrics used by some ethnic groups, *motka* fabrics and the so-called *khadi* woven with mill-spun coarse yarn. Once again, a small niche market persists, producing some traditional fabrics that retain a certain appeal among the populace.

The present position of the handloom industry as well as of the small-scale power loom industry is not known due to lack of data. Nevertheless, it would appear that despite dramatic reduction in numbers, the industry still persists within a niche market, showing some ability to adapt to change. The rate of decline of the establishments and of employment during 1990–2003 is estimated at 3.8 per cent and 1.31 per cent per annum respectively. This rate of decline accelerated over 2003–13 to 5.0 per cent and 6.80 per cent. The number of surviving handloom establishments in 2017 would be in the order of 45,000, compared to 100,000 in 2003 and 165,000 in 1990 (Latif 2019).

RNF: Explaining the Dynamics

The RNF sector has grown and is currently making a significant contribution to rural employment and income. Explanations of the factors underlying the rise in RNF have been alluded to earlier: the GR, micro-credit and non-farm enterprises, the exit from land-based work, and so on. Iqbal (2019) ran some regressions but did not find remittances significant in explaining RNF incomes or employment. In other words, while researchers have noted the expansion of RNF, explanations in terms of how RNF managed to take off are few. Based on this review, we put forward the following analysis.

RNF is unlikely to emerge on its own. It is much more likely to respond to growth and dynamism in the real economy and respond by providing goods and services needed by the real sectors. Thus, with the onset of the GR, new demand was created for a host of inputs and services that had to be traded, produced, maintained, transported and so on. Irrigation pumps needed to be procured, installed, maintained and serviced. Fertilizer and pesticides were in high demand – once again the entire supply chain for these inputs had to be set up throughout the country. Similarly, as agricultural mechanization speeded up, demand was created for power tillers, tractors, threshers and harvesters – again creating many new opportunities for work and livelihoods through linkage effects with procurement, distribution, repair, after-sales services and maintenance. Similarly, new kinds of entrepreneurship developed around irrigation equipment (and generally around agricultural machinery) leading to the emergence of a rental or lease market.

Apart from the GR, rural Bangladesh has also witnessed a number of other 'revolutions' that have not been adequately stressed. The 'Blue Revolution' in aquaculture has been phenomenal. On the back of aquaculture, numerous RNF activities emerged, related to capturing, processing, trading and storage of fish. Similar successes can be reported for poultry, dairy, mushrooms, flowers, fruits (local and exotic), horticulture – indeed, modern agriculture based on hydroponics and greenhouses has also emerged, even if these are still at an early stage of development.

Traditionally, livestock was an integral part of the subsistence farming system of Bangladesh with small surpluses sold at the local market to meet cash needs. Between 1991–92 and 2014–15, milk output increased 5.2 times (from 1,352 thousand tons to 6,970 thousand tons), meat production by 12.7 times (from 460 thousand tons to 5,860 thousand tons) and egg production by 7.2 times (from 1,517 million eggs to 10,995 million tons eggs). In more recent years (FY2009/10 – FY2019/20), the annual compound growth rates in milk, meat and egg production were 16.2, 19.8 and 11.7 per cent respectively – marking a slowdown but nevertheless recording a respectable performance.[10]

Begum and Alam (2014) analysed the actual headcounts and growth of livestock resources over a period of 60 years over 1949–2008. During this period,

The Rural Non-farm (RNF) Sector

the average annual growth rate in bovine population was 1 per cent per year and for small ruminants (sheep and goats) it was 5.2 per cent per year. A high annual growth was observed for poultry (7.4 per cent).

Similarly, in fisheries, Bangladesh has performed exceedingly well, ranking globally at the third position for inland capture fisheries and fifth in inland culture fisheries. Marine fisheries also have a small place in this sector comprising of industrial and artisanal fisheries that cater mainly to exports to the European Union. Between 1988–89 and 2012–13, total fish production increased by 4.1 times, from 841,000 metric tons to 3.41 million metric tons. The contribution of inland culture fisheries to total fish production was 21.8 per cent in the late 1980s – this share rose to 54.5 per cent by 2013. The contribution of inland capture fisheries has declined from 50.4 per cent to 28.2 per cent. At the same time, contribution of marine fisheries declined sharply, from 27.7 per cent to 17.3 per cent (Deb 2016). Overall trends in fisheries output are presented in Table 6.9, showing a slowdown in the last decade.

These changes were similar in principle with what we saw during the GR, with strong linkages with RNF employment, incomes and growth. The opportunities provided by expansion in the real sectors have been made much more accessible by the liquidity now available in the rural areas, in part assisted by domestic and international remittances, rural banking and microcredit. Thus, even if remittances did not directly generate RNF, it did so indirectly by stimulating demand in the real sectors, which in turn created demand for RNF services and inputs.

Public investments and the work of NGOs cannot be overlooked either. Investments in education, health, building community organizations of the poor, schools, roads, markets, rural electrification and solar home systems have all generated considerable RNF activity. Private-sector investments in agent banking, MFS, agro-processing industries, rice mills, storage units, mobile phone networks, and related economic activity, transport and construction companies, and growing rural demand for consumer durables have also joined the traditional NGO-led activities aimed at the poor and women

Table 6.9 Growth trends in fisheries output (compound annual growth rate [CAGR])

Period	1972–81	1982–91	1992–01	2002–11	2012–18
CAGR	2.5	3.0	7.4	5.7	4.6

Source: Estimates based on 'Aquaculture Production – Bangladesh', World Bank Databank, https://data.worldbank.org/indicator/ER.FSH.AQUA.MT?locations=BD&view=chart (accessed 27 November 2021).

in the rural areas as sources of employment and income. It is therefore not an accident that researchers have found that rural self-employment (agricultural and non-agricultural) has now given way to salaried work as the dominant type of RNF employment, ensuring greater predictability and stability in rural earnings. There was thus a convergence of many forces that served to dynamize agriculture, which in turn led to a dynamic RNF sector. While the early decades were difficult, with development finance severely hamstrung and overly dependent on foreign aid, gradually aid has been replaced by domestic resources as savings grew along with exports and remittances – finally doing what was unthinkable in the 1980s: Bangladesh was able to bridge, or at least narrow, the twin development gaps resulting from inadequate savings and scarce foreign exchange.

7

Industrialization and the Rise of RMG

The story is well known. Historically, Bangladesh exports were dominated by just one cash crop, namely jute, which accounted for nearly 90 per cent of total exports. Jute prices, however, experienced considerable volatility around a long-term secular decline in its terms of trade, imparting a high degree of uncertainty to export earnings. Remittance earnings opened up a much-needed additional source of foreign exchange, serving to lessen dependence on jute.

At the same time that remittances were beginning to flow in, in the late 1970s, crucial first steps were also being taken that would ultimately lead to the emergence of the apparels or RMG sector. Both remittances and RMG exports signalled a more open and accessible world market where poor, labour-abundant countries could find a niche on the basis of their comparative advantage. The global climate was more favourable for poor countries like Bangladesh, either by design or as the accidental consequence of advanced countries pursuing their own self interests.[1] Thus, once the RMG potential was demonstrated, the response from local entrepreneurs was lightning-fast.[2] The government, it must be underlined, rose quickly to take advantage of the opportunity to introduce incentives and policies to move things forward quickly for the RMG sector. Key initial movers who were close to the corridors of power played a crucial role in bringing the government fully on board. One could also argue that the government in the 1980s initiated a distinct change in its stance on 'socialism', which had earlier led to policy ambivalence and moved towards a more supportive role for private sector-led, capitalist development.

The Stylized Facts

The mid-1970s saw certain important changes in the world market for RMG. Advanced (importing) countries were getting increasingly worried about being swamped with low-cost clothes from East Asia, and as a precautionary move enacted the Multi-fibre Arrangement (MFA) in 1974, replacing the earlier Agreement on International Trade in Cotton and Textiles, 1964, under which country-specific quotas were imposed on major exporting developing countries.

The move was driven essentially by protectionist motives on the part of importers (the US and EU mainly) who were concerned about the effects on their own manufacturing industries. The major concern was with the group of Asian 'super-performers' whose market shares were expanding quickly. Quotas were imposed with this group in mind, especially by the USA. Major exporters like South Korea and Hong Kong had reached their quotas by the early 1980s. Subsequent MFA negotiations were aimed at preventing rapid growth in their exports (preventing sudden 'surges'), which opened up space for potential new countries to enter into this labour-intensive market that historically played an important role in fostering industrialization in many advanced countries including England, Japan and South Korea.

Daewoo, a South Korean firm, was the first to take a chance on Bangladesh, a country that had no quota restrictions and plenty of low-wage labour. The story of how it all began is well recorded.[3] There were already a number of garments houses in the country before the advent of *Desh* but these only managed to export small occasional consignments. These included Bond Garments, Reaz, Paris, Aziz Group, Sunmoon Group, Stylecraft and Aristocratic. These entities eventually were also able to convert themselves into modern, export-oriented factories.

How It All Began

Noorul Quader and Abdul Majid Chowdhury were an unlikely pair. Quader was a former bureaucrat who had become known for his role in the Liberation War, while Chowdhury came from a business background and was doing well in the new Bangladesh. They were of course interested in making money, but they also had this vague desire to do something for the country – a desire that was in fact widely shared at the time. Fortunately, Quader came into contact with the boss of a major garment's factory owner in Korea, namely the head of Daewoo Corporation. The timing was perfect as the Koreans and other East Asians were struggling with new rules under the MFA that restricted their exports to the US and European markets and were seeking to diversify their production bases. What now needed to be demonstrated was that Bangladesh could become a good source for RMG – a test that Bangladesh passed with flying colours. The technical assistance and hands-on training by Daewoo were crucial in getting things started off on the right note. Today, there are over 4,500 garment factories in Bangladesh with most tracing their lineage to the pioneering initiative of Quader, Chowdhury and the 128 Bangladeshis who travelled to Korea 30 years ago to be trained by Daewoo (Table 7.1).

Industrialization and the Rise of RMG

Table 7.1 RMG export trends (1983–84 to 2017–18)

Period	Number of Factories	RMG Exports (USD, mn)	Total Exports (USD, mn)	RMG Exports/ Total Exports (%)
1983–84 to 1987–88	485.2	202.368	974.49	19.1
1988–89 to 1992–93	1,003.6	917.932	1,861.92	47.9
1993–94 to 1997–98	2,320.6	2,622.892	3,893.672	66.5
1998–99 to 2007–08	3,407.4	4,545.012	6,013.378	75.6
2003–04 to 2007–08	4,309.4	7,983.118	10,614.47	75.1
2008–09 to 2012–13	5,282.8	16,672.88	21,204.7	78.6
2013–14 to 2017–18	4,377.6	27,368.41	33,395.36	81.9

Source: Bangladesh Garments Manufacturers' Association, BGMEA, https://www.bgmea.com.bd/ (accessed 5 December 2021).

The rest was history as can be seen from Table 7.2. Starting from scratch, it did not take long for the industry to take root and take off – all it needed was an initial helping hand followed by supportive government policy.[4] The figures show that there were more than 5,000 factories in operation in 2013 employing some 4 million workers with 57 per cent being women, when the Rana Plaza disaster struck. The fallout was clear – post-Rana Plaza, adjustments and compliance costs meant that around a thousand units had to close down. The increased firm concentration however did not affect exports, which continued to surge. Today, more than 80 per cent of Bangladesh exports are accounted for by RMG.

Output, Employment and Structure

Perhaps one of the most profound outcomes of the RMG success was the induction of large numbers of women in the workforce. The assumption that tradition-bound, Muslim women from ordinary, rural backgrounds could leave their rural comfort zones in such large numbers was unthinkable at the time. Thus ADB (2016: 1) observes:

> Traditionally, geographic mobility of poor women in rural Bangladesh has been remarkably limited: in a 1996 survey in the rural area of Matlab, 93% of women interviewed had never been to the local bazaar, 92% had never been to the local mosque, and 68% left their residential compound at most once a week (Anderson and Eswaran 2009). Effective restriction of mobility for women outside of the household can still be fairly severe today. In 2011, 44% of married women aged 20–24 said that they were not generally free to make decisions about visiting

their own relatives (BBS 2013d). A minority of women face even more severe restrictions. The same survey found that 22% of women were not free to travel to a health center either alone or with their children.

What it reveals is that women's attitudes and independence have changed even in the countryside, and people were more readily disposed to take on new challenges, new risks and embrace new opportunities. Little is known about how this attitudinal change came about, even though one could speculate that the grassroots activities of NGOs, the delivery of micro-credit and various development interventions often specifically focused on women are likely to have been critical. In the absence of rigorous analysis, it is difficult to say much more except to note that this little researched area may in fact hold the key to a true understanding of Bangladesh's development (see Chapter 9).

The exact number of workers in RMG and their gender composition is not known. Frequently, we are told that 80 per cent of RMG workers are women, especially those in the apparel sector, although it was not possible to locate any reliable source for this assertion. A micro-level study relating to RMG units located in and around Dhaka found the proportion of women outside the Dhaka export processing zone (EPZ) to be 61 per cent, while this figure was 77 per cent within the Dhaka EPZ in the 1990s (S. C. Zohir 2001). The figure given in BBS (2013) shows that women constitute 64 per cent of the workforce in the 'wearing apparel' sector – indicating a small increase over time. More recent estimates of women's share in RMG jobs have ranged from 46 per cent in 2017 (BBS), 53.2 per cent in 2016 (CPD) and 60 per cent in 2018 (BIDS–ILO).[5] While these estimates vary, one thing that everyone agrees with is that the share has been declining in recent years – most observers blaming technology and labour displacement for this tendency (Ullah and Akhter 2021).

RMG wages are rising and manufacturers have been trying to cut costs and raise productivity through technology upgradation. This process is gaining momentum and already some 20 per cent of firms (presumably larger ones) have completed this move. This has led to lower labour demand in general with the demand for (lower-end) women workers most affected.

This has also led to changes in the structure of RMG output towards higher value addition. In absolute (value) terms, all items recorded impressive gains. In terms of structure, the initial dependence on shirts and tee shirts have now given way to a much more evenly balanced portfolio with much of the restructuring coming from jacket and sweater production. It is also significant that these structural changes have occurred in the face of dramatic increases in value of output since 1993–94 (Table 7.2).

Table 7.2 Changes in structure of production of RMG in Bangladesh (1993–94 to 2018–19; USD, mn)

Item	1993–94 A	Col. %	2003–04 B	Col. %	% Rise A to B	2018–19 C	Col. %	% Rise B to C	Remarks
Shirts	805.3	65.01	1,116.6	24.84	38.7	2,324.9	9.33	108.2	Steady decline
Trouser	80.6	7.07	1,334.9	29.70	1,556.2	6,939.6	27.85	419.8	Sharp rise and stabilized
Jackets	126.9	10.25	364.8	8.12	187.5	4,384.1	17.60	1,101.8	Initial decline/sharp rise
Tees	225.9	18.24	1,062.1	23.63	370.1	7,011.3	28.14	560.1	Steady moderate rise
Sweater	–	–	616.3	13.71	–	4,255.9	17.08	590.9	Sharp rise
Total	1,238.7	100	4,494.7	100	262.9	24,916	100	454.3	–

Source: Based on BGMEA website, https://www.bgmea.com.bd/ (accessed 5 December 2020).

Policy Support

The role of policy support to RMG has been critical. From the very beginning, the commitment to RMG was strong. It was helpful that the new sector was led by people who were able to convince policymakers to come to its aid. While the needs of the sector were diverse, ranging from financing to raw materials, uninterrupted energy supply to infrastructure and port management, technology and compliance, the most important, especially in the early days, related to bank finance and working capital.

Sector leaders were able to quickly identify two particular areas of public policy, namely (*a*) the 'special bonded warehouse' system to allow duty-free imports to replace the existing, inefficient duty drawback system and (*b*) the 'back-to-back letter of credit' facility.[6] These mechanisms allowed RMG manufacturers to import their required inputs and intermediate goods quickly, without incurring duties, although the use of these policy instruments were not common in competing countries. The bonded warehouse arrangement allowed manufacturers to import all of the needed inputs without having to pay import duties, and the 'back-to-back letters of credit' allowed RMG exporters to use their original letter of credit (LC) as guarantees against bank loans to finance imports.[7] In the context of capital scarcity and a rudimentary capitalist sector, this was a brilliant way to facilitate growth of the sector.[8] The third element of incentive widely used was cash incentives for exports, which could only be claimed if the bonded warehouse facility was not availed.

The broad timeline for the various incentives is available from D. K. Roy (1993). In the 1980s, the government introduced the 'export performance licensing scheme', later known as 'export performance benefit scheme'. This was when there was a dual exchange rate in operation and a large gap between the official rate and the market rate. These schemes were intended to pass on a more realistic 'premium' exchange rate to exporters to make them competitive. These were withdrawn from January 1992 when a single, market-led exchange rate was introduced.

Bangladesh Bank also introduced a 'cash assistance scheme' that was used mainly by RMG exporters, especially those who were not covered under the bonded warehouse or duty drawback schemes. In the 1993–95 export policy, the incentive rate was set at a maximum of 25 per cent of local value added. These rates have since come down gradually to 4–5 per cent.

Exporters were given credit at a concessional rate in two ways: (*a*) if the period of repayment was within 180 days, concessions would apply – this provision was later relaxed by up to 270 days; (*b*) the interest rate structure was reformed to lie between 7.5 and 10.5 per cent with the instruction to stay at the lower bound for exporters (it appears though that the instruction was generally not followed [D. K. Roy 1993: 27]).

Special Bonded Warehouse

It is a form of temporary admission of imports into the country meant to be used only in export manufacturing. The term is variously used – special bonded warehouses (SBWs) in Bangladesh, export-only units in India, bonded manufacturing warehouses in Malaysia. There is substantial variation of the rules under which these operate.

In Bangladesh, bonded manufacturing status allows firms to bring imports into special warehouses, duty free, use these in manufactures and then export the output. The firms can also buy from domestic suppliers free of domestic excise, sales and other taxes. Participating factories must operate under the supervision of customs authorities, who check import and export containers coming in and going out of the factories. This policy allows the relatively high import tariffs to be offset and also saves firms the trouble and cost of claiming duty drawback on the duty-paid imported raw materials and inputs. This serves to level out the market for exporters who compete regionally and internationally.

Despite criticisms levelled against SBWs, there is little doubt that it has played a very prominent role in bolstering local firms wishing to enter the RMG global market. The issues most often discussed include denial of similar facilities to non-RMG exporters, thereby constraining the development of exports in general, and the complex set of rules and regulations that prevent access.[9]

Back-to-Back Letter of Credit

In 1980, the Bangladesh Bank gave permission for the use of back-to-back LCs along with SBW facilities to RMG producers–exporters, decreasing their working capital requirements and allowing duty-free access to inputs for the sector. Both these policy prescriptions were based on the prescription of leading local entrepreneurs. The innovation of the back-to-back LC system eliminated the need for foreign exchange for importing inputs, spares, and machinery for RMG as banks accepted the 'master LC' as collateral for releasing foreign exchange for intermediate imports. In 1993, the revised import policy of Bangladesh specified that the back-to-back LC cannot exceed 70 per cent of the mother LC, implying a net accrual of 30 per cent of total export value to the country in foreign exchange (see Table 7.3 for definition of terms such as LC and back-to-back LC).

Table 7.3 Back-to-back LC and master LC

Subject	Master LC	Back-to-Back LC
Definition	Master LC is prepared by the (foreign) importer–buyer to import goods from the (Bangladeshi) manufacturer	Back-to-back LC is opened by the (Bangladeshi) exporter–manufacturer to procure raw materials and other inputs for the production of exported (RMG) goods
Issuing bank	Master LC is issued by the importer's Bank	Back-to-back LC is issued by the exporter's bank
Types of LC	This is the original LC	This is the subsidiary LC
Purpose	To buy or import goods from the manufacturer	To buy or import raw materials or inputs for RMG from the suppliers

Source: D. K. Roy (1993).

A pervasive problem with all these schemes has been the exercise of discretionary powers by concerned authorities that has led to a degree of arbitrariness and discrimination in implementation. This has certainly led to extra costs and inefficiencies. In other words, poor governance certainly has had the effect of reducing benefits. In general, the constantly evolving policy regime has helped the RMG sector to keep it competitive despite severe challenges faced from time to time. These have included the MFA withdrawal of 2004, and the Rana Plaza debacle of 24 April 2013, which led to stricter demand for compliance with labour standards. All these moves served to raise costs in the face of stiff and growing competition in the world market. Bangladesh has competed mainly with low labour costs, but this advantage is now going out of steam: labour costs are rising, productivity is not keeping up and areas where potential gains could be reaped, for example, in more efficient customs procedures or removal of infrastructure bottlenecks at ports, show few signs of change. Thus, the country now appears to be moving into a new phase altogether. The old, time-tested approach in terms of policy support may no longer be adequate. There is the growing threat of robotics and technology that are eating into labour and employment shares. Global markets for Bangladesh are less friendly compared to its rivals like Vietnam. It is therefore important for Bangladesh to compete not on the basis of low wages alone but also through superior management, technology and productivity. A positive outcome attributable to the engagement with buyers' organizations like

ACCORD (Accord on Fire and Building Safety in Bangladesh) and Alliance for Bangladesh Worker Safety is that compliance levels have recorded laudable gains, with over 20 per cent of firms achieving full compliance in terms of meeting both labour and environmental standards. This makes Bangladesh's RMG sector virtually unassailable even if vulnerable to various market shocks. Unfortunately, the same cannot be said of other export sectors that have been in the 'promising' category for many years but failed to emerge out of the shadows of RMG. To an extent, the blame for this can be laid on the obsessive focus on RMG relative to all other sectors.

Backward Linkages: The Re-emergence of Textiles

The RMG story is well known but the phenomenal backward linkages that developed in the wake of RMG is no less fascinating. It provides an example of how the interplay of opportunity, entrepreneurship and policy support combined to unlock the considerable potential presented by RMG for backward linkage manufacturing of textiles. At the initial stages, RMG value addition was only 25–30 per cent. In recent years, this has ranged from 61 to 64 per cent. Today, 90–95 per cent of the yarn requirement of the RMG knitwear subsector is provided by the domestic industry while 40 per cent of the fabric demand from the RMG woven subsector is currently met locally (Kabir, Singh and Ferrantino 2019).[10] There is thus significant potential that remains to be tapped in the fabric subsector. Other accessories are largely domestically supplied. A beginning has also been made in the man-made fibre subsector which augurs well for the manufacture of higher-end products in the future.[11]

Bangladesh always had a large (relative to its small industrial base) textile sector producing for the domestic market under protection from competition by high tariffs and import quotas. The sector was affected by nationalization and entered a period of diminished activity under public ownership in the 1970s. The new government in 1982 under General Ershad began to reverse the process starting with denationalization of the Bangladeshi-owned textile mills in public hands.

As RMG exports took off in the 1990s, rising by some 600 per cent in a decade reaching USD 4.5 billion by 2000, the textile owners took note of the massive RMG demand for textile products generated and met almost entirely by imports. Various analysts suggested that Bangladesh did not have comparative advantage in production of yarn and fabrics as it did not grow much cotton, opposing domestic protection to the primary textiles sector (PTS) as being too risky. It was argued that Bangladesh would be better off with 'SAARC cumulation' whereby imports of raw material from within the South Asian Association for Regional Cooperation (SAARC) would qualify it to meet the 'rules of origin' (ROO) requirements for exports to the EU (World Bank 2006a). In fact, such a deal was signed between SAARC and the EU. This had generated controversy in Bangladesh where the RMG lobby and the textile lobby took diametrically opposed positions on the matter. Bhattacharya and Rahman (2000) provide a useful analysis of this controversy in some detail, noting that SAARC cumulation will be of marginal value to the RMG sector while the potential to hurt textiles is considerable. However, ROO were modified to allow two-stage conversion, which allowed this controversy to die down.[12]

What is important to note is that the government continued to provide determined support from the 1990s in a bid to improve value addition and stimulate the local industry. This was given a certain urgency with the withdrawal of the 1974 MFA that was coming to a close in 2005, ushering in new market opportunities as well as introducing additional risks. The fear grew that textile suppliers from countries like India and Pakistan would channel their products increasingly into their own domestic RMG industry, leaving Bangladesh's RMG industry hanging in a precarious position. If nothing else, the 'lead time' problem faced by Bangladesh could well become further aggravated so that local sourcing of intermediate goods needed for the industry would be highly desirable. This perception led to a closing of ranks between RMG and textiles, who have jointly lobbied a willing government for support. The two sectors have now merged into one textiles and clothing (T&C) sector with both forward and backward linkages occurring as a result of the marriage. Like the RMG pioneers of the 1980s, a new generation of textile entrepreneurs had emerged onto the scene by the mid-1990s (Lightcastle Partners 2020).

The rapid pace of this journey continued well into the new century despite the withdrawal of the MFA in December 2004, which was almost universally heralded as a moment of reckoning for the RMG industry for countries like Bangladesh (World Bank 2006a). However, Bangladesh's RMG run continued unabated even in the post-MFA era: the number of spinning mills increased from 197 in 2004 to 350 in 2009; the number of weaving mills increased from 278 to 400; dyeing and finishing units rose from 291 to 310; while the number of RMG units rose from 4000 to 5000.

In other words, this was another bright area of the Bangladesh economy that now contributes USD 21 billion to exports. It has been noted that this is a major policy success of the government which at one stroke has stimulated exports, increased value addition, diversified export earnings and can in fact be viewed as a rare example of successful import substitution that has led to the creation of a globally competitive industry (Sattar 2020; Kabir, Singh and Ferrantino 2019).

Some answers to the post-MFA puzzle were attempted by industry leaders (Ahmed 2013). These refer to management changes and innovations like the 'Lean Manufacturing System', which supposedly 'brought tremendous success in the apparel sector' as revealed through various key performance indicators (KPIs) such as line balancing (LB), work-in-process (WIP) inventory, labour productivity (LP), alter, reject and spot. Redwan Ahmed (2013) reports that LB and LP rose by about 11 per cent and 24.5 per cent while LB and LP, the WIP, alter, reject and spot reduced by about 85.4 per cent, 10.67 per cent, 33.34 per cent and 75 per cent respectively. Moreover, advocacy and campaigns were carried out amongst workers to forestall possible shocks resulting from work stoppages and strikes while wages and other facilities were improved. In addition, the government set up captive power plants and encouraged the private sector to invest in energy to resolve the frequent 'load-shedding' problem.

A more academic explanation for Bangladesh's 'unexpected and overwhelming success' is likely to be as follows: first, Bangladesh's basic advantage lay in its cheap labour and the ability to scale up volume that must be singled out as its primary advantage. The hourly wage rate in Bangladesh in 2008 was 0.22 cents compared to 0.33 cents for Cambodia, and 0.38 cents for Vietnam. Other competing countries like China and Turkey had much higher rates and would need higher export prices to compete.

Bangladesh has also quietly proceeded to diversify its export markets. In 1992, over 40 per cent of its RMG exports went to the USA, which reduced to 28 per cent in 2008 in the face of rapidly rising total exports diverted largely to the EU, where generalized system of preferences (GSP) privileges were available (Joarder, Hossain and Hakim 2010).

Last, but by no means least, Bangladesh's move towards a floating exchange rate regime in June 2003 has certainly imparted greater competitiveness to its largest export sectors, especially knitwear. Thus, Hossain and Ahmed (2009) refer to the first 10 months after floatation to be the 'honeymoon period' when rates were stable. However, by mid-2006, a depreciation of 20 per cent was recorded in nominal exchange rates bringing the real effective exchange rate (REER) quite close to the equilibrium exchange rate. Hossain and Ahmed (2009) also point to the significant association between RMG exports and international prices and incomes of importing countries, and their finding that a stable REER has a positive impact as well. In other words, opening up of the foreign exchange market to greater competition and the subsequent re-alignment of the exchange rate made Bangladesh's export sector much better equipped to deal with not only the post-MFA challenges but also, subsequently, the global financial crisis of 2007–09. Strictly speaking, what Bangladesh has done is to introduce what is known as 'dirty float' in central bank parlance, referring to a situation where the flotation is 'managed'. The dirty float system was introduced in May 2004 which subsequently was reclassified as a 'crawling peg' since 2010 – a situation where the exchange rate is allowed to fluctuate by small amounts (Table 7.4).

Post-COVID recovery measures are already having an impact on the exchange rates of trading partners like China and India, which may usher in an era of competitive devaluations. This should make Bangladeshi policymakers wary of a possible 'beggar thy neighbour' mood that might come into play, forcing Bangladesh to also follow suit. However, given Bangladesh's strong reserve position on the back of buoyant remittance flows even during the pandemic, pressures on the central bank to depreciate the currency are mounting – a move that it is continuing to resist. It is hoped that once recovery is underway, pent up imports and investments will be released, thereby helping to even out the potentially disruptive exchange rate movements that could otherwise occur.

The T&C sector has shown that given policy support and policy innovation designed with close consultation with the stakeholders can lead to exceptional results. Bangladeshi entrepreneurs have fought against the odds to carve out their shares in the global market with determination and an innovative spirit. This is once again a reminder that static comparative advantage plays into the status quo, while for countries like Bangladesh the goal must certainly be to wring out dynamic comparative advantages through purposeful policy innovations and pragmatic interventions. The advice from consultants, however, often tends to be based on static comparative advantage, which therefore needs careful review (Kabir, Singh and Ferrantino 2019).

Table 7.4 De facto classification of Bangladesh's exchange rate regime (2000–15)

Period	σe	$\Delta \sigma e$	σr	Regime
Jan 2000–May 2003	0.33 L	1.28 H	4.56 H	Adjusted peg
June 2003–April 2004	0.22 L	0.31 L	1.15 L	Inconclusive
May 2004–December 2006	1.05 H	1.23 H	3.65 H	Dirty float
Jan 2007–June 2008	0.15 L	0.18 L	5.97 H	Fixed
2010–15	1.8 H	0.05 L	5.79 H	Crawling peg

Source: Hossain and Ahmed (2020: 302).

Notes: H when value exceeds long-term estimates; otherwise = L. Long-term estimates: σe=0.98; $\Delta \sigma e$=1.16; r=4.15. σe: exchange rate volatility measured by monthly absolute percentage change in the nominal exchange rate (NER); $\Delta \sigma e$: volatility of exchange rate changes measured by the standard deviation of monthly percentage change in NER; σr: volatility of reserves measured by the absolute change of reserves. *De facto* regime classification methodology is derived from Levi-Yeyati and Sturzenegger (2005).

The Rana Plaza Fallout

The collapse of the Rana Plaza in Bangladesh in 2013 following on the heels of the Tazreen factory fire sent shock waves throughout the world, exposing poor working conditions and safety standards in Bangladesh's RMG industry. The outcry in consumer countries generated enormous pressure on retail brands and factory owners and a suitable governance response had become urgent. In a rare display of solidarity, leading brands in Europe and North America came together to form the Accord on Fire and Building Safety in Bangladesh (over 180 European brands) and the Alliance for Bangladesh Worker Safety (major US retailers), making it binding upon factories to raise safety levels to a satisfactory standard. To achieve this end, the first task was to carry out thorough safety and safeguard inspections in every factory – a huge task, but this is exactly what was mandated. Both initiatives involved independent inspection of all Bangladeshi suppliers and strict enforcement of the corrective action plans (CAPs) delivered. This rare initiative has received much attention from the academic literature and has been subjected to numerous analysis (for example, Donaghey and Reinecke 2017; Sinkovics, Hoque and Sinkovics 2016; Ashwin, Kabeer and Schüßler 2020).

Thus, the primary fallout of Rana Plaza was enforced safety inspections and the generation of the action plans. The next task was to implement these plans expeditiously. The alternative would have meant that brands and retailers would stop working with the suppliers and would eventually have to take their orders elsewhere. In addition, the US wasted no time before withdrawing its duty-free privileges to Bangladesh's RMG sector, promising to reinstate the GSP measures once compliance was met. The compliance pressure on suppliers, therefore, was enormous.

Compliance was costly, which in turn resulted in a number of repercussions: smaller firms who were already operating on wafer-thin margins had to close shop. The larger, better-resourced firms absorbed the costs and invested heavily in upgrading processes and technology, many turning into world-class, environmentally friendly production entities. Initial promises that brands would share in the costs of upgradation directly or through higher prices did not materialize. The suppliers and the government of Bangladesh were on their own and had to lift themselves up by their own efforts. At the same time, the work force had to endure greater pressures as wages stagnated. It has also been suggested that the power imbalance between brands and suppliers had become further aggravated as a result, ensuring that the ability of suppliers to negotiate better prices saw no improvement (Sinkovics, Hoque and Sinkovics 2016).

The data clearly shows the sharp decline in the number of RMG units following 2013 with the closing down of around 1000 factories almost overnight (see Table 7.1). The larger units survived and indeed many emerged into strong, highly compliant, technologically advanced operations, much better placed to compete in the world market. The downside was that the demand for unskilled labour and female labour fell significantly as a result with accusations of jobless growth gaining currency.

Today, once again the sector is faced with a grave crisis in the shape of the COVID-19 pandemic. There seems little chance of a quick recovery in demand from Western consumers. Nor is the US in a mood to reinstate the promised GSP privileges despite the much-lauded gains made in meeting RMG compliance standards, pointing now to new goal posts in the shape of permitting 'trade unions' and the right of labour to organize in the T&C sector. This is a sensitive area given the long and usually dismal story of public sector trade unions in the country. This has made both the private sector and the government wary of introducing 'traditional' labour unions. Nevertheless, it is important to allow labour the right to organize in a responsible manner while suppliers need to have the good sense to allow this space to prevent violence and conflict that has surfaced from time to time. In practice, this remains a serious weakness in not only RMG but the entire industrial sector of Bangladesh. In fact, in this respect, RMG fares better because of the presence of international stakeholders and a degree of local sensitivity to international criticism.

Bangladesh's share of the US market has declined steadily, displaced by Vietnam, although it has managed to improve its share in Europe as well as exploit new, non-traditional markets. At the same time, Vietnam has moved aggressively not only into the US market armed with duty concessions, but it is now also poised to do the same in Europe with which it signed a preferential trade agreement in August 2020. While the data is not available yet, it is thought that Vietnam may already have displaced Bangladesh from its second position in the global ranking of RMG producers (McKinsey 2021).

The solutions to RMG woes which continue to play a central role in Bangladesh's development are seen to lie in more technology, skills, infrastructure and reduction of freight and handling costs. While there is considerable scope for improvement in these regards, the crucial issue of market access – and the unfolding regional geo-politics – will need to be carefully observed. The outlook for market access through trade treaties does not look promising at the moment, although the emerging geo-politics in the region may throw up some opportunities to leverage its strategic location to some advantage. This is what Vietnam appears to have done with aplomb.

There are both dangers and opportunities here that must be carefully navigated. The emerging polarization with China with the Belt and Road initiative on the one hand and the US-led Quad involving India, Australia and Japan designed to contain China in the Asia-Pacific on the other may force Bangladesh into an uneasy position. For a small country flanked by powerful neighbours, a studied, neutral position may be hard to maintain for long. That however is what it must strive to achieve if it does not want to be crushed under the feet of quarrelling elephants.

8

Industrialization

Other Stories

Introduction

The popular narrative of industrialization of Bangladesh is focused almost solely on RMG. While RMG is certainly the jewel in the industrial crown, there are many other smaller sectors that have sprouted up in the country, many responding to growing domestic demand emanating from a newly emerging middle class. Some of these non-RMG manufactures are also being exported, and while their shares to total exports are small, taken all together, they play a significant role in the economy in terms of employment and value addition. The real significance of all these numerous, small-scale activities, however, is not how much they account for in terms of shares of GDP but whether and what potential these hold for future growth and expansion. This is important because for over 20 years Bangladeshi policymakers have been searching for signs of an additional one or two sectors that could impart further impetus to export growth and diversification. The growing industrial strength reflected in a number of sectoral and sub-sectoral activities could well mark a turning point for Bangladesh's industrial fortunes. Most importantly, it demonstrates that the country has acquired considerable skills and capacities to undertake a large variety of manufacturing and processing activities, and under the right circumstances (that is, incentives and policy support, including protection), it could expand quickly. In other words, this is proof of capability. What is needed now is for Bangladesh to leverage this experience to chart out new areas of dynamic comparative advantage. A precondition for this to happen would be a change in the mindset of policymakers to look beyond RMG and consider other potential sectors for privileged policy incentives.

These 'other sectors' are a combination of mostly new manufacturing areas along with a few traditional ones that are attempting to resurface once again, using new technology and fresh branding approaches. Among the latter, jute and especially leather goods are often touted as having great potential. However, the promise of rehabilitating them has been elusive, although the leather sector has seen a degree of new investments and use of improved technology, including effluent treatment plants to reduce environmental pollution. In the case of jute, achievements have been even less impressive. The jute and leather industries, nevertheless, have continued to chug along, even if slowly.

Other sectors of note include agro-processing and agribusiness, ceramics, automotive assembly, healthcare, ICT and outsourcing, light engineering, shrimp and fish processing, pharmaceuticals, plastics, renewable energy and energy-efficient technology, shipbuilding, telecommunications, construction, tourism and start-ups. The electronics assembly sector has begun to take off, responding to high domestic demand for consumer durables as exemplified by sales of colour television, refrigerators, smartphones, gas ovens, washing machines and air conditioners on the back of rising incomes. Similarly, the travel and tourism sector has recorded robust growth based on domestic tourism and international travel undertaken by Bangladeshis for work, medical treatment and entertainment.

While it is difficult to predict which particular market segment will forge ahead more quickly than others, there is little doubt that the country is poised for a breakthrough, perhaps across a number of markets simultaneously. Generally, two types of reasons are forwarded to explain why industrial diversification is not happening: (*a*) the policy focus is on RMG at the neglect of all other sectors and (*b*) high levels of protection do not provide any incentive to firms to try and diversify as returns from the domestic market are higher (Sattar 2020).

Studies that have attempted to examine Bangladesh's comparative advantage or identify priority sectors have generally used static 'revealed preference' frameworks or basically cherry-picked sectors that appear to be performing relatively well already, for example, like pharmaceuticals and ceramics. These exercises only reiterate the static claim where the country is 'revealed' to have comparative advantage in a few activities like jute goods, leather products and similar labour-intensive manufactures or services. This does not support a dynamic process whereby new, exciting areas of potential investment could be identified, the dream being that other new sectors will open up, much like RMG did in the 1980s and 1990s, that will carry Bangladesh to the next level of development. The search has been difficult and the course uncharted. The experience of East Asia shows that comparative advantage can be achieved or even be thrust upon a country – if this was not true, South Korea would not be exporting cars, for example, or Taiwan would not be selling sophisticated medical equipment today.

A recent USAID-funded study (USAID 2019) took a practical approach to the issue by focusing on a total of 16 areas of current economic activity to assess their dynamic potential. In other words, all 16 sectors were deemed to be doing well, and the policy question was which of these offered the greatest promise deserving of special policy support or encouragement.

While the Bangladesh government has, from time to time, designated various sectors as 'priority', in terms of policy and financial incentives, the main beneficiary has been the RMG and textiles sector, as already indicated. As far as new, priority sectors are concerned, the government appears to have taken the decision, in effect, to leave this to the market, banking in particular on SEZs that are being set up all over the country. The target is to create 100 SEZs in both the private and public sectors, inviting both domestic and foreign investors to take advantage of the infrastructure and incentives that will be provided. If properly implemented, this approach to industrialization could in fact be the best strategy available, allowing investors themselves to identify their priorities. Studies like that by USAID could play a useful role in helping investors to make up their minds.

The Emerging Industrial Landscape

The USAID Study

The 16 non-RMG sectors accounted for 6 million jobs and generated revenues worth close to USD 50 billion (USAID 2019). All these sectors are displaying double-digit growth. Of these, a few stand out, namely agribusiness (food processing), pharmaceuticals, light engineering, ICT and outsourcing, healthcare and tourism. These together account for around 10 per cent of the country's GDP while creating some 3.5 million jobs. The report projects revenues from these six sectors to reach more than USD 60 billion by the end of 2023. In terms of employment and share of GDP, this compares quite favourably with the RMG sector. The report observes that the agribusiness sector is 'thriving on a strong base of domestic backward linkage', generating revenues worth around USD 5 billion per annum, and has the capacity to generate employment for over 300,000 people, including women.

The healthcare sector is thought to have the capacity to generate annual revenues of over USD 11 billion by 2023 with the assistance of private sector actors. This assumes significant progress in addressing structural constraints originating in health infrastructure and generation of skilled workers and professionals, as well as putting in place a reasonable governance and regulatory regime.[1] That the potential is huge in terms of demand is underscored by the fact that large numbers of Bangladeshis travel outside the country, mainly to India and Thailand, for medical treatment. It is the supply side, reportedly mired in dubious transactions related to government procurement contracts for medical equipment and supplies, and the emergence of strong lobbies in the form of various associations of professionals aligned to political power blocs that have developed a strong interest in maintaining the status quo. There is inadequate political will to dismantle these lobbies.[2]

The pharmaceutical sector in Bangladesh is well developed, not only serving domestic demand but also making significant inroads into the world market. It generates revenues worth USD 2.5 billion per annum and employs over 170,000 workers.[3] Exports are still small but show genuine promise given steady increases in recent years, including in 2019–20, taking advantage of high demand for a variety of anti-viral drugs generated by COVID-19, including Remdesivir.[4] The main weakness of the sector is the benefits under Trade-Related Aspects of Intellectual Property Rights (TRIPS) that is set to cease subsequent to graduation out of LDC. This would result in the withdrawal of a key privilege that the sector currently enjoys, that is, the permission to produce patented drugs through reverse engineering, effective from 2030, assuming that LDC graduation occurs as per schedule in 2024. There is therefore some urgency for the sector to begin significant investments in research and development (R&D), as well as in skills and training – a difficult journey that appears to have begun.

Bangladesh IT and the outsourcing market recorded export earnings of USD 600 million in fiscal year 2017–18. The government has set a target of USD 1 billion in 2020–21 and USD 5 billion by 2025 – a target that would have seemed preposterous a few years ago but now seems achievable.[5] The potential is large but so are the constraints. The biggest advantage for Bangladesh is cheap, available labour. The weaknesses are many, including poor English-language skills, inadequacy of government support, infrastructure, education quality, security and privacy, and the data and intellectual property rights regime. The most crucial constraints are likely to be language and infrastructure to create the basic environment from which to move forward. The fact that it has begun the journey – albeit at the bottom rung of the ladder – gives us reason for cautious optimism.[6]

A related sector that has attracted attention relates to entrepreneurship around start-ups. 'Entrepreneurship development' as a sector is quite nebulous and broad. Entrepreneurship, driven by ICT- and IT-enabled business models, is considered to be one of the booming industries in Bangladesh, managing to attract investment funds totalling USD 268 million from early initiatives in 2013–19 (USAID 2019). These start-ups relate to e-commerce, MFS and ride-sharing companies creating employment, expanding markets and helping to build competitive, efficient markets that do not need to depend on face-to-face, personalised transactions. The importance of such a development is enormous.[7]

To date, the Information Retrieval and Information Technology Enabled Services (IR-ITES) sector is primarily based on domestic demand especially for software development for use by local businesses. The export component is small but growing and seems to hold good potential because of its alignment with Bangladesh's emerging comparative advantage.[8] It is doubtful, however, whether in a resource-constrained situation, the sector will be able to compete for policy attention with RMG, textiles and leather.

The tourism industry boasts around 7 million domestic travellers per annum, generating annual revenues of USD 5.3 billion in 2018–19. The number of international tourist arrivals over the period 1995–2019 shows considerable fluctuation over a low level. The highest point was reached in 2008 before beginning a steep decline and gradually recovering to between to 200,000–300,000 arrivals per annum in more recent years. There is a concern that the tourism data is deeply flawed. The government has decided to install a software called Advance Passenger Information System to get updated tourist data, which was due to be operative from mid-2020. 'The move came against the backdrop of criticism about lack of data from various stakeholders of tourism sector including tour operators, hoteliers, travel agencies, media, academicians and researchers' (*Financial Express* 2019b).

It is clear that Bangladesh, unlike its neighbours, has not been able to carve out a niche in the international tourism market. This is an area that has potential, especially for landlocked areas in the neighbourhood where there is a demand for access to the seaside (Figure 8.1).

The leather and leather goods industry is known to be the second-largest export earning sector for the economy of Bangladesh with a total market size of USD 2.9 billion, which is expected to reach USD 4.8 billion at the end of 2023. This highly labour-intensive sector directly employs around 200,000 people, while another 850,000 people are thought to be indirectly connected (ADB 2018).

The outlook for the leather industry may not be as rosy as depicted. Recent reports suggest stagnation and even decline in exports, and given that large-scale investments in the sector began as early as the 1970s, promises have not been kept. In other words, this traditional sector which seemed to hold much potential, and despite moderate achievements in the past, has remained stuck, beset by numerous problems relating to compliance with international standards, especially with regard to environmental safeguards, unstable raw material prices made worse by the continued smuggling of raw leather to India and the inability to develop backward and forward linkages.

The light engineering industry is another 'priority' sector that the government has emphasized. The sector plays a key supporting role for many industries, including cement, paper, jute, textiles, sugar and food processing and RMG (Swarna and Banik 2018). Based on buoyant domestic market demand,

Industrialization

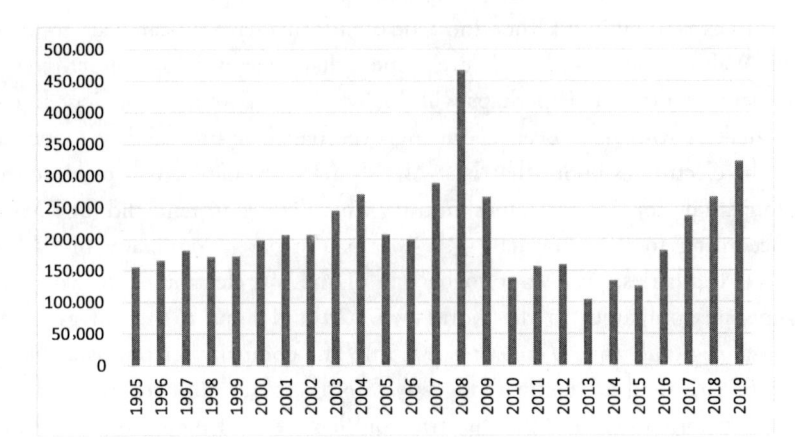

Figure 8.1 International arrivals (1995–2019)

Source: Based on World Bank tables ('International Tourism, Receipts (current US$)—Bangladesh', World Bank Databank, 16 March 2021, https://data.worldbank.org/indicator/ST.INT.RCPT.CD?locations=BD [accessed 2 January 2022]).

Note: See Trading Economics (2011):

> International inbound tourists (overnight visitors) are the number of tourists who travel to a country other than that in which they have their usual residence, but outside their usual environment, for a period not exceeding 12 months and whose main purpose in visiting is other than an activity remunerated from within the country visited. When data on number of tourists are not available, the number of visitors, which includes tourists, same-day visitors, cruise passengers, and crew members, is shown instead. The data on inbound tourists refer to the number of arrivals, not to the number of people traveling.

the sector has experienced exponential growth, currently generating revenues worth USD 3.1 billion and employment for over 800,000 people. Its performance in the export market, however, has been quite uneven, with total exports fluctuating around USD 300–500 million over the last decade. The market potential is excellent, but the sector needs to modernize to enhance productivity and quality in order to compete more effectively. This is perhaps best exemplified by the 'Waltonisation' process now underway in the country.

Walton is an electronic company that assembles a variety of consumer durables that are in great demand from a growing middle and affluent class (MAC) in Bangladesh. This sector has traditionally been dominated by international brands that are now having to make way for local assembly. Thus, the Waltonisation of the electronics market (and the entry of new domestic entities) has made this market interesting from the perspective of skill creation, import substitution and even potential exports. At the moment, the local brands are competing on price but also providing good-quality equipment that include television, refrigerators, washing machines, air conditioners and so on. Walton is already a dominant player in the television (27 per cent) and refrigerator (54 per cent) markets and is poised to expand rapidly. Other domestic brands that have appeared are trying to mimic Walton's success – a good development that bodes well for competitiveness and quality control. This perhaps will finally address a long-felt anxiety among policymakers who have been agonizing over Bangladesh's inability to benefit from the electronics boom that East Asia so deftly exploited. Is it possible that Walton can do for the electronics industry what Desh Garments did for RMG?

According to the chairman, RB Group, the parent company of Walton Hi-Tech Industries, 'We want to be one of the top electronics, telecom and automobile companies in the world by 2020 and hope to prevail as a true universal digital brand' (*Daily Star* 2015b). The company set out as a trading house in 1977 and has come a long way from there. It dominates the domestic market, exports to around 20 countries and has set itself high targets. A third-generation business family, RB Group has opened up an entirely new industrial sector with a new model. Unlike RMG, which began in collaboration with Daewoo of Korea, and later established strong domestic linkages, the Walton model grew on the basis of the emergent, affluent middle class and has begun to diversify into exports – confident that it could compete with price and quality. This is an exciting development – already many are emulating this model, and it does appear as if it could emerge as a vibrant sector. A key factor of course is the rise of China, which enabled the Waltonians of Bangladesh (and elsewhere) to emerge on the back of low-cost technology and intermediate goods imports. So, is the long wait now nearing an end? For several decades Bangladeshis have agonized over the question of why, unlike East Asia, the electronics industry has remained so elusive. Today, the country seems ready for electronics – the question really is whether the government is ready. Much will depend on the performance of industry leaders to persuade the government to align its policies with the needs of this sector. While the current government prides itself as being business friendly, it must also be true that not all businesses are created equal in its eyes. Finally, there is shipbuilding – which has also emerged as another new sector, currently valued at around USD 2.14 billion and growing steadily. The global market size is considerable, at USD 400 billion for the small-ship segment of the market in which Bangladesh operates. Bangladeshi shipyards have set a target to stake out at least 1 per cent of this market. How realistic is this?

Bangladesh is a maritime nation with 9,000 square kilometres of territorial waters and a 720-kilometre-long coastline. Bengal had a glorious maritime and shipbuilding tradition which continued well into colonial times.[9] The emperor Akbar (1506–1605) had a naval flotilla with headquarters in Dhaka (now capital of Bangladesh) comprising 3000 ships. Hunter (1876: 240) quotes Taylor, J. (1840) to report 'that such was the abundance of materials for ship-building in this country, that the Sultan of Constantinople found it cheaper to have his ships built in Sandwip in Southern Bangladesh than in Alexandria' apparently drawing on Frederici's travel reports of around 1565.[10] In the 17th century, the size of the Bengal flotilla rose to between 5,000 and 6,000 units, similar to the Chinese or the Arab *junk*s (Nath 2014). Mookerji (1912) also claims that ships made in Bengal saw action at Trafalgar under Nelson.

Thus, traditional shipbuilding, despite various upswings and downswings, was carried on in Bengal until around 1845, that is, until the advent of the steam engine and the gradual demise of wooden boats. Traditional boat builders are still to be found, locally known as *balaam*, relegated to the margins of what once was a prestigious and vibrant occupation demanding considerable skill and craftsmanship (Jansen et al. 1992).

So yes, shipbuilding is deeply rooted in the folk memory of the people of Bangladesh. They have moved into the sector with enthusiasm, instigated by their initial exposure to modern ships which began to be dismantled in large numbers along the Chittagong shore, giving rise to yet another labour-intensive, even hazardous occupation but which seemed to lead inevitably to shipbuilding as a 'new' industry in the country.[11] The country is already on the map as a shipbuilder carrying out orders from a variety of countries, including Germany and Singapore – signifying the acquisition of a certain level of capacity. This therefore is certainly another very interesting area that needs to be watched.

A comparative chart is provided in Table 8.1 demonstrating the potential of various non-RMG sectors to generate employment and revenues. Quite a few appear poised to stake out additional markets, both domestic and global. Constraints are well known: a combination of access to finance, technology, skills and issues related to fiscal governance and public infrastructure – the last particularly relating to standards and testing, and quality control.

Some economists blame excessive protection as a barrier to export diversification, suggesting that the hand of comparative advantage is not being revealed as a result as there is no incentive for manufacturers producing for the domestic market to improve their competitive edge (Sattar 2020). It can also be argued that a degree of protection has in fact enabled a large number of domestic manufacturers to emerge and is an opportunity for them to gain the knowledge and skills to address the demand of a market that is becoming increasingly sophisticated. Can this eventually lead to export competitiveness and export diversification? Walton suggests it can. Table 8.2 shows that there is considerable brand competition within the electronics market, both within domestic manufacturers and between domestic and foreign imports. The local brands appear to be steadily expanding the market and encroaching upon market share hitherto commanded by the foreign brands.

Table 8.1 Summary table of potential non-RMG sectors (2018–19)

Name of the Sectors	Current Employment in Million	Domestic Market (Million USD)	Export Market (Million USD)	Export No. of countries	Domestic Source of Prime Raw Material: Yes/No	Projected Market Size of 2023 in Billion USD	Growth Rate/ Annum (2015–19)
Agribusiness	0.3	3,545	635	144	Yes	8.23	15
Automotive/truck/buses assembly	0.05	13,890	1.5	1	No	32	21
Ceramic	0.0048	668.54	52	50	No	1.56	20
Healthcare	0.25	5,920	N/A	N/A	Yes	11.71	9.1
ICT and outsourcing	0.94	1,100	600	60	Yes	12	high
Leather and leather goods	0.6	1,900	1,000	84	Yes	48	–
Light engineering	0.8	3,125	356	33	Partially	12.06	–
Medical equipment	0.01	350	0.44	1	No	0.736	
Pharmaceuticals	0.172	2,440	103.46	127	No	7.6	7.7
Plastic	1.2	1,800	1,000	68	No	7.2	
Renewable energy and energy efficiency	0.001	512	N/A	N/A	Partially	3.7	
Shipbuilding	0.15	2,200	30.35	15	Partially	6	
Shrimp	0.85	370	431	20	Yes	1.3	
Telecommunication	0.245	3,800	N/A	N/A	Partially	5.08	–
Tourism	1.1	5,300	228	N/A	Yes	7.5	
	6.67	46,920.54	4,437.75	–	–	164.676	

Source: 'Comprehensive Private Sector Assessment' (USAID Bangladesh, June 2019), https://dec.usaid.gov/dec/content/Detail_Presto.aspx?vID=47&ctID=ODVhZjk4NWQtM2YyMi00YjRmLTkxNjktZTcxMjM2NDBmY2Uy&rID=NTUyNTU2 (accessed 4 December 2021).

Industrialization

Table 8.2 The electronic brand landscape

Product	Local Brand	International Brand
TV	Rangs, Walton, Vision, Singer, MyOne	Sony, Samsung, Panasonic, Toshiba, Philips, LG, Sanyo
Refrigerator	Walton, MyOne, Minister	Samsung, Whirlpool, Kelvinator, LG, Hitachi, Haier
Air conditioner	Butterfly, Walton	General, LG, Daikin, Gree, Carrier, Whirlpool
Home appliances	Walton, Electra, Singer, Eco+	Miyako, Sebec, Panasonic, Sharp, Steamfast

Source: 'Comprehensive Private Sector Assessment' (USAID Bangladesh, June 2019), https://dec.usaid.gov/dec/content/Detail_Presto.aspx?vID=47&ctID=ODVhZjk4NWQtM2YyMi00YjRmLTkxNjktZTcxMjM2NDBmY2Uy&rID=NTUyNTU2 (accessed 4 December 2021).

Bangladesh is beginning to diversify away from its almost total dependence on RMG and textiles. While no new, single sector can be identified yet as being of overwhelming importance, it can be safely said that quite a few interesting possibilities have reared their heads, demonstrating considerable potential to take the country to the next stage of industrialization and growth.

Pursuing Structural Economic Transformation

Policies

The path to industrial transformation has sought to be ushered in through the mechanism of 'industrial policies' enacted from time to time, meant to highlight priorities, indicate incentives and enable a legal basis for new manufacturing industries that could or should emerge. Traditionally, Bangladesh has always displayed a list of 'thrust' or priority sectors (and even 'high priority' industries) that would be encouraged, along with 'reserved industries', including cottage, micro, small, medium and large industries. These policies were useful from the point of view of laying out the overall stance of the government in terms of what it would support, what incentives might be available and what instruments are being deployed, including interest and exchange rate policies, licencing, degree of protection, and access to finance. The main goal was always how to expand investment – domestic and foreign.

Since 1971, a total of 12 industrial policies were announced – the last in 2016. These periodic exercises are interesting from the perspective of tracing the evolution of official thinking on how industrialization was to be promoted. Generally, these appear to have kept pace with the times, paying due attention to socialist economic planning in the 1970s, the role of state-owned enterprises, the pervasive licence and permit system, and the widespread use of quantitative restrictions to protect local industry from competition to the more recent obsession with exports, growth rates, market-determined interest and exchange rates, and promotion of entrepreneurship. Obviously, this kind of 'planning' is associated with intermediate regimes where there is an expectation that governments have a key role to play in economic development – even if that development must be led by the private sector.

How are industrial policies scripted? The core responsibility lies with the Ministry of Industries whose responsibility it is to come out with one at periodic intervals. At one level, this is a bureaucratic exercise implemented through a committee led by the ministry with members drawn from other relevant ministries like Planning, Finance and Commerce, but also including representatives of business associations and economists. The outcome of this process – the Industrial Policy document – upon approval, becomes the legal basis for industrial entrepreneurship, identifying areas, financing mechanisms and incentives. The task of taking the policy forward, that is, implementation arrangements, appears to be poorly defined if at all. Nevertheless, policy scope was usually kept broad to enable most prospective proposals to be accommodated.[12]

While this description represents the formal process quite accurately, the ground realities may be quite different and likely to have changed over the years. There are several types of influences that are brought to bear on policy – political influence, bureaucratic tradition and practice, and, lastly, the role of the private sector. The last, almost certainly, would mean dominant interest groups playing an active role to guide policy decisions in their favour from behind the scenes. It mattered little what actually the official policy documents contained. The balance and composition of these forces have fluctuated with the nature of the government of the time and, most critically, the personality and temperament of the leadership.

Up until the 1980s, the dominant forces shaping policy were political and 'military–bureaucratic' in nature. The private sector was too weak at the time to have much of an impact on economic governance issues. While some individual, private sector actors were already beginning to lobby successfully for policy change (most notably, Noorul Quader Khan, considered to be the father of the RMG industry in Bangladesh), these were exceptions. In the case of Mr Khan, a former bureaucrat, and a well-known freedom fighter, the ability to lobby reflected his close connection to bureaucracy as well as the politicians of the day.

The military-led leadership of the 1980s finally jettisoned socialism from policy and declared its commitment to private sector–led, market-driven growth as the key development strategy. Despite all the political mudslinging that political parties in Bangladesh typically engage in, this is one area where all major parties were in complete agreement. Socialism was forgotten, and the market paradigm, after some hesitation and self-doubt, came to rule. Bangladesh adopted structural adjustment policies in the 1980s and trade liberalization policies in the 1990s. In addition, the country moved to currency convertibility on its capital account, liberalized the exchange rate and the interest rate and divested some state-owned enterprises including jute mills. These were momentous changes that were bitterly fought over but which played a crucial role in ensuring macro stability, ushering in an enabling environment in which to save and invest. That this period coincided with the rapid increase in reserves from RMG exports and international remittances did not hurt either.

The SEZ Experience

Bangladesh has gained experience with SEZs through a number of export processing zones (EPZs) which have been present in the country since 1981. More recently, it undertook an ambitious programme of setting up 100 SEZs by 2025 under the direction of the newly constituted Bangladesh Economic Zones Authority (BEZA). Bangladesh has distinguished itself with a determined decision to set up the SEZ programme as part of its national economic strategy.

BEZA is led by the office of the prime minister – thus signalling its priority position – and is mandated to establish, licence, operate, manage and control economic zones in Bangladesh. BEZA's stated aim is to establish economic zones in all potential areas of Bangladesh including backward and underdeveloped regions in order to encourage rapid industrialization. In concrete terms, it has the stated intention to develop 100 economic zones across the country and create employment for 10 million people over 2010–25.[13]

BEZA is just one regulator among several involved in overseeing a broad class of economic zones in Bangladesh. In the same year as the founding of BEZA, the government also created the Hi-Tech Park Authority, and both were preceded by the Bangladesh Small and Cottage Industries Corporation (BSCIC) formed in 1957 – operating under the Ministry of Industries to support the small and medium enterprises (SME) sector, and the EPZs in 1981, as already noted.

The authority, composition and roles of BEPZA and BEZA are similar, as are their institutional set up and investment incentives. The two institutions share the same high-level staffing – their governing councils are both chaired by the prime minister and both include the key government ministers, the secretaries of the key ministries/divisions and the governor of the Bangladesh Bank. The primary differences between the EPZs and SEZs lie in the target investors and access to the domestic market.

The incentives provided to investors in the EPZs and SEZs both provide for income tax holiday, import duty exemption on intermediary input, tax exemption on dividends and royalties, repatriation of funds, relief from double taxation, full private ownership and facilitated access to foreign exchange, work permits, residency and citizenship. While the provisions are very similar, the incentive package offered to investors in SEZs is more attractive with regard to tax incentives: the progressively decreasing exemption rate drops to 50 per cent in the third year in EPZs and lasts for a total of 5–7 years, whereas in the SEZs the progressively decreasing exemption rate drops to 50 per cent in the sixth year and the scheme stretches out over 10 years, providing both slower reduction in tax incentives and longer tax incentive periods to the latter. However, under SEZs the exemption on dividend tax will only begin after this income tax holiday period is over. Another difference in the official regulation is that EPZ firms can sell only 10 per cent of their production to the domestic market versus 20 per cent for SEZ.[14]

Yunus and Mondal (2018) note that the SEZ programme has a much wider national perspective than the EPZ programme – at least in terms of its coverage and intentions. The main difference lies in the targeted investors and sales markets. In other words, EPZs primarily targeted FDI and export markets, while SEZs do not distinguish between domestic and foreign investment, and both are welcomed in the SEZs as developers and partners of BEZA. SEZs allow for a number of park ownership styles, including public, private, public–private partnership (PPP) and government-to-government (G2G), which may lead towards a more partnership-based approach to industrial development.

The Bangladesh private sector has responded with enthusiasm despite a lack of certainty around how the SEZ programme will unfold. Many business leaders have already obtained licences to develop private zones while others are keenly observing developments and positioning themselves to stake out a part of this pie. The most advanced SEZ is the private Meghna Industrial Economic Zone (MIEZ), which was granted a licence in 2017 and has completed basic construction work and the construction of several manufacturing sheds. Currently, three Meghna-owned companies are in production in the zone, with at least two foreign investors coming onstream in addition. As conveyed by the management, not having to deal with bureaucratic processes directly is one of the main advantages offered by private zones over public ones. Thus, a representative of a foreign company appreciated the pace of change and the excellent support from MIEZ in negotiating the complex bureaucratic processes involved (Murshid, Männlein and Hager 2019).

The most advanced government-owned zone is the Mirsarai SEZ, which, along with seven others, was reported to have been already completed (Sultana 2020).[15] BEZA is reported to have received investment proposals amounting to over USD 20 billion from 151 local and foreign business entities, the paper said, quoting BEZA officials. Around USD 4.8 billion is expected in the form of FDI from major international companies. Domestic and foreign investors are lured by a 'unique' opportunity to gain access to scarce land serviced with high-quality infrastructure and services and an environment that is expected to be business friendly. The SEZ initiative looks promising and may in fact usher in the next round of industrialization in Bangladesh. The process has not been marred by any significant social unrest or even unease arising from accusations of land grabbing or dispossession of local communities – an issue that is not uncommon with SEZ programmes in South Asia.[16]

The Regional Context and Some Important Lessons: A Digression

Like Bangladesh, India and Pakistan recently launched revitalized SEZ programmes following a history of early zone development. For India, the SEZ Act was adopted in 2005 despite having set up its first EPZ in 1965. In Pakistan an SEZ Act was passed in 2012, with the more than 100 zones set up in the 1970s. The comparison of these countries provides an interesting lens to view industrial policy due to their geographic proximity and history. Zone location, governance framework and land policy are common themes that are relevant across all three countries.

India, Pakistan, Bangladesh

India opened its first EPZ in 1965 in Kandla, in a very backward region in Kutch. According to Neveling's anthropological case study of the EPZ, this location was chosen for strategic reasons as it borders Pakistan and is home to a large number of refugees, although generally thinly populated (Nevelling 2014). Kutch received special development assistance and its new port was meant to compensate for the loss of Karachi. The zone never managed to take off due to its isolation and lack of basic infrastructure.

In a comparative study of EPZ performance in India, Bangladesh and Sri Lanka, Aggarwal underlined the Indian government's consistent inadequate preparation and conceptual weaknesses in setting up zones: lack of clear objectives, inadequate legal framework or administrative support. The zone authorities had limited power and customs, and FDI policies were rigid. Despite the poor experience with the first zone, India went on to establish five more in the 1980s. Again, their performance was less than remarkable: in 1998, total investment in the seven existing zones was only 0.33 per cent of total Indian manufacturing investment. Aggarwal (2004) suggests that India's EPZ programme was motivated by the need to promote exports in an attempt to earn more foreign exchange to offset the effects of the second oil shock.

The Pakistan experience was not much better, attributed to poor governance and rent-seeking behaviour of stakeholders, both public and private. Others have attributed failure to three principal causes: poor site selection, the absence of a facilitation framework and poor land management.[17] The location of industrial areas in Pakistan was decided on political grounds. For example, the provincial government of Punjab decided to locate one industrial estate in each district with total disregard to location suitability and its readiness for industrial development. Industrial estates situated in poor locations failed to attract the attention of investors despite large public spending. The same approach was reportedly being mooted for the new generation SEZ programme but was ultimately defeated by successful lobbies which demanded a more evidence-based location selection process supported by an integrated facilitation framework (Murshid, Männlein and Hager 2019).

In contrast, Bangladesh further developed its inherited industrial estates after separation from Pakistan and went on from there to build EPZs with moderate success. The BSCIC was first established in 1957 in the then East Pakistan. Industrial estates, aimed at small and cottage industries, took on an important role in the economy. According to Hossain et al. (2018), production from BSCIC firms accounted for 11.7 per cent of Bangladesh's total industrial production and 18.7 per cent of its total manufacturing production. Further, industrial estates in 2018 accounted for 9.5 per cent of total exports and 10 per cent of manufacturing exports, contributing to 8.8 per cent of employment and 21.4 per cent of SME employment.

Bangladesh located its first two EPZs in the dynamic urban areas: Chittagong in 1984 and Dhaka in 1993. Both performed well from the start and today account for more than 80 per cent of the enterprises operating in EPZs. However, those established in the 1990s in more backward areas were less successful. Today, of eight public EPZs, five performed well and three – namely those poorly connected to economic centres (capital city, ports) – failed to deliver.

The Indian economic liberalization programme began in 1991, which significantly improved zone governance (less control, simplified procedures). The first SEZ policy was announced in 2000 to be implemented by both central and state governments. However, it was not until 2005, when the government put in place the legal framework, that the private sector began to take interest.

While all 12 SEZs established in India between 2000 and 2005 were public initiatives, the 2005 Act triggered a new set of dynamics: by December 2017, a total of 204 zones were established, 70 per cent of which were private.

The number of Indian SEZs has been rising at an impressive rate ever since, bringing the total to perhaps over a thousand. Employment in SEZ rose from 134,704 in February 2006 to almost 2 million by March 2018, and investment increased from around USD 575 million to nearly USD 68 billion over the same period. This aggregate picture, however, was driven by a relatively few zones in more advanced states – many did not export or remained in limbo (Murshid, Männlein and Hager 2019). The land question was not properly handled, producing an outcry as the government took over land for SEZ without paying adequate compensation. The government response also appears to have been ill conceived, generating negative signals to investors.

At first sight it might appear that all three South Asian countries entered a new phase of SEZ development between 2005 and 2010. A closer look, however, shows that Bangladesh was an early leader in starting a modern and effective zone programme stretching back to the 1980s. India started EPZs merely as a way to compensate for its inward-looking strategy but later failed to fully commit to its zones. Bangladesh made EPZs a central tool for its new economic policy when it reoriented its development strategy starting from the 1980s. FDI was considered essential to promote exports and the vehicle for this was the EPZ model. EPZ investors, thus, were given a fully dedicated institution and a wide array of incentives from the beginning of the EPZ programme. Today, 70 per cent of investment in EPZs comes from 100 per cent foreign-owned enterprises and 10 per cent from joint ventures. More importantly, the EPZ experience has shaped the subsequent, very ambitious SEZ programme, which bodes well.

China

China is often thought of as the most successful innovator for SEZs, which played a crucial role in its remarkable development journey. Throughout China's more recent development history of reforms and opening up, beginning in 1978, the SEZs evolved to meet a variety of shifting economic challenges. Chinese SEZs enjoyed considerable political independence to experiment with reforms, and when successful, the lessons were scaled up nationally. This required an adaptive approach as well as the successful dissemination of policies by the highest authority (that is, the State Council). It is this dynamic approach that is missing when we depend mostly on static case study approaches to look for useful lessons rather than adopting a dynamic framework to draw these out and feed these back into policy.

This does not mean, of course, that there are no lessons to be learnt from China. China has also highlighted the issue of land grabbing, as has been seen in the South Asia region, pointing to a persistent risk from SEZ programmes.

In addition, not all Chinese SEZs were successful, with some mainland SEZs significantly underperforming in terms of firm productivity, compared to the successful coastal cases. In terms of inspiration, the pragmatism and adaptation of different types of targeted SEZs is a hallmark of the Chinese experience. It is this experimental approach that may be adopted in support of the widening industrial strategy in Bangladesh (Murshid, Männlein and Hager 2019).

Four SEZs were established in 1980: in Shenzhen, Zhuhai, Shantou and Xiamen, followed by 14 economic and technological development zones (ETDZs) in 1984, in coastal cities as well as in and around the various delta regions. By 2008 the number of ETDZs rose to 54. The Chinese continued to innovate both in terms of their own economic policy and with the concept of the SEZ. Thus, Fu and Gao (2007) remark that except for the first four SEZs, all other Chinese SEZs were more like autonomous jurisdictions rather than simply physical zones.

Key policy measures adopted by China include reduced corporate taxes (compared to the rest of China, including Hong Kong), the legalization of contract labour (and the right to fire workers as needed), allowing transfer of land use rights and devolution of power from the centre to the cities and zones – changes that were nothing short of revolutionary, in some cases requiring amendments to its constitution.

Investment in the SEZs flowed in, and by the end of 1981, the four zones together accounted for some 60 per cent of total FDI to China. This was initially dominated by investments coming from Taiwan and Macao, although subsequently US and EU investments also followed. However, it may be noted that the bulk of FDI was directed to Shenzhen, which alone accounted for 50.6 per cent of the share, while the other zones accounted for only around 3 per cent share each. Of particular interest is the observation by Alder, Shao and Zilibotti (2016) that the FDI went into new economic activity rather than generating an internal relocation from non-SEZ areas of the domestic economy. It may also be noted that Chinese domestic firms were also encouraged to enter into the SEZs to learn and gain experience from foreign firms.

Ironically, as successful policies gleaned from the SEZ experience were gradually disseminated and adopted in many other parts of the country, the SEZs themselves began to lose their uniqueness in terms of the special privileges that had originally set them apart. Thus, Yeung, Lee and Kee (2009) note, in 1992 when Deng Xiao went on his famous Southern Tour to re-emphasize his support for reforms, the SEZ mission had by then been largely accomplished. Whatever remaining distinguishing characteristics there were also vanished slowly, and by 2007 the new enterprise income tax law finally introduced a common national tax regime at 25 per cent while labour cost advantages that turned China into the factory of the world faded – paving the way for competitors like Bangladesh to make significant forays into the market. The SEZ innovation however continues (Martinek 2014): the Shanghai Pilot Free Trade Zone established in 2013 focuses on issues such as financial liberalization and RMB convertibility; many 'zones within zones' have been established to specialize in, for example, high-technology development. In other words, while mature zones are phased out, new ones are brought in to address new challenges.

Like the Chinese approach, the BEZA programme in Bangladesh has the potential for experimentation presented by the diversity of ownership structures, potential sectors and zone types. The case of China shows that zone-level innovation can support development of a dynamic industrial SEZ programme.

State-Owned Enterprises (SOEs)

The story of Bangladesh's struggle with industrialization will not be complete without some reference to nationalization in 1972 and the subsequent role that SOEs played or might have played, given that these had dominated the industrial landscape in the early years. Nationalization led to significant enlargement of public ownership of industrial assets, which rose from 34 per cent in 1969–70 to over 90 per cent in 1972. According to the World Bank (1994), some 305 entities, including factories, mills and financial institutions, came under public control by 1974.

Curiously, even as the government was trying to complete and consolidate the nationalization agenda, it decided on an expanded role for the private sector, which was evident from as early as July 1974. The monopoly in foreign trade was relaxed, foreign investment controls were slackened, ceilings on private investments in industry were revised upwards and a large number of smaller units that were abandoned were divested (World Bank 1994). Mollah (2020) reports that 114 units were sold by the government in 1974–75 for a total of BDT 41 million, with an average sale price of BDT 360,000.[18] These sales did not mark a policy reversal as the nationalization agenda covered larger enterprises. The government planners wished to retain some economic space within which the small and cottage industry entities could flourish.

Attempts at privatization have continued unabated at irregular intervals, undertaken by every government that came into power in the last 50 years. The results were generally disappointing, leading to a growing dilemma. Privatization per se was, it seems, not the cure that it was touted to be: it appears to have made no difference; in fact, some have argued that it made matters worse – neither efficiency nor productivity improved, profits failed to emerge and social contributions to employment, poverty or working conditions also remained elusive.[19] At the same time, large numbers of SOEs still continue to operate at varying degrees of inefficiency, widely perceived to exert an unwelcome burden on the public exchequer.

The mainstream SOE narrative is well known: these enterprises along with all other 'abandoned' properties were taken over by the government to protect and manage when their Pakistani owners left the country. In other words, there was no nationalization involved here – the SOEs were simply an outcome of war and displacement. This argument is generally correct, except that there was a significant segment under local (Bengali) ownership that included jute mills and tea plantations.[20] These enterprises were nationalized, as it became harder and harder immediately after liberation to ignore the loud calls for implementing some form of 'socialism'.[21]

Initially, the then leadership invited various former (non-Bengali) owners to come back and manage their abandoned enterprises. A few did, but by and large the opposition to hand back the industries to them was strong and became politically untenable at the time.[22] The management task therefore fell upon the bureaucracy to manage as best they could – which was of course not very well. They lacked the experience and the skills to run enterprises and soon notched up large losses requiring state funds to stay afloat. The matter was made worse by systematic predatory attacks in league with raw material and spare parts suppliers that turned these businesses into liabilities. The socialist goal that these would pave the way to industrialization and contribute profits to the exchequer remained a far cry.

The World Bank (1994) provides a good description of SOE status and performance in the early 1990s. There were four state-owned commercial banks, three insurance corporations, two agricultural banks and three development financial institutions (DFIs) at the time. The largest number of SOEs was in the manufacturing sector producing textiles, steel and engineering, food, chemicals and jute. The energy and power sectors were dominated by electricity production.

SOEs were able to generate only 8–10 per cent of their financing needs internally while the rest had to come from state coffers or as bank credit. The overall financial picture was dismal: the Bangladesh Power Development Board (BPDB) notched up the highest losses, followed by the Bangladesh Jute Mills Corporation (BJMC) and railways. Taken all together, aggregate losses of SOEs were around BDT 20 billion (USD 513 million at 1991–92 exchange rates). To put it in perspective, the annual development budget in 1991–92 was around BDT 75 billion, implying that the SOE losses were nearly 27 per cent of the Annual Development Programme (ADP).

Looking at it from another perspective, SOEs owed BDT 47 billion to banks, equivalent to 16 per cent of outstanding domestic bank credit, with around BDT 29 billion relating to the jute sector alone. Thus, if SOE losses could be prevented, significant development resources would have been released for deployment to more productive sectors.

Current Status

SOEs in general have expanded over time into more establishments, more jurisdictions and more complex roles, primarily in services and infrastructure development, which today includes mega projects, SEZs and quick-rental power projects. In this chapter, however, our focus is on industry, and it is to industrial SOEs that we must turn (Table 8.3). Challenges in this area appear to have proven insurmountable, and the drain on public resources continues unabated.[23]

Table 8.3 Profits and losses, manufacturing SOEs (1996–97 to 2018–19)

Corporation	1996–97	2000–01	2005–06	2010–11	2015–16	2018–19
Bangladesh Textile Mills Corporation (BTMC)	–163.26	–45.77	–36.19	–16.52	–24.29	–24.61
Bangladesh Steel and Engineering Corporation (BSEC)	–103.28	0.16	14.54	57.74	60.39	74.83
Bangladesh Sugar and Food Industries Corporation (BSFIC)	–65.29	–46.85	35.99	–170.62	–516.52	–981.96
Bangladesh Chemical Industries Corporation (BCIC)	–237.92	–155.01	–249.54	–434.9	–74.39	–911.43
Bangladesh Forest Industries Development Corporation (BFIC)	1.71	–15.2	23.01	63.99	8.15	–7.92
Bangladesh Jute Mills Corporation (BJMC)	–251.71	–380.36	–320.51	14.59	–656.3	–695.13

(Contd.)

Table 8.3 (*Contd.*)

Corporation	1996–97	2000–01	2005–06	2010–11	2015–16	2018–19
All state-owned industries (SOIs)	–819.75	–643.03	–532.7	–485.72	–1,202.96	–2,546.22
(SOI losses as % ADP)	6.56	3.67	2.25	1.38	1.28	1.47
ADP	12,500	17,500	23,626	35,130	93,894	173,000
(SOI losses as % SOE losses)	58.2	24.2	18.7	5.3	–	58.9
All SOE	–1,408.8	–2,659.4	–2,848.6	–9,191.5	+10,888.5*	–4,324.8
(SOE losses as % ADP)	11.3	15.2	12.1	26.2	(11.6)	2.5

Source: *Bangladesh Economic Review*, various years.

Note: *Between 2013–14 and 2017–18, for four years, SOEs posted profits dipping once again into red in 2018–19. SOEs contributed equivalent of 11.6 per cent of ADP to the exchequer in 2015–16 – clearly a rare event. Figures are crores.

The losses are dominated by three corporations, namely, Bangladesh Sugar and Food Industries Corporation (BSFIC), Bangladesh Chemical Industries Corporation (BCIC) and BJMC. Taken together, total losses in these state-owned industries (SOIs) represent nearly 60 per cent of losses incurred by the entire SOE sector, including those operating in utilities, services and infrastructure. However, in terms of assets, these SOI only account for 20 per cent of the total SOE share.

It is difficult to justify the existence of SOIs on economic grounds. There are almost no examples of a successful transformation of an SOI through privatization. The only 'good' example is that of Adamjee Jute Mills, which was converted into an SEZ, suggesting that a strategy that scraps the old, uneconomic SOI and redeploys its valuable assets (primarily real estate) into higher productivity investments would be the ideal way forward. If the government wants to retain some SOI on non-economic grounds, then that is another matter. There does not seem to be much pressure on the government to alter the status quo.

Indeed, strong vested interests have been created over the years that benefit from SOIs in various ways: as employees, as suppliers of raw materials and spares, as patronage givers and seekers – all of whom benefit from poor governance and inadequate supervision. There is no incentive for the management to improve efficiency given the regular government bailouts available every year. Thus, the leakages in the system remain wide open to chronic haemorrhage. The primary role of SOIs, therefore, can be deemed to be 'political' in nature.

The global literature on SOE or SOI has dwelt on the resurgence of 'state capitalism' with the rise of powerful state-owned companies across a wide range of contexts, especially in countries like Vietnam and China, which some have referred to as a new form of capitalism under state control (Nölke et al. 2015). The transformation has resulted in mixed or hybrid models (Bruton et al. 2015) leading to partnerships with private entities or various market-oriented adaptations. Scholars have noted that these new forms of state capital are performing well and are even beginning to take 'centre stage' (Musacchio, Lazzarini and Aguilera 2015).

Limited transformation has been witnessed in Bangladesh, particularly in the energy distribution sector, but these could hardly be described as transformative. Indeed, it is the persistence of the SOEs and especially the SOIs in Bangladesh that needs to be explained. One explanation would be that Bangladesh has not found the right model to transform its traditional SOEs, and the limited experience of privatization has not yielded positive results. Chinese or Vietnamese models have not received consideration nor have these been put forward as desirable models by international development organizations like the World Bank. Thus, the failure of privatization and the lack of a suitable alternative model have allowed Bangladesh's SOEs to retain its uneasy status quo. Perhaps it is time to look at the new forms of state capital as a solution to Bangladesh's SOE sector woes.

Lessons from East Asia

Bangladesh manufacturing and exports have remained overwhelmingly dependent on RMG and textiles. No other sector has appeared in the horizon that could replicate the RMG success despite promising developments. Some economists have argued that it might be best to leave it to the market to identify the next winner, but this approach proved futile. Dynamic comparative advantage could emerge on its own, although the East Asian experience suggests this can be achieved more efficiently through deliberate policy.[24]

More recently, 'the new structural economics' propounded by Justin Lin (2012) seeks to provide theoretical justification to this more aggressive interventionist approach. Lin begins with the premise that factor endowments do not remain static but undergo change as a country begins to transform over time. These changes demand corresponding changes in infrastructure – both hard and soft. Firms begin to face large externalities and transactions costs, implying the need for government intervention to upgrade and invest in infrastructure. The market, however, continues to determine core resource allocation decisions.[25]

A practical approach to assess dynamic comparative advantage for a country like Bangladesh may be to look at countries that are ahead by say 10–15 years in terms of their economic development progression. The structural transition of these countries over the past 10–15 years may then provide useful clues. In Table 8.4 we look at the economic structure of some East Asian countries when they were at the level of Bangladesh in terms of their per capita incomes (in 2010 USD prices).

The data is a stark reminder of how far ahead others in the region have moved up, although, apart from South Korea, they are still classified as developing countries with a fair distance ahead of them before they can be referred to as high-income countries. Even Vietnam, the closest development neighbour to Bangladesh in this group, is ahead by 10 years.

A comparison of the composition of Bangladesh's manufacturing exports with that of these countries at different stages of development may provide insights in terms of development paths, structural challenges and policy directions (Table 8.5).

Vietnam

Our nearest neighbour in terms of GDP per capita is Vietnam – a country that is a close competitor in the RMG exports sector for the second position in the world market. However, unlike Bangladesh's overwhelming dependence on RMG, Vietnam's export structure is far more diversified with its dominant export sector being 'machinery and electronics', which alone accounts for 40 per cent of exports. What is also striking is Vietnam's very large trade sector with total exports exceeding GDP (export–GDP ratio at 1.05). Vietnam's exports are more than five times larger than Bangladesh's, although its GDP is somewhat higher. Looking at it in another way, Vietnam exports much more capital goods

Table 8.4 Selected countries at Bangladesh's level in terms of GDP per capita

Country	Year	GDP Per Capita (Constant 2010 USD Prices)
Bangladesh	2019	1,288
Indonesia	1981	1,298
South Korea	1967	1,262
Thailand	1977	1,225
Vietnam	2009	1,251

Source: 'GDP per Capita – Bangladesh, Rep. of Korea, Thailand, Vietnam', World Bank Databank, https://data.worldbank.org/indicator/NY.GDP.PCAP.CD?locations=BD-ID-KR-TH-VN (accessed 4 December 2021).

Industrialization

Table 8.5 Bangladesh and selected East Asian countries, export structure (per cent)

Export Product	Bangladesh 2015*	Vietnam 2017	Thailand 2018	Indonesia 2018	South Korea 2018
Textiles and clothing	89.28	14.79	2.88	7.33	2.24
Footwear	2.48	7.26	0.29	3.1	0.12
Hides and skins	1.87	1.71	0.53	0.38	0.15
Animal	1.46	3	1.32	1.89	0.25
Food products	0.77	2.45	7.87	4.38	0.96
Machinery and electronics	0.73	40.2	30.97	8.17	43.16
Vegetable	0.63	7.12	5.01	14.82	0.14
Fuels	0.56	2.25	4.22	23.31	7.93
Transportation	0.52	1.63	13.12	4.37	13.96
Miscellaneous	0.44	7.51	3.63	2.12	5.42
Chemicals	0.32	1.5	5.29	5.05	8.39
Plastic or rubber	0.32	3.33	12.08	4.98	7.09
Metals	0.3	3.87	4.86	6.9	0.64
Wood	0.16	1.66	1.93	6.56	8.48
Stone and glass	0.14	1.2	5.58	3.55	0.92
Minerals	0.03	0.53	0.44	3.09	0.15
Capital goods	0.92	40.16	38.3	8.63	53.07
Consumer goods	93.41	36.8	34.3	38.05	22.91
Intermediate goods	3.07	12.66	21.57	27.42	23.39
Raw materials	2.6	10.25	5.8	25.45	0.62
Exports (billion, USD) in 2018	44.9	259.5	252.5	180.2	716.3
GDP (billion, USD) in 2018	274	245.2	506.5	1,042	1,721
Population, million 2018	161.36	95.54	69.43	267.66	51.61
Export–GDP ratio	0.164	1.058	0.498	0.173	0.416
GDP per capita	1,698	2,566	7,295	3,893.8	33,340

Source: Export structure data are from World Integrated Trade Solution (WITS) database, https://wits.worldbank.org/CountryProfile/en/Country/WLD/Year/2019/TradeFlow/Export (accessed 4 December 2021).

Note: *Bangladesh data provided for 2015 by WITS but the export structure in 2019 is not very different with 'textiles and clothing' at almost 90 per cent and 'footwear' at 2.49 per cent as given in ITC calculations based on UN Comtrade statistics (https://www.trademap.org/ [accessed 4 December 2021]).

compared to consumer goods, while Bangladesh exports primarily consumer goods. In addition, Vietnam is also a large exporter of primary commodities, especially rice.

Indonesia

Indonesia is next in terms of GDP per capita at around USD 3,900. What is immediately apparent is its large economy (over a trillion dollars), a huge population, rich mineral and natural resources and growing wealth. It has a low export dependence that is almost at Bangladesh's level. The export structure is well diversified into labour-intensive goods (textiles, footwear, food products), machinery and electronics, as well as primary commodities, mineral and natural resources (fuel, timber, rubber, palm oil). Its export structure is well balanced across raw materials and intermediate and consumer goods, although its capital goods sector is lagging well behind. Thus, in terms of structure, Vietnam appears better placed than Indonesia in terms of its export orientation, competitiveness and development of the coveted 'machinery and electronics' sector that has played such a catalysing role in East Asia. However, given Indonesia's size and resources, it enjoys a large domestic market which gives its economy stability and growth, both on the basis of exports and through leveraging its considerable domestic market.

Thailand

As demonstrated by its GDP per capita, Thailand is an upper middle-income country with a per capita income of around USD 7,300, which is more than four times that of Bangladesh, and 2.8 and 1.9 times that of Vietnam and Indonesia. Its raw material exports are relatively small, while capital goods, followed by consumer and intermediate goods, lead the way. The single most important export product category is machinery and electronics, followed by 'transportation' (cars, motorbikes, spares) and rubber and plastics. We see that clothing and footwear – items that are important for Bangladesh, Vietnam and Indonesia – play a minor role. In some ways, the Thai export structure looks quite similar to that of South Korea – the difference perhaps lies in value addition and the role of specialized R&D and cutting edge innovation in technology (semiconductors, ships, automobiles, high-value clothes), in the latter. Growth in Thailand has slowed and wages have risen too high for labour-intensive activities to be attractive. It is facing the 'middle-income trap' from which it must find a way out if it is to meet its objective of reaching high-income status by 2037 (World Bank 2020b).[26]

Korea Republic

South Korea attained 'high income status' by 1995 and displays the archetypal features of a developed economic structure that emerged relatively quickly through a deliberate, export-led strategy. Its export–GDP ratio of 0.416 is indicative of its balanced economic structure. Exports continue to play a crucial role with machinery and electronics and generally capital goods leading by far. Success comes with its own challenges. It has invested heavily in education, R&D and technology to help achieve competitiveness. In addition, it has created an excellent business environment which compares well even with the most advanced countries (Santacreu and Zhu 2018). There are twin threats that it now faces: stiff competition from lower cost China is gaining ground as China scales up investment in technology and R&D; and the unknown threat from the changing world economic order, of which the US–China trade war is a symptom.

Each of these countries used their comparative advantage to great effect while, at the same time, building on their advantages to enrich their factor endowments, skills and technology and to expand their economic spaces. They exploited their context-specific natural resources (for example, Indonesia) and their natural beauty and heritage-based tourism attractions (for example, Thailand, Vietnam). In particular, all relied initially on cheap, semi-skilled and skilled labour deployed in labour-intensive textiles, electronics, machineries and equipment, and gradually moving into much more sophisticated, technology-intensive production, such as integrated circuits, semiconductors, automobiles and ships. Underlying the progression, a close state–private sector compact was needed that formally and informally assisted the private sector to overcome constraints and challenges through credit, policy support and improving economic governance.

At Bangladesh's current stage of development, where it is poised to diversify into higher-value industry, there are numerous constraints. Foremost among these is a protection mindset in the RMG–textile sector and low-productive human capital. Both constraints need to be loosened, for the RMG sector has matured and should not have to rely on crutches any longer, while human capital investment in the context of the 'population dividend' must take the highest priority – especially when the country has few other resources that it can depend on.

The Flying Geese Paradigm (FGP)

To pose the question somewhat differently, the moot point is whether Bangladesh can be considered one of the latest countries to have joined the flock of 'Flying Geese' – and indeed whether the FGP still remains relevant some 60–90 years after it was first propounded.[27] This is the last of the great industrial development paradigms that has seen some modification over time and which appears to offer some insights into the industrialization process.[28]

The FGP compares the process of East Asian development to the flight pattern of a flock of wild geese which assumes an inverse V-shape as it collectively moves forward (Akamatsu 1962; Kojima 2000). Japan is the leading goose here, followed by the newly industrialized economies (Hong Kong, Singapore, South Korea, Taiwan), then by the Association of Southeast Asian Nations–4, or ASEAN-4, (Indonesia, Philippines, Malaysia, and Thailand), and finally the latest comers like China and Vietnam (Zhang and Ruan 2014). The core process is driven by rising costs of factors of production, especially labour, which forces firms and industries in more advanced countries to relocate to lower-cost areas. However, there may well be other considerations – benign or otherwise – stemming from international and regional political economy and geopolitics, as well as country specificity, that could hinder or accelerate outcomes generated by pure economic processes (Kasahara 2004; Wang 2004). The former, in particular, may be even more relevant today when the international economic system appears to be poised for a major shake-up in a bid to reverse globalization.

As predicted by the FGP, Bangladesh started off on the right note by managing to gain a foothold in labour-intensive manufacturing like clothing, textiles and leather goods. This is what Ozawa refers to as the first phase when 'Hecksher–Ohlin industries' develop (Ozawa 2009). In the second phase, heavy industries are built – namely steel and chemical industries. Bangladesh does not have any raw materials like iron ore or easily exploitable coal resources to manufacture steel directly. Interestingly, however, a large rerolling steel mill sector has developed which depends on scraps from the ship-breaking industry to produce steel. The sector has matured, giving way to large, automated production facilities that can produce high-grade steel. There are some 300 steel mills in operation, although the top 3–4 mills dominate the market. The country is self-sufficient in steel and the outlook is excellent given buoyant demand (Haque and Abdullah 2019).

Chemical industries have lagged behind despite growing demand from textiles and RMG for dyes and colorants – for which the country is mainly import dependent. This then is a 'deviation' from the model and probably attributable to the relatively slow growth of the leather segment – a sector that is a large consumer of chemical products. The current market for chemicals is over USD 2 billion and rising quickly – and could soon begin to attract attention from investors, especially foreign (Parvez 2019). In the case of Bangladesh, chemicals will likely cascade down into phase three.

The hallmark of phase three is the assembly of consumer durables like television sets, air conditioners, washing machines, refrigerators and automobiles. As we described earlier in this chapter, this phase has been initiated and, as indicated by the paradigm, is developing as expected. Production is mainly for the local market but increasingly forays into developing country markets are in evidence. The automobile sector has so far been nascent and is beginning to emerge as well.[29] The final phase is dominated by 'Schumpeterian' industries, which focus on R&D in cutting-edge technology to produce hi-tech electronic and manufacturing sectors (Ozawa 2001).

Kojima (2000), going by the experience of Japan, believes that FDI from the lead geese play a vital role in introducing capital goods and more advanced technologies and skills to the follower geese. Cheng (2011), Fan (2008) and Jou and Chen (2001) describes the transition process with reference to the footwear industry in Taiwan. The sector was booming in Taiwan in the 1960s, reaching its peak in the 1970s when Taiwan beat Italy to become the premier footwear exporter in the world. However, decline began from the mid-1980s as costs rose. The industry then looked for other investment destinations – moving gradually into China and Southeast Asia.

While the RMG story appears to comply much better with the FG model, initiated by a leading goose, that is, South Korea through FDI and technology transfer, and sharing of linkages to world markets, this did not happen for leather goods or footwear – a classic FG industry that played a key role in other East Asian countries.

In this case, we see a deviation from the model in Bangladesh – and one that possibly points out the reason for the inability of the leather goods sector to live up to its potential. There was scant FDI inflow into this sector from a leading goose – no one relocated to Bangladesh despite its clear comparative advantage in terms of abundant supplies of raw material and cheap labour. This only makes sense if there are non-economic factors at play. Two such factors come to mind: In the late 1980s to mid-1990s, when the Taiwanese were desperately looking for relocation opportunities for their footwear industry, Bangladesh was still 'invisible' to investors. The country suffered from an image as well as an infrastructure deficit. There may also have been resistance from the leather lobby to FDI from within Bangladesh at that time, leaving potential investors to turn away.

More recently, global compliance standards emerged as a steep binding constraint. There is new opportunity now due to China seeking to relocate its labour-intensive industries elsewhere. State initiatives of the type alluded to by

Gerchenkron or Kojima will determine if this succeeds.[30] Compliance initiatives and infrastructure have been taken up seriously and greater state commitment is in evidence. This has generated keen interest from leading brands in a number of countries in addition to those that are already sourcing from Bangladesh, including ABC-Mart, Adidas, Aldo, Esprit, Hugo Boss, H&M, Kate Spade, Kmart, Michael Kors, Marks & Spencer, Nike, Steve Madden, Sears and Timberland.[31]

FDI to this sector has been rising and seems set to rise well above USD 300 million in 2019–20, led by Japan, Taiwan and Vietnam.[32] Bangladesh appears to have finally fixed its image issues and successfully put its name on the FDI map. Much will depend on the role of the state in converting the renewed interest into expanded production and exports. The FGP seems well and alive, and all indications suggest that Bangladesh has joined the flock some ten years after Vietnam. A point that cannot be overemphasized is that a crucial role rests squarely on the leading goose, or perhaps geese, whose cooperation needs to be carefully cultivated. It is also clear that the lead goose will not remain constant but will change with time, over sectors or products, and by destination markets. In other words, FGP is a useful, stylized framework but should not be taken too literally. It provides a good, general description of recent industrialization in East Asia as well as useful insights to think about further evolutionary direction. However, each country has its own specific contexts and attributes that will determine its specific structure and the flight path.

Governance remains the great, unreformed area for Bangladesh and possibly poses the greatest challenge as well as holds out the most promise.[33] Commitment to governance reforms appears weak. On the other hand, there has been a transformation in the political will with respect to the private sector. While most governments have been broadly pro-business since the 1980s, there was always a certain amount of ambiguity as well as lack of trust in the private sector lurking just beneath the surface. Today, this has changed: the government has come out strongly in favour of business interests. It is no accident that leading businessmen in Bangladesh have become deeply embedded in governance, including assumption of top government offices in the country. While ordinary citizens may look askance at this change in political temperament, fearing whether it bodes well for genuine market-led development or will simply degenerate into expansion and consolidation of crony capital, there is little doubt that a strong, state role must come into play in support of the country's emerging dynamic comparative advantages. The worry is whether the pro-business stance sans reforms of the governance regime can actually deliver on the promise.

9

The Social Sector Puzzle

Let me only add ... that while recognizing the deep difficulties currently besetting the system – including the recent severe floods – I do not share the general sense of despondency, if not despair, concerning the prospects for the future. There are enough things, I am firmly convinced, within the control of the decision-makers of Bangladesh to convert present stagnation into satisfactory – though by no means spectacular – forward motion.

– Gustav Ranis, 'Brief Reflections on the Central Issues of Policy in Bangladesh'

The role of human resources in a country's development journey is crucial in supporting high-value agriculture, industry and services. We saw earlier that Bangladesh had chalked up considerable gains in social outcomes, especially in certain key indicators related to family planning, health, primary education, nutrition and women's empowerment. In fact, the most commented upon achievements of Bangladesh relates to its successes in the social sectors. Pointing to widely available governance indicators and corruption scores, especially emanating from the World Bank and Transparency International, observers have struggled to reconcile these positive social outcomes to the disappointing performance in governance.[1] This struggle intensified further given the relatively small public resources that were deployed to social sector programmes over the years (Chowdhury and Osmani 2010; Asadullah, Savoia and Mahmud 2014). The question to ponder over, therefore, is how these much-vaunted social outcomes were achieved, given acute resource constraints, poor political and economic governance and an uncertain aid regime within an unstable and depressed socio-economic environment.

The explanations attempted have generally referred to non-governmental actors, aid-supported interventions, low-cost solutions, attitudinal and behavioural changes, role of community organizations and a generally supportive role of the government.

Thus, Chowdhury et al. (2013) attribute the health sector performance to pluralistic health systems, women-focused interventions, family planning, oral rehydration therapy and immunization programmes, effectively delivered by trained community healthcare workers.

Asadullah, Savoia and Mahmud (2014) found no evidence to suggest that the performance was income mediated or support led, as some had indicated[2] and suggested that an inclusive approach combined with government and NGO efforts 'in all social sectors' were responsible: successful awareness campaigns were launched, low-cost innovations helped reduce fertility and child mortality rates, and gender parity in education was achieved through, for example, the 'Female Secondary School Stipend' programme.

S. Mahmud (2004) asserted that the achievements in health and fertility reduction were due to availability of contraceptives, preventive healthcare and low-cost methods until the mid-1990s – stating that the policy of 'more of the same' will not work any longer.[3] Much the same note is struck much later, by Mahmud, Asadullah and Savoia (2013), who specifically focused on the role of NGO-based approaches. They felt that this worked well within the limited confines of delivering low-cost solutions and simple motivational messages to poor, mainly female clients – which may not be of much further use when more complex challenges have to be addressed, pointing to the need for progress on the institutional front.

Hossain and Kabeer (2004) focus on the education sector to explore supply–demand factors underlying enrolment. The demand side was thought to originate, at the micro level, in affordability and parents' motivation in sending children, especially girls, to school. At the macro level, the authors felt that there was elite consensus towards mass education, especially of girls, as well as strong political commitment for this from all major parties.

The main demand-side interventions were various targeted stipend programmes of the government for girls established in the early 1990s. These were probably the biggest factor that helped in bringing the girls to school. Thus, the Food for Education (FFE) programme gave children from selected poor families a monthly wheat allowance in exchange for regular school attendance, reaching more than 2 million students by 1999. Similarly, the Female Stipend programme provided a cash incentive to parents who sent their daughters to attend secondary school (which also motivated them to send them to primary schools as well).

The huge demand that was unleashed required a robust supply-side response. This involved massive investment in schools, materials, teachers and administration, and was only possible because the state, donor agencies and the community responded well (N. Hossain 2004).

Hossain and Kabeer (2004) speculate that a more favourable social environment for girls' education took root quickly due to cultural and ethnic homogeneity and high population density that was conducive to quick transmission of knowledge and attitudes.[4] This argument glosses over the fact that conservative forces were always opposed to girls' education, and this is true even today. The interesting story here would be to try and understand how these opposing forces were overcome and prevailed upon, at the level of the community and the household – apparently without firing a shot! Despite much progress, however, secondary completion rate of girls remains weak, at less than 60 per cent – attributable to child marriage, school-based violence and household responsibilities (BANBEIS 2017).

Mahmud, Shah and Becker (2012) explore women empowerment from four dimensions using primary data from 128 villages: mobility, self-esteem, decision-making and control of resources. The authors report that 39 per cent of rural Bangladeshi women fare relatively well with the 'decision-making' dimension. Another 23 per cent have some 'control over resources', while 49 per cent feel that their opinions should be valued and another 29 per cent refuse to accept or justify intimate partner violence (reflecting on 'self-esteem'). Tellingly, only 5 per cent of women enjoy freedom of mobility. The low mobility score was unexpected given increasing participation of women in the labour force. Surprisingly, freedom of mobility did not increase with household wealth, although schooling and media exposure (for example, television) had a positive effect. Thus, while women's role in the economy and participation in education has increased dramatically, empowerment indicators appear to reflect strong, conservative behaviour at the household level. This actually suggests that while 'permission' is often required from husbands or fathers, especially in the context of work, education, mobility, life choices and so on, these are frequently granted, as indicated by the macro data. Once again, the more relevant question here may be what has caused changes in household attitudes, especially in dominant men sitting atop the patriarchy? This perspective unfortunately appears to be missing.

Before turning to each of the social subsectors for more detailed exploration, it is important first to look at the institutional foundations on which the social sector successes were grounded. We believe that a comprehensive exploration requires an examination of the evolution of rural development thought, institutional innovations and change at the community level, and interventions and practices.

The Evolution of Rural Institutions

Bangladesh in 2020 is still a rural country with just over 60 per cent of the population living in rural areas, although recent observers have noted the blurring of the rural–urban divide (Afsar and Hossain 2020; Toufique and Turton 2002).

In the early years, Bangladesh was overwhelmingly rural with over 90 per cent of the population residing in villages. Poverty was a rural phenomenon, disproportionately afflicting small and marginal farmers, wage labourers, artisans, petty traders, transport workers and women. Thus, development, and particularly social development in those days, was coterminous with rural development generally understood or defined in terms of the state of farm productivity, food security, nutrition, poverty, inequality, land ownership, wages and employment, health, education, family planning or women's welfare.

Ideas of development have played a central role in how priorities were established, objectives set, interventions undertaken and, ultimately, what institutions evolved. These ideas have tended to come from received wisdom often as part of an aid package or via technical assistance, such as under Village Agricultural and Industrial Programme, or V-AID, in the 1950s. Their successes depended on how well these became localized. The process of localization benefited from a professional approach, good management, research or action research inputs, and monitoring and evaluation, when present. The most important factor, however, was the quality of personal leadership. One is reminded here of Picketty's 'Switch Points' – a reference to the actions of a few people that can cause lasting change in a society's trajectory (Picketty 2017).

Thus, we saw the emergence of the Comilla Model in the 1960s that was launched on a pilot basis under the charismatic leadership of Akhtar Hameed Khan. Khan was a former civil servant who served under the British Raj, a cultured, well-read, 'modern' man who studied English literature at Cambridge and was well versed in the works of Rumi and other Sufi saints. He left the Indian Civil Service in 1945 in protest against the handling of the Bengal famine of 1944 by the British, worked for two years afterwards as a labourer and locksmith in a village near Agra, India, before finally accepting various teaching positions. He migrated to Pakistan at independence and was soon sent out as principal, Victoria College, Comilla in Bangladesh. In between, he took a year off to head the V-AID – an initiative that was funded and assisted by USAID.

Village Aid

V-AID was already billed as a participatory development approach 'from below' whose objective 'was to broaden the perspective of the small farmers as much as possible by instructing them in aspects of agriculture, irrigation, road construction, public health, basic education, cottage industry, co-operatives, and social recreation' through trained development agents (Mellema 1961: 12). The country was divided into 'Development Areas' with 20 village workers or trained agents assigned to each area. Some 5–10 of these workers were women who were required to complete a one-year training programme in V-AID institutes. Even after 60 years, V-AID sounds like any contemporary rural development effort, replete with all the correct buzzwords (like participatory development, development from below) and equipped with resources and trained field staff.

The programme, nevertheless, failed, and USAID withdrew all support, ending the programme in 1961 (Toufique 2017). V-AID showed how difficult it was to focus on small farmers – a lesson that would take years to fully comprehend. It also demonstrated the difficulty of working in an area-based programme without adequate local institutions to provide support from below – again something that would begin to be better understood much later. The idea of using well-trained village workers as extension agents was excellent but much depended on what extent they were from the local area and suitably embedded in the community structure.

Comilla Model

After V-AID came the much-heralded Comilla Model (CM): 'In all of South Asia ... the Comilla programme has been the most successful of all the schemes and projects designed to further rural development' (Blair 1978: 77).[5] The initial success of the model in transforming the fate of small farmers who joined the cooperative movement within the experimental zone of the Kotwali Thana led to its scaling up and roll-out after liberation through the auspices of BRDB, despite the fact that weaknesses of the CM were already beginning to be articulated in the 1970s.

The CM consisted of four distinct but integrated components, backstopped by a fifth element – field action research. These four components were (*a*) a strong training wing (Thana Training and Development Centre – TTDC), (*b*) a traditional public works programme to create employment and at the same time develop local roads and improve drainage (Thana Drainage and Roads Works Programme), (*c*) an irrigation component to distribute surface water pumps to farmer groups (Thana Irrigation Programme) and (*d*) its 'hallmark' Cooperative Project, whereby specific target groups would be organized at the village level and federated at the *thana* (sub-district) level.

The main innovation of the CM was its last component, that is, the cooperative project. The village was considered to be the heart of rural economic activity where small and medium farmers were to be brought together and transformed into modern, capitalist farmers free from the exploitation of large farmers and moneylenders. Each village cooperative elected a 6-to-12-member management committee represented by a manager and a 'model farmer' who maintained close links with the Thana Central Cooperative Association (TCCA).

The TCCA functioned as a resource and training hub where managers and model farmers from the surrounding villages would regularly gather and participate in training sessions. They in turn would go back to their villages and disseminate their knowledge to others. While most activities were highly subsidized, the hope was that one day these would become self-sustaining.[6] Cooperatives were not limited to farmers, but eventually separate ones were formed for transport workers, artisans (handloom), carpenters, butchers and so forth.

The CM generated plenty of excitement.[7] The pilot (trial) phase produced excellent results. Problems began to accumulate as the programme was scaled up and expanded and ran into further trouble after liberation when governance weakened, resources declined and influential large farmers took the opportunity to take over the cooperatives – many of which had already accumulated significant savings. This also engendered an environment of non-compliance with rules and large-scale loan default by borrowers.[8]

The departure of Khan, a return to 'business as usual' bureaucracy and a mediocre leadership combined with heightened scarcity of resources and trained staff meant that what was possible within a small 'pilot' area was impossible to replicate on roll-out. Under these circumstances, it was not possible to prevent elite capture as 'village study' type research had already warned.

Nevertheless, the CM broke new ground and stimulated further analysis and experimentation with new ideas. It had grappled with the use of trained Imams of mosques as well as village midwives as agents of change – the use of the latter in family planning in particular was something that succeeded well later on as part of other initiatives.

The CM experimented with separate cooperatives for occupational groups like rickshaw pullers and artisans – the broad message here was that target groups needed to be at a similar level of socio-economic development for such initiatives to succeed. This lesson was incorporated in the design of later initiatives by NGOs and government, including by BRDB and Grameen.

The CM also demonstrated the potential for mobilization of savings and loans by small farmers. It also demolished the widespread idea of the poor, ignorant peasant farmer who needed to be prodded and cajoled into adopting modern technology. Thus, A. H. Khan (1974: 64) recalls: 'Listening to the managers of the village societies, I could not picture to myself the dull, apathetic, legendry peasant who is to be pushed and prodded. On the contrary, I saw the servicing agencies being pushed and prodded and even kicked by intelligent and alert farmers.'

Another key element highlighted by the CM was the need for continuous training of village workers and managers. This idea was also adopted in subsequent

GO–NGO programmes where we have seen substantial resources being deployed to set up training centres (for example, by BRAC, Grameen and BRDB).

In other words, the CM as a project floundered, but as a generator of ideas and innovations it made a major contribution to how rural development ideas took root in Bangladesh.

Many of these ideas were carried over into the BRDB platform and their 'integrated rural development' approach (and by the government in general), which adopted a strategy of physical infrastructure development, including rural roads, storage and markets, irrigation, minor drainage and flood control works and employment of the rural poor, often in specific zones like *char*s, *haor*s and the hill tracts of Chittagong which suffer from specific types of disadvantages and stress (Mandal and Das 2010; Toufique 2017).[9]

Simultaneously, other government agencies were already involved in family planning, child immunization and other preventive measures like safe water and campaigns against open defecation. In the 1990s and later, a major thrust was also given to rural electrification and solar home systems along with speeding up work further on toilet usage, feeder roads, and education of girls driven by stipend-based programmes.

Initially, NGOs began with cooperatives, for example, as seen in the work of BRAC in the early 1970s which was a period of intense NGO experimentation that soon pointed to other directions.

The NGO Revolution

The NGO revolution in Bangladesh has been much commented upon (Lewis 1997, 2012, 2017; Davis 2006; S. Zohir 2004; S. Rahman 2006). It certainly does mark a paradigm shift in how rural development is viewed today in Bangladesh and across the developing world. This revolution is characterized by the proliferation of NGOs and community-based organizations (CBOs), and by the intense experimentation that they were engaged in and the powerful new ideas that they brought to the table for implementation.

Nevertheless, it still needs to be emphasized that the NGOs did not work in a vacuum. Indeed, they picked up from where others left off, and most notably where the CM left off. They were helped along in their work by foreign donors who provided both financial and technical support, by government agencies that were supportive even if sometimes uneven in the quality of their support, and by the rural population with whom they worked closely and whose loyalty they won. The most important feature of Bangladeshi NGOs was the fact that the biggest and most innovative of these were all indigenous, led by charismatic, committed and fiercely patriotic NGO leaders who emerged from the ashes of war.

The NGO heydays now appear to be over, but in the meantime they can claim to have permanently altered Bangladesh's rural development landscape. In the process they have had to learn the art of survival in a complex social and political-economy landscape – ever careful not to trod over too many toes and learning to negotiate the economic and social landscape while at the same time staying clear of the political landscape. Some mistakes were made – and when that happened, a stiff penalty inevitably ensued.[10] Some observers have suggested that the apolitical stance was encouraged both by donors and the government and did not bode well for the emergence of a flourishing democracy (S. Rahman 2006; Lewis 2017).

In terms of institutional evolution of NGOs, the major milestones need to be highlighted. After a brief tryst with cooperative ideas and an integrated-type approach influenced by the CM, most NGOs entered into a 'conscientization' phase that extended up to the late 1970s. This clearly reflected the profound influence of 'village studies' carried out by both foreign and Bangladeshi scholars in the late 1960s and 1970s – a tradition that can be traced back much further. Let us take a brief pause here to take stock of this important body of work.

Ideas of rural development have been gaining momentum slowly over many years.[11] An early influential analysis of the socio-economic context of Bangladesh was conducted by Ramakrishna Mukherjee (1948) using primary data from six villages. An idea of both long-term and short-term change was provided using recall observations (for 1922), as well as field survey data for a six-year period ending in 1944 (Mukherjee 1948: 670). The picture portrayed is one of rapid decline in land ownership shares of the small and medium households, with the top households sitting atop a pyramid of poverty and inequality – a picture not too different from that of rural Bangladesh of the 1970s.

Village studies carried out in the 1960s tended to be centred on socio-economic conditions of a particular village or cluster of villages.[12] These were carried out within the tradition of field-based rural sociological, anthropological or socio-economic research providing a detailed narrative of rural conditions related to wealth, land, power and state of the poor. The 1970s witnessed further intensification of village-based research but this time with a greater focus on development concerns, in addition including demography, family planning, social change, education and social structure – these represented 46 per cent of the research catalogued by Saqui and Akhtar (1987) for this period.

Thus, for example, we have:

> A quiet violence today stalks the villages and shanty towns of the Third World, the violence of needless hunger. In this book, two Bengali-speaking Americans take the reader to a Bangladesh village where they lived for nine months. There, the readers

meet some of the world's poorest people – peasants, sharecroppers and landless labourers – and some of the not-so-poor people who profit from their misery. The villager's poverty is not fortuitous, a result of divine dispensation or individual failings of character. Rather, it is the outcome of a long history of exploitation, culminating in a social order which today benefits a few at the expense of many. (Hartman and Boyce 1983: 1)

This genre was quite popular at the time, both among visiting and resident academics, and appears to have had great influence on NGO policy. The influence of Paulo Freire is also evident here, particularly in developing suitable pedagogical material for the poor (Fateh 2020).

Thus, the 'conscientization' approach adopted by NGOs became popular in the 1970s. This consisted of internalizing the 'exploitation' narrative within programmes and the development of suitable pedagogic material to take to target groups. The message was that their poverty and disadvantages were not their own fault but lay in the exploitative economic and political power structures at the local level. They therefore needed to unite as a group to resist and protect their rights and, indeed, to proactively demand their rightful share of resources and benefits.

However, this phase did not last long, although some NGOs, notably BRAC, retained some key aspects, particularly in its education programmes, after suitable deradicalization of its contents (Rafi 2003; Fateh 2020). It must be remembered that this was also the period when the pro-Maoist Naxalite Movement was raging in neighbouring West Bengal and was beginning to spill over into Bangladesh. This must have persuaded everyone – NGOs and donors – to tread the ground carefully, as the government kept a close watch.

Thus, the major NGOs to emerge in the 1970s were Rangpur Dinajpur Rural Service (RDRS)[13] based in northwest Bangladesh, which initially worked with war refugees on the Indian border in 1971; BRAC, which had worked with fisherfolk communities in northeastern Bangladesh immediately after 1971; and Proshika.[14] Gonosasthya Kendro under Dr Zafrullah Choudhury was also active in 1971, when it had set up medical camps along the border to treat freedom fighters, later focusing almost entirely on the health sector, including promoting the idea of barefoot paramedics.

By 1977, BRAC had abandoned its cooperative experiments and began setting up 'Village Organizations' (VO) for the poor consisting of 20–25 members per group, federated into broader associations. A widely used land ownership criterion was used to recruit members, thereby ensuring that only poor and very poor households were eligible for inclusion. In the meantime, Professor Yunus was already testing out his ideas of micro-credit in Chittagong and would soon begin setting up the early versions of Grameen *samiti*s consisting of 10–12 poor women per group. The 'group' journey had begun and with it a new rural development journey with VO or *samiti* as the central grassroots entity through which ideas, services and interventions would be routed. Two main lessons from the CM were incorporated in the process: a strict target group approach was identified to prevent elite capture and groups were supported by the 'NGO umbrella' to thwart any takeover efforts by the rural power structure. In other words, by the end of the 1970s, significant institutional evolution of NGOs had already taken place.

The success of the Grameen model in the early 1980s generated intense excitement because a new paradigm shift seemed to be indicated. The Grameen approach resolved a number of issues: the poor, especially poor women, were able to use collateral free small loans and, more importantly, repaid their loans on time; Grameen *samiti*s were homogeneous, and members supported and monitored each other and also guaranteed repayment, so that loan default that plagued the formal banking system and all manner of rural credit provided by the government virtually disappeared; and lastly, the group solidarity backed up by Grameen management was strong enough to prevent the local power structure from encroachment and sabotage. Given the huge response to their programme, it was evident that as an entry point into rural development, use of microfinance and savings mobilization was extremely effective. These key messages were rolled out and most NGOs including BRAC and Proshika, and others like ASA that came later, internalized and adapted these quite readily within their own community activities as well as into their popular training programme curricula.

Thus, the Bangladeshi 'NGO model' was established and proliferated, providing a powerful grassroots presence for the poor and for disadvantaged women throughout rural Bangladesh. Indeed, the 'samitization' process further expanded, even into urban areas. Eventually, many years of micro-credit experience and successful financial intermediation led to the emergence of new norms. Repayment was no longer an issue – all (poor) borrowers displayed high repayment rates, irrespective of the institutional regime faced, as part of this new norm (S.R. Osmani 2016).

The 1980s and the 1990s saw heightened NGO activity as existing ones expanded and new, donor-supported NGOs took off. Research has shown that NGO expansion responded to social needs of the people rather than profits (Salim 2013). While total NGO numbers have never been accurately counted, figures have ranged from under 2,000 for those registered with the NGO Bureau of the government (and able to receive foreign funds) to upwards of 20,000 if one includes those that are unregistered (Davis 2006; S. Zohir 2004).

The proliferation of NGOs has been attributed to natural disasters, donor support and the existence of a strong society in a weak state (Korten 1990; Hasan 1993; Kabeer, Mahmud and Castro 2010; S. C. White 1999; Arifeen et al. 2013).

This transformed institutional landscape must be acknowledged as the basis upon which successful social intermediation programmes were anchored, allowing synergies to be captured across micro-interventions, including micro-credit, micro-enterprises, savings, health, education and fertility behaviour. It is with this firm understanding that we can now move to a more sectoral inquiry. However, at this point, and before going into sub-sectors, it would be instructive to see how, in the meantime, the research agenda was responding.

By the 1980s there were several hundred international development agencies scattered throughout Bangladesh (Gross and Selim 1983) supporting numerous small-scale social sector interventions. These agencies funded a specific type of research – usually related to some aspect of performance or field intervention. Saqui and Akhtar (1987) reported 241 studies for the 1980s of which over 50 per cent were thought to be directly related to the development process. Typically, these studies explored agriculture and land use issues, adoption and capacity use of modern irrigation, government policy, nutrition, health, labour, family planning and women.

The topics addressed provide us with a flavour of the broad range of engagement that was witnessed at the time. Thus, we have Mannan (1982) examining project villages with a view of assessing poverty and childcare, and child development interventions, while Arif (1984) directs his attention to village resources and resource utilization (using derelict village water tanks or ponds as an example) – an issue that was keenly debated in the 'self-reliance' literature that had briefly appeared at the time. In the same vein, Mahbubullah (1984) evaluates the impact of water control structures (polders) in reducing crop production risk and encouraging investment in rice farms – the sort of 'impact-evaluation' studies that would proliferate over the next two decades as Bangladesh struggled with the twin problems of food production and flood control – areas where the role of the state was paramount, historically.

M. A. Chen (1983) is already beginning to take a harder look at the role of women in a traditional, rural environment and is reporting clear signs of change that led her to believe that 'a quiet revolution' was underway with women at its centre. Curiously, at around the same time, Hartman and Boyce (1983) discover a different kind of stillness – one that is generated by poverty and hunger. Chen's quiet revolution remained quiet for a while as much of the subsequent research seemed to resonate with the tone and tenor set by Hartman and Boyce.

Thus, we have S. M. N. Alam (1983) discussing marginalization, pauperization and agrarian change 'in two villages' – the findings distinctly evocative of Mukherjee's work in the 1940s as well as that of Jahangir (1979).

The transition from the 1970s to the 1980s witnessed an attempt to develop a broader theoretical framework within which to explore processes of inequality and exploitation given the nature of rural social structure, agrarian relations and the mode of production (Westergaard 1985; de Vylder 1982; Van Schendel 1981; and Wennergren, Antholt and Whitaker 1984). These forays into agrarian research were deeply influenced by the work of Alavi (1975) and others on the mode of production debate in Indian agriculture and more specifically, the debate on the transition from feudalism to capitalism in Punjab and elsewhere.[15]

The reality of transition in South Asian agriculture is undeniable, with most observers seeing in this different stages of capitalist development (or underdevelopment) characterized by backward feudal and semi-feudal forms co-existing alongside advanced capitalist forms in different parts of the broader region. The same could be said of the transition in Bangladesh which began later than in India but started to gain momentum in the 1980s. It was these 'backward' agrarian forms that rightly commanded quite a bit of attention, especially in the late 1970s and 1980s (M. A. Huq 1976; Haque et al. 1977; Jahangir 1979; Januzzi and Peach 1980; Wood 1981; K. Siddiqui 1982; S. M. N. Alam 1983; H. Z. Rahman 1986).

Thus, rural development was generally seen to depend on two major planks: (*a*) introduction of modern agriculture, which was being held back by socio-economic and structural constraints and (*b*) social attitudes and norms that militated against the poor and women. If progress were to be made, then these two types of barriers had to be taken down. It is likely that these constraints have been overstated.[16]

While the 1970s and 1980s witnessed a huge amount of cerebration over what conceptual and 'theoretical' approaches were appropriate for building a rural development strategy, the practice and field experimentation moved in parallel. One is reminded of the warning by Robert Chambers (2014) that poverty and its causes are likely to be misunderstood by 'outsiders' who lack familiarity with local conditions in rural areas. The initial burst of research outputs in the 1970s and 1980s originated with left-leaning 'outsiders' whose perceptions and diagnosis of rural poverty and deprivation may have been biased if not misleading. With hindsight it can be correctly asserted that the left-radical diagnosis of rural conditions in Bangladesh was misplaced. The forces thought to be arrayed against NGOs were certainly a lot less deadly than was believed as opposition that surfaced from time to time remained localized and scattered and never really amounted to a major threat at any time. NGOs in fact were able to emerge as a powerful, new local arbitrator with suitable connections with government and, most importantly, rich and powerful countries. They were thus a force to contend with at a time when the state was weak, and aid dependence was high.

By the 1990s, some of the experimental interventions in the field like micro-credit, integrated rural development programmes and grassroots organizations to serve as vehicles for deploying services matured. The micro-credit revolution led by Professor Muhammad Yunus soon became the watchword of rural development in Bangladesh, giving birth to a new, powerful tool for poverty reduction and women's empowerment.[17]

Thus, the state-led struggle against food insecurity and natural disasters combined with the NGO-led battle against poverty and its correlates at the level of the household and community, reaping the benefits from the substantial synergy that existed between the two. Other influences were also beginning to exert an influence stemming from new frontiers that were opening up in the form of employment opportunities abroad and the emergence of RMG. Taken together, these were strong modernizing forces at work that displayed an openness to new experience: 'Readiness for social change, a sense of efficacy (the opposition of fatalism), and the valuing of technical skills' (Inkeles and Smith 1974: 23–25, quoted in Abdullah 2000).

Critique of Microfinance

The popularity and appeal of microfinance drew scholars in large numbers to the subject, all interested in further exploring the vigorous claims being made by protagonists of microfinance such as M. Hossain (1988b), Pitt and Khandker (1998), Mahmud and Osmani (2016), and Khandker, Khalily and Samad (2016a). A strong counter-literature began to take shape, first generated by the social anthropologists (A. Rahman 1999, 2004; L. Karim 2008, 2011) and later by a heterogeneous group of quantitative economists expressing serious reservations, including Roodman and Morduch (2009), Morduch and Roodman (2011), Armendáriz and Morduch (2010), Duvendack et al. (2011) and Banerjee et al. (2015). Methodological questions figured prominently in these discussions such as how impact should be assessed with major contributions from Hulme (2000) and Banerjee et al. (2015).

The main outcomes that received the bulk of attention relate to poverty and its correlates and women's empowerment. The disagreements that arose are non-negligible. What seems largely missing from this literature is the broader dynamics of change due to micro-credit – that is, factors that serve to facilitate or confound impact and pathways, and the role played by contexts, models, institutions and actors. The range of conclusions have ranged from extremely negative (Galbraith 2017) to moderately positive (King 2020; Woutersen and Khandker 2014; Mahmud and Osmani 2016; Quibria 2012). All others have generally said that outcomes were slight or even negative.

The debate among empirical economists was prompted by Morduch and Roodman (2011, 2014) who re-examined the Bangladesh data used by Pitt and Khandker (1998) and tried to replicate their results but appeared to obtain findings that were very different, and thus coming out with the conclusion that not only was micro-credit not beneficial but it in fact was detrimental for users.

Pitt and Khandker (2012) stoutly defended their findings. They countered by saying:

> Roodman and Morduch's claims are based on seriously flawed econometric methods and theory and a lack of due diligence in formulating models and interpreting output from packaged software. On the basis of Roodman and Morduch's preferred two-stage least squares regression, an alternative calculation of the standard errors would lead one to conclude that the problem with Pitt and Khandker is that they underestimate the positive and statistically significant effect of women's credit on household consumption ... the methods of Roodman and Morduch are shown to bias the findings in the direction of rejecting the results of Pitt and Khandker.

The authors go further into the technical discussion relating to the choice of instruments, programme eligibility rules and validity of exclusion restrictions to essentially dismiss the criticisms, claiming 'The results originally reported in the Pitt and Khandker paper hold up extremely well in this new analysis' (Pitt and Khandker 2012: 1).

The controversy has principally revolved around the best methodology with which to isolate the impact of micro-credit on household welfare and has gone through several phases in pursuit of a 'better' way to solve the identification and endogeneity problem that can confound observed causality because of unwittingly selecting better off clients, better off areas or self-selection of clients with hidden or unobservable characteristics that influence outcomes. Given these well-known technical problems in using non-experimental or observational data, the obvious solution was seen to lie in true 'randomized control trials' or an RCT design – a technique that has been in use in the sciences for many years but tried out relatively recently in the social sciences, initially led most famously by Banerjee et al. (2015) in Hyderabad, India, and with others following suit.[18]

These too cast substantial doubt on the positive impact of micro-credit. The involved technical debate that arose has been explored at length by Mahmud and Osmani (2016) as well as Khandker, Khalily and Samad (2016a). For our purposes, here what needs to be highlighted is that methods matter and contexts matter. One could argue that researchers like Banerjee applied RCT to micro-credit programme evaluations inappropriately. RCT is suitable for evaluation of programmes like conditional cash transfer (CCT) but micro-credit is not CCT – it is a loan that is disbursed steadily over a period of 18 months and requires several years afterwards for impacts to be realized (and measurable). The problem is RCT is typically not suited for evaluation beyond two years of its introduction.[19] In the context of Bangladesh, where microfinance is pervasive, there is little scope to deploy RCT to a microfinance study since experimental conditions would be virtually impossible to meet.

Thus, the large scholarly literature can be said to have generated mixed results with both positive and negative results widely reported with each side appearing to have developed well-entrenched positions – one that will have to be disentangled by new, methodologically and empirically watertight research. In the meantime, the position that this author has taken is that Bangladesh benefited significantly from microfinance even while acknowledging that some countries in Africa and other places may not have been similarly impacted. The diverse results need to be better understood, and quite apart from technique it is vital also to understand contexts, intervention models, covariant factors like local food security and food prices, the nature of grassroots institutions, motivation and mobility. The most important point however is to note that micro-credit in Bangladesh proved to be a potent entry point with which to reach out to and mobilize the rural poor, especially women, thereby promoting the difficult task of building grassroots institutions. While we may debate about the role of micro-credit per se, its wider role as an enabling vehicle of socio-economic change should not be lost sight of in this quarrel. It would be useful if future research explores micro-credit from this broader perspective.

Health

Any explanation of health outcomes should begin with the exploration of a number of key issues: (*a*) fertility decline and the debate around how this was achieved, especially in the 1980s and 1990s; (*b*) preventive campaigns centred around water sanitation, child immunization and vitamin A supplementation; (*c*) 'low cost' curative solutions like oral rehydration therapy (ORT) for diarrhoea; (*d*) the state of orthodox curative-care services; (*e*) outreach approaches used to reach target groups in their homes (for example, through traditional birth attendants – TBA, or *dai*s). The last component has been discussed earlier and will not be repeated.[20]

An element that also needs to be mentioned here is the role of the 'drug policy' adopted by the government, and its groundbreaking role in Bangladesh, making it possible to provide essential medicines cheaply to the population (Chowdhury and Osmani 2010).[21]

The Unexpected Fertility Decline

As soon as the dust of war, instability and turmoil of the 1970s began to settle, Bangladesh turned its attention to the two most urgent, 'Malthusian' issues of the time: food shortages and population control. As noted earlier, by the end of the 1970s, Bangladesh did manage to put in place the basic family planning infrastructure with which to initiate a large-scale, supply-driven programme. The main approach was to motivate the population using trained fieldworkers – in this case, mostly locally recruited village midwives, or *dai*s, who would then hand out contraceptive supplies at the doorsteps of their clients. Under the programme, each acceptor household had to be visited by the *dai* at least once in two months – in other words, the main strategy was supply driven at that stage of socio-economic development. This was supported by the establishment of family welfare centres (FWCs) up to the union level. A demand-driven phase would require changes in education, income, attitudes and women's empowerment judging by the experience of other countries, including China, Kerala, Sri Lanka and Indonesia, and was some distance away (A. A. Abdullah 2000; Easterlin 1975; Abadian 1996; Saharty, Ahsan and May 2014). Two other factors have been cited in the Bangladeshi literature as being important in reducing fertility, namely urbanization and the rising age at marriage of women (Khan and Raeside 1994).

Cleland et al. (1994: 1) begins the introduction to their study as follows:

> Much has been written about how fertility falls in the course of economic development; relatively little is known about how fertility can fall in its absence. As a setting where demographic transition has begun despite social, economic, and institutional circumstances that are unfavorable to reproductive change, Bangladesh represents an apparent anomaly. Bangladesh is alone among the world's 20 poorest countries as a site where fertility decline has begun.

The authors go on to observe that fertility decline as measured by the adjusted total fertility rate (TFR) was dramatic, from around seven births per woman in the 1960s and early 1970s to well under five in 1990. At the same time, a series of contraceptive prevalence surveys (CPSs) revealed that adoption of contraception ('prevalence') rose from 3 to 40 per cent by the late 1980s. These findings were surprising because these were unexpected: the literature produced complex arguments to explain why such a decline is unlikely, in addition to invoking the more usual, 'traditional, conservative, agrarian outlook' that would thwart any such process. Cleland et al. (1994) have painstakingly sifted through the alternative data sources and have been able to establish that despite any major changes in economic structure, education, incomes or women's empowerment, the TFR declined sharply and this was largely to be attributed to the family planning programmes of the government and NGOs.[22]

The decline began in the late 1970s and picked up speed in the mid-1980s. In the process, several types of fertility differentials began to emerge: (*a*) urban residents had higher contraceptive use, (*b*) a small elite of better educated women married to white-collar husbands had lower fertility and (*c*) there was a notable absence of a link between fertility and land ownership or living standards. It would appear that all socio-economic groups reduced their fertility rates at around the same time and to the same extent – a dramatic finding indeed in the light of slow socio-economic progress during that period.

While Cleland et al. (1994) do acknowledge the role of women's mobility and household decision-making power in affecting fertility, they miss some obvious changes already under way: the rise of grassroots organizations and the intense 'modern' messages that women were being exposed to by NGOs – Chen's *A Quiet Revolution* may also be noted in this context (M. A. Chen 1983). At the same time, RMG and labour migration were also beginning to exert influence over rural lives and livelihoods (A. A. Abdullah 2000). In other words, in addition to a latent contraceptive demand carried over from the 1960s, important attitude-shifting changes were under way that facilitated the relatively smooth adoption of contraceptives by rural women in Bangladesh.[23]

A. A. Abdullah (2000: 138–40) makes another crucial observation that reflects the dramatic change in social attitudes, especially women's attitudes that were underway at the time, when he talks about '*purdah* meets factory' – a reference to the massive response from young rural women taking up urban factory work in RMG. He notes:

> Clearly, factory work of this kind represents for most of these women, and for their families, a fundamental rupture with what women are 'normally expected to do' and further working in factories under (non-kin) male supervision and with male co-workers, all this must outrage the norms of *purdah*, of female seclusion and modesty, and call down general condemnation....

He wryly observes that this could be considered an 'epic confrontation between the quintessentially modern, the capitalist world system, with its local manifestation, the modern factory, and the quintessentially traditional, the institution of *purdah*' in which the modern won almost without resistance – reinforcing our earlier assessment that the Western-centric, left-leaning literature frequently overstated the difficulties of development or 'modernization' by endlessly reinforcing a particular stereotype, as a 'traditional, conservative and largely Islamic society' that must now be laid to rest.

As far as fertility was concerned, the period after 1990 fell into a routine stride, with the TFR continuing to decline steadily, now helped along by both supply- and demand-side developments, allowing Bangladesh to reach a TFR of 2 and a contraceptive prevalence rate (CPR) of over 63 per cent projected to reach 75 per cent by 2020, and a population growth rate of 1.5 per cent (Lutz 2017).

Of Low-Hanging Fruits and Low-Cost Solutions

Key turning points in major health outcomes may be noted: child mortality (for children under 5) began its steep descent from 1980; immunization coverage accelerated in 1986–88 and displayed spectacular rise in 1990–95; child under-nutrition began to decline from 1992, in particular indicators related to underweight, stunting and mid-upper arm circumference (MUAC) – the impact on wasting came later, beginning from 1995; maternal mortality rates began to decline from 1980 but accelerated in 1988 and displayed a pronounced descent from 2000, while antenatal care began registering an improvement from 1997. In the context of development turning points across numerous indicators, the period between the mid-1980s and mid-1990s seems particularly poignant.

Chowdhury et al. (2013) writing in the *Lancet* puts forward a number of reasons to explain the exceptional performance in the health sector of Bangladesh, 'despite economic poverty', and these include a pluralistic health system, women placed at the centre of the strategy as beneficiaries and as outreach workers, highly focused upon family planning, child immunization along with vitamin A supplementation and ORT, within an overall 'primary healthcare' (PHC) framework. Others have noted a strong government commitment, generous donor support, key partnerships with a vibrant NGO sector, and community mobilization (Abed 2013).

Bangladesh's strong, early commitment to family planning allowed it to move quickly into its PHC phase as agreed under the Alma-Ata Declaration. In addition, Bangladesh's health outcomes can also be attributed to successful public health interventions like safe drinking water, quite early on (WHO 1978). Other major campaigns in the sanitation sector would come later in particular, those promoting 'total safe sanitation' to eliminate open defecation and ensure basic sanitary safety. Thus, Qimiao and Azad (2017) in a blog post note:

> Indeed, there is much to emulate in Bangladesh's remarkable progress in recent years in the field known as WASH – water, sanitation access, and hygiene. Today, 98 percent of the population gets drinking water from a technologically improved source – water which comes from a manmade structure – up from 79 percent in 1990. Bangladesh also largely succeeded in providing access to basic sanitation. It is estimated that only three percent of the population practice open defecation, down from 34 percent in 1990, thanks to behavior change campaigns and the building of many new toilets.

All the major campaigns starting from the early years under PHC involved delivering well-designed interventions to rural homes, especially to rural women and their children. As already demonstrated, the grassroots institutions were in place and the government needed to align its local level infrastructure with that of partner NGOs. This was perhaps the most important institutional shift that the government engineered.

There was no great resistance to these shifts to speak of. The only difficulty was presented by natural conditions where groundwater depth was too low, or its quality was compromised by salinity or arsenic deposits with some regions of the country especially hard hit (southern Bangladesh for salinity, Sylhet and Chittagong districts for arsenic). This was further compounded by fears of other types of contamination of drinking water. The World Bank (2018a; 2018b) reports that 40 per cent of improved sources of drinking water are contaminated with E. coli – a major cause of diarrheal diseases. E. coli was also present in tap water in urban homes at rates not very different from water in open village ponds (around 80 per cent).[24]

Frequent reference is made in the literature to the role of 'low cost solutions', principally ORT, in striking a major blow against a widespread and highly debilitating cause of ill health, namely diarrhoea (Asadullah, Savoia and Mahmud 2014; Mahmud, Asadullah and Savoia 2013). The therapy was innovated in International Centre for Diarrhoeal Disease Research, Bangladesh (ICDDRB) and scaled up nationally and, once again, delivered by the GO–NGO aligned institutional framework that we have already noted a number of times. Therefore, conceptually, there is nothing more to be said here in terms of further explanations.

However, notions of 'low hanging fruit and low-cost solutions' as explanations appear to underrate the enormity of what was accomplished. All these interventions or campaigns hinged on massive, grassroots institutional change that occurred over several decades with contributions by many actors. The resources that have gone into it must have been enormous.

Secondly, innovations like ORT took years to discover and fine-tune involving the work of many researchers, much experimentation, testing and piloting before being ready for scaling up, requiring the existence of an institution like ICDDRB. Similar observations could be made for other programmes like child immunization or distribution of hand pumps. The real issue here, therefore, is likely to be governance rather than costs (costs in any case were being borne largely by donors), and one could put forward the hypothesis that success depended on approaches and strategies that required basic, low-intensity governance rather than complex governance-intensive arrangements.[25] If correct, the successes reported in the health sector would have to be attributed mainly to simple, well-integrated governance structures that were able to deliver quickly and effectively even in remote locations. Therefore, it is the governance problem that was effectively resolved for more basic, supply driven interventions that made such a difference. This also explains the Bangladesh governance paradox. The implication here is that more complex health challenges where suitable partnerships between NGOs and the public sector did not emerge, where community mobilization did not take place, and governance mechanisms were top down, bureaucracy driven and had little chance of being successful. This must be abundantly clear from even a casual glance at the entire public sector curative health infrastructure and the complete disarray it has found itself in, so starkly exposed by COVID-19.

Before turning briefly to curative health, we may observe that the urban areas were generally left out of the PHC programme until 1998. Curiously, when urban-based PHC was introduced, implementation responsibility was given to the Ministry of Local Government, Rural Development and Cooperatives (LGRDC) which lacked the experience, although it was apparently legally mandated to provide these kinds of services in urban areas.

Lack of capacity of this ministry to address urban health services became quickly apparent. For example, in 2013–14, the infant mortality rate, which in urban areas overall was 34 per 1,000 live births and 40 in rural areas, was almost 70 in urban slums – a pattern that was also reflected in the under-5 mortality rate and the maternal mortality rate. A contracting-out (CO) mechanism was then adopted at the behest of the ADB which funded the Urban Primary Health

Care Project (UPHCP). It was hoped that this would lead to decentralized management responsibilities and involvement of municipal bodies in managing contracts given to partner NGOs. Involving partner NGOs was a step in the right direction but was not enough. Strong local institutions were not easy to build in an intrinsically unstable and fluid demographic context. Moreover, the history of urban NGOs was more recent, and they tended to be poorly resourced and lacked the well-tested, effective institutions that evolved in rural areas.

In addition, factors like the choice and composition of the management committees at the municipal or corporation level entrusted with implementation led to complications that resulted in disempowering local government institutions. Thus, integration of CO processes into the broader national health system did not happen due to politics and power dynamics, and unwarranted interference in project management.[26] This was a far cry from the experience of rural PHC with its strong grassroots institutions, partnerships and community mobilization approach, the lessons of which were not obviously learnt.

The State of Curative Health Care

The public curative health system in Bangladesh belonged to an entirely different order. This was based on onsite management of facilities and service provision to patients. A national-level structure has existed for decades extending up to the district, *upazilla* (sub-district), union and ward level. General and specialized public hospitals were present in districts and cities, including teaching hospitals with the capacity to undertake complex treatments like sophisticated surgery. There also exists a large, mixed bag of private sector entities comprising mostly poorly equipped and managed facilities with a veneer of 4–5 hospitals that could be regarded as adequate, even good. The overall state of the curative healthcare system in Bangladesh is perhaps best reflected in the large number of patients who go out of the country for medical reasons, especially when faced with complications, even minor ones. This is true for the non-poor and particularly for the better off population. The destination is mostly India but for the rich the preference is Singapore, Thailand or Malaysia.

The main reasons, according to recent research, are relatively lower cost of surgery (India), qualified and experienced doctors, proper nursing care, and modern, technically superior facilities (Medhekar and Ali 2012; Mamun and Andaleeb 2013). One estimate for 2017 suggests that Bangladeshi patients spent around USD 350 million in 2016–17 in India alone.[27]

The nature of morbidity is also changing rapidly, which has implications for the orientation of the sector (Table 9.1).

Table 9.1 Prevalence of morbidity per '000 population between 2000 and 2012

Year	Arthritis	Diabetes	Heart Disease	Cancer
2000	4.7	2.7	1.6	0.4
2012	14.0	7.8	3.3	0.6

Source: BBS (2001b, 2013a), cited in Begum and Mahmood (2017).

The prevalence of non-communicable diseases is seen to be on the rise. For example, arthritis increased from 4.7 per '000 to 14.0; diabetes from 2.7 to 7.8; heart disease, 1.6–3.3; and cancer, 0.4–0.6. Notably, while persons with lowest asset quintiles experienced relatively higher proportion of most traditional (communicable) diseases, the opposite has been the case for the non-communicable ones. Better off individuals experienced the highest incidence of diseases like diabetes, arthritis and blood pressure.

In terms of availability of healthcare personnel, it appears that Bangladesh faces a health workforce crisis due to shortages across the board as well as an inappropriate skill mix and inequitable distribution (Ahmed et al. 2011; Begum and Mahmood 2017).

The number of registered nurses in 2016 was estimated at 38,452. The number of doctors, on the other hand, was 61,921, yielding a doctor to nurse ratio of 1:0.62 – well below the recommended 1:2 ratio by WHO.

The number of medical technologists in 2016 was 3,249 – including laboratory technicians, radiology and imaging, radiotherapy, physiotherapy, dental assistants, and sanitary inspectors. In addition, there were 7,330 medical assistants designated as sub assistant community medical officers, giving us a total number of around 10,600 technicians. Other categories of technical staff are health assistants, health inspectors and assistant health inspectors, who make up some 22,600 persons.

There are over 11,000 registered pharmacists in the country working from drug stores who are often the first point of contact for many common illnesses and are sometimes referred to as informal healthcare providers.

Begum and Mahmood (2017) have made some supply–demand estimates for various categories of skills, as of 2016:

- *Doctors* – oversupply by nearly 11,000
- *Nurses* – acute shortage by nearly 100,000
- *Technicians* (selected categories) – shortage of 6,500

The government has adopted a new strategy now to promote universal healthcare (2012–32). Not a great deal of progress has been made until 2020 although it is likely that the COVID-19 experience will serve to refocus attention on health on a priority basis. The task ahead is enormous given a move towards service delivery in onsite facilities, severe lack of trained, motivated medical staff, especially nurses, and a narrow fiscal space. A major governance–institutional breakthrough will be needed.

Women's Empowerment and the Feminization of Education

Bangladesh has been commended on its education sector performance. Its performance in the field of girls' education at both the primary and secondary levels has been singled out as particularly praiseworthy (Sosale, Asaduzzaman and Ramachandran 2019). As discussed, rural women have been specifically targeted as beneficiaries by both NGOs and the government from early on, which quietly resulted in changed attitudes, behaviour and perceptions, as we have argued. This has been crucial in gradually engaging women and men in a process of modernization and openness to ideas and influences. Potent symbols of such influence include women and girls riding motorbikes and bicycles in rural areas in the late 1970s and 1980s, and the subsequent display of girl power as factory workers. In other words, women and girls were ready for education and only needed a small push in the right direction. This came mainly through government–donor supported initiatives aimed at getting children, especially girls, into school at both the primary and secondary levels. NGOs like BRAC participated in the challenge through vibrant non-formal education streams.

There are a number of initiatives that have been adopted by the government for promotion of both primary and secondary education. The overall objectives are similar: to increase enrolment, attendance and reduce drop out, and involve a cash element. Additional objectives include nutrition (when midday school meals are given or a food allocation was provided), pro-poor when targeted to disadvantaged locations, and preventing early marriage for female secondary or higher secondary students. In other words, all these stipend-based programmes would fall under the so-called CCT programmes.

The 'Education for All' objectives led to the introduction of the Food for Education (FFE) programme which was launched in 1993. Its successor, the Primary Education Stipend Programme (PESP), came into effect in 2002. Both these programmes led to increased enrolment and attendance of primary school aged children from poor families (Ahmed et al. 2005). In 2016, the programme was universalized. The success of the midday meal pilot programme for poor areas led to its expansion to all 16.4 million primary school students in the country. The snack (fortified biscuits) is designed to meet 67 per cent of the calorie needs of the children.

Similar stipend programmes were designed for secondary and higher secondary students with a special focus on girls. Apart from the size of the stipend, other criteria are fairly similar across programmes. It should be noted that the Madrasa stream of education was included in these campaigns. The other stream is the NGO non-formal schools whose designs took particular trouble to be pro-women. The competency outcomes of these schools were excellent when compared to those in the formal schooling sector.

The 'Female Secondary School Assistance Project' (FSSAP) started in the 1990s and was instrumental in promoting gender parity. It began as a pilot and was then expanded into a nationwide programme. FSSAP was a well-coordinated effort to increase girls' enrolment and retention in secondary schools by providing stipends and tuition waivers. This provided the foundation to introduce a second-generation stipend programme for the most disadvantaged children, 55 per cent of whom were girls.

Despite the impressive numerical gains in basic educational indicators, quality aspects have lagged behind. Subsequent projects like the ADB-funded Secondary Education Development Programme (SEDP) (2007–12), SEDP (2018–22) and Transforming Secondary Education for Results (TSER) have incorporated quality concerns through attention to teacher training, relevance of the curricula, improving management as well as promoting key behavioural changes. Under the Adolescent Girl's Programme, the Ministries of Health and Education have joined forces to address the issue of retention of girls in school. It will address menstrual management, create separate sanitation facilities and provide female students with cash incentives to attend school.

The stipend programmes were able to address the demand-side problems and act as powerful incentives to parents to send their children, especially girls to school. The supply-side issues were autonomously resolved through institutional and attitudinal changes, as discussed earlier. A point to note is the sustained donor assistance to the education sector that has evolved along with the strong government commitment in evidence.

While some observers have spoken of an 'elite consensus' (Hossain and Kabeer 2004) in favour of education, especially girls' education, to explain the sharp supply response, one could just as easily attribute it to adoption of modernizing influences in the relatively open socio-cultural environment that has characterized Bengal, especially maritime (Eastern) Bengal – now Bangladesh – for many millennia.[28] Thus, Sarao (2012: 34) describes medieval Bengal as 'a potpourri of fast shifting beliefs and social allegiances, religious questing, and social and geographical mobility, making it a world of genuine syncretism of belief and conduct perhaps more multifaceted than elsewhere in the subcontinent'.[29]

In more recent times, women and girls showed that they were willing to adopt contraception, take up micro-enterprises or join RMG factories, migrate abroad as maids, and even take to agricultural work that was traditionally a male preserve. Thus, a stipend-driven opportunity to send children to school could not but fail to prompt a quick and massive response.

Nutrition

Nutrition is a complex variable, and its improvement depends on many factors, including income, education and knowledge, health, fertility changes, safe water and sanitation. The most fundamental influence on nutrition, however, is likely to stem from agricultural performance in a country like Bangladesh, where it has historically accounted for the bulk of employment, income and food supplies. In addition, one would expect programmatic interventions that address nutritional targets to also have an effect.

Among Bangladesh's many successes, one that has gone largely unnoticed has been its dramatic reduction in child malnutrition. Headey (2013) reported that over the period 1997–2007 Bangladesh achieved one of the fastest, most sustained reduction in child underweight and stunting prevalence in contemporary history (at 1.1 and 1.3 percentage points per annum respectively). Interestingly, rural performance was even better compared to urban performance.

Although the decline was only slightly below the much-applauded case of Thailand in the 1980s (Heaver and Kachondam 2002), it was somewhat better than the acclaimed success stories of Brazil, Mexico, and Honduras (World Bank 2006). In other words, despite having lower incomes, Bangladesh outperformed many countries, including neighbours like India and Pakistan.

A major study (Headey and Hoddinott 2016) examined the link between Bangladesh's GR and child nutrition. This is possibly the first study that looks at Asia's GR from a nutritional perspective. The study confirms Bangladesh's rapid growth in rice yields and production and links this to weight gain in children as well as an earlier introduction of solid foods for infants. The most important factor in this context is likely to have been the smoothing of intra-year consumption with the emergence of the major *boro* winter rice crop in addition to the dominant *aman* rice crop. However, the authors point to lack of dietary diversification – an area that they recommend for policy interventions from both the supply and demand sides.

Headey et al. (2014) in fact suggest that the nutritional gains noted earlier have been due to broader, economy-wide developments. They come to this conclusion based on data from the annual DHS for 1997–2011. Their findings are highly instructive: The biggest roles are attributed to rapid wealth accumulation and considerable rise in parental education. Secondary factors are reported to be health, sanitation, the dramatic reduction in open defecation, and reduced fertility rates. These findings are well supported by the general literature.[30] What is disappointing, however, is that the study found very little evidence of impact attributable to the major national nutrition programmes of the government, like the Bangladesh Integrated Nutrition Programme 1995–2004 (BINP) and the subsequent National Nutritional Programme (NNP).[31]

UNICEF (2013b) provides a useful framework to analyse nutritional outcomes. There are 'basic determinants' (policies, culture, agro-ecology) that lead to 'intermediate' determinants (household food security, reduced morbidity), which in turn affect the 'immediate determinants' – that is, food intake and utilization.[32] In the case of Bangladesh, we can think of the GR and family planning as creating the basic environment upon which other income sources could leverage and expand. This provided further motivation for adoption of education, health, and sanitation to expand, which together led to the 'immediate' outcomes.

Conclusion

Over the years, a multi-pronged strategy evolved fortuitously, involving state and non-state actors, market and non-market based solutions and diverse supply-side approaches which evolved through a trial and error process, whereby promising approaches were retained and further developed and eventually scaled up – usually by the state but also by the largest NGOs. In other words, a variety of grassroots, aid-supported development approaches coalesced to generate a set of (mostly rural) dynamics that set off a number of active processes that led to the emergence of new norms and values, new forms of 'voice', new forms of local institutions, which led to the adoption and proliferation of effective, easy-to-adopt social and health innovations.

The most important change of all was that in social attitudes and a willingness to embrace change and adopt technology and ideas, and to boldly seek opportunities wherever they were. The available literature, unfortunately, has given scant attention to this important area.[33] Some have also speculated that cultural homogeneity, density of population and close-knit social groups allowed for a quick transmission of information.[34]

Many hurdles had to be crossed on the way as the obstacles seemed numerous, intractable, and deeply embedded in the social structure – or at least that is what the pundits and experts ordained. Thus, war had to be waged on multiple fronts: ignorance and illiteracy, forms of patriarchy that were stifling women's agency, gender discrimination, child marriage, unfavourable land ownership and tenancy systems, exploitative rich farmers, landlords and moneylenders who presided over backward forms of 'interlocked' markets, and of course regressive religious beliefs and attitudes that prevented women from adopting family planning or from working outside the home. It seemed that all such factors presented deep-seated hurdles that would keep Bangladeshi society forever in an arrested state of underdevelopment.

Bangladesh for most of its history has been rural and agricultural in character, and therefore, the battle for development had to begin in the rural hinterlands. This is what happened as early development efforts primarily targeted farmers, especially small and medium farmers, before the focus of attention expanded to include the landless, poor and women. In Chapter 3, we reported on the success of the GR, whose impact was felt far beyond food production and consumption. The GR was broad based and created a positive environment within which social innovations could take root and spread – a process that was supported by concerted interventions by government and non-governmental actors. One of the outcomes of this process was the emergence of new grassroots institutions beginning with the CM and followed in the 1970s and 1980s by a variety of CBOs including the Grameen-led 'samiti' and BRAC-led 'village development organizations'. The newly formed BRDB borrowed extensively from Comilla to formulate an 'integrated rural development programme', which they expanded nationally.

We have argued that the evolution of these institutions needed to be viewed as part of a historical struggle to build grassroots institutions in rural Bangladesh, beginning with V-AID in the 1950s. Their absence was keenly felt, leading Khan to observe:[35]

> The Academy's first concern was to improve the quality and scope of rural administration. In this field the Empire had left a poor legacy. The Imperial symbol was the Police Station. We erected a new symbol – the Thana Training and Development Centre. Offices of the so-called nation building departments – Agriculture, Animal Husbandry, Fishery, Health, Education, etc – were housed together in a spacious new building. For intensive planning and coordination, a local government council was created at the thana level and also located at the Centre. (Khan 1974: 11)

Already in this model we note the presence of key components of any rural development programme – training, sector-specific focus (for example, agriculture, fisheries) and the inclusion of health and education alongside these production-oriented objectives. Thus, any attempt to understand Bangladesh's success with social sector objectives and interventions must focus on the institutions that serve as the vehicle for delivery of services, ideas, and inputs. In other words, the effectiveness of a model depends on the underlying institutional arrangements. In Bangladesh, their emergence began with the public sector in the 1950s and 1960s, supported by foreign money and technical assistance, but further evolution and adaptation occurred mostly at the hands of NGOs – once again supported by donors – leading to unprecedented change in the Bangladesh countryside in later decades.

10

Dhaka: Capital Formation

Urbanization, Competition and the Rise of a Business Class

Introduction

The majority of modern activities and transactions are concentrated in the capital cities of developing countries: It is where the bulk of the formal sector employment is generated. This is also where one would encounter relatively more women in the labour market and, generally, a superior standard of living in terms of health and well-being, literacy, women's status, and social mobility, as well as access to public services. The capital is also where one would expect to find museums, art galleries, film industries, theatres, fashion houses, and other important cultural centres.

Many developing areas are undergoing rapid urbanization, and this has been particularly true for the city of Dhaka, the capital of Bangladesh, where rates of urbanization have been high.[1] Such growth is not devoid of economic logic, as has been pointed out.[2] Generally, high urbanization rates are a positive indication suggesting strong economic performance. Urbanization and city growth are caused by different factors, including rural–urban migration, natural population increase and horizontal expansion. However, the fundamental cause relates to patterns of economic expansion and structural transformation in the case of sustained urbanization as has been witnessed in Dhaka.

While urbanization is powering economic growth, it is also generating formidable challenges of management and sustainability. With forecasts that more than half of Bangladesh's population may be living in urban areas by 2040 from the current level of nearly 40 per cent, these challenges are set to become even more complex.

The story of urbanization in Bangladesh is mainly a story about Dhaka, its premier, indeed primate city and the centre of the administrative, political, cultural, and economic life of the country. There are other towns and cities as well, of which Chittagong in the southeast and Khulna in the southwest are the most important and serve as the country's maritime gateways to the world. Chittagong is much larger than Khulna and was given the name Porto Grande by the Portuguese and was once considered the most prosperous city in the 'Kingdom of Bengala' (*Encyclopaedia Britannica* 2021). This chapter, however, focuses mainly on Dhaka, which has become Asia's fastest-growing megacity in the 21st century, alone accounting for around 40 per cent of the national economic pie and more than a third of the nation's urban population (Afsar and Hossain 2020).

Historically, Dhaka's fortunes have fluctuated due to political or strategic changes, from at least the Mughal times to 1971, by which time Bangladesh became an independent state after separating from Pakistan. After 1971, the rapid expansion of Dhaka was driven by economic and demographic forces, including globalization, rural–urban migration and feminization of the labour force employed in RMG.

This chapter focuses mostly on post-1971 Dhaka's meteoric rise to megacity status. It may be well to remember that 400 years ago Dhaka had faced a similar challenge when it was the capital of Mughal Bengal.

Mughal Dhaka

Dhaka was transformed from a nondescript urban settlement in Eastern Bengal into the capital city of Subah Bangal (Mughal Bengal) in either 1608 or 1610 (A. Karim 1964). This was the centre of a vast administration with a jurisdiction stretching from the border with Arakan (now Rakhine State in Myanmar) in the southeast, to West Bengal and major parts of Bihar, Orissa and eventually Assam. Dhaka's status as the pre-eminent city in the region continued generally uninterrupted for the next 100 years. The rise and fall of historical Dhaka can be gauged from its population history in Table 10.1.

The Bengal economy flourished under Mughal rule, especially after liberating the port city of Chittagong from the Arakanese–Portuguese occupation, when Dhaka became the most important trading and manufacturing centre in the Mughal Empire. Bengal in general, and Dhaka in particular, emerged as a proto-industrial region making a name for itself as a major centre for the manufacture and export of cotton and silk textiles, as a shipbuilding hub with ships being made for domestic use and exports, and as a source of saltpetre used in gunpowder, for steel, grain and other agricultural produce. Some reports suggest that Bengal at the time was the richest province of the Mughal Empire and contributed around half of its GDP.

Eaton (1996) cites Fray Sebastião Manriques, a traveller who was in Dhaka in 1640, as stating that it is a 'Gangetic emporium', with a population of over 200,000. Recalling that the population of Gaur, the former capital, had been estimated at only 40,000 at the height of the Sultanate's power around 1515, one sees how rapidly the Mughal capital must have grown in the 30 years since the arrival of Islam Khan, the new Mughal *subedar* (governor). Manrique was especially impressed with the city's wealth. He wrote:

Dhaka: Capital Formation

> Many strange nations resort to this city on account of its vast trade and commerce in a great variety of commodities, which are produced in profusion in the rich and fertile lands of this region. These have raised the city to an eminence of wealth that is actually stupefying, especially when one sees and considers the large quantities of money which lie principally in the houses of the Cataris [Khatri], in such quantities indeed that, being difficult to count, it is usual commonly to be weighed. (Luard 1929)

Such a booming economy would obviously draw many foreign traders to Dhaka. European companies including the English, French and Dutch were granted permission to trade. Traders and bankers from upper India and Persia were in evidence in sizeable numbers. The most enterprising foreign community to set up shop at this time were the Armenians, who soon constituted a powerful trading community in Dhaka. By the standards of the time, the population of Dhaka was large – perhaps close to a million.[3] To put this in perspective, the population of Dhaka was only 240,000 in 1941 – a time when its role was that of a small town located in a remote hinterland (Table 10.1).

The Mughal governor of Bengal most credited for the prosperity of the region was Shaista Khan, who ruled for 24 years and by all accounts ruled wisely and justly, pacified unrest led by disgruntled chieftains, took back control of Chittagong from the Arakanese and re-established peace all over lower, riverine

Table 10.1 Population and area size of Dhaka city (1608–2001)

Year	Periods	Population	Area (Square Kilometre)
1608	Pre-Mughal	30,000	2
1700	Mughal period	900,000	40
1800	British period	200,000	4.5
1867	British period	51,636	10
1872	British period	69,212	20
1881	British period	80,358	20
1891	British period	83,358	20
1901	British period	104,385	20
1931	British period	161,922	20
1941	British period	239,728	25
1951	Pakistan period	411,279	85
1961	Pakistan period	718,766	125
1974	Bangladesh period	2,068,353	336

Sources: J. Taylor (1840), BBS (1977, 2001a), Government of Bangladesh (1997), accessed from S. Hossain (2008).

Bengal which had suffered massive devastation and depopulation at the hands of marauding Arakanese and Portuguese pirates.

Given the economic boom of Dhaka (and the province, more generally), one would have expected a much heavier, more eloquent architectural footprint relating to Mughal rule. This did not happen. A. Z. Morshed (2019) attributes this to the Mughal image of Dhaka as a city that is far from the heart of the empire, located in a difficult and climatically challenged region, suitable perhaps as an important frontier outpost but not as a place for Taj Mahals or a Shalimar Garden.

Dhaka's Mughal journey came to an end in 1717 when Murshid Quli Khan, the *subedar* at the time, decided to take the capital to a place called Murshidabad, on the banks of the river Bhagirathi in West Bengal, which he named after himself. This new capital would be short-lived with the defeat at Plassey at the hands of the East India Company and the relocation of the capital to Calcutta after 1757.

What is not clearly understood is why the capital was shifted in the first place – especially when the economy was apparently doing well. There may have been strategic reasons, especially after eliminating the threat from Arakan. There was a growing military threat – from the Marathas in the West who were testing the might of the Mughals in the Deccan and increasingly looking eastwards to Bengal. It is likely that these factors led to the relocation of the capital to Murshidabad from where these threats could more easily be dealt with. As it turned out, the Maratha attacks could be delayed but not prevented: the Maratha light cavalry known as the *bargir-giri*[4] unleashed terror and devastation in the West Bengal countryside that lasted 10 years starting from 1740, when an estimated 400,000 people may have perished (Marshall 2006).

Colonial Dhaka

The rationale for Dhaka's location cannot be understood without reference to its hydrology. It is a 'hydrological' city – surrounded by low, flood-prone wetlands and rivers on all sides, situated in the centre of Eastern Bengal, which gave it easy access via the numerous waterways to all parts of the vast floodplains that make up Bangladesh. Access was however seasonal as in the dry months many rivers dried up and vast stretches of the countryside remained cut off from the administrative centres. In Dhaka, settlements grew sequentially along the riverbanks – a natural response from builders and planners of the time. This river-front character of the old city has undergone much dilution but is still in evidence today (I. Ahmed 2016).

During the colonial period, Dhaka continued its journey as a backward, remote 'rural' destination far from the provincial capital of Bengal located in

Calcutta (now Kolkata). Life was slow, following the rural-agricultural and seasonal rhythms of the Bengal monsoons. The heat and humidity could not have made it popular for the Europeans, although most accounts suggest that apart from the British, who manned the higher echelons of the military as well as administrative, education and police services, there was a significant foreign community of traders, bankers and moneylenders as well. The Armenian community was rich and retained a significant presence from their first arrival in Dhaka around the turn of the 17th century.

Colonial Dhaka retained the old town as it was found, which remained the site of its principal residential neighbourhoods, for locals. The Ramna area along with a large park, the Dacca Club, the Gymkhana Club, the racecourse, university buildings and residential quarters for the British were established north of the old town, a few kilometres away. This was the heart of modern, colonial Dhaka.

At this period in its history, the most important civil institution to be set up was the Dhaka University in July 1921. The university attracted an excellent faculty drawn initially from British teachers and quickly emerged as a significant academic powerhouse. This was the only centre of higher learning in Eastern Bengal – an area where the majority of the population were Bengali Muslims (58 per cent of an estimated 30 million people)[5] who tended to be rural, agrarian and relatively deprived from access to modern education. The significance of Dhaka University, therefore, cannot be overstated. For the first time, this remote, backward area would now have easier access to higher education and would no longer need to send their wards to distant Calcutta. The university would also play a central role in the development of an urban middle class which would play a crucial role in nation formation within 30 years. This was a major political concession made to East Bengal and was not without strong discordant voices in Calcutta that appear to have been opposed fearing diversion of budgetary sources away from Calcutta University or perhaps reflecting communal biases.[6]

Dhaka soon emerged into a sleepy little university town with teachers and students on bicycles, halls of residence filled up with students from the rural hinterland, and *adda* in the adjoining tea stalls. The concept of the university that was mimicked, successfully for a while, was that of Oxford and Cambridge, with residential colleges ('halls'), a system of tutorials and a growing prestige as a centre of excellence.

However, Dhaka remained small and provincial, even if the presence of the university was beginning to have a modernizing impact. The population of Dhaka in 1951, barely four years after independence from Britain, was a mere 411,279 (UN Statistical Office 1955: 178). This is eloquent testimony to its inconsequential size and provincial makeup. The seeds of change, however, had already been planted.[7]

Capital of East Pakistan

The emergence of East Pakistan once again gave Dhaka another opportunity to rise after some 350 years as the capital of the new province of East Pakistan (population 41.3 million in 1951). Transport consisted mainly of horse-driven hackneys but there were cycle rickshaws as well along with pushcarts and bikes. The number of motorized vehicles was few and far between as were telephone lines that were in three digits. A smattering of abandoned military vehicles duly restored were also to be seen, left over by the Allies serving in the Burma front in the Second World War.

In terms of culture, clothes, attitudes and norms, the people of Dhaka at the time were not particularly distinguishable from rural folks of a similar class. Those who migrated from India, especially from a city like Calcutta, were more sophisticated in their appearance, their accent and clothes – setting a new standard or role model for the locals.

There was also an indigenous group of people in Old Dhaka who evolved over the centuries through their interaction and service with the Muslim elites including Pathan and Mughal rulers, and later the new 'Nawabs of Dhaka' – the latter position created by the British for the chosen loyalty! This satellite group known as the *dhakaiya*s were witty and spoke a mixed blend of Urdu and Bengali to give Dhaka a distinct character in terms of not just language but also culture, food, attire and demeanour.

As a provincial capital it attained a certain prestige and importance, drawing people from all persuasions to its centre, including a large inflow of Muslim migrants from adjoining West Bengal and Bihar, estimated at around 1.5 million – many of whom settled in Dhaka. On the other hand, there was a sizeable outflow in the other direction, with Dhaka Hindus largely drawn from the upper castes leaving for West Bengal.[8]

Thus, while the Muslim immigrants brought with them skills, expertise, experience and capital, there was simultaneously a gaping vacuum left by the departure of the professional, middle-class Hindus, especially from urban spaces like Dhaka and Chittagong, that would take years to fill. Overnight, there was a dramatic change in the urban social–professional landscape that affected education, health, administrative services and the bureaucracy where caste Hindus dominated. In other words, the politics of partition resulted in the emergence of new types of spaces that would have to be filled: vacant houses, abandoned or unoccupied land, jobs, services and economic activities. It is these spaces that the nascent Muslim middle classes aspired to fill, and the immigrant Muslims competed for.

In other words, Dhaka's elite Hindu *bhadrolok*[9] neighbourhoods emptied out and was filled by a new emerging Muslim middle class that began to converge into the city from all over rural Bangladesh and beyond. In all other respects, Dhaka continued to behave as if nothing happened. In this new, emerging landscape, poor immigrant concentrations sprouted up in some designated as well as undesignated areas while better off Muslims attempted to make lucrative deals with well-to-do departing Hindus who were selling off their houses and property at presumably heavily discounted prices. The principal of exchange was also common then with departing individuals and arriving individuals mutually agreeing to exchange their properties in India and Dhaka. There is little doubt that these processes were chaotic, ad hoc, unsupervised and carried out frequently under stress. Once these uncomfortable dealings and demographic adjustments were completed, the journey of Dhaka or Dacca (as it was then called) as the provincial capital could begin in earnest.

The Bihari immigrants from the Indian province of Bihar as well as from other north Indian provinces formed a separate ethnic element in Dhaka as also in some of the other cities and towns of the province. These were ordinary folks who were displaced by partition, generally of poor education and modest means. They were housed in designated areas of Dhaka in its northern fringes and constituted a vibrant community that also had an impact on Dhaka's cuisine.

The beginnings of a new mercantile class were also in evidence principally drawn from the traditional Indian Muslim trading communities who arrived from northern and western India, Calcutta and even from British Burma – where resurgent Burmese nationalism caused many Indian Muslims to flee. This group emerged as a small, well-networked elite who brought with them some capital and expertise in trade and business – skills sorely lacking in post-colonial Dhaka. They had connections in the corridors of power in the central government in Pakistan based in Karachi, Rawalpindi, and later Islamabad some 1,000 miles away that facilitated their businesses through dealings in licences and permits, as well as loans from state-owned banks.

Thus, the 1950s and 1960s saw important changes: the economy grew slowly but steadily and depended overwhelmingly on agriculture, especially rice and jute. Jute and jute products were the main exports that led to the establishment of jute mills in the public sector as well as in the growing private sector. These represented the main face of modern industry at the time. In this scenario, demand for labour was limited so demand pull was not the dominant force behind rural–urban migration. While a certain flow of persons going to the city for higher education, white-collar employment or better health services always existed, the main drivers of rural–urban migration were push factors that emanated from acute poverty, and displacement and dislocation due to riverbank erosion and storms and floods that occurred with regular frequency.

There was a half-hearted attempt by the military government of General Ayub Khan to create a local capitalist class in East Pakistan patterned after the capitalist class in West Pakistan. General Ayub had usurped power in 1958, staging a bloodless coup to remove a democratically elected government. In his attempt to seek allies and friends, he tried somewhat half-heartedly to promote a capitalist class, or at least the rudiments of one in the eastern wing in the mid-1960s. The methods chosen were familiar: licences awarded to the chosen and various inducements, including a protected market for investors, bank loans, underpriced capital and foreign exchange. Ayub's belated strategy to create stakeholders among the local elite succeeded to a limited extent but as an initiative it was too little and came too late. The unrest in the east had already begun.

On 21 February 1952, the police fired into a crowd of students protesting the imposition of Urdu as the state language (thereby ignoring Bengali which was the language of the majority) near Dhaka University, killing several students and injuring many. This was the beginning of the end. The sparks of Bengali nationalism had been ignited, eventually growing into a wildfire by the mid-1960s. It was not enough anymore to achieve linguistic parity but also parity in all spheres, particularly political and economic. There was a strong sense of deprivation arising from the extraction of resources from the east that went into investment in the west – processes duly documented by Bengali economists (Sobhan 2015; N. Islam 2003).[10] The political movement for autonomy gained momentum under the leadership of Sheikh Mujibur Rahman and his Awami League, and the famous six-point agenda was proclaimed (Rashiduzzaman 1970; Kabir 1998; Baxter 1974; Choudhury 1972, 1973). Thus, almost like a Greek tragedy, a collision course took over – inexorable, clear and inevitable in its outcome.

As the politics of the region were getting transformed, sociocultural changes were also afoot. The period of the 1960s saw the coming of age of a new, much more confident, and mature middle class consisting of teachers, civil servants, lawyers, doctors, cultural activists, musicians, writers and poets. This class was much more modern in outlook, far less sectarian, believed in democracy, equity, Western education and Bengali values in addition to Islamic ones. The 1960s, in fact, saw a kind of brief renaissance among Bengalis in East Bengal centred in Dhaka, where song, music, dance, short stories and poetry were turned into a powerful medium of political protest. It was an exciting time that witnessed a sudden gush of Bengali pride and emotional outpourings that have been repressed for centuries. Thus, alongside the political movement led by students who remained a central piece of the story until the war broke out in 1971, there grew a powerful cultural movement that complemented and reinforced the political movement manifold. This was totally spontaneous, a *gonojagoron*, or mass awakening, that simply could not be rolled back. It would not be untrue to say that the movement went completely into the hands of the street activists, students and ordinary people with the politicians forced to follow rather than lead.

By the time of liberation from Pakistan, the immigrant, Urdu-speaking business elite acquired considerable economic clout, dominating the upper reaches of trade and industry. They enjoyed close cultural and emotional links to West Pakistan and were able to establish strong networks with the ruling elite there, which helped them to benefit from the permits and licences that were awarded by the central government to cronies. This group, like the Hindus earlier, would soon find themselves at peril. Identified as being pro-Pakistani, an independent Bangladesh would not look kindly upon them. Most abandoned their homes and businesses located in the upmarket residential areas of Gulshan and fled for their lives. And once again there was a mad scramble for abandoned properties that were taken over by armed groups and powerful individuals. It is not clear to what extent such occupation was legalized later. Many of the more prominent structures were later taken over by the government.

Two other Dhaka-based groups of the time need to be mentioned – not because of their large numbers but because of their roles in the Dhaka economy and society at the time. These were the Anglo-Indians of Dhaka and the tiny Chinese presence. The small Anglo-Indian community was best known for their work in the railways but later gravitated towards work in airlines and travel agencies. They were also great entertainers and musicians – helping to inject a cosmopolitan flavour into an otherwise provincial setting. The Chinese were even fewer in number but had an enduring influence: they introduced Chinese restaurants, laundries, and shoe-making shops to Dhaka. Chinese restaurants had soon become immensely popular. Even though the Chinese moved away gradually after 1971 – mostly to Australia and Canada, as did the Anglo-Indians, their cuisine is alive and well, continuing to thrive and evolve on the back of a steadily rising per capita income and introduction of world-class restaurants manned by chefs from the mainland. Chinese cuisine constitutes the major food experience of those dining out in Dhaka today.

Thus, while independence in 1971 came as a great blessing, it entailed untold suffering and sacrifice in terms of blood and tears; the experience had a profound influence on certain visible and hitherto integral sections of Dhaka society which disappeared quietly and became lost forever. When we walk the streets of Dhaka, it is somewhat sad to imagine all those former inhabitants who had once called it home – European and Armenian traders, Marwari bankers, Hindu doctors, teachers and lawyers, Englishmen and Anglo-Indians, and non-Bengali immigrants from North India – all of whom have since been long gone. If one looks closely, evidence of their presence can be found in the nooks and corners of the city – its food, architecture, names of streets or neighbourhoods, in churches and cemeteries, and ill-kept monuments, along with an occasional descendant whose forefathers had decided to stay on or perhaps were too poor to leave.

As independent Bangladesh emerged in 1971, Dhaka, the capital city, assumed an altogether new importance. The quiet city of just around a million began a new journey that would lead it to its ultimate destiny as a megacity, with a population exceeding 21 million.

Towards Mega Dhaka

Urban studies in Bangladesh have tended to be based on Dhaka with the available literature traditionally focused on settlement patterns ('slums'), rural–urban migration, and poverty.[11] Later studies have tended to focus on specific groups, especially women workers and children (UNICEF 2013a, 2019; Kabeer and Mahmud 2004). One particular study made a rare attempt to provide a comprehensive account of 'socio-economic changes' in Dhaka city over the period 1985–2005, using fragmented survey data in addition to observations based on personal experience (Siddiqui et al. 2010). The study examined socio-economic transformation of Dhaka in the context of the broader political and economic changes, the competition for resources and the rise of new elites that have come to characterize the city in the last 50 years. Although a rare and brave attempt, the study is fragmented, incoherent and unconvincing, switching uneasily between micro data, personal observations and sweeping judgements. The attempt was altogether far too ambitious in scope although rather limited in terms of delivery.

The population of Dhaka was a mere 335,000 in 1951, growing at 2.38 per cent per annum – a rate that is close to the overall population growth rate in the region (Table 10.2). As the capital of East Pakistan, it received a shot in the arm and began to attract fresh blood. The city's population rose some fourfold in the next 20 years, of course from a low base, to reach 1.37 million just before the country's separation from Pakistan – growing at that time by a whopping 10.8 per cent per annum.

Subsequently, the growth rate began to slowdown but in the meantime the base had increased, resulting in rapid increases in the size of the city population. By the end of the 1970s, it grew to 3.27 million – an increase of 2.4 times over 1970, and each decade saw major additions, doubling in 1990 over the

Dhaka: Capital Formation

Table 10.2 Population of Dhaka city (1951–2020)

Year	1951	1960	1970	1980	1990	2000	2010	2020
Population (million)	0.335	0.543	1.373	3.265	6.621	10.285	14.731	21.005
Growth rate (%)	2.38	4.44	10.85	8.02	7.27	4.51	3.62	3.56

Source: 'Dhaka Population (Demographics, Maps, Graphs)', 14 March 2021, https://worldpopulationreview.com/world-cities/dhaka-population (accessed 6 December 2021).

1980 level to reach 6.6 million, exceeding 10 million in 2000, and 21 million today. These figures refer to what is called the Greater Dhaka Area while the city itself is estimated to have a population of 7 million. It is one of the most heavily populated cities in the world, with a density of 23,234 people per square kilometres and a total area of 300 square kilometres.

Satellite data suggests that there was an 81.5 per cent increase in the built-up area of the city over the period 1989–2014. As expected, considerable reduction in vegetation, agricultural land and water bodies also occurred during this 25-year period (Morshed, Yorke and Zhang 2017).

In other words, Dhaka's physical and demographic landscape have been fundamentally transformed. The process has been rapid, converting Dhaka into a crowded, bustling mega metropolis. Other towns also grew but these are much smaller areas by comparison.[12]

It has been suggested that despite the high population density of Dhaka, its economic density is relatively low compared to comparable metropolitan areas in Asia. The concentration of GDP is estimated by the World Bank at USD 55 million per square kilometre, compared to say USD 88 million for Bangkok and USD 269 million for Singapore (Roome, Gapihan and Lee 2019). What is perhaps more worrying is that economic density may even have declined in Dhaka – between 1996 and 2010, as seems to be indicated by night-time light intensity as well as economic census data (Roome, Gapihan and Lee 2019).

Bangladesh's prime minister has reiterated the goal of reaching upper-middle-income status by 2031. The role of the urban economy, especially the Dhaka economy, will be crucial if that goal is to be achieved. This might in fact require an even higher rate of urbanization than what Bangladesh is currently experiencing – at least in terms of raising the level of economic density or value addition per square kilometre of Dhaka space.

The question that the country will have to face is what kind of urbanization it should pursue. One approach could well be to make the 'economic' mountains grow taller – that is to say, focus more on the metropolitan areas and core districts of Dhaka and Chittagong. Alternatively, urbanization could be allowed to proceed through expansion of smaller urban centres and small towns.

Given Bangladesh's small geographic area which historically suffered from isolation and poor connectivity due to the numerous rivers and the absence of all-weather roads – constraints that have receded although not entirely gone – it may be time now to consider a multi-town approach to urbanization. This would have the advantage of relieving congestion and pollution of Dhaka, enabling it to become a more liveable urban space. This might be a better option than putting all eggs in one major, megacity basket.[13]

However, let us now return to Dhaka's new story – its journey as the capital of an independent country ruled for the first time in a thousand years by the inhabitants of Bengal. The focus here is not so much on the 'Dhaka is a urban nightmare' theme – there is an abundance of that type of material for those interested[14] – but much more on how its inhabitants came to be, to compete, cope and indeed thrive in their beloved Dhaka, despite the 'nightmare'.

Competition has increased manifold in scale and intensity over the years: competition for physical, social, political, cultural and economic space that in turn determines access to scarce tangible and intangible resources like wealth, power, privileges, promotions and even national awards. The rise of a new country and a new capital city opened up vast opportunities for fame and fortune. Individuals from different socio-economic groups therefore vied against one another for a place under the rising Dhaka sun. While some were better positioned and networked than others, it was by no means the case that fresh deals could not be struck even by those of more modest circumstances or by more recent settlers. Thus, both urban elites and sons of the rural gentry or rich peasantry educated in the city jostled for key positions in this urban environment. Success required negotiating a complex maze of obstacles and challenges and a certain creativity using whatever capacities, capabilities and endowments one was able to garner. A main element of success was one's ability to belong – to have a powerful patron or 'elder' (*murubbi*) and an ability to persuade.[15]

Before the advent of the Pala dynasty in Bengal in the seventh century, the region was engulfed in unprecedented lawlessness as various chieftains fought for dominance. Law and order broke down and a general predatory regimen ensued – a period that is referred to as 'Matsyanyaya', or Law of the Fishes, where the big fish devours the small.[16] Without governance and law and order, the tendency would be to revert back to such lawlessness. In a context where governance is not impartial and systematically differentiates between individuals, groups, vested interests and political affiliation facilitated by *tadbir*, elements of Matsyanyaya would tend to surface from time to time – possibly across competing groups.

These are the concerns that have motivated us as we wade through the historical evolution of Dhaka since 1971. As Aristotle reportedly said, 'A city is composed of different kinds of men; similar people cannot bring a city into existence.'[17] In today's context we would probably want to substitute 'men' with individuals and fluid 'interest groups' constantly coalescing, breaking up and regrouping to sustain, retain or expand their share of the proverbial pie in the face of emerging challenges and opportunities. It is these fluid socio-economic and political dynamics that have made Dhaka what it is today.

New Elites
1970s Dhaka: The Beginnings

The war had ended, and independence was achieved. In the immediate aftermath, Dhaka was filled with soldiers, journalists, returning Mukti Bahini boys, students and opportunists of all shapes and hues. There were armoured cars, military vehicles, cars and rickshaws on the road – all displaying the new Bangladesh flag. The atmosphere was jubilant, emotional, electric – with more than a hint of danger in the air. Occasional gunshots and discharge of automatic weapons would still resound, particularly after nightfall. There were reports of residual resistance, occasional casualties, looting, raping and accidental explosion of UXOs (unexploded ordnances). In these chaotic circumstances, no one knew who was in charge initially – it took five days for the Awami League–led government in exile to relocate to Dhaka. The new government found it hard to manage. It made frequent appeals for surrender of arms, but no one paid heed, until, that is, the return of Sheikh Mujibur Rahman on 10 January 1972 from prison in Pakistan.

Law and order challenges were the first priority – there is little doubt that the opportunity was used for personal gain or to settle old scores. Houses and property were occupied on the grounds that these belonged to departing Pakistanis or their collaborators; vehicles were commandeered and used for raucous joyrides; there was a general air of bravado with an 'anything goes' attitude. The most predatory appeared to be fake freedom fighters who quickly armed themselves after the fall of Dhaka on 16 December 1971 and set about perpetrating criminal activities including kidnapping for ransom and looting – immediately dubbed as members of the '16th Division'. The problem was that it was not easy to verify who was fake and who genuine.

Thus, Bangabandhu's early repatriation from Pakistan was heaven sent. He immediately assumed power and exercised his authority and his considerable charisma to take on several key challenges: (*a*) He disarmed the freedom fighters of the Mukti Bahini and various other auxiliary and guerila units including the Kader Bahini and the Mujib Bahini – powerful guerilla units that could potentially threaten stability, together numbering perhaps up to 200,000, who responded to his appeal and came forward to ceremonially lay down arms in his presence; (*b*) He presided over the departure of the entire Indian Army from Bangladesh on 12 March 1972 within two months – another major achievement in the context of rife speculation at the time that the Indians may remain for much longer to ensure that their strategic interests are not jeopardized, especially after all the sacrifices that they made. Bangabandhu's presence and clear command over the situation must have convinced India that it was alright to withdraw; and (*c*) He enacted the constitution, styled after the Indian constitution, where the four pillars of nationalism, secularism, democracy and socialism were incorporated, and Bangladesh was declared as a 'Peoples' Republic'.[18] These were monumental tasks which served to lay down the basic preconditions for Bangladesh's journey forward. If Bangabandhu had not returned so quickly, the history of Bangladesh may have been quite different.

In the meantime, the competition for power and 'space' began to intensify. The immediate beneficiaries and intermediaries of this space were the politicians and civil servants on the one hand, and the military and the broader private sector on the other. The distribution of spoils would have to go through a complex, loosely organized, informal system of *tadbir* and threat – an important factor being loyalty to the regime in power. These transactions tended to be highly personalized – a feature that remains alive and well. To paraphrase Dasgupta (2016), it was important to observe to what extent the relationship between institutions of the state and that of the private sector were critical for the process of capital accumulation in the post-1971 environment, with the caveat that these would typically be mediated by powerful, elite men from the political–bureaucratic–military nexus.

This was a new country so there were many opportunities and coveted spaces available for negotiation. Some wanted promotions, some wanted trade and business opportunities or lucrative postings. The nationalized enterprises also became a focal point of competition not only for the top positions but also for the money-making opportunities through the supply of raw materials and spare parts. There were also smaller enterprises that the government wanted to get off its hands, which too were available for negotiation.

This competition was not limited to individual attempts to seek privileges but often took on a more organized shape. Suitable platforms were constructed for the purpose under the freedom fighter banner initially but later in the name of various auxiliary components of the ruling political party that happened to be in power at any given point. While these institutions were meant to bolster support for the ruling regime particularly through control and dominance of the streets as needed, it also proved to be a useful mechanism with which to extract rent in their spare time. Leadership of these institutions, therefore, became sites of keen competition and contestation.

Bangladesh was heavily dependent on aid which financed imports of key commodities: (*a*) petroleum and petroleum products, (*b*) fertilizers and raw materials for fertilizers, (*c*) edible oil and oil seeds, (*d*) import policy financing, (*e*) development imports, (*f*) revenue imports, (*g*) feasibility studies and (*h*) project financing (Islam 1991). The most important was food aid, which was received in wheat, mainly under the USAID PL 480 programme. Over the period 1972–90, the contribution of aid as a percentage of GDP remained above 6 per cent. These aid-imports generated a complex web of direct and indirect benefits, creating further opportunities to traders, brokers, dealers, shipping agents, in addition to spawning a huge aid-dependent bureaucracy.

The first blight to strike Bangladesh after liberation was the 1974 famine whose after-effects reverberated through Dhaka. Alamgir (1980: 128–29) reports: 'By the end of August, the whole of Bangladesh turned into an agonizing spectacle of confusion and human suffering. With the addition of the flood, it was 1943 re-enacted. Streams of hungry people (men, women and children), who were nothing but skeletons, trekked into towns in search of food'. Further, reports suggest that there was a sharp rise in unclaimed dead bodies in the streets of Dhaka – perhaps up to 700 each month.[19]

The 1974 famine took its toll not only in terms of human misery and death but also undermining credibility of the ruling elite and was an important factor behind the subsequent upheavals witnessed in Dhaka, beginning with the assassination of Sheikh Mujib in 1975.

Dhaka turned into a hotbed of conspiracies, coups and counter coups, and further killings that would keep the country, and Dhaka in particular, in a perpetual state of political uncertainty for the rest of the decade. Whatever the political implications of these changes, it was clear that new interest groups would now be on the ascendant and would push out the older interest groups to the fringes.[20]

The 1970s also witnessed the emergence of another interesting fledgling group known at the time as the 'briefcase businessmen'. There was a large demand, immediately after the war, for many kinds of raw materials for supply to SOEs, including chemicals, yarn, cement, spares and so on. Thus, anyone who could get a contract to supply these could quickly make a lot of money from commissions from their international suppliers or 'principals'. This was a new business opportunity and those with connections and influence entered into this space quickly. The leading ones among them were people who had some exposure to the nature of the business from their salaried positions as managers or senior executives of now-abandoned, Pakistani businesses.[21] Some of these briefcase-carrying gentlemen did well but very few invested their new-found wealth, presumably preferring to stash it away in a safe offshore location.[22]

An example of how connections, location and history can combine to usher in enormous success may be cited here for illustration:

Group A is a well-known brand in Bangladesh with investments in numerous fields from RMG to pharmaceuticals, textiles to ceramics, and banks to LPG plants. It began as a modest trading house in the 1970s although even before liberation, the group owners – the R brothers – had significant family property in the shape of a jute mill that was later nationalized. The elder R was even offered a job by the government to run the mill as 'Managing Director', which he turned down and decided to focus on other opportunities.

Group A was originally owned by a European who was the agent of an airplane manufacturer who knew the Rs well and to whom he sold the business before he left the country. The R brothers immediately realigned their business strategy. They were able to access bank finance relatively smoothly which helped them to enter into the most profitable business of the moment – supplying clothes, food, edible oil and other essentials to a major parastatal, namely, the Trading Corporation of Bangladesh (TCB).

Given the acute foreign exchange crisis then, the brothers pleaded to be allowed to make the imports through barter deals, using Bangladesh's cash crops, such as jute and tea. They approached Bangabandhu, who refused the request, as the two items were reserved for government procurement. He, however, signalled that other 'non-traditional' items could be used instead. The brothers then successfully introduced the use of fish bones and frog-legs for the first time in place of jute or tea for barter deals.

The ability of Group A to mobilize bank financing lay in their close networks among the elite as well as their genuine entrepreneurial spirit. Today, it is one of the biggest 'group of companies' in the country with a turnover exceeding a billion dollars.[23] This story is certainly not unique in Bangladesh's contemporary history.

Two other examples may be readily cited. The first relates to the origins of one of the biggest leather goods manufacturer and exporter of the country, whose career began in a multinational bank in Dhaka. This young banker had come in contact with a Frenchman who was bringing in planeloads of chemicals for various public sector (SOE) clients. The business was doing well, and he needed help. At this point the young banker was approached if he wanted to partner up, and he promptly left his coveted salaried position in the pursuit of greater glory. This was the 'break' that led to the emergence of an industry leader in Dhaka.

A rather different perspective is provided by a humble entrepreneur, Mr A, a producer of cheap hand-rolled indigenous cigarettes, or *biri*, made from special dried leaves. This gentleman was the archetypal self-made man – with little education, no capital and hardly any social, political or elite connections, who still managed to build one of the largest business conglomerates in the country, recently signing a USD 1.5 billion deal with Japan's JT Group to whom he sold his tobacco interests.[24] It must be said that his journey began in colonial times so that by 1971 he already had a bit of capital to play with.

The use of easy bank loans with the intention of creating a business class had also begun by this time. Aid-financed specialized banks[25] began to invite applications for setting up 'industries' and those with a bit of capital came forward. These financing facilities looked the other way when investors came with proposals that showed highly inflated costs of machineries and equipment ('over-invoicing') knowing full well that the extra amount would be needed as working capital. Even default was generously dealt with – apparently with donors willingly participating in this charade (Sobhan 1991).[26]

Old Elite Capital and Old Capital

There are not many instances of old elite capital succeeding in the new climate. Those that survived the trauma of the 1971 war struggled initially and eventually had to yield to the younger, much more aggressive newcomers. The old elite were successful in a particular milieu that was rapidly becoming extinct. The new country, the new politics and the new power brokers presented new dynamics and new opportunities that needed different skills to negotiate with or around – which old elite capital found difficult to handle.

According to M. M. Akash (1987) cited in Siddiqui et al. (2010), there were 16 Bengali-owned elite business houses in the 1960s, and at the time of liberation the richest Bangladeshis owned an estimated 70–80 jute, textile and sugar mills, one bank and a few insurance companies. Another study reports that Bengali-owned businesses owned 53 per cent of fixed assets but only 28 per cent of industrial assets (Sobhan and Ahmad 1975). A. Riaz (1993) weighs into this debate with even more detailed data. He reports that by the late 1960s, public development banks (like Industrial Development Bank of Pakistan and Pakistan Industrial Credit and Investment Corporation) had provided financing to Bengali businessmen, as follows, apparently as part of President Ayub Khan's somewhat belated strategy to generate support in the Eastern Wing: 36 for jute mills, 25 for textile mills, 1 for a sugar mill; 16 loans to large jute traders; 12 to the inland water transport sector; 12 for insurance companies and 1 for a bank. There were 3 Bengali-owned banks in all. Thus, Riaz maintains, that by the late 1960s, a super-rich class of Bengalis had already emerged, located mostly in Dhaka but a few in Chittagong.

All of the Bengali-owned mills were nationalized in 1972 along with abandoned Pakistani-owned enterprises. In a way this made it difficult for the newly emerging pre-1971 Bengali elite capital to survive, although a few did succeed depending on their 'contacts'. Group A described above would certainly fall in this category.

Another excellent example is Group B, which began in 1958 as a small pharmaceutical firm. By the 1970s they had generated some capital but could still be described as a struggling, unremarkable entity. Their big breakthrough came after the enactment of the National Drug Policy, 1982 – a game changing piece of legislation that released immense entrepreneurial potential. Today, it is one of the largest conglomerates in Bangladesh with a turnover exceeding a billion dollars.

A somewhat unusual success story is perhaps that of the I Group – a leading business house dating back to the 1950s. Their ancestral roots were in Iran from where they had moved to India during British rule – drawn to Calcutta, which was then the capital of British India, later moving to Rangoon when it was being governed from Bengal, and finally settling in nearby Chittagong and Dhaka after eviction from Burma. There were other prominent (non-Bengali) business houses that relocated to the then East Pakistan from Rangoon at around the same time.

These, in particular, continued to thrive even in the new Bangladesh because of their ability to keep up with the times, to adapt and also because of their ability to handle succession issues over generations. The most important survival factor was perhaps their close relationship with Bangabandhu who, after 1971, had insisted that they return to Bangladesh.[27] There were a few other non-Bengali business houses that were similarly rehabilitated later on.

Thus, despite the turmoil, violence and famine of the 1970s, Dhaka was undergoing a reawakening with a new-found energy and sky-high aspirations that began to fundamentally realign and reshape its political and socio-economic landscape. The old rules and the old networks had become moribund. The new ones were still in the making so that there was plenty of space here for the brave, the aggressive and the desperate to make a fortune. Others would have to be content with somewhat less.

The uncertainty and instability of the time also resulted in a large-scale emigration of the sons of the elite and the upper middle classes. They saw no future in their Dhaka and were desperate to go abroad, usually in the name of 'higher studies'. While no numbers are available, it would be true to say that an entire generation of the urban, better-educated, more talented young people of the time left the country in droves, leaving Dhaka distinctly poorer in terms of its human capital base.

As those who could left the country, there was a flow in the opposite direction as a large number of Bengalis who were stranded in Pakistan during the war were now returning. These included 40,000 military personnel and unspecified numbers of bureaucrats, teachers, doctors, bankers, businessmen and students – altogether perhaps numbering 200,000 (Weinralib 1973). This was a significant addition to the human resources available to the new country, and especially to Dhaka, with the potential to make a significant contribution.

Another paradigm shift took place in the education sector: all English-medium schools were asked to convert to Bengali medium as the language of instruction. This set into motion a trend towards a steady erosion of English-language competence, especially in Dhaka where there existed significant capacity in English-medium instruction. Thus, a 200-year engagement with the language was put on hold only to be relaxed many years later, and then only selectively, and after much slippage in the level of English-language competence.

Thus, the 1970s saw both creation and destruction: old elite capital struggled hard and was pushed gradually to the margins, while the time had now come for old (non-elite) capital as well as brash new capital to fill up the vacuum. Political, economic and social spaces were being realigned to accommodate the new, emerging dynamics that were afoot.[28]

The 1980s: Game Changers and New Elites

Three major dynamics were put in motion by the early 1980s that would revolutionize Bangladesh's development trajectory and lay down the foundations of its emergent urban business class: first, the RMG sector was launched and it was beginning to arouse keen interest; second, migration of workers to the Middle East was growing; and third, the National Drug Policy was enacted by President General Ershad. The broad economic philosophy of Bangladesh moved decisively away from even the slightest nod to one of its constitutional pillars – 'socialism', which was quietly jettisoned, although still remaining in the books. Instead, Bangladesh adopted the IMF-led structural adjustment policies since 1982, thereby embarking on a process of adjustment and liberalization which was successfully carried out without major adverse effects (Gotur 1991; H. Rahman 1992).

General Ershad increasingly began to play the religion card, hoping thereby to garner some support from a particular section of society. He went as far as to amend the constitution to introduce Islam as the state religion, contravening the original, secular nature of the constitution.

On the political front, General Ershad struggled almost non-stop to achieve legitimacy, which he never quite managed to do. He held two presidential elections and a parliamentary election between 1985 and 1988, each time winning with a massive majority. Each time his elections were boycotted by the major political parties, leaving him with Pyrhhic victories bereft of political value. He eventually had to leave office in the face of massive street demonstrations in 1990.

Despite the inherent instability and uncertainty during Ershad's rule spanning much of the 1980s, the new economic dynamics referred to earlier did not stand still and indeed received considerable support and encouragement. People close to Ershad were well placed to benefit particularly from public sector contracts and ownership of denationalized industries.

International Migration

On the economic front, unprecedented opportunities arose before the nascent business classes in Dhaka and elsewhere. While international migration was mostly a rural phenomenon and therefore did not have a direct impact on Dhaka, its indirect effects nevertheless were enormous. A whole class of new 'manpower exporters' came into being. There was a scramble for orders for men to be fed into the frenetic petrodollar economies of the Middle East. Given the rate of expansion of manpower exports, the demand for brokerage services was large. These were poorly regulated, often exploitative and unscrupulous in their dealings resulting in one of the highest costs of migration per worker in the region (Afsar and Hossain 2020; RMMRU 2017). Nevertheless, necessary institutions and networks developed – primarily in the informal, private sector – and these were able to channel as many workers as was required from host countries, initially to the Middle East but later extending to East Asia (RMMRU 2017).

International migration generated large fortunes. There were numerous other spinoffs as well, the most significant being those related to the huge demand for brokerage services covering all aspects of the recruitment trade – obtaining visas and passports, issuing air tickets, arranging various documents and permissions, and selling employment contracts. Specialized training facilities also began to develop to better equip potential migrants including training in language and culture of host countries. The other side of the coin consisted of remittance flows that helped prop up the BOP. At the household level, it stimulated consumption and began to exert pressure on land prices. The large brokerage houses that were able to obtain lucrative employment visas from host partners sold these at highly marked up prices to ever-willing migrants. This became one of the fastest methods of making money in the 1980s and 1990s. This, however, was a business that lacked in respectability so that those who accumulated capital in this way would be eager to invest in other, more respectable areas.

The overwhelming grip of informal brokers or agents (*dalals*) over the migration process has been aptly described by RMMRU (2017), which reveals that there is no way out for migrant families other than to go to *dalals* who process the work permit or visa that is needed to work abroad. Even family visas for relatives of migrants are processed through these agents. In fact, the report observes that it is nearly impossible to migrate without the help of *dalals* who play a crucial role in the entire recruitment–migration process.[29] It is difficult to assess exactly how many agents operate in this area or what their turnovers are. Given the scale of migration – around 200,000 in 1995 and rising to over 700,000 in 2019 (BBS 2019, 2011)– the scale of their operations is immense, generating a significant class of streetsmart, efficient, economically mobile group, some of whom undoubtedly have become very rich. The richest among them would be undoubtedly based in Dhaka or perhaps Chittagong.

Pharmaceuticals

The pharmaceutical sector was under the complete control of MNCs in Bangladesh until 1982, when the National Drug Policy was enacted by General Ershad.[30] This was a paradigm shifting piece of legislation that succeeded in wresting control over the sector away from multinational corporations (MNCs). These companies produced drugs with API (active pharmaceutical ingredients) imported from their own parent companies at highly inflated prices. The new policy resulted in an opening up of the market. All existing licencing agreements with MNCs were revoked. Almost overnight, local pharmaceutical companies found the cost of their raw material imports drop to one-fifth of the previous level – revealing the extent of market distortion that MNCs had created.[31] Those local companies that were well positioned in the market already quickly responded to the opportunity. Square Pharmaceuticals, for example, became the number one company in the sector in just three years. Many others entered the fray to turn Bangladesh's pharmaceutical market into a unique success story.

According to Tapan Choudhury, director of Square, 'The sector is highly controlled and strictly regulated – there is no scope for manufacturers in this sector to cheat on quality or prices that are set by the government and carefully monitored.'[32] This has demonstrated that good governance is possible although there have been one or two scandals that erupted over the quality of drugs, for example, for children's paracetamol. The regulatory body, the Directorate of Drug Administration, is well reputed as a body that carries out its mandate with due diligence.[33] The sector enjoys policy support that allows duty free imports of raw materials and machinery and has now reached a point where significant exports to the US and EU markets are being made. It began as a USD 40 million industry in the early 1980s and by 2000 it reached 700 million. Today the market size stands at over USD 3 billion and industry leaders expect this to double in the next five years (J. Chakma 2020).

With the rise of pharmaceuticals, Dhaka witnessed the emergence of a new professional class of pharmacists, scientists as well as that of a skilled labour force able to work in an increasingly high-tech, modern environment.

The new business opportunity attracted attention from successful businessmen from other sectors. For example, BEXIMCO, which began as a trading house, now invested not only in RMG but also in pharmaceuticals, emerging as a top player in both. In the future, companies like Square and BEXIMCO would also be diversifying further into newer territories including textiles, banks, insurance, cosmetics and shipping – setting the tone and pattern of development of ambitious Bangladeshi business houses who, whatever their early origins, gradually gravitated to wherever opportunities were to be found. And of course, there seemed to be endless opportunity for those who were already well entrenched.

The new business environment also saw the departure of a number of MNCs who may have found the new environment less to their liking – certainly, it did not seem to be due to profitability issues (Zahid 2019).

Quite apart from the business opportunities provided by the National Drug Policy, the real beneficiaries were ordinary people who now had access to drugs at a fraction of the previous cost. Such developments are rare in any country's history. There is little doubt that cheap, affordable drugs had a significant impact on Bangladesh's much-applauded health sector performance.

RMG and Entrepreneurship

The momentum in RMG expansion was preceded by important changes in rural attitudes, especially among women. Fertility was declining as poor, illiterate women were 'miraculously' responding to contraception campaigns. Women were also the main beneficiary of micro-credit which had now become the most popular entry point for rural development projects. At the same time, the migration-led rush to the Middle East was accelerating and significant remittances were beginning to flow back into the countryside. These were major changes in an erstwhile quiet, traditional rural economy.

The arrival of RMG onto the scene was timely as witnessed by the large labour supply–response from rural women who flocked to urban centres, mainly to Dhaka, for industrial employment. Before this, the only opportunity of wage work for women was in domestic work where pay was low and the hours unregulated. This took the form of an avalanche that began with a trickle, which today has grown into a sea of 4.4 million workers, 80 per cent of whom are thought to be female although other sources suggest that the share may have dropped since the 1990s to around 55–60 per cent (ILO 2020).

Thus, the 1980s saw a growing number of women workers who began to alter Dhaka's demographic pattern. These were mostly young women under 29, generally single, poorly educated and almost entirely rural, who had to find accommodation with friends and relations in the various *bustee*s or shanties in the city.[34] The character of Dhaka streets began to alter. Once where few women were visible now a steadily increasing number were to be seen walking back and forth from their homes to the factories in small groups. A small economy also began to grow around these newcomers to the society who now had a bit of disposal income to play with.[35]

The game-changing role of the RMG sector was not in evidence even by the end of the 1980s. For example, Bakht and Bhattacharya (1991) and Sobhan (1991) in a rare review of the progress of industrialization in the 1980s make no mention of RMG or textiles at all, although the dynamics had already begun. Similarly, in their book on Dhaka based on survey material, Siddiqui et al. (2010) fail to record the presence of the women RMG workers in their 1985 survey. It would take a little longer for RMG to reveal its true power.

The 1990s: Taking Off

The period particularly after 1995 was decisive in leading Bangladesh towards its next, high-growth phase. After the unceremonious departure of General Ershad from power, a caretaker government took over the reins to oversee elections. By all accounts, the caretaker formula which was introduced and written into law delivered a 'free and fair' election – proving that credible elections can be held in a poor country. The right of centre, the BNP, came to power with 140 seats in parliament out of 300 while the main opposition, the AL, had obtained 88 seats. Ershad's Jatiya Party (JP) had 35 seats while the right wing Jamaat-i-Islami (JI) obtained 18 seats. This created space for the two smaller parties to influence the balance in parliament. This was significant for both JP and JI who were fighting for survival and therefore needed to demonstrate credibility. These elections appear to have enabled just that.

Given Ershad's nearly decade-long rule, one would expect that a whole new class of beneficiaries were created from the ranks of his loyalists that consisted of people from the usual mix of sources – bureaucracy, military, civil society and some who had deserted other parties to join him. They would now have to lie low for a while and regroup later to resurface. The top leadership would have sufficient resources to tide over these temporary difficulties. In fact, opportunity came sooner than expected as after his fall in December 1990, and serving a jail sentence, he re-emerged as a pivotal political figure. This allowed Ershad and his party cadres to regain relevance, to survive, and in some cases, even to thrive. More importantly, it provided Ershad and his party with a modicum of safety and security to their persons, as well as to the considerable wealth that they reportedly accumulated.[36] In particular, Kochanek (1993) reports that although corruption is widely perceived to be high in Bangladesh, the Ershad regime stood out as perhaps the most corrupt in the country's history.

On the economic front, as macro-economic stability was achieved on the back of economic liberalization policies adopted with strong encouragement from the IMF–World Bank, growth picked up, with the annual compound growth rate rising to 4.8 per cent in the 1990s compared to 4.4 per cent in the earlier decade. Per capita income remained low at USD 370 compared to the South Asian average of USD 440 and the low-income country average of USD 410 (Bakht, Yunus and Salimullah 2002).

While the politics of the day kept the populace entertained, the business community became fully alert to the potential of RMG. The business models had become familiar by now and the ease of entry and the relatively small amount of capital needed attracted entrepreneurs by the hundreds. As discussed earlier in Chapter 7, the use of the back-to-back LC to finance RMG-related imports played a crucial role in enabling the all-important working capital problems to be solved. The data is self-evident and illustrates this dramatically: In 1983–84, RMG exports were just beginning, totalling USD 31.6 million (3.9 per cent of exports). This rose to just over USD 624 million in 1989–90 and over USD 4.3 billion in 1999–2000 (around 76 per cent of exports). Today, in 2019–20, RMG exports have exceeded USD 27 billion, accounting for 83 per cent of all exports.[37]

The RMG success laid the foundation for the development of Bangladesh's independent entrepreneurial class. The pioneers saw the opportunity and used all their influence to bring about conditions which allowed even complete novices to enter the sector. They came from every occupation: retired civil servants and army officers, university professors, small businessmen with some capital. Of course, entry required a certain amount of capital which the entrepreneurs were able to raise in a myriad number of ways. An important component of this is believed to be from sale of land whose price, in the meantime, had risen by leaps and bounds. The traditional leniency that one came to almost expect from the public sector banks did not disappoint.

By the end of the decade, Dhaka was literally surrounded by garments factories often operating from makeshift premises hurriedly setup to keep pace with the rapid demand. There was inadequate attention given to compliance details, including safety measures. In the 1990s, these had not yet become matters of international concern. Those who had one factory wanted to set up another and their successes drew more people into the business. There was a lot of foreign interest as well, but it seems this sector was unofficially declared as being only for locals. The trade associations and business leaders informally influenced the government to discourage 'opening up too soon', raising fears that this could swamp the indigenous development initiatives in evidence. The argument was that foreign investment should go into areas in which locals could not, for technical or other reasons. A few large foreign investors do operate in RMG, but these are generally in the EPZs.

The sector is dominated by Bangladeshi capital, unlike say in many East Asian countries where foreign investment is often central. Both Cambodia and Vietnam are excellent examples of this. However, greater foreign investment in Vietnam, mainly Chinese capital, appears to have led to more product diversification and higher value added compared to Bangladesh.

RMG success also led to strong backward linkages leading to a phenomenal growth in textiles output, allowing the RMG industry to source most of its yarn and a significant part of its fabric requirement locally instead of from imports and generating a second round of intense industrialization. This story is worthy of note because of the strong interplay of entrepreneurship and policy support that enabled the rise of textile manufacture. These backward linkages took root from the mid-1990s onwards. Thus, between RMG and textiles, the Dhaka business class expanded manifold with the entry of both new capital and older trade capital into the sector.

Gradually, as discussed earlier, many new sectors began to emerge including construction and real estate, led by public infrastructure investments and private demand for factories and housing – in turn setting in motion the manufacturing of construction material like steel and cement. The services sector soon followed suit, including growing private investment in banks, insurance companies, and later in telecom and media. The Dhaka Stock Exchange was also launched anew in this period. In other words, suitable reforms were carried out by the state to enact regulations to allow private banks and regulate the Dhaka Stock Exchange through the Securities and Exchange Commission, hoping to breathe new life into these moribund sectors.[38]

Important developments occurred not only in the financial sector but also in telecom with at least two new mobile phone companies given a licence to operate – in 1994 and 1996 – breaking the monopoly of the lone cell phone company (Citycell) until then.[39]

The 1990s therefore set the stage for the emergence of Bangladesh's conglomerates referred to locally as 'Group of Industries'. Those with capital and the right connections soon headed out to lobby for licences to set up banks, television channels, FM radio stations, newspapers and so on – spreading out in many directions. These were now becoming rich, powerful and numerous enough to influence politics and policy. The worry though is that it is indicative of growing concentration of wealth, narrowing avenues for new entrepreneurship, growing crony-tainted capital and perhaps a precursor to the emergence of oligarchic trends.

Dhaka in the New Century

The new century began with fresh elections under another caretaker government, once again resulting in a transfer of power – this time from the AL to the BNP in 2001. While the two parties have an intense, even visceral dislike for each other, their economic philosophies and class interests have come to be identical. This unstated consensus tends to be disrupted from time to time due to factional tensions, patronage and *tadbir*, which could put businesses too close to the opposition in disadvantage. Thus, when a particular party comes to power, the occasion is a celebration by its leaders as well as its rank and file – all of whom expect to be well rewarded for their role in bringing their party to power. These raw aspirations can easily get out of hand, especially during the initial euphoria of victory, and thus needs to be carefully managed.[40]

The new century saw the intensification of trends that began earlier in the 1990s with a number of sectors gaining particular momentum, including private commercial banks, media and television, telecom, travel and tourism, ICT and start-ups, MFS, electronics and light engineering, consumer durables, e-commerce – the last receiving a huge boost from COVID-19. The important thing about these new sectors was that younger, new, ideas-based investors came forward and gave a boost to existing capital that was already beginning to look old, tired and uninspired.

Even among older capital, there was a distinct leadership change among many groups, from first generation pioneers to their better-educated, more polished, IT-savvy progeny with a foreign (generally US) degree in business or IT. In other words, the character, nature, and demographics of the elite were undergoing change in Dhaka. On the other hand, the sea change outlined in terms of the qualitative and quantitative expansion of businesses operating mostly from the capital, also implied changes down the line – to the emergence of a new, much larger, urban middle class and a vast proletarian labour force – each group sharing the city's resources and services in its own distinct, insulated and unequal way.

Major political changes emerged that threatened to put an end to the see-saw power sharing arrangement that had developed after each election conducted under the caretaker formula. The caretaker government that took over in 2006 to oversee the next election extended its three-month tenure to two years with the support of the military – ostensibly to clean up corruption. While most observers felt that this in fact did produce some initial results, the move quickly became mired in controversy with allegations of corruption involving the caretaker government itself as well as its military backers.

When finally elections were held and the new AL government came back to power with a landslide victory, it took the bold step of scrapping the caretaker formula altogether on the ground that it was 'undemocratic'. The AL has remained in power ever since, in the meantime consolidating its political position considerably. It has won every election subsequently, with a landslide victory every time! Whatever the fate of democracy as a result, one thing is certain: the political stability experienced by Bangladesh for a period of over 12 years has yielded a 'peace dividend' in the form of sustained economic growth unprecedented in its history.

The prolonged AL rule has also meant that the business classes close to the AL have prospered much more than others. Thus, past finance ministers have sometimes had to go on record to state that they were under pressure to grant licences for banks, for example, on 'political grounds' – having a licence to operate a bank had by then become one of the most sought-after status symbols and milking cow combined, much favoured by crony capital (*New Age* 2018). A similar story could be told for other sensitive sectors, like the media – which too became almost completely dominated by those close to the ruling regime. The crony control over banks and other sensitive sectors like the media was not merely just a sharing of patronage but was also meant to consolidate political power.

Group Dynamics: The Rise of Conglomerates

A database has been constructed from secondary sources including newspaper reports and supplements, as well as relevant websites to piece together a development narrative of some of the major Bangladeshi conglomerates. There are 44 conglomerates in the database which constitute some of the largest entities. It is uncertain how many such entities there are altogether, although it is likely that these 44 represent a significant proportion, perhaps a third or more of the total.[41] The data reported are based on a series of reports on the 'giants of industry' published throughout 2012 by a prominent vernacular business daily *Bonik Barta*.

This data was compiled and updated by reviewing other published material and visiting group websites (see Table 10A.1 to this chapter).

The data obtained includes the historical trajectory of company formation and expansion, core areas, expansion along value chains, export orientation, role of the RMG-textiles sector, employment and turnover, and location – specifically whether located in or around Dhaka. A number of observations emerge from the data, as discussed here.

Unexpectedly, we find quite a significant number of groups whose origins, often humble, actually date well back to pre-Liberation times. A total of 14 groups (31.8 per cent) fall into this category. Others emerged in the 1970s–90s, but their numbers tapered off quite dramatically after 2000. The decadal distribution was 15.9 per cent (1970s); 27.3 per cent (1980s); 20.5 per cent (1990s). Only two entities traced their origin to after 2000.

Dhaka and its surroundings were the preferred destination for most enterprises. However, 9 groups (20 per cent) are based in Chittagong, the port city that is a major commercial and shipping centre. The concentration of business activity in both these cities but especially Dhaka has changed the character and composition of its inhabitants.

The other common assumption often made is that the RMG and textile sector that dominates exports is also the basis of resurgent capitalism in the country. While that may well be true, it is interesting to note that RMG and textiles do not have such a large footprint on the activity of these conglomerates. A total of 9 groups (20 per cent) were found to have core engagement with RMG and were heavily concentrated in its value chain. However, 22 groups (50 per cent) had some exposure to RMG or textiles even if this was not their main sector of interest.

Initial capital appears to have been generated primarily through trading and shopkeeping (38.6 per cent). Only 5 groups made their initial money through RMG and only 1 generated capital from labour exports. In general, each group had almost 20 companies in its portfolio (ranging from 3 to 38). Although there is a clear tendency to remain within its core value chain initially, most groups appear to have expanded in many directions from shipping, real estate to agribusiness, tourism or finance. Within value-chain units as a percentage of total units per group is 43 per cent (Table 10A.1).

These 44 conglomerates constitute some of the major business houses that dominate the economic and business landscape of Dhaka and Chittagong. It is likely that the number of big entities has grown since further expanding their economic footprint in newer directions or along new value chains. The total number of 'large' business groups today, in 2020, as noted earlier, is likely to exceed 100.[42] On average, they employ over 18,000 workers and have a turnover in excess of BDT 4,800 crores (around half a billion dollars).

It was found that a third of the older groups are in decline or embroiled in legal trouble with financiers for defaulting on loans or falling out among the successors over control of shares. In some cases, a clear political hand is noticeable as well. Thus, two entities, namely Partex Holdings and Meghna Kha, have separated from the parent group. Another three along with Partex Holdings are in disarray, clearly on the decline due to political–legal–financial misalignments. These include Crystal Group, Pacific Group and SA Group.[43]

The Middle Class

Concern about the state of the middle class is universal. There is, however, no universally accepted definition of what constitutes this elusive concept. Definitions that have been attempted range from a wholly subjective set of criteria to a highly specific income measure, and everything else in between. Therefore, before setting out to explore how the Dhaka middle class has evolved, it is important to clarify who or what constitutes the middle class as specifically as possible. Three dimensions are often referred to in this context: an economic dimension measured by income ('cash'), an educational dimension ('credentials') and a social dimension (approximated by 'culture').[44]

Karl Marx and Frederick Engels thought of the middle class as consisting of uninspiring individuals lacking in ingenuity while others have taken a more positive view.[45] Economists have tended to focus mainly on income in constructing a definition of the middle class but even there the options advanced are numerous.

Easterly (2001) used a relative definition of middle class as those between the 20th and 80th percentiles of the income distribution; Birdsall, Graham and Pettinato (2000) take the middle class to be those within 75 per cent to 125 per cent of the median income distribution; Banerjee and Duflo (2008) chose an absolute definition in terms of consumption (between USD 2 and USD 10 [2005 PPP USD]); Kharas and Gertz (2010) examine a richer set of individuals making between USD 10 and USD 100 (2005 PPP USD) per day, and so on.

A middle class *bhadrolok* social segment has been in existence in Bengal but centred in Kolkata for over 200 years, especially among Bengali Hindu upper caste folks – the term however referred to not only economic status but perhaps more importantly to educational, social and cultural status. It reflected a person who was economically well off or at least solvent, was educated, often 'Western' in orientation although Bengali in outlook, and who, as a gentleman, would not engage in manual labour. In fact, the *bhadrolok babu* constituted the backbone of the British colonial administration in Bengal. A similar *bhadrolok* class also emerged later among the Muslims of Bengal (and in what is today Bangladesh).[46]

The Muslim *bhadrolok* class was much smaller in number and was not able to reproduce fast enough in modern Bangladesh, particularly after 1971 in the face of rapid economic, demographic and social changes. While the new, emergent middle classes acquired the economic power of the *bhadrolok*, the associated social and cultural norms and practices may not have had time to ferment. In other words, today's middle class is mostly new, upwardly mobile and a product of the economic transformation brought on by globalization and a new division of labour. While it has had reasonable access to what is generally considered to be a declining quality of education, it is perhaps less 'Western' in its values, less urbane and perhaps less secular than their *bhadrolok* counterparts. Thus, the few attempts to assess the size of the middle class in Bangladesh have been made to assess the size of *this* economic middle class (B. Sen 2010; ADB 2010).

From South Town to North Town

The new middle class expanded quickly and contributed to a new demographic shift in which the character of the neighbourhood, or *para*, changed. The *bhadrolok*s were concentrated in the old town, south of the Ramna area of Dhaka and the High Court. These areas were then regarded as upmarket residential districts with quiet lanes, single-storeyed bungalow-style houses with large verandahs and front and back courtyards. The northern fringes of Dhaka were occupied by farmlands as well as a large military cantonment.

The first major housing project undertaken by the government was the Azimpur Estate where apartment buildings were constructed for First and Second Class government officers – the former in the more spacious 'new colony' and the latter in the 'old colony'. The colonies were vast consisting of several hundred four-storeyed structures with two apartments on each floor. This was where the bulk of the Dhaka government officer class was concentrated – indeed it would not be wrong to refer to this group as *bhadrolok*s. The Azimpur Estate was also the first-generation apartment housing complex in the country but became a model for similar developments in other areas of town, for example, for Dhaka University teachers in the Ramna area.

In the 1950s and 1960s, two other major housing development projects were taken up, namely the Dhanmondi Residential Area and the Gulshan Model Town. The concept was to acquire and develop farmland, install utilities, establish 'plots' and then hand these out on long-term leases to different beneficiaries. Unlike in Azimpur where one was a tenant, these developments allowed the *bhadrolok*s to actually own the land on which they could construct their homes. The owners were bureaucrats, military officers, prosperous businessmen, politicians, university teachers, doctors and lawyers – that is, everyone who had influence or could curry favour, or *tadbir*.[47] The owner–residents of Dhanmondi and Gulshan formed the basis of the new elite. Other developments also sprouted up – for Biharis north of Dhanmondi, in Mohammedpur and Mirpur, and for the middle-middle and lower middle classes, in Uttara, further north.

The class mobility route had now taken a spatial dimension. The most important recognition of this became one's residential address. An aspiring and ambitious person would come to Dhaka from the village and find a foothold in the old town first. Once he had done well, his dream would be to move to Dhanmondi or even to Gulshan – the latter being the ultimate statement of arrival. In reality, the move happened in stages: first to the old town, then to Azimpur or some other intermediate zone like the university campus housing for teachers, or to solid middle-class areas like Elephant Road, Mirpur or Uttara, and then on to Dhanmondi or Gulshan. This slow movement became accelerated. It was evident that the new middle class had money and there was a massive pent-up demand for housing in Dhanmondi and Gulshan, and indeed all over town. This led to the apartment construction boom where landowners joined up with real estate investors to construct multi-storeyed apartments for sale – an entirely new concept in the 1980s and 1990s. While it was no longer possible to buy land in Dhanmondi or Gulshan because of the exorbitant price inflation, the middle-middle and upper middle classes could now aspire to at least buy an apartment in these areas.

Most of the original Dhanmondi residents moved to Gulshan or abroad after selling their land to developers or making an apartment-share deal, while people from everywhere else, especially from the old town, came in droves and settled in the new apartments that mushroomed there. In other words, the residents of Gulshan (and the adjoining Banani and Baridhara) now house the old elite *bhadrolok*s as well as the new business elites, along with younger, successful professionals from the private sector. The character of Dhanmondi began to change – consisting of left-behind *bhadrolok* mixed up with the new middle class competing for social recognition. The old town and other areas throughout Dhaka came firmly under the control of the lower and middle-middle classes.

In the process, however, apartment complexes of various sizes and price ranges arose, completely dominating the Dhaka residential landscape. The quiet Dhaka consisting mostly of one- or two-storeyed houses of the 1970s–90s has disappeared. There are now two types of accommodation – in apartments and in shanties. And thus, the apartment residents are all middle class – ranging from the lower middle class to the upper-upper middle class. Even the rich elite now live in apartments – very large ones of course – located in the best areas of town in North Dhaka.

The government's sale of land to *bhadrolok*s has been a regular feature of official policy that continues to be practiced to this day. The number of plots, the size of land or its quality and location – all reflect the status of the beneficiary and his or her location in the patronage pecking order. These lands are distributed at well-below market rates and immediately upon distribution command a price that is many times that of the government price. In fact, this has been an important avenue of 'creating' capital for the *bhadrolok* class that requires little more than appropriate connections or a high-status occupation.

It is difficult to assign numbers but a study by B. Sen (2010) and a cross-country study from ADB (2010) estimates the size of the national economic middle class at around 20–22 per cent in 2010 compared to 9 per cent in 1992. Sen adopted an income definition of USD 2–3 per capita per day as describing a middle-class person and an income of USD 3–4 for an upper-middle-class person – with middle class and middle income seemingly confounded. The definition used by the ADB (2010) defines middle class, again in terms of per capita income as those who earn USD 2–20 per day.[48] The proportion of the population with a per capita income of USD 2–4 was described as vulnerable middle class and estimated at 16.4 per cent while those falling in the range of USD 4–20 were the non-vulnerable middle class estimated at only 3.9 per cent. The ADB study estimates that the middle class increased at a slower pace than suggested by Sen, by just over 8 per cent instead of 11 per cent.

The Labour Force Survey 2016–17 gives us another perspective on the middle class by enabling us to review what proportion of those employed are engaged in white-collar occupations. We note that of the 4.57 million women in the labour force, 27 per cent were in white-collar occupations. In aggregate, total employment was 16.9 million of which 17.7 per cent were in white-collar occupations (Table 10.3).

As to be expected, there is a difference in estimates due to definitional differences used but these appear to be consistent. After some 10 years of sustained growth of 6–8 per cent, the size of the economic middle class in 2020 is likely to be at least 30 per cent for the country as a whole, and possibly as high as 50 per cent for Dhaka city.[49]

B. Sen (2010) also attempted to construct a middle-class profile: Around 48 per cent were employed in the private sector, 96 per cent had a bank account, over 24 per cent had a fixed deposit, more than 61 per cent had an internet connection, 49 per cent owned urban land, 33 per cent owned a flat and

Table 10.3 White-collar occupations (2016–17), urban areas

Occupational Category White Collar	Total Number ('000)	Per Cent	Women Number	Per Cent
Managers	647	3.82	74	1.62
Professionals	1,353	7.99	522	11.42
Technicians and associate professionals	556	3.33	84	1.84
Clerical support workers	436	2.57	79	1.73
Sub total (white collar)	2,992	17.66	759	16.61
All occupations	16,943	100	4,570	100

Source: Based on BBS (2019).

31 per cent received a rental income. A significant proportion had a preference for English-medium education for their wards (23.5 per cent).

These attempts at assigning a number to the middle class does little justice, however, to the broader, more nuanced concept of the *bhadrolok* middle class – a class which appears to have diminished in relative terms, and perhaps even in absolute terms. A trend towards a regeneration of this class would serve to create a more enlightened, urbane culture that would be pro-democratic, more liberal, more tolerant and more sophisticated. Such a class would be a tremendous socio-economic asset to the civic life of the city and the nation.

Profile of the Dhaka Middle Class in 2021

An attempt was made to update the profile of Dhaka's middle class through an online survey conducted in March 2021 launched from the Facebook page of BIDS. A wide range of middle-class neighbourhoods were targeted, obtaining responses from a total of 5,150 respondents (households). The profile of this sample is provided in Table 10.4 covering education, employment, income, assets and culture.

The sample respondents are generally male (92 per cent), relatively young with an average age of 35 years with over a fifth who are students and a third who are seeking employment. They belong loosely to the economic middle class encompassing both the vulnerable low or lower middle class, comprising 51 per cent with monthly incomes of at least BDT 20,000 (USD 234) or the non-vulnerable middle class with a monthly income of over BDT 50,000 (USD 585) – comprising 49 per cent. The average family size of respondent households is 3.72, that is, considerably lower than the national average given a younger demographics and a significant number of single-member households (31.2 per cent).

Table 10.4 Dhaka: Profile of the middle class

Variable	Per Cent*	Remarks
Age (years)	35.8	
Gender (male)	92	
Education		
Medium (Bangla)	98.2	
Education above HSC	43.02	Respondents are young with many still studying
Education above BA	8.99	
Father's education (above HSC)	75.1	Father's education better reflects 'status'
Father's education (above BA)	15.2	
Mother's education (above SSC)	48.8	
Mother's education (above HSC)	22.4	
Grandfather's education (above HSC)	22.4	
Income above BDT 30K per month	61.7	
Income above BDT 50K per month	48.8	
Accommodation		
Own apartment	33.6	
Years in Dhaka	17.8	
Years in current address	8.9	
Lives alone	31.2	
Employment		
Public	13.7	
Private	41.6	
Own business	33.6	
Rental income	11.2	
Assets		
Car	11.2	
Fridge	76.8	
Land	46.4	
Motorbike	33.5	
Smartphone	80.8	
TV	65.6	

(*Contd.*)

Dhaka: Capital Formation

Table 10.4 (*Contd.*)

Variable	Per Cent*	Remarks
Computer	75.9	
AC	11.2	
Culture		
Own books	73.6	
Read English books	46.4	
Read Bangla books	95.2	
Participate in cultural events	53.6	
Newspaper subscription	88.2	
Liberal papers		
Daily Star (English)	52.3	Surprising finding – rising interest in English
Prothom Alo (Bengali)	57.7	
Jugantor (Bengali)	25.2	
Music		
Own musical instrument	19.2	
Wi-fi	83.9	
Listen to music	88.2	
Nazrul	70.3	Surprising finding – generally associated with a more 'Islamic' orientation
Rabindranath	39.7	Generally associated with a more secular, 'Bengali' orientation
Modern Bengali	62.2	
Band	60.3	
Western pop	30.6	
Bollywood	23.5	Interesting finding – generally thought to be widely popular

Source: Online survey conducted by author.
Note: *Or as indicated.

In terms of education, 43 per cent of respondents have passed high school (Higher Secondary Certificate, or HSC) and 9 per cent have a bachelor's degree. Among respondents' fathers, 75 per cent have a high school degree and over 15 per cent have a graduate or post-graduate qualification. This does not mean that younger people are less qualified; it simply reflects that a large number of respondents are still studying (22.4 per cent). Education of respondents has been overwhelmingly in Bengali-medium schools. However, among the 1,152 school-going children reported by respondent households, 50 per cent study in English-medium schools with little difference between sons and daughters on this score.

The respondents have reported living in Dhaka for over 18 years on average and in their current address for more than nine years. In other words, they are not recent arrivals from the countryside and generally came to Dhaka with their parents at a young age.

Employment is provided overwhelmingly by the private sector as salaried workers (42 per cent) or as self-employed businessmen (33.6 per cent). Public sector employment accounts for only 13.7 per cent of jobs. In other words, self-employment in small businesses appears to have emerged as an important and presumably rising category, easing somewhat the pressure for public sector jobs – which, however, continues to dominate the job market in aspirational terms even though in practice only a small number of aspirants can be absorbed annually in public administration.

The hallmark of a rising middle class is its acquisition of consumer durables. The sample reported widespread access to Wi-Fi (84 per cent) and ownership of laptops or computers and smartphones (76 per cent and 81 per cent). Ownership of a fridge and colour television (TV) came next at 77 per cent and 66 per cent – presumably, many are relying on the internet to access TV shows and other types of media on their phones or computers as well. Interestingly, ownership of urban land was 46.4 per cent – slightly lower than what Sen reported in 2010. Other assets reported include motor bikes (33.5 per cent), cars (11.2 per cent) and air conditioners (11.2 per cent).

The cultural profile of the middle class is also an important aspect of its maturity and character. This was captured by exploring access to books, newspaper reading habits, musical preferences, and engagement with cultural events.

Ownership of books was reported by 74 per cent of respondents with 46 per cent stating that they read English-language books and 95 per cent reporting reading Bengali-language books. At the same time, over 88 per cent reported subscribing to a newspaper – most commonly the Bengali-language *Prothom Alo* (57 per cent) followed by the English-language *Daily Star* (52 per cent). It was interesting to find the relative popularity of liberal, more independent-minded newspapers on the one hand and the high appeal for an English-language newspaper as well on the other. The first reflects the desire for objective, broadly liberal news media able to criticize the government while the latter, in addition, to have a better familiarity with English.

Other important newspapers reported were *Bangladesh Protidin* (29.7 per cent), *Jugantor* (25.2 per cent), *Kaler Kantha* (4.5 per cent), *New Age* (4.5 per cent) and others (25.2 per cent). These together comprise of a wide spectrum of political and ideological positions encompassing far-right religious sentiments as well as left-leaning or pro-government voices.

The musical taste of the respondents is also quite revealing. The most popular are Nazrul songs (70.3 per cent) followed by 'modern Bengali songs' (67.7 per cent) and local band music (60.3 per cent). The more sophisticated songs of Rabindranath Tagore have a rating of 39.7 per cent, while Western pop and Bollywood songs have ratings of 30.6 per cent and 23.5 per cent. Around 20 per cent of respondents also reported owning a musical instrument.

In other words, the middle class appears to be well informed, with good access to the media including social media, is liberal minded, prefers Bangladeshi band music to Western or Bollywood music and also shows a marked preference for Nazrul songs over, say, songs of Rabindranath – a symbolic marker for a growing preference perhaps for a greater Islamic cultural orientation as opposed to those who tend to identify with more 'Bengali' or secular values. This is a broad generalization based on a middle class understanding of sociocultural markers in the Bangladeshi context.

Thus, a strong economic and cultural middle class has emerged and expanded dramatically over the last 50 years. This middle class is far more diverse and prone to adopt modern consumer durables and appear to be in sync with modern culture (represented by Band music) but still anchored in more traditional cultural forms (represented by Nazrul and Rabindranath songs, as well as 'modern' Bengali songs).[50] This class remains broadly anti-establishment, in keeping with the ethos of the pre-1971 period (reflected in the type of newspaper subscriptions).

The Working Class

The Dhaka shanty towns have grown enormously as a result of the economic boom fuelled by industrialization, expansion in storage, transport and construction, as well as the expansion in trade, transport and services. This meant a transformation from largely informal employment of the workforce to more formal employment, although even today formal employment as a proportion of total employment in the economy remains small (Afsar and Hossain 2020; Siddiqui et al. 2010).

Dhaka's working classes appear to consist of garment workers, other industrial workers, workers engaged in transport services like rickshaw pulling, drivers of buses and autorickshaws, mechanics and repairmen, domestic workers, Fourth

Class employees of the government, equivalent staff in the private sector and vast numbers of self-employed people like petty traders, retail workers, small shopkeepers and so on. They tend to concentrate in the shanties, although some from among them may be found in apartments living under sublet arrangements or in shared 'messes' in lower-end accommodation. Afsar and Hossain (2020) report reduced congestion in the shanties, better quality of accommodation in terms of construction material used and improved quality of services with regard to utilities and sanitation in the face of rising incomes. This is reflected in reduction of poverty which had fallen to 35 per cent in 2010 compared to 50 per cent in 1998 and 90 per cent in 1991 (Afsar and Hussain 2020: 291). The impression is that basic household equipment like electric fans, fridge, television and mobile phones have also become objects of familiarity even in the shanties (Table 10.5).

The shanty population has experienced an explosion, rising to 5 million in 2012–13 from 1.1 million in 1996. More recent estimates are not available; one would expect this figure, however, to be hovering around 7–8 million in 2020. It is interesting to note that the numerous shanties are scattered all over town often in marginal, lowlands with houses built on stilts, or government-owned land, typically controlled by local gangs who construct flimsy rooms for renting out. Utility services are informally provided as formal connections cannot be given to addresses that are not officially recognized.

The shanties are thus located in both upmarket neighbourhoods as well as in poorer ones, depending on where suitable spaces could be found and taken over. There is a strong preference for the inhabitants to be located in areas that are within walking distance to their place of work, and given poor urban planning and enforcement, commercial, industrial and residential spaces, including shanties, are interwoven together in the same physical spaces.

The official policy towards shanty towns is terribly inconsistent. There are periodic drives to evict people from 'illegally' occupied land which is sometimes required for building a road, freeing up a canal or construction of government offices. At other times, these are half-hearted moves that cause temporary dislocation, even distress, only for the *status quo ante* to be quickly resumed.

Table 10.5 Number of shanties and their population in Dhaka

	1976	1996	2012–13
Shanties	10	2,156	4,966
Population	10,000	1,100,000	5,000,000

Sources: Nazrul (1996); UNICEF (2013a).

There is also the fact that the labour force located in the shanties are needed by businesses and the economy, and any attempt to move them out *en masse* will not be acceptable to the powerful business lobbies.

And a Growing Grey Zone?

As with any large, complex city, there is crime – at one extreme there is white-collar crime conducted through financial scams and embezzlement of public finances through connivance and default, and crimes committed by manipulating public procurement rules, for example, and at the other, crimes that involve drugs, smuggling, trafficking, kidnap and ransom. It is reasonable to assume that these are conducted within networks of power, influence and money, with well-delineated jurisdictions and rules for sharing the proceeds. While the specific sector will differ, the basic mechanism for extracting rent is familiar: intermediaries mediate every large transaction – stronger the intermediary, more lucrative the transaction, and the spoils are then shared out in proportion to power and authority within the network. This is an area that exists, appears to be extensive and involves vast sums of money, if various media reports are to be believed.[51] This is only mentioned in passing but no analysis or attempts to provide further evidence one way or the other will be made. Suffice it to say, the emergence of a powerful, 'honest and self-righteous' *bhadrolok* class would be useful to battle a phenomenon which one hopes has not proceeded beyond repair.

Conclusion

Dhaka has grown from a sleepy provincial town to a roaring metropolis, and is the political, cultural and economic heart of the country contributing some 40 per cent to the national GDP. This is not surprising as the population of Dhaka is larger than that of many countries. It is the centre of urban-based industrialization duly supported by a vast and complex transport, storage, handling and financial infrastructure.

The socio-economic and cultural character of Dhaka has also changed. There is now a relatively large, well-entrenched rich business class led by a super-rich segment consisting of powerful conglomerates – which did not exist in the 1970s and 1980s. The middle class too has grown dramatically in structure and composition. It had consisted of a small, educated segment of the population deriving their livelihoods from employment in the public sector supplemented by a significant flow of food and other agricultural produce from their villages as rent from their agricultural land. Today, this middle class is vast, consisting of a significant professional segment of bankers, teachers, lawyers, business executives, journalists in electronic and print media, in addition to white-collar factory workers, technicians, small entrepreneurs and service-sector providers. In other words, there was a time when the old middle classes were closely networked. Currently, this is impossible as there are many middle classes in Dhaka today, each operating within their own sphere.

The working-class character has also changed. The shanties are numerous but better equipped with services. Dire poverty no longer stands out and unemployment is low. In fact, while the dominant profile of shanty dwellers in the past consisted of transport workers, petty traders and low-income service providers, today the dominant category consists of industrial workers in addition to transport sector operatives and low-income salaried workers in the private or government sector.

In other words, despite all the challenges that Dhaka faces as a least 'liveable' city with one of the worst air quality levels in the world, it has performed a stellar role in supporting Bangladesh's 50-year journey towards economic prosperity.

Annex

Table 10A.1 Firm level data on large firms and conglomerates collated from the daily *Bonik Barta* and company websites

SL	Name of Group	Year of Establishment	Employees	Turnover	No. of Companies in Group	RMG/ Textiles units – number	Number of Exporting Units	Whether RMG/ Tex core	No. of Units in Value Chain	Location: Dhaka =1	Initial Business	Major Investment Sectors
1	ACI	1992	9,147	6,948	20	0	4	No	11	1	Chemicals	Agribusiness; RMG; Shipping
2	Akhtar	1976	n/a	5,000	17	1	1	No	9	1	Furniture shop	Real estate; RMG
3	Akij	1950	70,000	20,000	34	1	1	No	4	1	Making handmade *bidi*	Textiles; Real estate; Agribusiness; Shipping
4	Ambia	1965	3,000	n/a	24	4	2	No	7	2	Construction	Construction; Ship breaking; Steel
5	BSM	1985	3,000	1,500	9	2	2	No	2	2	Trading in spices	Textiles; Banking; Real estate; Shipping
6	Deshbandhu	1989	15,000	n/a	27	4	9	No	9	1	Trading in fertilisers	Textile; Real estate; Shipping
7	East Coast	1977	n/a	n/a	32	0	2	No	12	2	Oil trading	Banking; Shipping; Real estate
8	Essack	1955	1,390	n/a	5	0	0	No	2	2	Brick making	Shipping; Real estate

(*Contd.*)

Table 10A.1 (Contd.)

SL	Name of Group	Year of Establishment	Employees	Turnover	No. of Companies in Group	RMG/Textiles units – number	Number of Exporting Units	Whether RMG/Tex core	No. of Units in Value Chain	Location: Dhaka =1	Initial Business	Major Investment Sectors
9	IFAD	1985	3,000	6,375	12	0	0	No	10	1	Auto imports	Transport; Agribusiness; Food
10	FMC	1995	1,500	n/a	18	0	1	No	16	2	Shipping	Shipping; Construction; Agro-processing
11	Janata Jute	1967	10,000	450	3	0	3	No	3	1	Jute trade	Jute mill; Cold storage
12	Mir	1968	4,000	427	22	1	1	No	6	1	Construction	Construction; Real estate; ICT
13	Impress	1978	222,237	4,263	35	9	9	Yes	9	1	Advertising	Media; Textiles; ICT
14	Incepta	1999	7,800	2,755	5	0	0	No	5	1	Pharmaceuticals	Pharmaceuticals
15	Bengal Group	1969	10,000	9,461	30	3	3	No	12	1	Plastics	Textile; Real estate
16	Otobi	1975	5,000	450	9	1	1	No	7	1	Gift shop	Furniture
17	Multimode	1981	2,500	n/a	26	1	1	No	7	1	Shipping	Shipping; Textile; ICT; Real estate
18	Kazi Farms	1996	10,000	1,200	9	0	1	No	6	1, 3	Consultancy; RMG	Poultry; Media

(Contd.)

Table 10A.1 (Contd.)

SL	Name of Group	Year of Establishment	Employees	Turnover	No. of Companies in Group	RMG/ Textiles units – number	Number of Exporting Units	Whether RMG/ Tex core	No. of Units in Value Chain	Location: Dhaka =1	Initial Business	Major Investment Sectors
19	Saif Power	1997	3,000	388.5	11	0	0	No	5	1	Trading in machinery	Power; Real estate
20	S. Alam	1985	7,000	17,223	50	4	4	No	n/a	2	Trade and transport	Transport; Steel; Banking; Real estate; Agro-processing; Shipping; Textiles
21	West Marine	1994	3,500	228	6	0	0	No	6	2	Shipping services	Shipping and yards
22	Unique	1984	25,000	n/a	19	0	0	No	7	1	Manpower exports	Manpower; Travel; Tourism; Hospitality; Real estate
23	United	1978	7,800	n/a	32	1	1	No	10	1	Construction	Shipping; Real estate; Spinning mills
24	Paragon	1993	4,000	800	20	0	0	No	15	1	Printing press; Poultry	Agribusiness; Tea; Poultry

(Contd.)

Table 10A.1 (Contd.)

SL	Name of Group	Year of Establishment	Employees	Turnover	No. of Companies in Group	RMG/Textiles units – number	Number of Exporting Units	Whether RMG/Tex core	No. of Units in Value Chain	Location: Dhaka =1	Initial Business	Major Investment Sectors
25	Runner Group	2000	n/a	950	9	0	1	No	2	1	Motorbike imports	Motorbike; Real estate; Construction; Energy
26	Phoenix Finance	1995	n/a	n/a	9	5	5	Yes	5	1	Insurance	Finance; Textile; RMG; Steel
27	Intraco	1969	n/a	n/a	25	0	0	No	7	1, 2	Hotel; Trading	Tourism and hospitality; Energy; Pharmaceuticals; Agribusiness
28	Purbani Group	1973	6,000	800	11	9	9	Yes	9	1	Trading	RMG; Textile;
29	LabAid	1989	5,000	850	11	0	0	No	6	1	Healthcare; Diagnostic centre	Health; Education
30	GP	1996	2,400	14,365	1	0	0	No	1	1	Telco	Telco
31	Asian Apparels	1951	30,000	n/a	28	24	24	Yes	24	2	Utensil trading	Textile; Banking; Agro
32	Envoy	1984	21,000	3,400	33	17	17	Yes	17	1	RMG	Textiles; Real estate; Banking

(Contd.)

Table 10A.1 (Contd.)

SL	Name of Group	Year of Establishment	Employees	Turnover	No. of Companies in Group	RMG/Textiles units – number	Number of Exporting Units	Whether RMG/Tex core	No. of Units in Value Chain	Location: Dhaka =1	Initial Business	Major Investment Sectors
33	Ha-Meem	1984	50,000	4,675	29	25	21	Yes	25	1	RMG	RMG; Textiles; Media
34	Islam Garments	1985	21,000	1,450	20	20	20	Yes	20	1	RMG	RMG; Textiles
35	Mohammadi	1986	10,000	850	21	11	11	Yes	11	1	RMG	RMG; Textiles; Energy; Real estate
36	Shanta	1988	200	590	15	5	5	Yes	5	1	RMG	Real estate; Banking
37	Meghna	1976	35,000	21,250	38	0	0	No	12	1 ++	Trading	FMCG; Economic zones
38	Meghna Ka	2003	n/a	n/a	13	0	0	No	4	1	Condensed milk	FMCG
39	Parex Group	1962	10,000	3,536	24	1	1	No	9	1	Furniture	Furniture; FMCG
40	Parex Holdings	1962	n/a	n/a	n/a	n/a	n/a	n/a	n/a	n/a	Trading	Textile; Real estate; Banking; Agro-processing; Ship breaking IN DECLINE

(*Contd.*)

Table 10A.1 (Contd.)

SL	Name of Group	Year of Establishment	Employees	Turnover	No. of Companies in Group	RMG/ Textiles units – number	Number of Exporting Units	Whether RMG/ Tex core	No. of Units in Value Chain	Location: Dhaka =1	Initial Business	Major Investment Sectors
41	Crystal	1900	n/a	n/a	n/a	n/a	n/a	n/a	n/a	n/a	Shipping	Textile; Shipping; Banking; Real estate
42	Mostofa Group	1952	6,000	n/a	21	1	1	No	n/a	2	Cloth trade	Textile; Real estate; Banking; Agro-processing; Ship breaking
43	Pacific	1968	n/a	n/a	n/a	n/a	n/a	n/a	n/a	n/a	Electronics	Electronics and telecommunication
44	SA Group	1988	n/a	n/a	n/a	n/a	n/a	n/a	n/a	n/a	Cloth trading	Textile; FMCG

Source: Compiled from information in *Bonik Barta* and the company website.

Conclusion

Despite the Odds

The odds against Bangladesh were heavily stacked as the country faced war, devastation, floods, famine and severe political instability beginning in 1971 and continuing off and on for at least two decades before reaching a semblance of stability. In addition, the country faced a huge burden of poverty, malnutrition and hunger but was bereft of resources with which to tackle these. Despite such grave handicaps, the country registered sharp progress across a large number of fronts, recording improvements in health and education, nutrition and poverty, women's empowerment, water sanitation and food production. It was able to begin the process of export-led industrialization as in other parts of Asia, shedding its aid dependence and 'basket case' image, growing steadily at around 5 per cent in the 1990s and over 6 per cent from the early 2000s. This sustained, stable macroeconomic performance, the rapid pace of industrialization and a growing indication of economic diversification suggests that Bangladesh has spread its wings to join the 'flying geese' flock of Asia as its latest member behind Vietnam, having in the meantime achieved 'club convergence' in its immediate South Asian vicinity.

Food and Population

The GR had already transformed the agriculture of countries like Mexico, Philippines and Punjab (in India and Pakistan). Initially, the GR was focused on wheat but the success of the Philippines, which experienced large rice productivity increases, held out promise for impoverished rice-growing areas in South Asia.

However, for the GR to succeed, preconditions were required, including irrigation and transport infrastructure, rural roads, and complementary inputs like chemical fertilizers and seeds needed to be made available and accessible to farmers. Here, the public sector backed by donors and suitable policy reforms was able to rise to the challenge, despite the widespread reports of poor governance.

This, along with fertility declines, constituted Bangladesh's main achievement of the 1980s and 1990s – one that was central to its development journey.

The impact of the GR was immense: on rural wages, on food prices and consumption, and on poverty, and the government budget and BOP – the last resulting from a much-reduced need to make large food imports. This also created the basis on which Bangladesh's industrialization, which was sputtering in fits and starts, could actually take off. There were other concomitant factors that coalesced around this time imparting further stimuli to a journey that had already started.

The role of the donor community should also be duly acknowledged. Irrigation, flood control and drainage were financed mostly by donors, especially the World Bank and ADB but also by bilateral donors like USAID, DFID and JICA. Technical assistance from these agencies was important in terms of taking the reform agenda forward and supporting the quest for food self-sufficiency. The same is certainly true for the population control programmes.

A direct consequence of the success in agriculture was the expansion of the RNF sector, which, aided by the influx of remittances sent from the Middle East by expatriate workers, provided a major boost to employment, wages and productivity.

Food Markets

The improvement in agricultural performance and generally the rural economy was marked by exogenous developments in roads and infrastructure, mobile telephony, rural finance and remittances, which transformed rural markets by reducing risk, improving information flows and reducing transactions costs. The role of endogenous traditional market institutions, in other words, played a strong role in supporting the GR.

Going forward, the traditional market will have to confront the challenge of the rise of a growing supermarket segment in the country. The crucial question is whether the traditional market will survive by adapting and meeting the demands of this emerging segment or ultimately take a back seat to a more dynamic, efficient supply chain that overtakes it. This is an important area of both empirical and analytical research with far-reaching policy implications. For the moment it seems modern retail has not affected traditional market chains significantly, but as per capita incomes rise, some degree of polarization already in evidence will certainly deepen.

International Migration

In the context of the story of Bangladesh, the role of remittances has not only been entirely positive and complementary but indeed critical to the various other development efforts initiated by the government (food, family planning and infrastructure), the non-government (education, health, grassroots institutions, micro-credit) and the private sector (RMG). The immediate impact of remittances was to ensure a significant, more predictable flow of scarce foreign exchange to complement meagre export earnings and unpredictable aid, thereby having a stabilizing impact on the BOP and reserves.

At the household level, remittances increased savings and investment, and generally had a positive impact on poverty and livelihoods, even if indirectly. While it was frequently observed that remittances were not being 'productively' used, the increased household spending that resulted, nevertheless, helped stimulate the local economy through increased demand as well as some diversification of agriculture into cash crops and aquaculture.

RMG-Led Industrialization

What is important to note is that the government continued to provide determined support in a bid to improve value addition and stimulate the local industry. This was given a certain urgency with the withdrawal of the 1974 MFA, which ended in 2005, ushering in new market opportunities as well as introducing additional risks. The fear grew that major textile suppliers from countries like India and Pakistan would channel their products increasingly into their own domestic RMG industry, leaving Bangladesh's RMG industry hanging precariously in the balance. If nothing else, the 'lead time' problem faced by Bangladesh could well become further aggravated so that local sourcing of intermediate goods needed for the industry would be highly desirable. This perception led to a closing of ranks between RMG and textiles that jointly lobbied a willing government for support. The two sectors have now merged into one textiles and clothing sector with both forward and backward linkages occurring as a result of the marriage. Like the RMG pioneers of the 1980s, a new generation of textile entrepreneurs had emerged onto the scene by the mid-1990s.

The rapid pace of this journey continued well into the new century despite the withdrawal of MFA in December 2004, which was almost universally heralded as a moment of reckoning for the RMG industry for countries like Bangladesh (World Bank 2006). However, Bangladesh's RMG run continued unabated even in the post-MFA era, notching up new records.

In other words, textiles emerged as another bright area of the Bangladesh economy, contributing over USD 21 billion to exports in 2020. This is a major policy success of the government which at one stroke has stimulated exports, increased value addition and diversified export earnings. It is a rare example of successful import substitution that has led to the creation of a globally competitive industry.

Bangladesh has also quietly proceeded to diversify its export markets. In 1992, over 40 per cent of its RMG exports went to the USA, which reduced to 28 per cent in 2008 in the face of rapidly rising total exports diverted largely to the EU where GSP privileges were available (Joarder, Hossain and Hakim 2010).

Bangladesh's move towards a floating exchange rate regime in June 2003 also served to impart greater competitiveness to its export sector, especially knitwear, by bringing the REER quite close to the equilibrium exchange rate. The opening up of the foreign exchange market to greater competition and the subsequent realignment of the exchange rate regime made Bangladesh's export sector much better equipped to deal with post-MFA challenges and subsequently with the global financial crisis of 2007–09.

Other Industries

The popular narrative of industrialization of Bangladesh is focused almost solely on RMG. While RMG is certainly central, there are many other smaller sectors that have sprouted up, many responding to growing domestic demand emanating from a newly emerging middle class. Some of these non-RMG manufactures have also begun to be exported, and while their shares to total exports are small, they play a significant role in the economy in terms of employment and value addition taken together. The real significance of all these numerous, small-scale activities, however, is not how much they account for in terms of shares of GDP but whether and what potential these hold for future growth and expansion.

Some of these emerging sectors include agro-processing and agribusiness, ceramics, automotive assembly, healthcare, ICT and outsourcing, light engineering, shrimp and fish processing, plastics, renewable energy and energy-efficient technology, shipbuilding, telecommunications, construction, tourism and start-ups. The electronics assembly sector has begun to take off responding to high domestic demand for consumer durables as exemplified by sales of colour TV, refrigerators, smartphones, gas ovens, washing machines and air conditioners on the back of rising incomes. Similarly, the travel and tourism sector has recorded robust growth based on domestic tourism and international travel undertaken by Bangladeshis for work, medical treatment and entertainment. While it is difficult to predict which particular market segment will forge ahead more quickly than others, there is little doubt that the country is poised for a breakthrough, perhaps across a number of markets simultaneously.

Conclusion

In the Asian Flying Geese Flock?

All indications suggest that Bangladesh has joined the flock some 10 years after Vietnam. A point that cannot be overemphasized is that a crucial role rests squarely on the leading goose, or perhaps geese, whose cooperation needs to be carefully cultivated. It is also clear that the lead goose will not remain constant but will change with time, over sectors or products, and by destination markets. In other words, FG is a useful, stylized framework but should not be taken too literally. It provides a good, general description of recent industrialization in East Asia as well as useful insights to think about further evolutionary direction. However, each country has its own specific contexts and attributes that will determine its specific structure and flight path.

While the RMG story appears to comply much better with the FG model, initiated by a leading goose, that is, South Korea through FDI and technology transfer, and sharing of linkages to world markets, this did not happen for leather goods or footwear – a classic FG industry that played a key role in other East Asian countries.

In this case, we see a deviation from the model, in Bangladesh, and one that possibly points out the reason for the inability of the leather goods sector to live to up to its potential. There was scant FDI inflow into this sector from a leading goose – no one relocated to Bangladesh despite its clear comparative advantage in terms of abundant supplies of raw material and cheap labour. This only makes sense if there are non-economic factors at play. Two such factors come to mind: In the late 1980s to mid-1990s when the Taiwanese were desperately looking for relocation opportunities for their footwear industry, Bangladesh was still 'invisible' to investors. The country suffered from an image as well as an infrastructure deficit. There may also have been resistance from the leather lobby to FDI from within Bangladesh at that time, leaving potential investors to turn away.

More recently, global compliance standards emerged as a steep binding constraint. There is new opportunity now due to China seeking to relocate its labour-intensive industries elsewhere. Compliance initiatives and infrastructure have been taken up seriously and greater state commitment is in evidence. This has generated keen interest from leading brands in a number of countries in addition to those who are already sourcing from Bangladesh.

Bangladesh appears to have finally fixed its image issues and successfully put its name on the FDI map. Much will depend on the role of the state in converting the renewed interest into expanded production and exports.

Social Sectors

A multi-pronged strategy evolved, involving state and non-state actors, market, and non-market, based solutions and diverse supply-side approaches which evolved through trial and error. In other words, a variety of grassroots, aid-supported development approaches coalesced to generate a set of (mostly rural) dynamics that led to the emergence of new norms and values, new forms of 'voice', new forms of local institutions and the adoption and proliferation of effective, easy-to-adopt social and health innovations.

The most important change of all was that in social attitudes and a willingness to embrace change and adopt technology and ideas, and to boldly seek opportunities wherever they were. Many hurdles had to be crossed. Thus, war had to be waged on ignorance and illiteracy, patriarchy, gender discrimination, child marriage and exploitative rich farmers, landlords and moneylenders who presided over backward forms of 'interlocked' markets. Regressive religious beliefs and attitudes were also thought to keep women in purdah. These hurdles would seemingly keep Bangladeshi society forever in an arrested state of underdevelopment.

Early development efforts like the Comilla Model primarily targeted farmers, especially small and medium farmers, before the focus of attention expanded to include the landless, the poor and women. In the 1970s and 1980s a variety of community-based organizations arose, including the Grameen-led *samiti* and BRAC-led 'village development organizations'. Bangladesh's success with social sector objectives depended crucially on these kinds of institutions. In Bangladesh, these institutions began with the public sector in the 1950s and 1960s supported by foreign money and technical assistance. Further evolution and adaptation occurred mostly at the hands of NGOs – once again supported by donors, leading to unprecedented change in the Bangladesh countryside in later decades, and reflected in numerous social and economic outcomes.

Dhaka and the Rise of a Business Class

Dhaka has grown from a sleepy provincial town to a roaring metropolis. It is the political, cultural and economic hub of the country, and the centre of urban-based industrialization.

The socio-economic and cultural context of Dhaka has evolved. There is a large, well-entrenched, prosperous class that has emerged, led by powerful business conglomerates – which did not exist in the 1970s and 1980s. The economic and cultural middle class too has evolved. It consisted of a small, educated segment of the population in the 1960s–1990s. Today, this middle class is vast and diverse, including white-collar factory workers, technicians, small entrepreneurs and service-sector providers. In other words, old social networks have declined while new ones are taking shape.

The working-class character is also in flux, with shanties proliferating although much better equipped with services now. Dire poverty no longer stands out and unemployment is low. The profile of shanty dwellers has also changed. In the past they consisted of transport workers, petty traders and low-income service providers. Today, the presence of industrial workers is striking, in addition to transport sector operatives and low-income salaried workers in the private or government sector.

In other words, despite all the challenges that Dhaka faces as a least 'liveable' city, it has performed a stellar role in supporting Bangladesh's 50-year journey towards economic prosperity and the evolution of a strong business class.

The Policy Regime

Bangladesh's move towards a more open, liberalized economy was hotly debated each step of the way but was ultimately accepted as the principal development paradigm, with good effect. As part of Pakistan in the 1950s and 1960s, a strategy of 'import substitution' for industrialization (ISI) had been promoted in line with the prevailing orthodoxy. Thus, the 'developmental state' sought to usher in industrialization by giving protection to Pakistan's fledgling industry through a combination of measures including tariffs, quotas, licences, subsidized foreign exchange and cheap state-mediated loans to entrepreneurs. As part of Pakistan at the time, Bangladeshi entrepreneurs were generally left out of this strategy as much of the investment was directed to West Pakistan. As the main foreign exchange earner, the role of Bangladesh was to help (West Pakistani) industrialization by providing subsidized foreign exchange earned from jute exports.

After Liberation, Bangladesh explicitly adopted 'socialism' as its economic development philosophy, which had by then become a popular demand from across the political spectrum. Bangladesh's socialism was never explicitly defined and may at best be thought of as 'work in progress', as the fledgling nation was groping its way forward. Given time, this pragmatic trial-and-error approach may have delivered a set of policies commensurate with the essential ethos behind the demand for socialism expressed at the popular level. There was an abundance of post-war idealism that reflected sentiments of shared prosperity, equity, redistribution of wealth and the need to ensure basic food and shelter for the impoverished population.

In practice, the only 'socialist' achievement of Bangladesh was the nationalization of industries and enterprises in 1972. The short-lived attempt to forge a one-party state in February 1975 may have been the forbearer of other interventions that would attempt to take the socialist agenda forward. However, 'socialism' was not the only agenda that had gained currency; the demand for democracy was just as potent – the two ideals sitting uncomfortably with each other demanding mutual accommodation – a contradiction that perhaps was too fundamental to be easily resolved. The quest for justice on the one hand and the desire for liberty on the other have been at ideological loggerheads for generations, one side arguing for a robust role of the state as a precondition for development while the other considering a strong state role as anathema, inevitably paving the way to autocracy.[1]

Perhaps, with time, Bangladesh would have found a way around these 'irreconcilable' issues. The hurried floating of BAKSAL (the new party launched by Sheikh Mujibur Rahman in 1975, which was a kind of an umbrella party incorporating all like-minded parties under its fold, not unlike the one-party model of governments in various socialist states) and the abolition of all other parties created an uproar among an unsensitized but highly critical civil society. It is likely that various anti-Liberation forces belonging to the right and the left along with cold-war 'enemies' that disapproved of Bangladesh's close Soviet ties would want to exploit this crack that opened up. Thus, with the assassination of the Sheikh, socialism too came to a premature end on 15 August 1975. Democracy did not fare much better either.

The immediate post-1975 years saw a marked shift towards military-led authoritarian regimes that espoused capitalist, free-market economic policies and sought to develop a local entrepreneurial class similar to what was attempted by Pakistan in the 1950s and 1960s (E. Ahamed 1978). Thus, without the rallying cries of socialism or democracy, these regimes sought to anchor themselves on a development agenda where a market-led approach as encouraged by donors and multilateral bodies like the World Bank seemed most attractive. This paradigm shift also resulted in a larger flow of aid resources to both the government and NGOs. Attempts by successive governments to dismantle the large, nationalized enterprises sector through privatization produced poor results.

Within the broad market-led paradigm that was now the new mantra, specific policy discussions and decisions appear to have been initiated by aid agencies led by the World Bank combined with a pragmatic adoption of policy advice by the governments in power.

Conclusion

Thus, major policy advocacy initiatives with the full weight of the Washington-based international financial institutions (IFIs) began in earnest with the adoption of structural adjustment policies in the 1980s, and trade liberalization policies and substantial reduction in subsidies to agriculture and to food parastatals in the 1990s. Further steps were taken to open up what was almost a closed economy by reduction of protection levels to domestic industry and tariff reforms as per WTO mandates. In the new millennium we saw the introduction of the World Bank–IMF-led poverty reduction strategy papers which replaced the normal five-year plans, starting with the Interim Poverty Reduction Strategy Paper (IPRSP) for 2003–05, the National Strategy for Augmented Poverty Reduction-I (NSAPR-I) for 2005–08, and the NSAPR-II for 2009–11 before returning back to the five-year plans for periods beyond 2011. These were years of relatively high growth – a trend that was carried into and indeed further augmented in the 6th and 7th five-year plan periods covering the period until 2020. The various PRSPs and the 6th plan also ran in parallel with the millennium development goals (MDGs), while the sustainable development goals (SDGs) have been aligned with the 8th plan.

In other words, there has been a sustained engagement from the international development community over many decades and taking different forms. The earlier conditionality-driven policy advocacy appears to have been replaced by a softer approach that encourages buy-in into international agreements, for example, those related to MDGs and SDGs. Bangladesh has not hesitated to enter into these agreements, displaying an openness that is possibly not common.

Thus, despite earlier theoretical attempts to justify liberalization without giving a role to the state, the neoliberal orthodoxy once again created space for state intervention quite deliberately, in support of market-led development. In this respect, Bangladesh turned out to be a good student that was receptive to much of the advice stemming from Washington, resulting in macroeconomic stability and a high, sustained GDP growth rate. This new orthodoxy had no quarrels with the NGO sector and in fact supported NGOs because of their key role in occupying a mostly rural space from which the government was absent or thinly represented – a space that was important to protect from a possible red revolution or perhaps from Islamic fundamentalists.

The combination of agricultural and rural growth, fast-paced industrialization, unprecedented migration of labour from rural areas to the city and abroad, and parallel progress in health, education and empowerment of women through government and NGO interventions resulted in broad-based growth that trickled down fast enough to reduce poverty and malnutrition.

There were of course important domestic stakeholders who too had a hand or at least a say in policy discussions. Local researchers in the 1970s and 1980s had been vocal against World Bank policies, but this began to alter and by the end of the 1990s the bulk of the research community had fallen in line. The other and by far the most important actor was the private sector, which by the 1990s had matured sufficiently to be able to call some shots. Powerful private sector lobbies emerged on the back of the RMG revolution, and subsequent deepening and expansion of Bangladesh's capitalist class. These lobbies were based in the various business chambers led by the apex Federation of Bangladesh Chambers of Commerce and Industries (FBCCI). This class further consolidated both economic and political power and is now better placed than ever before to ensure that their interests are well served by a government that openly considers itself pro-business, with key business leaders even serving as members of parliament and as influential ministers.

As the country develops further and gains in confidence, it will increasingly determine its policy stance not from received wisdom in the form of policy advice from Washington and its allies but from the needs of its own, indigenous capitalist class. The question that could be asked is whither poverty and, especially, inequality? Poverty has responded well to both growth and targeted interventions. Inequality in incomes has grown to worrying levels, although ameliorated somewhat by the rather sluggish growth in consumption inequality. In other words, apart from a faint hope that inequality will be resolved in the process of development, there is no strategy or clear thinking around what to do to address the problem, nor does there seem to be sufficient grassroots activity that could demand a greater share of the pie.

The overall policy stance designed to open up the economy to make it competitive and supportive of an export-led industrialization strategy has now become embedded into Bangladesh's economic philosophy. There is no guarantee, however, that strong lobbies that have emerged and are now led by billion-dollar conglomerates cannot or will not reverse this strategy in favour of short-term exigencies or narrow self-interests. The safety valve that now requires to be nurtured in earnest is transparency, accountability and a genuine move towards democracy if the goal of 2041 – to emerge as an egalitarian, high-income country – is to be taken seriously.

Control over Economic Space

Bangladesh is lucky to have created its own indigenous capitalist class and thereby occupy its precious economic space with indigenous capital. It is imperative that this economic dominance be always protected. History tells us that once such space is destabilized by foreign capital, a country's sovereignty can become compromised, and further, such displacement can rarely be reversed. Thus, while FDI is encouraged, the policy of protecting strategic or basic sectors for indigenous capital is a sound idea so that FDI is coaxed towards critical sectors where new technology and new innovations are urgently needed.

In fact, instead of focusing separately on FDI as such, Bangladesh should seek to encourage both domestic and foreign investment, and generally to redirect the large outflows of domestic capital that goes offshore every year because of the perceived insecurity and lack of confidence among local investors who thereby seek to diversify their portfolio to reduce risk. In any case, FDI has had a chequered career in Bangladesh, and even if things were to turn around, for example, because of the facilities extended by the SEZs, it is likely that local capital will drive growth in the foreseeable future. There is much that the state can do to facilitate this trend, including improving property rights and judicial reforms in support of binding contracts and agreements.

A more recent worry revolves around growing crony capital which at times overlaps with criminal capital that is contributing to an undetermined but possibly large black economy. This inevitably brings up the issue of governance – an area in which Bangladesh has made little progress.

Governance

The weakest link in Bangladesh's governance development is its lack of progress in establishing a strong, impersonal political market. This requires strong, credible political institutions to be nurtured to enable not just a smooth transfer of power at regular intervals but also to make the government accountable and transparent to the people. This has taken a beating that has resulted in a certain underlying disquiet that may affect investment and development as well as equity objectives. The political economy of Bangladesh is currently precariously poised between a weak polity and a strong economy – a tension that one hopes will remain contained for sufficiently long enough to restore the polity to a more sustainable level. It is this basic weakness that institutional reforms need to redress, through reforms in law enforcement, judiciary, revenue collection and key regulatory bodies. An impersonal, merit-based incentive regime therefore remains a pipe dream with most deals and transactions of any significant size determined primarily by non-market arrangements. It is therefore high time to review the nature of a developmental state in the process of rapid development and move forward with urgent but difficult governance reforms that can deliver on complex, high-value-added projects.

On this journey Bangladesh will be able to count on a mature business class, a skilled farming community, a young population and a significant pool of educated and skilled women and men in the labour market. In addition, the domestic market supported by a growing middle class is set to expand rapidly, while the potential regional and global market opportunities for Bangladesh appear unlimited. The problem for Bangladesh will remain a supply-side problem for a long time. That is why Bangladesh's key challenges relate to human development, infrastructure, skills and governance, which are going to act as the basic drivers of future growth and development.

The dream of all Bangladeshis will continue to be to build a *sonar bangla*, or 'golden Bengal', whose contours will keep changing with the times. It will no longer be enough to ensure that everyone has two meals a day or to eliminate poverty defined in minimalist terms. The new *sonar bangla* will demand much more – it will demand prosperity, equity, freedom and an end to corruption. This will in turn require massive investments in human development, infrastructure, technology and machines. This journey will be hard without a supportive and enlightened political economy and impersonal, merit-based institutions. The climate change challenge and climate migration, the Fourth Industrial Revolution, looming land, energy and water shortages, and growing regional and geo-political tensions in the Bay of Bengal will sorely test the country's ability to safeguard its vital economic and strategic interests. Bangladesh has a long record of effectively battling the odds. It cannot take this ability for granted without addressing fundamental reforms.

Key Development Lessons

Bangladesh's development has been the outcome of complex forces brought together by a process of engagement among state and non-state actors – both national and international, operating at different levels – the micro and household level, the meso level (markets and institutions) and the macro policy level. Key non-state actors have been the donors or international development partners, the NGOs who closely depended on them for financing, and from the 1990s onwards, an expanding business class which began to exert confidence and clout.

The most important stakeholders were the farmers and ordinary women in the early stages of development who responded well to economic and non-economic incentives and opportunities that were on offer. Their response was overwhelming, although in the case of agriculture it was slow initially because the new, GR technology and farm incentives were being tweaked as farmers gradually gained familiarity with the technology. The lag in adoption generated

Conclusion

considerable agony as the nation pondered over whether the GR would succeed, and even if it did, whether it would benefit all farmers and not just the rich ones. Of course, even though delayed, it did arrive, and it brought with it shared growth and greater food security for everyone.

In the case of women, their swift and unequivocal response to the newly introduced family planning methods took scholars and policymakers by surprise, upsetting current notions of 'structural' constraints imposed by Islam, tradition and norms. It too arrived with a vengeance and carried all segments of society, the rich and the poor, the educated and the uneducated, along with it. This was the precursor to further gains by women through access to education, health services, industrial and agricultural employment, and micro-credit. As with family planning, whenever women and girls were presented with new opportunities, their response was always robust, although each time this seemed to confound Western-centric scholars who were at pains to understand how this happened. The latest such response has been the interest shown by women in working abroad as housemaids, even in the Middle East where a number of countries have already stopped sending female workers to, in the face of grave human rights violations.

There is little discussion in the literature on the potential role of a wrong or erroneous diagnosis of constraints to rural development that for decades have hammered out ideas of 'structural constraints' stemming from land and asset ownership inequality, tradition and belief systems, or embedded in power relations superimposed on 'precapitalist' forms of exploitation (for example, through interlocked markets). Generally, this important but fringe literature often derived from studies performed in particularly backward regions of India was uncritically foisted on rural Bangladesh as well. That some of these forms did exist in certain parts of Bangladesh or even more widely is beyond question. What however appears to have emerged (with hindsight) is that these constraints were overrated and over-emphasized – and thus when peasants and women embedded within these supposedly severe structural constraints actually responded rather well to newly presented opportunities without too much persuasion, it left observers 'surprised'.

While the factors behind women's receptiveness to emerging opportunities and ideas are complex, there is little doubt that the early dissemination of simple messages directed to women through the agency of trusted local actors played a vital role. Grassroots institutions like the *samiti* were important in these kinds of initiatives.

In pursuing the basic goals of food and population control, and rural development in general, the government had remained steadfast and unrelenting, progressing by fits and starts through pragmatic actions driven by field lessons as well as by theoretical or ideological positions. In addition, the traumatic experience of the 1974 famine would undoubtedly have imparted a particular urgency to these goals. Thus, for example, in agriculture we saw considerable experimentation with irrigation technology, and after much effort, finally arriving at low lift pumps and shallow tube wells as the irrigation technology of choice. The final push towards mass adoption of irrigation was facilitated by adoption of trade liberalization policies by the government, resulting in a dramatic fall in machinery and equipment prices that was immediately translated into massive private sector investment in irrigation equipment.

These developments, along with the micro-credit revolution in rural Bangladesh and the rapid rise of a remittance economy beginning from the late 1970s, began to transform rural life and livelihoods. The rural economy began to receive large inflows of financial resources, which in turn led to unprecedented dynamism of the rural farm and non-farm sector including in what has been termed the 'blue revolution' along with dramatic growth in poultry and feed. These momentous changes had a palpable impact on nutritional standards, especially of children.

If agricultural and rural development constituted one leg of Bangladesh's journey, the other came from the RMG-led industrial revolution which created large-scale employment opportunities for rural women who once again vigorously responded to the new, urban-based 'global market' opportunities, in turn contributing to an additional flow of remittances into the countryside alongside the remittances flowing in from abroad from their male counterparts. The developments in the rural sector set in motion classic, textbook contributions to industrialization, through the release of rural surplus labour of both women and men, by easing the foreign exchange constraint and expanding the domestic market. The success of rural development, and in particular food production, reduced the need for expensive food imports, thereby reducing the drain on foreign reserves. It had a stabilizing influence on inflation that was mainly food-price led.

There is a tendency to suggest that Bangladesh's RMG success is attributable to 'globalization'. In reality, the instinct on the part of the major player, the USA, was quite the opposite. The US was worried about cheap Asian imports and imposed an export quota on the more successful Asian countries like South Korea and Taiwan. This prompted the South Koreans to look elsewhere to relocate their factories and chanced upon Bangladesh, which had not yet entered this market. In other words, the US policy simply led to the unintended effect of diverting production from one Asian country to another, and instead of reducing overall exports from Asian locations, it unexpectedly benefited Bangladesh.

Conclusion

The US followed suit by imposing quotas on Bangladesh as well, but by that time Bangladesh's RMG had taken off.

Once a foothold was gained in the market, the RMG sector grew by leaps and bounds, forging lateral and backward linkages all the way to the manufacture of textiles as 'deemed exports' to feed the giant RMG sector. In the process, the country acquired skills and expertise not only in manufacturing but also in banking, finance, transportation, shipping, insurance and international trading. The sector has moved towards compliant factories and technology-driven productivity gains. These have created the pre-conditions for diversification and expansion into other sectors based on both domestic and international market demand. There is little doubt that RMG allowed a large class of 'intermediate' or medium-sized, independent entrepreneurship to develop in the country, which may ultimately prove to be its most important contribution.

Thus, what emerged was a powerful, integrated set of dynamics that reinforced each other and brought about new opportunities through expanded markets and reinvigorated labour demand, leading to new areas of investment and growth. This helped the process of industrialization take root and consolidate, paving the way for further diversification and expansion – clear, unmistakable indications of which have been noted.

Bangladesh's 'traditional' markets have played a major, although silent, role in the process of development. In this book, we have demonstrated the strength of the rice market – arguably the largest market in the country by far and have demonstrated its resilience and strength, and its ability to change and adapt quickly to resolve emerging market challenges. This pace has remained undiminished, and it is fair to assume that generally Bangladeshi market institutions are strong and dependable, and have ably supported Bangladesh's development journey.

As industrialization progressed, the necessary financial infrastructure also emerged quite rapidly including banks, insurance companies and mobile finance. Despite some serious governance issues that confront the sector and instances of muddled policy faux pas, the sector has ably supported industry and trade, although weaknesses that are well known will require redressal without further delay.

Development resources came from aid, remittances and exports along with domestic resource mobilization. However, the role of state institutions, governance and political institutions were of limited relevance. Thus, looking to the future, the key challenge will be to avoid the (lower) middle-income trap which will require reforms of political markets and governance, reduction of the democratic deficit, ability to ensure market access, upgrade its human resource base and promote independent capital.

Last Words

The world is changing rapidly and at the same time becoming less and less predictable. It appears that the future world economy, and possibly every sphere of life from medicine to forecasting techniques, will be driven by digital technology and new forms of knowledge. Solutions to problems will depend crucially on knowledge creation and access, and one hopes that such knowledge will not become a monopoly of a few countries. To ensure that countries like Bangladesh are not left out of knowledge and technology loops, it will be important to invest heavily in this area.

Given an uncertain future – pandemics, sea-level rise, global economic crises – the best strategy for a country like Bangladesh is to enhance its human capital: the resilience, flexibility and adaptability of its people and its institutions. It is in this context that we have stressed the importance of macro-governance and political reforms. Bangladesh still remains a fractious and divided country where basic ideological issues are unresolved and thus continue to pose a threat to political stability. Given entrenched positions of the adversaries, resolution will be hard but not impossible.

While the rise of Bangladesh's business class has been remarkable, there is a danger that crony and criminal capital may become ascendant, driving out independent capital. That would be a huge blow to our developmental aspirations and must be thwarted. Once again, this new political economy tendency can be contained by squarely encouraging independent capital and a strong civil society. The most important factor for the future however will be the pace and direction of political reforms and whether Bangladesh can reposition itself as a responsible democracy.

Notes

Introduction

1. According to the United Nations High Commissioner for Refugees (UNHCR) estimates available on 1 December 1971, there were 6.79 million refugees in different camps. In addition, there were another estimated 3.13 million refugees who had taken shelter with friends or relatives (Zamir 2017).
2. For example, Chowdhury et al. (2013).
3. For example, Asadullah, Savoia and Mahmud (2014); Ahmed, Greenleaf and Sacks (2014).
4. For example, by Ban Ki Moon, former UN Secretary General (*Daily Star* 2019).
5. Her basic approach is to use the political settlement or social compact framework to back her claim that an 'elite consensus' was reached following the 1974 famine to enshrine social protection in policy. She also credits mass rapes in 1971 with a diminished patriarchy that enabled women a certain degree of freedom. The rationing system in Bengal developed after the 1944 famine and a version of it still exists. It is not clear what is gained by suggesting that a new consensus emerged in 1974. The food security need of the country was well known and was prominently written into the *First Five-Year Plan* well before the famine. Further, to link mass rape to patriarchy is problematic, for, if correct, one would be hard-pressed to understand how patriarchy has survived in South Asia and indeed across much of the world.
6. See Hasell and Roser (2017); Purkait et al. (2020).
7. The early, post-Liberation entrepreneurs were mainly 'brief case' businessmen who were essentially able to obtain patronage and strike deals to earn commissions as suppliers of mainly aid-financed imported raw materials, food grains, intermediate and final goods for which the market was expanding rapidly given the magnitude of scarcities in the economy.
8. Strictly speaking, Grameen is not an NGO but from its inception behaved as one and may therefore be treated as an NGO for the purposes of this book.
9. This has been discussed at length by a number of authors, including Asadullah, Savoia and Mahmud (2014), Raihan (2008), Khondker and Raihan (2004), Begum and Shamsuddin (1998), Annabi et al. (2006) and Bayes, Hussain and Rahman (1995).

Chapter 1

1. The COVID-19 pandemic may force the government to seek to postpone graduation depending on how adverse its economic impacts might turn out to be. The initial fears of economic devastation have, however, begun to recede as the economy appears to be experiencing a V-shaped recovery following record remittance inflows and a trend towards normalization of exports, especially of RMG.
2. See 'GDP per Capita – Bangladesh', World Bank databank, https://data.worldbank.org/indicator/NY.GDP.PCAP.CD?locations=BD (accessed 11 November 2021); also see Roome, Gapihan and Lee (2019).
3. See 'GDP per Capita Growth – Bangladesh', World Bank Databank, https://data.worldbank.org/indicator/NY.GDP.PCAP.KD.ZG?locations=BD (accessed 11 November 2021); also see Jha (2005).
4. *Bangladesh Economic Review 2020* (Government of Bangladesh 2020), table 2.7.
5. The *Bangladesh Economic Review 2020* quotes an investment figure of 31.75 per cent for 2019–20 and 31.57 per cent for 2018–19.
6. Domestic tourism is robust and has grown exponentially. There is also some evidence of encouraging trends in international tourism – see Chapter 8.
7. The next triennial review by the Committee for Development Policy (CDP) to determine Bangladesh's graduation prospects will be held in February 2021. According to a report in the *Financial Express* dated 12 August 2020, 'To overcome the adversity of the economic distortion (due to COVID), the Bangladesh government may consider deferring graduation status from 2024 to 2027 considering the global economic fallout....' The argument against postponing graduation would be that this would also likely delay much-needed reforms to improve the investment climate, tackle corruption and improve the crucial performance of regulatory bodies.
8. The Indian journey would be considered atypical, in the light of the bulk of international experience, and could raise questions on the sustainability of this strategy over the longer term and its potential to transform it to a high-income country.
9. Some observers have noted that South Asia, and Bangladesh in particular, display a perverse form of structural change where services, rather than manufacturing, have come to prematurely dominate the economy, raising questions of whether the region was experiencing premature de-industrialization (for example, Dani Rodrik, speaking at SANEM International Development Conference, 1–3 October 2020). This now appears to be set to change, at least for Bangladesh.

10. The initial onslaught was hard, and the health system seemed almost in tatters, unable to deploy adequate personnel, oxygen, masks, and personal protective equipment (PPE), and to make matters worse, it was riddled with corrupt practices related to procurement, testing and certification – duly exposed by the media.
11. See, for example, Heady and Hoddinot (2016); Headey et al. (2015); Srinivasan, Zanello and Shankar (2013); and Nisbett et al. (2017).
12. See the seminal contribution on the topic by Ahmed, Haggblade and Choudhury (2000).
13. It may be noted that while many NGOs worked in health, education and in the area of 'conscientization', the dominant activity was micro-credit, which focused on women's groups ('samiti') and relied on female as well as male organizers and outreach staff. Thus, the NGO presence was crucial in transforming social attitudes towards women in employment in rural Bangladesh. The simple act of women on bicycles and motorbikes was momentous under the circumstances of the time and had become common in rural areas, although it is rare in the towns and cities even today.
14. *Gender Development Index*: The GDI measures gender inequalities in achievement in three basic dimensions of human development – health (measured by female and male life expectancy at birth), education (measured by female and male expected years of schooling for children and mean years for adults aged 25 years and older) and command over economic resources (measured by female and male estimated GNI per capita); *Gender Inequality Index (GII)*: Reflects gender-based inequalities in three dimensions – reproductive health, empowerment and economic activity. Reproductive health is measured by maternal mortality and adolescent birth rates; empowerment is measured by the share of parliamentary seats held by women and attainment in secondary and higher education by each gender; and economic activity is measured by the labour market participation rate for women and men. The GII can be interpreted as the loss in human development due to inequality between female and male achievements in the three GII dimensions (Table 1.10).
15. For a particularly forceful argument in the context of the GR, see Lipton and Longhurst (1989).
16. The notable exception is the oft-repeated claim that trade liberalization and open-market policies were key, which at best is a partial appreciation of a much more involved set of dynamics as discussed in subsequent chapters.
17. See F. Ahmed (2004) for a useful discussion of definitions used over time.
18. Official estimates based on HIES data.
19. For example, see Hossain and Sen (1992); Rahman and Hossain (1995); Sen and Hulme (2004); Osmani and Latif (2013); and Khandker and Samad (2014).

20. See F. Ahmed (2004) for a concise definition of CBN.
21. Many researchers advocate looking at consumption and income inequality as representing two different aspects of welfare: consumption reflects individual or household standard of living while income reflects level of resources available (McGregor and Barooah 1992; Johnson, Smeeding and Torrey 2005). If a choice had to be made, consumption would possibly be considered more important for a poor country than income. For a discussion on rural consumption and income inequality, see Osmani and Sen (2011).
22. For example, see Quibria (2019); Asadullah, Savoia and Mahmud (2014); Basu (2018); Sawada, Mahmud and Kitano (2018).

Chapter 2

1. Amartya Sen in his famous book *Poverty and Famines* has written in detail on the 1974 famine in Bangladesh arguing that the famine was not due to food availability decline (FAD) but because of entitlement failure, especially of poor, agricultural workers who were unable to find work (A. Sen 1980; Sen 1982).
2. The Russian response was quick, professional and free. The United Nations (UN) was apparently mulling over a possible response but had indicated that this would require time (Kamal 2014). No other offers were at hand.
3. According to a merchant mariner who was sent to take charge of the Mongla Port in January 1972,

   > The entirety of Pussur River was in chaos, being devasted and damaged by the Indian Air Force bombings and strafings 3–4 days before Final Victory. All the port launches, tugboats, and Pilot Vessels were damaged and put out of commission.... Fairway anchorage and passage to Hiron Point were badly mined by Indian as well as Pakistan Navies during the war. Many ships, ocean-going and on coastal trades were sunk or damaged.... (Hossain et al. 2020)

4. Datta (2012) quotes the official figure of 10 million; A. J. Taylor (1979) quotes a figure of 8 million.
5. See Ravallion (1982: 75):

   > Probably the most important immediate cause of starvation during the 1974 famine in Bangladesh was a sharp drop in the food purchasing power of agricultural earnings. Past work has attempted to explain this in terms of conditions in food markets. This paper reports an econometric investigation of wage movements before and after the famine which reveals a significant structural break in the short-run

response of wages to prices at the time of the famine. Without this change in labour market conditions, real wages would have remained fairly stable during the famine.

6. The Bangladesh War of Independence took a toll on the Pakistan economy as well. A study on the war's consequences estimated that the indirect costs of the conflict were USD 14.08 billion and had a significant long-term negative impact on both countries. The year 1971 was marked by a steep decline in Pakistan's GDP annual growth rate, from 11.6 per cent in 1970 down to 0.47 per cent in 1971, followed by three years of economic recession. In the period directly after the war, the country was internationally isolated both politically and economically. For instance, the US pressured the World Bank into withholding loans to Pakistan until it formally recognized Bangladesh, in 1974. Furthermore, Pakistan's trade relations with other countries suffered from its refusal to recognize Bangladesh. In retrospect, the Pakistani government acknowledged that the country 'has certainly not performed to potential or initial expectations' and attributed the derailing of the promising developments of the 1960s to wars with India (1965) and Bangladesh and to a 'chequered political history'.

7. Despite the intense volatility of the period, some progress was made in exports and manufacturing, which in turn boosted revenues, allowing development expenditures to triple by the end of the decade, riding on the back of a sharp rise in aid flows.

8. These estimates are based on the periodic HIES and assumes a calorie-based norm of 2122 ('poverty I') and 1805 ('poverty II').

9. See World Bank (2020a: 8):

> The Plan document identified specific population activities for six other ministries, besides the Ministry of Health and Family Welfare, essentially reflecting a Whole-of-Government Approach to this critical issue. For example, the Ministry of Rural Development was tasked with promoting women's employment, as well as functional and family planning literacy, through rural cooperatives. The Ministry of Agriculture introduced population and nutrition education in their extension programs. The Ministry of Education incorporated population education in academic curricula and also created a Department of Population Sciences at Dhaka University, while the Ministry of Information disseminated information promoting fertility regulation through various mass media channels. These ministries developed projects to implement activities supporting family planning, and Population Control Committees were formed at national and sub-national levels to coordinate action across sectors under the broad ambit of a National Population Council, led by the Prime Minister.

10. Based on adjusted 1974 and 1981 census data.
11. *Thana* is the lowest level administrative unit.
12. Per cent of currently married women using contraception rose from 7.7 per cent to 18.6 per cent over 1976–81. Contraception use among younger women was found to rise more quickly.
13. The military itself was going through a process of change and adaptation with the core membership drawn from regular Bengali units of the Pakistan Army that had rebelled and formed the Mukti Bahini (Liberation Army). After liberation, diverse elements constituting the Mukti Bahini along with new paramilitary outfits were inducted into the military along with Bengali officers and men who were in Pakistan and repatriated in 1972. Thus, there were all manner of tensions and rivalries that quickly emerged at independence setting various factions and groups against each other, leading to the assassination of Sheikh Mujib and subsequent power struggles.
14. See S. S. Islam (1984); Maniruzzaman (1980).

Chapter 3

1. For Bangladesh, food always translated as meaning rice, and the thrust of food policy over much of the last 50 years was squarely on the rice sector.
2. A recent study finds that uncompetitive features are emerging in the face of a powerful automatic milling sector (Rahman et al. 2020).
3. It is interesting to note that Bangladesh diverged sharply from India in this respect starting from the 1980s. While India retained a very large, expensive and inefficient PFDS for food, Bangladesh chose to go for targeting and improving efficiency (Banerjee et al. 2014).

Chapter 4

1. This chapter is an updated version of K. A. S. Murshid (2014).
2. For example, CM (1994); Harriss-White (1997, 1999, 2008); also see Bhaduri (1983) for an Indian perspective.
3. For example, North (1990, 1998); Platteau (1994a, 1994b); Kumar and Matsusaka (2009); also see K. A. S. Murshid (1997) who disputes Platteau's position on the need for generalized morality.
4. Eklas Miah of Messrs Eklas Miah Enterprise, interviewed in Noakhali on 26 July 2010.
5. There is little doubt that MFS have, by 2020, displaced other forms of money transfers (Murshid et al. 2020).
6. See M. Hussain (1988a); Ahmed (2004); and Talukder (2005) on agricultural performance; and Ahmed, Haggblade and Chowdhury (2000) on reforms.

Chapter 5

1. Hossain and Lowy (1990) tried to explain the late start of Bangladeshi migration to the Middle East in terms of the uneasy diplomatic relations with a number of Arab countries, especially Saudi Arabia after the split with 'Muslim' Pakistan in 1971 and Bangladesh's espousal of secularism. This may have been true for Saudi Arabia more than any other country given its close ties to Pakistan and delay in recognizing Bangladesh. However, within a few years, pragmatic policies took over on both sides.
2. President Ziaur Rahman is sometimes credited with playing an important role in expediting migration of workers in the late 1970s to the Middle East, particularly to Saudi Arabia on the back of improved relations and a distinct right-wing political shift in policy (R. Roy 2017).
3. The market gave rise to a large number of 'manpower businesses' (recruiting agents) that were set up to supply labour to foreign entities for a fee. Fees were also charged (informally) from would-be migrants keen to work abroad, enabling some of these agents to generate very large profits in what is widely considered to be highly exploitative terms.

Chapter 6

1. The Kerala experience, however, appears much more positive – see Eapen (2001).
2. Bakht (1996) describes RNF as dominant and growing, with traditional cottage industries on the decline but manufacturing led by small-scale industry increasing quickly. The other two major areas for RNF were trading and personal services.
3. Observers are much more prone to talk about the achievements of the RMG sector, the GR, international migration and remittances, or the role of the NGO sector in health, education and gender rights in the context of Bangladesh's development journey.
4. One study used unit data from LFS 2013 (Khandker et al. 2016b) to arrive at an estimate of 43.5 per cent for RNF.
5. There is a strong debate on the role of international and urban–rural remittances on rural households revolving around fungibility (that is, whether the source of income matters) and impact on household welfare including human capital and poverty. In the context of Bangladesh, the two types of flows operate in slightly different markets separated by class, gender, size of remittances and therefore usage, which appear to have resulted in differential impacts in terms of magnitude but similar impacts in terms of the nature of

effects (consumption, investment tendencies, human capital and poverty) – see for example Akhter and Islam (2019); Chowdhury and Radicic (2019).
6. Gautam and Faruquee (2016) observe that while labour and manual employment have increased in RNF, employment in business and skilled services has declined.
7. While the story of micro-credit and remittances flowing into rural areas is well known and recorded, there are other dynamics at work whose role have been less noticed. Just as the GR dynamized the RNF sector in the 1990s, later successes in aquaculture (Blue Revolution – see Rashid and Zhang [2019]), poultry, fruits and vegetable farming, the rise of a significant market for domestic flowers, investment in modern agro-processing including automatic rice mills and the effects through employment and employment linkages, transport services, packing, sorting and grading, along with the rise of food supermarkets, created unprecedented work opportunities. This story, as argued earlier, requires to be systematically addressed.
8. Chittaranjan looms are semi-automatic looms used to weave coarse and medium cloth.
9. Casual observation suggests that even the *salwar-qameez* is on the wane, replaced by a form of long, loose dress combined with a shawl and head-wrap – an innovation that would perhaps be considered 'Islamic'. These 'fashion trends', however, do not have a simple interpretation and deserves separate inquiry by social anthropologists, and is almost certainly a reflection of deeper, underlying social and economic changes.
10. These growth rates were calculated using data from the Department of Livestock (DOL 2020).

Chapter 7

1. The US and EU were anxious to be seen to protect their domestic markets from excessive foreign competition in the RMG sector at the cost of local jobs, and therefore imposed country-specific quotas. When these quotas were exhausted, countries like Korea began to outsource production to countries like Bangladesh where quotas remained largely unutilized. This was the initial entry point for Bangladesh, and once sufficient experience was gained, progress was unstoppable. The Multi-fibre Arrangement (MFA) was then enacted under the World Trade Organization (WTO) to phase out quotas completely by 2004. Despite dire predictions, it had little effect in arresting the RMG growth in Bangladesh. EBA privileges from EU and Canada played an important role in sustaining Bangladesh's progress, while even without quotas and duty-free status in the US market Bangladesh learned to compete.

Notes

2. This was all the more noteworthy given the absence of a local entrepreneurial class at the time.
3. See, for example, 'Richard Nixon, Kimchi And The First Clothing Factory In Bangladesh' (episode 499, WWNO, New Orleans Public Radio), https://www.wwno.org/2013-11-29/episode-499-richard-nixon-kimchi-and-the-first-clothing-factory-in-bangladesh?_amp=true (accessed 28 November 2021); 'Tracing History: A Journey Well Clothed', Apparel Resources, 1 February 2013, http://apparelresources.com/business-news/sourcing/tracing-history-a-journey-well-clothed/ (accessed 28 November 2021; and Mostafa and Klepper (2009).
4. There were obstacles from global markets even at this early stage. Harris et al. (2000: 26) observe:

> ... the first surge of growth in 1983–84 when its share of world clothing exports to developed countries was barely 0.2 per cent (and to the US, 0.32 per cent) led to formal complaints by the UK, France and the US, and for a period, a suspension of imports (with severe damage to the industry). Later, the European Union disputed duty preferences claimed by Bangladesh exporters on the grounds that the fabric and yarn used in the garment exports was not made in Bangladesh - a remarkable defiance of the logic of a global economy based upon comparative advantage, and an attempt to force Bangladesh back into economic nationalism. The exporters, those who survived, learned the nimbleness required to circumvent these obstacles.

5. Cited in Jahan (2019).
6. The duty drawback system allows exporters to import after paying appropriate duties upfront and later claiming refund after proof of export – a system that is inefficient, time-consuming and associated with significant transactions costs. This system is still in use for non-RMG exporters who face considerable hurdles in obtaining access to bonded warehouse facilities (for example, see http://documents.worldbank.org/curated/en/275881537421782651/text/Export-Diversification-through-Bonded-Warehouse-Reforms.txt [accessed 28 November 2021]).
7. Back-to-back LC is a negotiable instrument obtained from the buyer that can be used by the recipient to open a secondary LC to import from suppliers of inputs. Banks usually require securities or collateral before issuing an LC. The original LC is used as collateral. A back-to-back letter of credit is opened against export letters of credit. Banks provide up to 80 per cent of the export LC to finance the back-to- back LC.
8. Competitors like Vietnam and Cambodia do not appear to use similar arrangements, mainly perhaps because of the dominant position of FDI in

their RMG sectors. Given a budding entrepreneurial class and severe capital constraints in Bangladesh, the context was quite different and required the use of innovative policies.

9. See World Bank (n.d.); and http://documents.worldbank.org/curated/en/275881537421782651/text/Export-Diversification-through-Bonded-Warehouse-Reforms.txt (accessed 28 November 2021):

> It appears that there are around 320 Statutory Rules and Orders (SRO), meeting minutes and instructions governing the SBW regime, 248 of which are not even recorded. Most of the instructions have been drafted to support the operation of SBWs in the RMG sectors. When applied to other sectors, the rules have the effect of being less favorable and, in some cases, a barrier to seeking an SBW license.

10. The breakdown for value addition in knitwear is estimated as follows: spinning 17 per cent; weaving 15 per cent; knitting 18 per cent; dyeing and finishing 15 per cent; knitted garments 28 per cent (cited by Kabir, Singh and Ferrantino [2019], quoting Bangladesh Textile Manufacturers Association – BTMA).
11. Bangladesh's biggest foreign investor in RMG is Youngone Corporation of South Korea, which has already invested in this growing area and has announced plans for larger investments in three additional factories in the Korean export processing zone (KEPZ) (*Textile Today* 2021).
12. Initially, in the early 1980s, the European community (EC) defined its ROO in terms of stage 2 for knit products and stage 3 for woven products, defined as follows: stage 1 refers to conversion of raw cotton to yarn; stage 2 refers to conversion from yarn to fabric; while stage 3 refers to conversion of fabric to RMG. However, as Bangladesh had little backward linkages for RMG in existence at the time, the EC quotas went largely unutilized. As Bhattacharya et al. (2000) point out, generalized system of preferences (GSP) utilization rate of Bangladesh began to deteriorate – moving from 43.2 per cent in 1994–95 to only 27.3 per cent in 1996–97 due to the inability to comply with the three-stage and two-stage conversion requirements of EC. Further, ROO issues came into prominence following EC allegations that exporters were claiming GSP falsely. Eventually, the EC ROO was modified to allow stage 2 conversion for both the knit and woven sectors – and that is where matters currently stand.

Chapter 8

1. COVID-19 has exposed the poor governance infrastructure of the health sector in the public as well as the private domain. Hospitals were found operating without a licence or with expired licences, and even rudimentary inspections

Notes

revealed gross mismanagement and indiscipline – leading the government to actually stop inspections fearing further public disquiet and a possible backlash.

2. Under these circumstances, one would have expected the private sector to fare better – unfortunately, that too did not happen. Except for a very small, very expensive enclave within the private sector that has developed relatively recently, and which provides an acceptable quality of healthcare services, all others offer services that, let us say, leave much to be desired.
3. Some reports put the figure at USD 3.45 billion in 2017 ('Bangladesh: Healthcare and Pharmaceuticals', Export.gov, 12 October 2018, https://legacy.export.gov/article?id= Bangladesh-Healthcare-and-Pharmaceuticals [accessed 16 March 2021]).
4. Exports totalled USD 73 million in 2014–15 rising to USD 136 million in 2019–20.
5. There is a buzz around Bangladesh's ICT potential with top consultancy firms like AT Kearney forecasting very positive outcomes for the country's new, emerging sector (as reported in Lightcastle 2019).
6. To put this in context, the wage rate in the far more mature Indian IT outsourcing sector is USD 20 an hour as against USD 8 an hour in Bangladesh.
7. North (1998, 1981); also see Murshid (2014).
8. See, for example, Lightcastle (2020).
9. Ancient temple sculptures in Java testify about various kinds of ships 'the people of Lower Bengal built and used in sailing to Ceylon, Java, Sumatra and Japan in pursuits of their colonizing ambition, commercial interests, and artistic and religious missions' (Mookerji 1912: 156).
10. Berthet (2015) reports that this information is cited in numerous studies but could not be found in the transcriptions in Federici's account that he examined (Robert 2021).
11. The length of the coastline dedicated to ship breaking increased from 2 kilometres in the 1980s to more than 12 kilometres in 2012, reflecting the dominant position of Bangladesh in this sector – underpinned by huge domestic demand for scrap steel and other recycled parts (Sujauddin et al. 2015).
12. This was discussed with two economists who participated in the special committees set up to draft the industrial policy – one in 2016 and the other in the later 1990s. It was their impression as well that these documents were essentially ornamental, consisting of wish lists cobbled together after discussions with various stakeholders. What was significant was the complete absence of the big, powerful, interest groups in the country who ignored this completely – reinforcing the suggestion (personal communication from Dr Nazneen Ahmed, member of the Committee on Industrial Policy, 2016, who was deeply associated with drafting and finalizing the report).

13. Writing this in 2020, this goal seems unreal, and not just because of COVID-19.
14. However, SEZ firms appear to be able to sell freely on the domestic market – provided they pay required import duties on imported materials at the moment of sale. In fact, one company admitted that they were following a 'niche market strategy', by focusing first on local markets and expanding progressively with the potential for future exports – a strategy that by no means is limited to just one entity (Murshid, Männlein and Hager 2019).
15. If correct, this is excellent progress – a visit to some of these sites in 2018 revealed that only very basic works had been initiated.
16. Mr Paban Choudhury, executive chairman, BEZA, indicated in an interview that land for SEZ was typically low-productive, government-owned (*khas*) land which were taken up after suitable identification, for infrastructural development.
17. See Murshid, Männlein and Hager (2019: 64), which cites an interview with Sameeh Ullah.
18. The exchange rate in 1974 and 1975 were BDT 8.2 and BDT 12.2 per USD.
19. The exception was the Adamjee Jute Mill set up by the Dawoods on 245 acres of land on the banks of the river Sitalakkhya in 1950. This became the largest jute mill in the world. The government decided to shut down the old, neglected, poorly maintained factories, got rid of the workers amicably through a golden handshake, and converted the sizeable real estate on which the factory was sitting into an EPZ. This was a complex and expensive exercise, creating employment for around 65,000 in 10 years (2009–19) and widely acclaimed as a success. It was, however, not duplicated. It may also be pointed out that Adamjee was not privatized but allowed to be taken over and managed by BEPZA – a successful parastatal.
20. Howlader (2015) reports a total of 76 Bengali-owned units at the time – 75 in jute and textiles and one sugar mill.
21. Mollah (2020: 13) observes: 'Nationalization of the Bengali-owned jute and cotton textile industries was an outcome of the ideological conviction of some members of the ruling party and of the handful of economists working at the Planning Commission during that time.'
22. Among those non-Bengali business families who stayed or came back include the Ispahanis, Mohammed Bhai of Bengal Group, Tabani who owned Coca-Cola but could not get it back – but did get his rexin factory back – and Bawani, who came too late to get back his jute mills. Incidentally, all these businessmen were carrying out very profitable businesses in Rangoon, where their ancestors had migrated from different parts of British India when Burma was administered from Calcutta but relocated to East Pakistan after the British left in 1947 (information provided by Ajmal Kabir who belongs to a

prominent business family in the country and who was a personal witness to many of these changes in the 1970s).
23. For example, see report by Kashem (2020) in the *Business Standard* based on a finance ministry report.
24. The South Korean automobile industry is a notable example.
25. Also see Lin (2016); Monga and Lin (2019).
26. World Bank (2020b) suggests a comprehensive set of reforms that will enhance investment, improve productivity growth, develop human capital, encourage women's participation in the labour market and raise the efficiency of public capital if Thailand is to move out of upper middle-income country (UMIC) status by 1941.
27. The 'Flying Geese' concept was originally developed by Akamatsu (1935, 1937, 1962) and further expanded and elaborated most notably by Kojima (1960, 1970, 1995, 2000).
28. See Mathews (2006) for a good review of the various development paradigms starting from Rosentein Rodan, Albert Hirschman and Alexander Gerchenkron, as well as a strong defense of FGP. We may also note Balassa's stepladder model from 1982, which appears to vindicate FGP given the close likeness of the two. For a dissenting voice, see Bernard and Ravenhill (1995).
29. Byron and Chakma (2020) reported that Japanese auto-giant Mitsubishi Corporation has inked a deal with the state-owned Pragati Industries to produce Bangladesh brand cars, for which there is already a big local market.
30. Fishlow (2003) interprets Gerchenkron's position on the role of the state as follows: state intervention is able to compensate for various inadequacies that prevent investment, including lack of capital, skilled labour, entrepreneurship and technological capacity. This is what the Bangladesh government must seriously address in the leather sector.
31. See report by Refayet Ullah Mridha in Mridha (2020).
32. See Bangladesh Bank FDI data at https://www.bb.org.bd/econdata/fdi.pdf (accessed 4 December 2021).
33. Bangladesh has consistently performed poorly in most governance indicators relating to corruption, bribery, ease of doing business, contract enforcement, rule of law (see, for example, *Ease of Doing Business Rankings*, World Bank, 2021, https://www.doingbusiness.org/en/rankings (accessed 27 December 2021); Agrawal and Salam (2019).

Chapter 9

1. The most widely used indices are the World Governance Index (WGI) covering six separate indicators (see Kaufmann, Kraay and Mastruzzi 2010) and the

Corruption Perception Index (CPI) for the public sector from Transparency International.
2. For example, see A. Sen (1992).
3. In the context of fertility reduction and its causes, the intense debate that was generated in the 1990s appears to have reached a stalemate with supply-side explanations perhaps enjoying a slight edge over demand-side explanations.
4. Ethnic homogeneity and high population density have not prevented vertical factions and intense political divisions, the former frequently based on local allegiances. A better explanation would be in terms of expanding social networks and local institutions that facilitated exchange of ideas and knowledge.
5. For Khan's personal take on the CM, see his lucid account after his retirement in A. H. Khan (1974).
6. 'Gradually your cooperative will accumulate a substantial amount. It will also get cheap loans for you. Ultimately, through your cooperative, you will become your own financier' (A. H. Khan 1974: xx).
7. See, for example, Blair (1978); Raper (1970).
8. For example, see Abdullah, Hossain and Nations (1976); Bose (1974); B. Ahmed (1972); K. M. Rahman (1976); Manjur-ul-Alam (1978); and Toufique (2017).
9. This led to substantial improvement in farm productivity but failed to address equity issues (Abdullah, Hossain and Nations 1976).
10. Reference here to Professor Yunus' attempt to float a political party; the virtual elimination of Proshika and other NGOs with a more radical agenda – see Lewis (2012, 2017).
11. See, for example, Wali (1904); Mukherjee (1948); Qadir (1960); Bertocci (1970); S. Rahman (1960); Bhattacharya and Natesan (1932); Adnan (1990); Saqui and Akhtar (1987).
12. For example, see Wallace and Harris (1989); Bertocci (1970); S. Rahman (1960); and Qadir (1960).
13. RDRS was established in 1972 to assist the people of greater Rangpur–Dinajpur region through relief and rehabilitation programmes. Since 1997, RDRS became a national development organization. RDRS is an associate programme of Lutheran World Federation (LWF) and Department for World Service (DWS), Geneva.
14. This is how the organization describes its origin:

> PROSHIKA officially came into existence in 1976. After the liberation war ended in 1971, in the wake of that devastation, Canadian University Service Overseas (CUSO), Logistic Centre Dhaka, was operating relief work in Bangladesh. For better operation of relief work CUSO used to organize the youth groups that were committed to socio-cultural and economic development, and also enlightened with the spirit of the

war. Eventually, they realized that relief work was not the permanent solution of socio-economic development of the rural sector. Hence, the idea shifted from the relief work to building up a Bangladeshi organization through which social and economic development work could be implemented making it a social and economic wheel to reach down trodden, poor and destitute people of the country in the most efficient way possible. Keeping this idea in mind a group of youth decided to setup a Bangladeshi organization, which came to be known as PROSHIKA. It was a Bangladeshi NGO created by the united effort of many committed young people who worked in the CUSO in 1975. ('Proshika: A Brief', https://proshikabd.com/notice/History_of_PROSHIKA.pdf [accessed 5 December 2021])

15. This debate was triggered by an article by Ashok Rudra and his co-researchers in the late 1960s (Rudra, Majid and Talib 1969) which attempted to characterize Indian agriculture as semi-feudal. A host of Indian Marxist economists led by Utsa Patnaik deliberated on the issue, with Patnaik essentially arguing that there was a distinct *tendency* towards capitalist farming especially in such advanced areas as Punjab while others continued to stress that the dominant character of Indian agriculture remained feudal or semi-feudal. A comprehensive review of this debate is provided by Alice Thorner (1982) and later by Nadkarni (1991), H. Z. Rahman (1989) and Patnaik (1990), among others.

16. A. A. Abdullah (2000) notes that large-scale participation of women in RMG factory work could be considered a victory of the forces of modernization against 'purdah', in which the battle appears to have been won effortlessly by the former. In fact, as others have noted, *purdah* actually changed and adapted to accommodate factory work and remains very much a part of the 'cultural realm' – its parameters, always contested, are constantly being modified and made compatible, in this case with factory work (Siddiqi 1991; S. C. White 1992).

17. Some of the more influential work include Yunus (1999); Bornstein (1997); A. Rahman (1999); M. Hossain (1988b); Hulme and Mosley (1996a, 1996b); Hulme and Arun (2009). Thus, Hulme and Arun (2009: 163) note:

> The Grameen Bank holds an iconic position in the world of micro finance. It is credited with proving that the 'poor are bankable'; the Grameen model has been copied in more than 40 countries; it is the most widely cited development success story in the world.... At the end of February 2008 it had 7.4 million clients and outstanding loans of US$545 million.

18. See, among others, Crépon et al. (2015) for Morocco, Agelucci, Karlan and Zinman (2015) for Mexico, Attanasio et al. (2015) for Mongolia and Tarozzi, Desai and Johnson (2015) for Ethiopia.

19. I am grateful to Shahid Khandker for clarifying this argument through a personal communication.
20. One should also bear in mind that there are wider cross-cutting developments that have major health implications, for example, progress in girls' education and women's empowerment, role of microfinance, or growing rural incomes.
21. Two studies that provide excellent introductions to the state of health systems in the country are Osman (2008) and BHW (2010).
22. The authors acknowledge a small role of rising age at marriage and urbanization as well.
23. For example, see Lutz (2017), who resurrects the old education–fertility debate in a new guise.
24. Though most people have access to a toilet, 40 per cent of the population use shared, rudimentary sanitation facilities with a meagre 28 per cent with access to a hand washing station equipped with soap and water. Hence, the battle now needs to be taken to the next level to ensure safe sanitation (UNICEF 2019).
25. More specifically, low-intensity governance refers to the grassroots-based service delivery programmes developed by NGOs and adopted by both GO–NGO programmes that generated viable, low-cost, simple and effective governance solutions.
26. For example, Islam et al. (2018).
27. For example, see Maswood (2017).
28. Thus, Buddhism arrived peacefully in Bengal and appeared to have gained particular favour among the people of Eastern Bengal, where great monasteries and centres of learning were established. Bengali monks like Sri Atish Dipankar who was born in Vikrampura on the outskirts of Dhaka, the capital city of Bangladesh, is accredited with the spread of Buddhism to Tibet. Unfortunately, there is very little literature on the subject. A notable exception is Mitra (1954) and more recently Sarao (2012). The retreat of Buddhism began with the defeat of the Buddhist Pala dynasty by the Chola–Sena kings of south India, and the Hindu revival that it prompted. The fate of Buddhism in Bengal was finally sealed with the Turkish conquest and the destruction of monasteries that were mistaken for forts. Apparently, massive conversions to Islam followed, spurred on by Sufi-saint preachers who may have found a fertile ground among disgruntled Buddhists resentful of the hold of Brahmanical Hinduism over their lives (Rasul 1986; Chakma 2011). Unlike Buddhism, Islam did not require elaborate temples, statues or monasteries or even a laity, allowing it to spread quietly. Given the dispersed habitation and difficult terrain of Eastern Bengal, this remained a well-kept secret for hundreds of years. It was not until the first ever population census of Bengal undertaken by the British in 1872

that the Muslim presence became evident (H. Beverly 1874). That in fact the majority of the population of East Bengal was Muslim created shockwaves of disbelief and consternation all around. This is how quietly Islam entered upon the scene. This brief history points to considerable maturity and awareness of a population that had always shown itself ready to adopt and adapt to new ideas and new opportunities.

29. See also Eaton (1996); Tarafdar (1965).
30. For effects of income on nutrition, see Behrman and Deolalikar (1987); Haddad et al. (2003); Headey (2013); Heltberg (2009); Smith and Haddad (2000). The link to education is explored in Burchi (2012); Headey (2013); Thomas, Strauss and Henriques (1991); Webb and Block (2004). In the case of demography and family planning, see Headey (2013); Horton (1988); Jensen (2012). For gender empowerment and cultural norms, see Jayachandran and Pande (2013); Pande (2003), For improved sanitation, see Humphrey (2009); Lin et al. (2013); Spears, Ghosh and Cumming (2013). For health service utilization, see Headey (2013).
31. For example, see Hossain, Duffield and Taylor (2005); H. White (2005); Levinson and Rhode (2005).
32. Also see Black et al. (2013).
33. For an exception, see Osmani (2016).
34. For example, Asadullah, Savoia and Mahmud (2014).
35. Akhtar Hamid Khan – founder-director of the Comilla Academy and originator of the cooperative-based Comilla Model (1959–71).

Chapter 10

1. Dhaka population quadrupled between 1974 and 1990, growing at 9.2 per annum; since 2000, the growth rate has been generally around 3.6 per cent – still considered high (Afsar and Hossain 2020).
2. For example, Cohen (2006).
3. Another report estimates the population at over 500,000 by the early years of the 18th century even with the transfer of the Bengal capital from Dhaka to Murshidabad (Ray 2010: 16).
4. Hence the reference to the word 'bargi' in children's rhymes where it enjoys the status of a bogeyman, serving to remind us of that dark period.
5. The numbers relate to the 1901 Census of East Bengal and Assam, which belonged to one unified administrative unit.
6. The matter is well documented, for example, see Mazid (2012); also, Banglapedia (2015c). The financial concerns may not have been far-fetched. Ahmad (1981: 134) talking about Calcutta University, observes:

In spite of repeated requests by the University, drawing Government attention to its 'critical and embarrassing' financial difficulties, the Education Minister refused any increased grant to the University in his budget for 1922–23. Dacca University, which had started functioning in July 1921, received a grant of Rs. 9,00,000 while Calcutta had only its annual recurring grant of Rs. 1,41,000. The Minister denied any charge of partiality to Dacca and accused Calcutta University of 'thoughtless expansion'.

7. On 26 February 1923, the then governor of Bengal and chancellor of Dacca University, Lord Lytton, said at the convocation of the graduates of 1922: 'I have already stated in public that in my opinion this university is Dacca's greatest possession and will do more than anything else to increase and spread the fame of Dacca beyond the limits of Bengal or even of India itself' (quoted in Hashan 2020).
8. Numbers of such migrants are not known, not even approximately (Rahman and Schendel 2013) – reflecting what Shelly Feldman (1999) refers to as the 'Silence of East Bengal' and the erasure of the East Bengal voice.
9. Loosely defined as educated, upper- and middle-class Bengalis (Rahman and Schendel 2013).
10. East Pakistan's deprivation was not denied by Pakistani leaders like President Yahya Khan or even his predecessor Ayub Khan as reported by Choudhury (1973: 229) in his personal account of 'The Last Days of United Pakistan'. Choudhury was closely associated with Yahya's inner circle and therefore had a ringside view of the behind-the-scenes political manoeuvres leading up to the breakaway of East Pakistan to form Bangladesh, noting in particular that unlike Ayub, Yahya was not 'master of his own house'.
11. For example, Alamgir (1973); Nazrul Islam (1973, 1976); Ahsan, Hussain and Ahsan (1987); and Begum (1997, 1999).
12. The population of Chittagong (officially Chattogram is over 5 million and that of Khulna, less than a million).
13. This concept has undergone some examination by young architects of the Bengal Institute (*Daily Star Supplement* 2018).
14. For example, Afsar and Hossain (2020); Rashid (2000); Swapan, Zaman and Ahsan (2017); and Dewan, Haider and Amin (2014).
15. The word *tadbir* is frequently employed to refer to lobbying – with the sort of lobbying determined by the task at hand starting from just being nice (if you are favoured) to tearful supplication or disbursement of adequate speed money to get the *tadbir* done.
16. This was before the rule of the Palas (AD 750–850) following the end of the rule of Shashanka in Bengal (K. Islam 1966).

17. Aristotle, *The Politics*, quoted in Sennett (1996 : 13), cited in Ahmed (2016).
18. This usage is generally seen in socialist states and was incorporated into the Bangladesh constitution probably in deference to its dalliance with socialism in the initial years.
19. Reported by the US embassy using data obtained from Anjuman-e-Mufidul Islam – a charitable organization well known for its work in this field (US Embassy report, Dhaka [1974], cited in N. Hossain [2017]).
20. These 'resources' varied from access to contracts in trade or construction, bank loans at low cost (that would never be repaid) down to control over transport cartels, government lands and even the sidewalks that would be let out to vendors for a price.
21. For example, the agent for Sony Electronics was a Pakistani who had left and the offices were then taken over by his Bengali manager, who in turn sold shares of the business to his friends. This entity then participated in tenders floated by SOEs and government corporations for the import of various commodities including foodstuffs and steel billets. Given their connections, major deals were struck. Similarly, owners of 'Ameejee Valeejee and Sons Pvt. Ltd' and the agent for Siemens also abandoned their businesses and left, and local managers took over and began competing for contracts (based on an interview with a senior, well-connected banker and leading businessman, Mr Ajmal Kabir).
22. This can be attributed to the author's personal familiarity with many of the principal characters involved.
23. Based on interviews with Salman F. Rahman of BEXIMCO and Ajmal Kabir. It may also be noted that Mr Rahman spent time in prison when the 'wrong government' was in power, and today he has successfully emerged as an influential member of parliament from the ruling Awami League, and an adviser to the prime minister in charge of private sector development.
24. This is the largest deal ever in Bangladesh by the private sector – see *Dhaka Tribune* (2018).
25. Bangladesh Shilpa Rin Sangstha (BSRS) and Bangladesh Shilpa Bank (BSB) were the two major banks raised particularly to channel industrial financing to potential entrepreneurs.
26. Thus, when Mr Akijuddin had mustered enough courage to venture into a bank in the early 1970s, the bank manager, after talking to him at length, offered to help. Indeed, he went out of his way to arrange a substantial loan even when there was no collateral on offer. The banker had a 'hunch' about Akij as sometimes bankers are wont to do, and decided to back him (reported by Musa Miah, senior journalist–reporter, *Bonik Barta*). While there is little doubt that such heartwarming incidents did occur, the more usual story would be one where the manager would require a certain percentage of the loan as an inducement for approval.

27. In the uncertain situation of the time, and the fact that they were not Bengali speaking and therefore in danger of being identified with the retreating Pakistanis, the Ispahani clan had fled the country. Their patriarch had taken shelter in Calcutta from where they he was monitoring developments. My key respondent, Ajmal Kabir, informed that Bangabandhu had sent word to him to return.
28. Old (Bengali) capital did not survive the new times – even when they got their factories back. They could not get them off the ground – the times had changed and 'they did not have the fire in them' (key informant Matin Choudhury, former chairman of the Textiles Association). They were older and their children were unable to rise to the occasion, frequently falling apart due to sibling rivalries. At the same time capital accumulation was taking varying shapes – for example, trading in PL480 grains or trading and shopkeeping, and bribe money for selected members of officialdom (specific examples are being withheld).
29. The RMMRU (2017) report provide the following data from a survey: *dalal*s provide information of jobs (57 per cent), obtain work visas (7 per cent), obtain passports (32 per cent), provide official smart cards (72 per cent), arrange medical tests (70 per cent), arranged flight tickets (85 per cent) and so on.
30. As has often happened in Bangladesh, the role of key individuals has often driven change sometimes from the most unexpected of places. Thus, Sir Abed was the founder of BRAC, the largest NGO in the world; Mohammed Yunus founded the Grameen Bank and led the micro-credit revolution; Akhtar Hameed Khan founded the Comilla Model of rural development. In a similar vein, the role of Dr Zafrullah Choudhury, founder of the prominent health-based NGO Gonoshasthya Kendro, in leading the initiative and mobilizing support and finally persuading General Ershad to push it through must be acknowledged. In an interview with the *Multinational Monitor* (2002), Choudhury recounts the saga which is a must-read if one is to understand how real-world policymaking works.
31. Based on an interview with Tapan Choudhury, Director of Square Pharmaceuticals – one of the most successful drug companies in the country.
32. Personal interview with Mr Choudhury on 22 December 2020.
33. This is particularly heartening to note given widespread governance problems in other sectors.
34. Most women, especially at the early stages, came into the workforce through pre-existing contacts already working in the factories so that relocation was relatively smooth (Begum 1999; Siddiqui et al. 2010)
35. Interestingly, leading cosmetic brands began to target this emerging market by introducing 'mini packs' of shampoo, 'fairness creams', toothpaste and soap

that cost just a few *taka* and well within the purchasing power of this new proletariat.
36. See Quah (1999); Kochanek (1993). Paul (2010) raises the question of a positive relationship between economic growth and corruption.
37. Data from BGMEA, 'BGMEA Export Performance', https://www.bgmea.com.bd/export-performances/4 (accessed 6 December 2021).
38. The Bank Company Act, 1991, empowers the Bangladesh Bank to issue licences to carry out banking business in Bangladesh. The Dhaka Stock Exchange is managed under the Company Act, 1994, the Security and Exchange Commission Act, 1993, Security and Exchange Commission Regulation, 1994, and Security Exchange (Insider Trading) regulation of 1994.
39. The establishment of the mobile phone monopoly was perhaps one of the most naked examples of crony capitalism in Bangladesh.
40. Attacks on the person or property of opposition leaders as well as attacks on minorities suspected to have voted for the other side have been seen during these times. The *New Humanitarian* (2014) quotes a minority leader, Mr Dasgupta, after the 2014 elections: 'One of the major reasons for the attacks is occupying land and assets. If repeated attacks take place, Hindus will migrate and this will help local [lawbreakers] to occupy the lands....'
41. The prime minister's private sector development advisor (and a key business leader) thinks that there are more than 100 large groups of this type so that our assumption is likely to be biased towards the lower side.
42. Based on an interview with the private sector adviser to the prime minister, who himself is a leading businessman. 'Large' is defined as entities with a turnover of around a billion dollars.
43. The owners of the Pacific Group who had benefited from their political ties from the former regime of Khaleda Zia in the 1990s and early 2000s have lost their 'crony' privileges and find themselves embattled. The owners of Crystal Group and SA Group seem to suffer from legacy issues, extreme bank exposure, default and generally poor management.
44. For example, see Krueger (2012); Reeves (2018).
45. For example, Stein and Charters (1990).
46. See, for example, Riaz (1993); T. Murshid (1995).
47. There was a compensation system for the original landowners which was inadequate and poorly managed.
48. ADB (2011) and B. Sen (2010) have used the poverty line as the cut-off point for the poor and the middle class.
49. This is purely conjectural based on an interesting piece of evidence related to newspaper readership in 2016–17, which was 26.5 per cent for the country as a whole and 42.2 per cent for urban areas. Clearly, given that Dhaka is the

primate city, this proportion would be even higher for Dhaka. The assumption is that newspaper readership is a strong characteristic of the middle class.

50. Although popularly described as 'modern' to distinguish from earlier genres, these became popular with the Kolkata-based Bengali cinema of the 1950s–60s, and drew a large following in Bangladesh.

51. Siddiqui et al. (2010: 202) has a section which describes some of these extractive mechanisms in his discussion on 'primitive capital accumulation'. The criminal underbelly I am referring to can no longer be swept under such terminology, as that particular phase of accumulation has now passed.

Conclusion

1. Today an accommodation of sorts has emerged with even the World Bank espousing an indispensable state role in fostering development. Thus, it notes, 'Development without an effective state is impossible … an effective state – not a minimal one' (World Bank 1997: 18), though it added that the role should be facilitative, not directive, that it should complement markets, not replace them – this was the 'post-Washington Consensus' where a balance between the market and the state, and a role of civil society in governance was envisaged (Fine 2001; Fine and Rose 2003).

Glossary

adda	informal socializing in places like tea-stalls or parks
aman	rainy season rice crop
aratdar	middleman or broker who plays a central market role in Bangladesh
aus	rice crop grown in between the *aman* and *boro* crops
balaam	traditional boat builder
bepari	itinerant trader operating to connect producers to mills, wholesale or retail
bhadralok	the educated middle-class
bharkiwala	petty paddy processor at village level
biri	hand-rolled indigenous cigarettes
boro	dry season rice crop
bustee	poor urban areas or 'slum'
char	sandy shoals created by riverine action
crore	local unit = 10,000,000
dadon	a traditional cash advance stipulating repayment in kind (for example, rice or paddy)
dai	traditional birth attendants
dalal	middleman, generic name
dhakaiya	the original inhabitants of Dhaka as opposed to those who migrated there later from the hinterland
dhaner upore	similar to *dadon* but specific to cash for paddy
faria	petty trader at village level
gonojagoron	mass awakening
haor	a wetland ecosystem in the northeastern part of Bangladesh which is a bowl- or saucer-shaped shallow depression, also known as a backswamp
hawala	traditional, informal international money transfers that bypass the formal financial system
junk	traditional Chinese sailing vessel of ancient unknown origin, still in wide use; high-sterned, with projecting bow, the *junk* carries up to five masts on which are set

	square sails of panels of linen or matting flattened by bamboo strips
khadi	coarse handloom cloth made of cotton
khas	government-owned fallow land on which no one else has any property rights
lac	local unit = 100,000
lungi	a type of sarong that originated in the Indian subcontinent; the multi-coloured *lungi* is a men's skirt usually tied around the lower waist below the navel
maund	local unit for weight = 40 kilograms
motka	a rough handloom silk made out of waste mulberry silk without even removing the gum
murubbi	respected elder
purdah	veil
salwar-qameez-dupatta	traditional dress worn by both women and men in southern Asia: *salwar*s are loose pajama-like trousers with legs wide at the top and narrow at the bottom; *kameez* is a long shirt or tunic; *dupatta* is a long scarf often used to cover a woman's head
samiti	club or group
sari	principal outer garment of women of the Indian subcontinent, consisting of a piece of often brightly coloured, frequently embroidered, silk, cotton, or, in recent years, synthetic cloth 5–7 yards long
subedar	governor
tadbir	canvassing or persuasion as in seeking favour
thana	police station or area under a police station
upazilla	sub-district

References

Abadian, S. 1996. 'Women's Autonomy and Its Impact on Fertility'. *World Development* 24 (12): 1793–1809. https://doi.org/10.1016/S0305-750X(96)00075-7.

Abbot, J. C. 1962. 'The Role of Marketing in the Development of Backward Agricultural Economies'. *Journal of Farm Economics* 44 (2): 349–62.

Abdullah, A. A. 2000. 'Social Change and "Modernization"'. In *Bangladesh: Promise and Performance*, edited by R. Jahan, 129–47. Dhaka: University Press Limited.

Abdullah, A., M. Hossain and R. Nations. 1976. 'Agrarian Structure and the IRDP Preliminary Considerations'. *Bangladesh Development Studies* 4 (2): 209–66.

Abed, F. H. 2013. 'Bangladesh's Health Revolution'. *Lancet* 382 (9910): 2048–49.

Adams, A. M., A. Rabbani, S. Ahmed, S. S. Mahmood, A. Al-Sabir, S. F. Rashid and T. G. Evans. 2013. 'Explaining Equity Gains in Child Survival in Bangladesh: Scale, Speed, and Selectivity in Health and Development'. *Lancet* 382 (9909): 2027–37. https://doi.org/10.1016/S0140-6736(13)62060-7.

Adams Jr, R. H. 1998. 'The Political Economy of the Food Subsidy System in Bangladesh'. *Journal of Development Studies* 35 (1): 66–88.

ADB. 2014. 'Bangladesh: Irrigation Management Improvement Project'. Text, Asian Development Bank, 30 June 2014. https://www.adb.org/projects/45207-002/main.pam.pdf. Accessed 25 December 2021.

———. 2016. 'Women at Work'. ADB Briefs no. 68, October 2016, Asian Development Bank and International Labour Organization. https://www.adb.org/sites/default/files/publication/203906/women-work.pdf. Accessed 25 December 2021.

———. 2018. 'Developing the Leather Industry in Bangladesh'. ADB Briefs no. 102, November 2018, Asian Development Bank and International Labour Organization. https://www.adb.org/publications/bangladesh-developing-leather-industry. Accessed 25 December 2021.

———. 2020. 'Bangladesh: Irrigation Management Improvement Project: Resettlement Plan'. South Asia Department, Manila. https://www.adb.org/projects/45207-002/main. Accessed 25 December 2021.

Adler, N. 2001. *International Dimensions of Organisational Behavior*. 4th ed. Cincinnati, OH: South-Western College Publishing.

Adler, N., and F. Ghadar. 1991. 'Strategic Human Resource Management: A Global Perspective'. In *Human Resource Management: An International Comparison*, edited by R. Pieper, 235–59. New York: Walter de Gruyter.

Adnan, S. 1990. *Annotation of Village Studies in Bangladesh and West Bengal: A Review of Socioeconomic Trends over 1942–88*. Comilla: Bangladesh Academy of Rural Development.

Afsar, R., and M. Hossain. 2020. *Dhaka's Changing Landscape: Prospects for Economic Development, Social Change, and Shared Prosperity*. New Delhi: Oxford University Press.

Aggarwal, A. 2004. 'Export Performance of EPZ in India'. ICRIER Working Paper no. 148, New Delhi, India.

Agrawal, R., and K. Salam. 2019. 'South Asia's Year in 10 Charts'. *Foreign Policy*, 24 December 2019. https://foreignpolicy.com/2019/12/24/south-asia-year-10-charts/. Accessed 25 December 2021.

Ahamed, E. 1978. 'Development Strategy in Bangladesh: Probable Political Consequences'. *Asian Survey* 18 (11): 1168–80.

Ahmad, Z. 1981. 'Education in Bengal 1912–1937'. PhD diss., School of Oriental and African Studies, University of London. https://eprints.soas.ac.uk/33783/1/11010556.pdf. Accessed 25 December 2021.

Ahmed, A. 2005. *Comparing Food and Cash Incentives for School in Bangladesh*. International Food Policy Research Institute, Tokyo: United Nations University.

———. 2006. 'Do Education Incentive Programmes Work? Evidence from IFPRI Studies in Bangladesh'. Paper presented to the conference on 'What Works for the Poorest? Knowledge, Policies and Practices', BRAC Centre for Development Management, Rajendrapur, Bangladesh, 2–5 December 2006.

———. 2016. 'Bangladesh Integrated Household Survey (BIHS) 2015'. International Food Policy Research Institute (datasets), Washington, DC.

Ahmed, A. U., P. Dorosh, Q. Shahabuddin and R. A. Talukder. 2010. 'Income Growth, Safety Nets, and Public Food Distribution'. Prepared for the Bangladesh Food Security Investment Forum. https://citeseerx.ist.psu.edu/viewdoc/download?doi=10.1.1.1064.6951&rep=rep1&type=pdf. Accessed 25 December 2021.

Ahmed, B. 1972. *Who Decides: Role of Managing Committee in A. C. F.* Comilla: BARD.

Ahmed, F. 2004. 'Practices of Poverty Measurement and Poverty Profile of Bangladesh'. Economic Working Paper Series no. 54, Asian Development Bank (ADB).

Ahmed, F., Y. Arias-Granada, M. E. Genoni, M. Yanez-Pagans, N. Yoshida, D. Roy and A. Latif. 2019. 'Description of the Official Methodology Used for Poverty Estimation in Bangladesh for 2016/17'. Background paper for the Bangladesh Poverty Assessment 2010–2016/17, World Bank, Washington, DC.

References

Ahmed, F., C. Dorji, S. Takamatsu and N. Yoshida. 2014. 'Hybrid Survey to Improve the Reliability of Poverty Statistics in a Cost-Effective Manner'. World Bank Policy Research Working Paper no. 6909, SSRN Scholarly Paper ID 2462335; Issue ID 2462335. https://papers.ssrn.com/abstract=2462335. Accessed 25 December 2021.

Ahmed, F. Z., A. Greenleaf and A. Sacks. 2014. 'The Paradox of Export Growth in Areas of Weak Governance: The Case of the Ready-Made Garment Sector in Bangladesh'. *World Development* 56 (April): 258–71. https://doi.org/10.1016/j.worlddev.2013.11.001.

Ahmed, I. 2016. 'Dhaka: Stressed but Alive!' In *Building Resilience in Cities under Stress*, edited by F. Mancini and A. Ó. Súilleabháin, 13–23. New York: International Peace Institute.

Ahmed, J. U. 1982. 'The Farm Wage and Land Market Situation under Comilla Cooperative Programme'. *Bangladesh Development Studies* 10 (1): 1–22.

Ahmed, M., S. R. Nath, A. Hossain, M. Kabir, A. Kalam, M. Shahjamal, R. N. Yasmin and T. Zafar. 2005. 'Quality with Equity: The Primary Education Agenda'. Education Watch 2004/4, Campaign for Popular Education (CAMPE), Bangladesh.

Ahmed, N., Z. Bakht, P. A. Dorosh and Q. Shahabuddin. 2007. 'Distortions to Agricultural Incentives in Bangladesh'. Agricultural Distortions Working Paper Series no. 48481, World Bank, December 2007.

Ahmed, R. 2001. *Retrospects and Prospects of the Rice Economy of Bangladesh*. Dhaka: University Press.

———. 2004. 'The Rice Economy of Bangladesh'. *Economic and Political Weekly* 39 (4): Article 4.

Ahmed, R., S. Haggblade and T. E. Chowdhury (eds.). 2000. *Out of the Shadow of Famine: Evolving Food Markets and Food Policy in Bangladesh*. Washington, DC: International Food Policy Research Institute (IFPRI).

Ahmed, Redwan. 2013. 'An Analysis of the Change and Volatility in the Apparel Industry of Bangladesh after MFA Era'. *Journal of Textile and Apparel, Technology and Management* 8 (1): 1–11.

Ahmed, S. 2004. *Microcredit in Bangladesh: Achievements and Challenges*. Mimeo. https://scholar.google.com/scholar?hl=en&as_sdt=0%2C33&q=Microcredit+achievements+challenges+Bangladesh+Ahmed%2C+S.&btnG=. Accessed 25 December 2021.

Ahmed, S. M., M. A. Hossain, A. M. RajaChowdhury and A. U. Bhuiya. 2011. 'The Health Workforce Crisis in Bangladesh: Shortage, Inappropriate Skill-Mix and Inequitable Distribution'. *Human Resources for Health* 9 (1): 1–7.

Ahmed, T., and B. Sen. 2018. 'Conservative Outlook, Gender Norms and Female Wellbeing: Evidence from Rural Bangladesh'. *World Development* 111 (November): 41–58. https://doi.org/10.1016/j.worlddev.2018.06.017.

Ahsan, R. M., S. Hussain and E. Ahsan. 1987. *Rural Urban Dynamics: Household Economic Strategies, Migration and Agricultural Development in Bangladesh*. Report submitted to Bangladesh Agricultural Research Council, Dhaka.

Akamatsu, K. 1935. 'Waga Kuni Yomo Kogyohin No Susei'. *Shogyo Keizai Ronso* 13: 129–212.

———. 1937. 'Waga Kuni Keizai Hatten No Sogo Benshoho'. *Shogyo Keizai Ronso* 15: 179–210.

———. 1962. 'Historical Pattern of Economic Growth in Developing Countries'. *Developing Economies* 1: 3–25. https://doi.org/10.1111/j.1746-1049.1962.tb01020.

Akash, M. M. 1987. *Bangladesher Orthoniti O Rajniti: Shamprotik Probonotashamuha [Economy and Politics in Bangladesh: Recent Trends]*. Dhaka: Jatiyo Shahitya Prakashani.

Akhter, N., and M. D. Islam. 2019. 'The Impact of Migration and Migrant Remittances on Household Poverty in Bangladesh'. *Asian Development Perspectives* 10 (1): 43–59.

Alam, Md. M., and M. A. Haque. 1976. 'Rural Power Structures and Cooperatives in Relation to Modernization in Agriculture'. In 'Exploitation and the Rural Poor: Working Paper on the Rural Power Structure in Bangladesh'. Bangladesh Academy for Rural Development, Comilla, 215–36.

Alam, S. M. N. 1983. *Marginalization, Pauperization and Agrarian Change in Two Villages of Bangladesh*. UMI. https://www.proquest.com/openview/d8d33da e8935d7e94052074b1f678b9b/1?pq-origsite=gscholar&cbl=18750&diss=y. Accessed 25 December 2021.

Alamgir, M. 1973. *Problems of Urbanization in Bangladesh*. Dhaka: Bangladesh Institute of Development Studies. Mimeo.

———. 1980. *Famine in South Asia: Political Economy of Mass Starvation*. Cambridge, Mass.: Oelgeschlager, Gunn & Hain.

Alauddin, M., and C. Tisdell. 1991a. 'The "Green Revolution" and Labour Absorption in Bangladesh Agriculture: The Relevance of the East Asian Experience'. *Pakistan Development Review* 30 (2): 173–88.

———. 1991b. 'Welfare Consequences of Green Revolution Technology: Changes in Bangladeshi Food Production and Diet'. *Development and Change* 22 (3): 497–517. https://doi.org/10.1111/j.1467-7660.1991.tb00423.x.

Alavi, H. 1975. 'India and the Colonial Mode of Production'. *Economic and Political Weekly* 10 (33/35): 1235–62.

References

Alder, S., L. Shao and F. Zilibotti. 2016. 'Economic Reforms and Industrial Policy in a Panel of Chinese Cities'. *Journal of Economic Growth* 21 (4): 305–49.

Alderman, H., and D. D. Headey. 2017. 'How Important Is Parental Education for Child Nutrition?' *World Development* 94 (June): 448–64. https://doi.org/10.1016/j.worlddev.2017.02.007.

Alvaredo, F., L. Chancel, T. Piketty, E. Saez and G. Zucman. 2017. 'Global Inequality Dynamics: New Findings from WID.world'. *American Economic Review* 107 (5): 404–09. https://doi.org/10.1257/aer.p20171095.

Alwang, J. 1991. 'A Literature Review of Public Food Distribution in Bangladesh'. International Food Policy Research Institute, Working Paper on Food Policy in Bangladesh no. 1, Washington, DC. https://pdf.usaid.gov/pdf_docs/pnabk843.pdf. Accessed 25 December 2021.

Anderson, S., and M. Eswaran. 2009. 'What Determines Female Autonomy? Evidence from Bangladesh'. *Journal of Development Economics* 90 (2): 179–91.

Angelucci, M., D. Karlan and J. Zinman. 2015. 'Microcredit Impacts: Evidence from a Randomized Microcredit Program Placement Experiment by Compartamos Banco'. *American Economic Journal: Applied Economics* 7 (1): 151–82.

Annabi, N., B. H. Khondker, S. Raihan, J. Cockburn and B. Decaluwe. 2006. 'Implications of WTO Agreements and Unilateral Trade Policy Reforms for Poverty in Bangladesh: Short versus Long-Run Impacts'. World Bank Policy Research Working Paper no. 3976, World Bank Publications.

Armendáriz, B., and J. Morduch. 2010. *The Economics of Microfinance*. Cambridge, Mass.: MIT Press.

Arif, F. 1984. 'Renovation of Derelict Tanks (An Experience of Utilization of Rural Resource in Bhawanipur Mouza)'. Rural Development Academy, Bogura, Bangladesh. http://www.rda.gov.bd/sites/default/files/files/rda.portal.gov.bd/page/639b0c9d_722b_4604_bb16_30d3bc4f563b/2021-09-25-07-11-a8d8387ec66eb1bfcb24dcfce8b82dfe.pdf. Accessed 25 December 2021.

Arifeen, S. E., A. Christou, L. Reichenbach, F. A. Osman, K. Azad, K. S. Islam, F. Ahmed, H. B. Perry and D. H. Peters. 2013. 'Community-Based Approaches and Partnerships: Innovations in Health-Service Delivery in Bangladesh'. *Lancet* 382 (9909): 2012–26. https://doi.org/10.1016/S0140-6736(13)62149-2.

Aristotle. n.d. *The Politics*. Quoted in Richard Sennett, *Flesh and Stone: The Body and the City in Western Civilization*, 13. New York: W. W. Norton & Company, 1996.

Arnold, F., and N. M. Shah. 1986. *Asian Labor Migration: Pipeline to the Middle East*. Boulder, CO: Westview Press.

Arrow, K. 1969. 'The Organization of Economic Activity: Issues Pertinent to the Choice of Market versus Nonmarket Allocation'. In *The Analysis and Evaluation of Public Expenditure: The PPB System*, 1:59–73. US Joint Economic Committee, 91st Congress, first session, Washington, DC: US Government Printing Office.

Asadullah, M. N., A. Savoia and W. Mahmud. 2014. 'Paths to Development: Is There a Bangladesh Surprise?' *World Development* 62 (October): 138–54. https://doi.org/10.1016/j.worlddev.2014.05.013.

Asaduzzaman, M. 1979. 'Adoption of HYV Rice in Bangladesh'. *Bangladesh Development Studies* 7 (3): 23–52.

Ashwin, S., N. Kabeer and E. Schüßler. 2020. 'Contested Understandings in the Global Garment Industry after Rana Plaza'. *Development and Change* 51 (5): 1296–1305. https://doi.org/10.1111/dech.12573.

Attanasio, O., B. Augsburg, R. De Haas, E. Fitzsimons and H. Harmgart. 2015. 'The Impacts of Microfinance: Evidence from Joint-Liability Lending in Mongolia'. *American Economic Journal: Applied Economics* 7 (1): 90–122.

Azad, Md. A. K., and F. Qimiao. 2017. 'Towards a Cleaner Bangladesh: Safe Water, Sanitation, and Hygiene for All'. *World Bank Blogs*, 15 September 2017. https://blogs.worldbank.org/endpovertyinsouthasia/towards-cleaner-bangladesh-safe-water-sanitation-and-hygiene-all. Accessed 25 December 2021.

Bain, J. S. 1959. *Industrial Organization*. New York: John Wiley and Sons.

Bakht, Z. 1996. 'The Rural Non-farm Sector in Bangladesh: Evolving Pattern and Growth Potential'. *Bangladesh Development Studies* 24 (3/4): 29–73.

Bakht, Z., and D. Bhattacharya. 1991. 'Investment, Employment and Value Added in Bangladesh Manufacturing Sector in 1980s: Evidence and Estimate'. *Bangladesh Development Studies* 19 (1/2): 1–50.

Bakht, Z., M. Yunus and M. Salimullah. 2002. *Machinery Industry in Bangladesh*. IDEAS Machinery Industry Report no. 4, Institute of Developing Economies Advanced School, Japan.

Banerjee, A., E. Duflo, R. Glennerster and C. Kinnan. 2015. 'The Miracle of Microfinance: Evidence from a Randomised Evaluation'. *American Economic Journal: Applied Economics* 7, no. 1 (January): 22–53.

Banerjee, A. V., and E. Duflo. 2008. 'What Is Middle Class about the Middle Classes around the World?' *Journal of Economic Perspectives* 22 (2): 3–28.

Banerjee, O., T. Darbas, P. R. Brown and C. H. Roth. 2014. 'Historical Divergence in Public Management of Foodgrain Systems in India and Bangladesh: Opportunities to Enhance Food Security'. *Global Food Security* 3 (3): 159–66. https://doi.org/10.1016/j.gfs.2014.06.002.

Bangladesh Bank. 1975. 'Annual Balance of Payments 1974–75'. Statistics Department, Bangladesh Bank, Dhaka.

———. 2020. 'BOP Data Publication of 1973–74 and 1974–75'. https://www.bb.org.bd/econdata/bop.php. Accessed 25 December 2021.

———. n.d.-a. 'BOP Provisional Data 2020'. Accessed 10 January 2021. https://www.bb.org.bd/econdata/bop.php.

References

———. n.d.-b. 'Provisional Per Capita GDP and Growth Estimate for 2020'. National Accounts Statistics, Bangladesh Bureau of Statistics, Ministry of Planning, Dhaka. https://bbs.portal.gov.bd/sites/default/files/files/bbs.portal.gov.bd/page/cdaa3ae6_cb65_4066_8c61_d97e22cb836c/2021-02-18-15-16-35d82ae9286826fe79472d8be1777b73.pdf. Accessed 25 December 2021.

Bangladesh Bureau of Educational Information and Statistics (BANBEIS). 2017. *Pocket Book on Bangladesh Education Statistics 2017*. Dhaka: Ministry of Education, Government of Bangladesh. http://lib.banbeis.gov.bd/BANBEIS_PDF/Pocket%20Book%20on%20Bangladesh%20Education%20Statistics%202017.pdf. Accessed 25 December 2021.

Bangladesh Bureau of Statistics (BBS). 1975. *Statistical Yearbook of Bangladesh 1975*. Dhaka: Ministry of Planning, Government of Bangladesh. www.bbs.gov.bd. Accessed 25 December 2021.

———. 1977. *Bangladesh National Population Census Report 1974*. Dhaka: Ministry of Planning, Government of Bangladesh.

———. 1991. *Statistical Yearbook of Bangladesh, 1991*. Dhaka: Ministry of Planning, Government of Bangladesh. http://www.epb.gov.bd/. Accessed 25 December 2021.

———. 1997. *Bangladesh Population Census 1991: Urban Area Report*. Dhaka: Ministry of Planning, Government of Bangladesh.

———. 1981. *Statistical Yearbook of Bangladesh 1981*. Reproduction and Documentation Branch, R. D. P. wing, Secretariat, Dhaka: Ministry of Planning, Government of Bangladesh. www.bbs.gov.bd. Accessed 25 December 2021.

———. 1991. *Statistical Yearbook of Bangladesh 1991*. Dhaka: Ministry of Planning, Government of Bangladesh. www.bbs.gov.bd. Accessed 25 December 2021.

———. 1992. *Report on Integrated Annual Survey of Non-farm Activities, 1989–90*. Dhaka: Ministry of Planning, Government of Bangladesh. www.bbs.gov.bd. Accessed 25 December 2021.

———. 1993. *Twenty Years of National Accounting of Bangladesh, 1972–73 to 1991–92*. Dhaka: Statistics Division, Ministry of Planning, Government of the People's Republic of Bangladesh.

———. 2001a. *Population Census 2001: Preliminary Report*. Dhaka: Ministry of Planning, Government of Bangladesh.

———. 2001b. *Health and Morbidity Status Survey 2000*. Dhaka: Statistics and Informatics Division, Ministry of Planning, Government of the People's Republic of Bangladesh.

———. 2011. *Statistical Yearbook of Bangladesh 2011*. Dhaka: Ministry of Planning, Government of Bangladesh. www.bbs.gov.bd. Accessed 25 December 2021.

———. 2013a. *Health and Morbidity Status Survey, 2012*. Dhaka: Statistics and Informatics Division, Ministry of Planning, Government of the People's Republic of Bangladesh.

———. 2013b. *Survey of Manufacturing Industries, SMI 2012*. Dhaka: Ministry of Planning, Government of Bangladesh.

———. 2016. *Preliminary Report on Household Income and Expenditure Survey 2016*. Dhaka: Ministry of Planning, Government of Bangladesh. www.bbs.gov.bd. Accessed 26 December 2021.

———. 2018. *Handloom Census*. Dhaka: Ministry of Planning, Government of Bangladesh. http://data.bbs.gov.bd/index.php/catalog/186. Accessed 27 November 2021.

———. 2019. *Statistical Yearbook of Bangladesh 2019*. Dhaka: Ministry of Planning, Government of Bangladesh. www.bbs.gov.bd. Accessed 26 December 2021.

———. 2020a. *Gross Domestic Product (GDP) of Bangladesh 2019–20(p)*. Dhaka: Ministry of Planning, Government of Bangladesh. http://www.bbs.gov.bd/. Accessed 26 December 2021.

———. 2020b. *Gross Domestic Product (GDP) of Bangladesh 2019–20(p)*. Dhaka: Ministry of Planning, Government of Bangladesh. http://www.bbs.gov.bd/. Accessed 26 December 2021.

———. n.d. *Household Income and Expenditure Surveys 2000, 2005, 2010, 2016*. Survey Data. Dhaka: Ministry of Planning, Government of Bangladesh.

Bangladesh Finance Division Economic Adviser's Wing. 2005. *Bangladesh Economic Review, 2005*. Dhaka: Ministry of Finance, Government of the People's Republic of Bangladesh.

———. 1982. *Bangladesh Economic Survey, 1981–82*. Dhaka: Ministry of Finance, Government of the People's Republic of Bangladesh. https://books.google.com.bd/books?id=E9-yzQEACAAJ. Accessed 26 December 2021.

———. 1993. *Bangladesh Economic Survey, 1992–93*. Dhaka: Ministry of Finance, Government of the People's Republic of Bangladesh.

Bangladesh Garments Manufacturers and Exporters Association (BGMEA). 1983. 'BGMEA Export Performance Data'. https://www.bgmea.com.bd/. Accessed 26 December 2021.

———. 2021. 'BGMEA Export Performance Data'. https://www.bgmea.com.bd/site/digest/4. Accessed 26 December 2021.

'Bangladesh Nutrition Data'. n.d. UNICEF Data. https://data.unicef.org/dv_index/. Accessed 16 March 2021.

'Bangladesh Trade Indicators'. 2015. WITS Data. https://wits.worldbank.org/CountryProfile/en/Country/BGD/Year/2015. Accessed 15 March 2021.

Banglapedia. 2015a. 'Bangla Language'. 31 March 2015. http://en.banglapedia.org/index.php/Bangla_Language. Accessed 26 December 2021.

———. 2015b. 'Matsyanyayam'. http://en.banglapedia.org/index.php/Matsyanyayam. Accessed 26 December 2021.

———. 2015c. 'University of Dhaka'. https://en.banglapedia.org/index.php/University_of_Dhaka. Accessed 6 December 2021.

References

Barkat, A., A. Osman and S. K. Sen Gupta. 2014. *In the Corridors of Remittance: Cost and Use of Remittances in Bangladesh*. Dhaka: ILO.

Bass, G. J. 2013. *The Blood Telegram*. Gurgaon: Random House India.

Basu, K. 2018. 'Why Is Bangladesh Booming?' *Brookings*, 1 May 2018. https://www.brookings.edu/opinions/why-is-bangladesh-booming/. Accessed 26 December 2021.

Bauer, P. T. 1957. *Economic Analysis and Policy in Underdeveloped Countries*. Virginia: Duke University, Commonwealth Studies Center.

Baulch, B., J. Das, W. Jaim, N. Farid and S. Zohir. 1998. *The Spatial Integration and Pricing Efficiency of the Private Sector Grain Trade in Bangladesh: Phase II Report*. Institute of Development Studies, May 1998, Sussex, UK.

Baxter, C. 1974. 'Constitution Making: The Development of Federalism in Pakistan'. *Asian Survey* 14 (12): 1074–85.

Bayes, A., I. Hussain and M. Rahman. 1995. 'Trends in the External Sector: Trade and Aid'. Chap. 8 in *Experiences with Economic Reforms: A Review of Bangladesh's Development*, edited by R. Sobhan. Dhaka: Centre for Policy Dialogue and University Press Limited, 1995.

Begum, A. 1997. *The Socio-Economic Condition of Pavement Dwellers of Dhaka City*. Research Report no. 150, Bangladesh Institute of Development Studies, Dhaka.

———. 1999. *Destination Dhaka: Urban Migration; Expectations and Reality*. Dhaka: The University Press Limited. http://www.uplbooks.com.bd/book/destination-dhaka-urban-migration-expectations-and-reality. Accessed 26 December 2021.

Begum, A., and R. A. Mahmood. 2017. 'Labour Market and Skill Gap Analyses: Health Care (Nursing and Health Technician)'. Chap. 9 in *BIDS Study Report: Labour Market and Skill Gap in Bangladesh; Macro and Micro Level Study*. Dhaka: Finance Division, Ministry of Finance, Government of the People's Republic of Bangladesh.

Begum, S., and A. F. M. Shamsuddin. 1998. 'Exports and Economic Growth in Bangladesh'. *Journal of Development Studies* 35 (1): 89–114. https://doi.org/10.1080/00220389808422556.

Behrman, J. R., and A. B. Deolalikar. 1987. 'Will Developing Country Nutrition Improve with Income? A Case Study for Rural South India'. *Journal of Political Economy* 95 (3): 492–507.

Bernard, M., and J. Ravenhill. 1995. 'Beyond Product Cycles and Flying Geese: Regionalization, Hierarchy and the Industrialization of East Asia'. *World Politics* 45 (2): 171–209.

Berthet, S. 2015. 'Boat Technology and Culture in Chittagong'. *Water History* 7 (2): 179–97.

Bertocci, P. J. 1970. 'Elusive Villages: Social Structure and Community Organization.' In *Rural East*, edited by S. M. Nurul Alam, 21–42. Dhaka: University Press Ltd.

Beverley, H. 1874. 'The Census of Bengal'. *Journal of the Statistical Society of London* 37 (1): 69–113.

Bhaduri, A. 1983. *The Economic Structure of Backward Agriculture*. London; New York: Academic Press.

Bhattacharya, D. 1996. 'The Emerging Pattern of Rural Non-farm Sector in Bangladesh: A Review of Micro Evidence'. *Bangladesh Development Studies* 24 (3/4): 29–74.

Bhattacharya, D., and M. Rahman. 2000. 'Experience with Implementation of WTO-ATC and Implications for Bangladesh'. CPD Working Paper 7, Centre for Policy Dialogue.

Bhattacharya, N. C., and L. A. Natesan. 1932. *Some Bengal Villages: An Economic Survey*. Calcutta: Calcutta University.

Bhuiya, A., P. G. Datta and A. M. R. Chowdhury. 2013. 'Health Progress and Research Culture in Bangladesh'. *Lancet* 382 (9906): 1699. https://doi.org/10.1016/S0140-6736(13)62394-6.

BHW. 2010. *Bangladesh Health Watch Report 2009: How Healthy is Health Sector Governance?* BRAC University. http://dspace.bracu.ac.bd/xmlui/handle/10361/597. Accessed 26 December 2021.

Birdsall, N., C. Graham and S. Pettinato. 2000. 'Stuck in a Tunnel: Is Globalization Muddling the Middle?' Brookings Institution Center Working Paper no. 14, Washington, DC.

Black, R. E., C. G. Victora, S. P. Walker, Z. A. Bhutta, P. Christian, M. de Onis, M. Ezzati, S. Grantham-McGregor, J. Katz, R. Martorell and R. Uauy. 2013. 'Maternal and Child Undernutrition and Overweight in Low-Income and Middle-Income Countries'. *Lancet* 382 (9890): 427–51. https://doi.org/10.1016/S0140-6736(13)60937-X.

Blair, H. 1978. 'Rural Development, Class Structure and Bureaucracy in Bangladesh'. *World Development* 6 (1): 65–82.

Bora, J., N. Saikia, W. Lutz and A. Jaarsveld. 2019. 'Revisiting the Causes of Fertility Decline in Bangladesh: Family Planning Program or Female Education?' Working paper, International Institute for Applied Systems Analysis. https://doi.org/10.13140/RG.2.2.14876.23681

Bornstein, D. 1997. *The Price of a Dream: The Story of the Grameen Bank and the Idea That Is Helping the Poor to Change Their Lives*. Chicago: Chicago University Press.

Borooah, V. K., P. P. McGregor and P. M. McKee. 1991. *Regional Income Inequality and Poverty in the United Kingdom: An Analysis Based on the 1985 Family Expenditure Survey*. Dartmouth, UK: Dartmouth Publishing Company.

Bose, S. R. 1973. 'The Price Situation in Bangladesh: A Preliminary Analysis'. *Bangladesh Economic Review* 1 (3): 243–68.

———. 1974. 'The Comilla Co-operative Approach and the Prospects for Broad-Based Green Revolution in Bangladesh'. *World Development* 2 (8): 21–28. https://doi.org/10.1016/0305-750X(74)90003-5.

References

Bruton, G. D., M. W. Peng, D. Ahlstrom, C. Stan and K. Xu. 2015. 'State-Owned Enterprises around the World as Hybrid Organizations'. *Academy of Management Perspectives* 29 (1): 92–114.

Burchi, F. 2012. 'Whose Education Affects a Child's Nutritional Status? From Parents' to Household's Education'. *Demographic Research* 27 (July): 681–704.

Byron, R. K., and J. Chakma. 2020. 'Cars Made in Bangladesh on the Way'. *Daily Star*, 1 September 2020. https://www.thedailystar.net/business/news/cars-made-bangladesh-the-way-1953853. Accessed 26 December 2021.

Camerer, C. F. 2003. *Behavioral Game Theory: Experiments in Strategic Interaction*. Princeton, New Jersey: Princeton University Press.

Cardenas, J. C., J. Stranlund and W. Cleve. 2000. 'Local Environmental Control and Institutional Crowding Out'. *World Development* 28 (10): 1719–33.

Centre for Urban Studies. 1976. *Squatters in Bangladesh Cities: A Survey of Urban Squatters in Dhaka, Chittagong and Khulna, 1974*. Dhaka: CUS.

Chakma, J. 2020. 'Bangladesh on Track to Becoming a $6b Pharma Market by 2025'. *Daily Star*, 16 November 2029. https://www.thedailystar.net/business/news/bangladesh-track-becoming-6b-pharma-market-2025-1995741. Accessed 26 December 2021.

Chakma, N. K. 2011. 'Buddhism in Bengal: A Brief Survey'. *Bangladesh E-Journal of Sociology* 8 (1): 37–44.

Chalfin, B. 2004. *Shea Butter Republic: State Power, Global Markets, and the Making of an Indigenous Commodity*. 1st ed. Routledge. https://doi.org/10.4324/9780203496534.

Chambers, R. 2014. *Rural Development: Putting the Last First*. London: Routledge.

Chami, R., C. Fullenkamp and S. Jahjah. 2003. 'Are Immigrant Remittance Flows a Source of Capital for Development?' IMF Staff Papers no. 189, 55–81. SSRN Scholarly Paper ID 880292; Issue ID 880292. https://papers.ssrn.com/abstract=880292. Accessed 26 December 2021.

Chattopadhyay, P. 1972. 'On the Question of the Mode of Production in Indian Agriculture'. *Economic and Political Weekly* 7 (53): A185–92.

Chen, L. C., M. Rahman, S. D'Souza, J. Chakraborty and A. M. Sardar. 1983. 'Mortality Impact of an MCH-FP Program in Matlab, Bangladesh'. *Studies in Family Planning* 14 (8/9): 199. https://doi.org/10.2307/1966412.

Chen, M. A. 1983. *A Quiet Revolution: Women in Transition in Rural Bangladesh*. Cambridge, Mass.: Schenkman Pub. Co.

Cheng, C. P. 2011. '"Internal Goes before International": A Historical Analysis of the Governance Structure of Taiwan Footwear Industry'. *Journal of Social Sciences and Philosophy* 23 (1). https://doi.org/10.6350/JSSP.201103.0015.

Choudhry, S., and S. Basher. 2002. 'The Enduring Significance of Bangladesh's War of Independence: An Analysis of Economic Costs and Consequences'. *Journal of Developing Areas* 36 (1): 41–55.

Choudhury, G. W. 1972. 'Bangladesh: Why It Happened'. *International Affairs (Royal Institute of International Affairs 1944–)* 48 (2): 242–49. https://doi.org/10.2307/2613440.

———. 1973. 'The Last Days of United Pakistan: A Personal Account'. *International Affairs (Royal Institute of International Affairs 1944–)* 49 (2): 229–39.

Chowdhury, A. M. R., A. Bhuiya, M. E. Chowdhury, S. Rasheed, Z. Hussain and L. C. Chen. 2013. 'The Bangladesh Paradox: Exceptional Health Achievement Despite Economic Poverty'. *Lancet* 382 (9906): 1734–45. https://doi.org/10.1016/S0140-6736(13)62148-0.

Chowdhury, Dr Z. 2002. 'Essential Drugs and Health for All: Healthy Innovations from Bangladesh'. *Multinational Monitor* 23, no. 6 (June). https://www.multinationalmonitor.org/mm2002/062002/interview-chowdhury.html. Accessed 26 December 2021.

Chowdhury, N. 1986. 'Public Foodgrain Distribution System in Bangladesh in the Post-liberation Period: A Historical Profile'. *Bangladesh Development Studies* 14 (3): 67–95.

———. 1987. 'Seasonality of Foodgrain Price and Procurement Programme in Bangladesh Since Liberation: An Exploratory Study'. *Bangladesh Development Studies* 15 (1): 105–28.

Chowdhury, O. H., and S. R. Osmani. 2010. 'Towards Achieving the Right to Health: The Case of Bangladesh'. *Bangladesh Development Studies* 33 (1/2): 205–73.

Chowdhury, M., and D. Radicic. 2019. 'Remittance and Asset Accumulation in Bangladesh'. *Journal of International Development* 3 (6): 475–94.

Chun, N. 2010. 'Middle Class Size in the Past, Present, and Future: A Description of Trends in Asia'. Asian Development Bank Economics Working Paper Series no. 217. https://doi.org/10.2139/ssrn.1688710.

Central Intelligence Agency. 2012. *World Factbook 2012*. CIA.

Clark, G. 1994. *Onions Are My Husband: Survival and Accumulation by West African Market Women*. Chicago, Illinois: University of Chicago Press.

Cleland, J., J. F. Phillips, S. Amin and G. M. Kamal. 1994. 'The Determinants of Reproductive Change in Bangladesh: Success in a Challenging Environment'. World Bank Regional and Sectoral Studies, The World Bank, Washington, DC.

Cohen, B. 2006. 'Urbanization in Developing Countries: Current Trends, Future Projections, and Key Challenges for Sustainability'. *Technology in Society* 28 (1): 63–80. https://doi.org/10.1016/j.techsoc.2005.10.005.

Colson, E. 1974. *Tradition and Contract: The Problem of Social Order*. Portsmouth, New Hampshire: Heinemann.

Coulmas, F. 2017. *An Introduction to Multilingualism: Language in a Changing World*. Oxford: Oxford University Press.

References

Crawford, S. E. S., and E. Ostrom. 1995. 'A Grammar of Institutions'. *American Political Science Review* 89 (3): 582–600. https://doi.org/10.2307/2082975.

Crépon, B., F. Devoto, E. Duflo and W. Parienté. 2015. 'Estimating the Impact of Microcredit on Those Who Take It Up: Evidence from a Randomized Experiment in Morocco'. *American Economic Journal: Applied Economics* 7 (1): 123–50.

Crow, B. 1999. 'Researching the Market System in Bangladesh'. In *Agricultural Markets from Theory to Practice: Field Experience in Developing Countries*, edited by B. Harriss-White, 115–50. London: Palgrave Macmillan UK. https://doi.org/10.1007/978-1-349-27273-0_5.

———. 2001. *Markets, Class and Social Change: Trading Networks and Poverty in Rural South Asia*. London: Palgrave-Macmillan.

Crow, B., and K. A. S. Murshid. 1994. 'Economic Returns to Social Power: Merchants' Finance and Interlinkage in the Grain Markets of Bangladesh'. *World Development* 22 (7): 1011–30. https://doi.org/10.1016/0305-750X(94)90145-7.

Daily Star. 2018. 'Rethinking Urban Spaces: Dhaka and Beyond; Re-imagining Urban Nodes in Dhaka'. 22 February 2018. https://img.thedailystar.net/supplements/rethinking-urban-spaces/reimagining-urban-nodes-dhaka-1538062. Accessed 26 December 2021.

———. 2019. 'Bangladesh Role Model for Developing Nations'. 26 November 2019. https://www.thedailystar.net/business/news/bangladesh-role-model-developing-nations-1832041. Accessed 16 November 2021.

———. 2020a. 'Leather Turning into a Big Draw for Foreign Investors'. Report filed by Refayet Ullah Mridha, 13 October 2020. https://www.thedailystar.net/business/news/leather-turning-big-draw-foreign-investors-1977121. Accessed 26 December 2021.

———. 2020b. 'Unitex Group to Splash Out Tk 650cr on New Ventures'. Report filed by Jagaron Chakma, 18 October 2020. https://www.thedailystar.net/business/news/unitex-group-splash-out-tk-650cr-new-ventures-1979769. Accessed 26 December 2021.

Daily Star Supplement. 2018. 'Rethinking Urban Spaces'. 22 February 2018. https://www.thedailystar.net/rethinking-urban-spaces-dhaka-and-beyond. Accessed 26 December 2021.

Dasgupta, C. 2016. 'State and Capital in Independent India, Infrastructure and Accumulations'. Cambridge books, Cambridge University Press, January 2016.

Datta, A. 2012. *Refugees and Borders in South Asia: The Great Exodus of 1971*. London: Routledge.

Davis, J. K. 2006. 'NGOs and Development in Bangladesh: Whose Sustainability Counts?' In *Global Poverty: Sustainable Solutions*. Proceedings of the Anti-Poverty Academic Conference with International Participation, Institute for Sustainability and Technology Policy, Murdoch University, Perth.

Dawson, P., and P. Dey. 2002. 'Testing for the Law of One Price: Rice Market Integration in Bangladesh'. *Journal of International Development* 14 (4): 473–84. https://doi.org/10.1002/jid.888.

De Meza, D., and D. C. Webb. 1992. 'Efficient Credit Rationing'. *European Economic Review* 36 (6): 1277–90.

De Vylder, S. 1982. *Agriculture in Chains. Bangladesh: A Case Study in Contradictions and Constraints*. London: Zed Press.

Deb, U. 2016. 'Agricultural Transformation in Bangladesh: Extent, Drivers and Implications'. 15th National Conference of the Bangladesh Agricultural Economists Association (BAEA) on 'Transformation of Agricultural Sector in Bangladesh: 21st Century', Bangladesh Agricultural Research Council (BARC) Auditorium, Dhaka, Bangladesh, 22–23 January 2016.

Deichmann, U., F. Shilpi and R. Vakis. 2009. 'Urban Proximity, Agricultural Potential and Rural Non-farm Employment: Evidence from Bangladesh'. *World Development* 37 (3): 645–60. https://doi.org/10.1016/j.worlddev.2008.08.008.

Department of Fisheries, Bangladesh. 2018. *Annual Report 2018*. Dhaka: Ministry of Fisheries and Livestock, Government of Bangladesh.

Department of Livestock. 2020. *Livestock Economy at a Glance 2019–20*. Dhaka: Ministry of Fisheries and Livestock, Government of Bangladesh.

Devine, J., I. Basu and G. Brown. 2017. 'Governance, Rights and the Demand for Democracy: Evidence from Bangladesh'. In *Politics and Governance in Bangladesh: Uncertain Landscapes*, edited by I. Basu, J. Devine and G. Wood, 86–107. 1st ed. London: Routledge.

Dewan, A. M., M. R. Haider and M. R. Amin. 2013. 'Exploring Crime Statistics'. In *Dhaka Megacity: Geospatial Perspectives on Urbanisation, Environment and Health*, edited by A. Dewan and R. Corner, 257–82. Dordrecht: Springer.

Dewey, K. G., and R. J. Cohen. 2007. 'Does Birth Spacing Affect Maternal or Child Nutritional Status? A Systematic Literature Review'. *Maternal and Child Nutrition* 3 (3): 151–73. https://doi.org/10.1111/j.1740-8709.2007.00092.x.

Dhaka Tribune. 2018. 'Akij to Sell Tobacco Business to Japanese Firm for $1.5 Billion'. 7 August 2018. https://www.dhakatribune.com/business/2018/08/07/akij-to-sell-tobacco-business-to-japanese-firm-for-1-5-billion. Accessed 27 December 2021.

Directorate of Primary Education (DPE). 2019. *Annual Primary School Census (Draft) 2019*. Dhaka, Bangladesh: Ministry of Primary and Mass Education, Government of Bangladesh. https://mopme.gov.bd/sites/default/files/files/mopme.portal.gov.bd/publications/4a81eee1_4fff_4c20_ab68_282c1db70caa/2.10.1%20APSC%20(2).pdf. Accessed 27 December 2021.

Dodwell, H. 1929. 'The Travels of Fray Sebastian Manrique. Vol. II. Edited by Lt-Col C. E. Luard. Hakluyt Society, 1927'. *Bulletin of the School of Oriental and African Studies* 5 (2): 388–90. https://doi.org/10.1017/S0041977X00122840.

Donaghey, J., and J. Reinecke. 2017. 'When Industrial Democracy Meets Corporate Social Responsibility: A Comparison of the Bangladesh Accord and Alliance as Responses to the Rana Plaza Disaster'. *British Journal of Industrial Relations* 56 (5/6): 14–42. https://doi.org/10.1111/bjir.12242.

Dorosh, P. A., and Q. Shahabuddin. 1999. 'Price Stabilization and Public Foodgrain Distribution: Policy Options to Enhance National Food Security'. Food Management and Research Support Project Working Paper no. 12, Dhaka.

Drèze, J., and A. Sen. 2012. 'Putting Growth in Its Place'. *Yojana*, 12 January 2012. https://www.insightsonindia.com/wp-content/uploads/2013/09/putting-growth-in-its-place.pdf. Accessed 27 December 2021.

Duvendack, M., R. Palmer-Jones, J. G. Copestake, L. Hooper, Y. Loke and N. Rao. 2011. 'What Is the Evidence of the Impact of Microfinance on the Well-Being of Poor People?'. EPPI-Centre, Social Science Research Unit, Institute of Education, University of London.

Eapen, M. 2001. 'Rural Non-farm Employment: Agricultural versus Urban Linkages: Some Evidence from Kerala State, India'. *Journal of Peasant Studies* 28 (3): 67–88.

Easterlin, R. A. 1975. 'An Economic Framework for Fertility Analysis'. *Studies in Family Planning* 6 (3): 54–63.

Easterly, W. 2001. 'Middle Class Consensus and Economic Development'. *Journal of Economic Growth* 6 (4): 317–35.

Eaton, R. M. 1996. *The Rise of Islam and the Bengal Frontier, 1204–1760*. Berkeley: University of California Press.

Economist. 2012. 'Bangladesh and Development: The Path through the Fields'. 3 November 2012. https://www.economist.com/briefing/2012/11/03/the-path-through-the-fields. Accessed 27 December 2021.

El-Saharty, S., K. Z. Ahsan and J. F. May. 2014. 'Population, Family Planning and Reproductive Health Policy Harmonization in Bangladesh'. World Bank, Washington, DC. © World Bank. https://openknowledge.worldbank.org/handle/10986/20663. Licence: CC BY 3.0 IGO.

Encyclopedia Britannica. 2021. 'Chittagong: History, Population, and Facts'. 14 March 2021. https://www.britannica.com/place/Chittagong. Accessed 27 December 2021.

Escobal, J. 2005. *The Role of Public Infrastructure in Market Development in Rural Peru*. Published PhD diss., Development Economics Group, University of Wageningen, Holland.

Faaland, J., and J. R. Parkinson. 1976. 'A Development Perspective for Bangladesh'. *Bangladesh Development Studies* 4 (1): 49–66.

Fafchamps, M. 2004. *Market Institutions in Sub-Saharan Africa: Theory and Evidence*. Cambridge, Massachusetts: MIT.

Fafchamps, M., and B. Minten. 1999. 'Relationships and Traders in Madagascar'. *Journal of Development Studies* 35 (August): 1–35.

Fan, L. Y. 2008. *Networks Competitive Advantages of Taiwan Footwear Industries*. Taiwan: Nanhua University.

Farruk, M. O. 1970. *The Structure and Performance of the Rice Marketing System in Bangladesh*. New York: Cornell University Press.

Fateh, M. 2020. 'A Historical Analysis on Bangladesh Rural Advancement Committee (BRAC) and Abed's Reception of Paulo Freire's Critical Literacy in Designing BRAC's Functional Education Curriculum in Bangladesh from 1972 to 1981'. Thesis, Queens University, Kingston, Canada. https://qspace.library.queensu.ca/handle/1974/27558.

Feldman, S. 1999. 'Feminist Interruptions'. *Interventions: International Journal of Postcolonial Studies* 1 (2): 167–82. DOI: 10.1080/13698019900510291.

Ferdous, J. 2016. 'Bureaucracy in Bangladesh: Past, Present Experiences and Future Expectations'. *Public Policy and Administration Research* 6 (4): 1–10.

Financial Express. 2019a. 'BD to Attract $10b Investment from UAE'. 15 September 2019. https://www.thefinancialexpress.com.bd/economy/bangladesh/bd-to-attract-10b-investment-from-uae-1568528946. Accessed 27 December 2021.

———. 2019b. 'Remittance Inflow Increases by 31.75pc in November'. 10 December 2019. https://www.thefinancialexpress.com.bd/public/economy/bangladesh/remittance-inflow-increases-by-3175pc-in-november-1575292338. Accessed 27 December 2021.

———. 2019c. 'Tourist Arrivals Rise in Five Years'. 19 October 2019. https://thefinancialexpress.com.bd/economy/tourist-arrivals-rise-in-five-years-1569469201. Accessed 27 December 2021.

Fine, B. 2001. 'Neither the Washington nor the Post-Washington Consensus: An Introduction'. In *Development Policy in the Twenty-First Century: Beyond the Post-Washington Consensus*, edited by B. Fine, C. Lapavitsas and J. Pincus, 17–43. 1st ed. London: Routledge.

Fine, B., and P. Rose. 2003. 'Education and the Post-Washington Consensus'. In *Development Policy in the Twenty-First Century*, edited by B. Fine, C. Lapavitsas and J. Pincus, 171–97. London: Routledge.

Fishlow, A. 2003. *Review of Alexander Gerschenkron, Economic Backwardness in Historical Perspective: A Book of Essays*. University of Wisconsin: EH.Net Economic Services.

Fu, X., and Y. Gao. 2007. *Export Processing Zones in China: A Survey*. Geneva: ILO Report.

Galbraith, J. K. 2017. 'Foreword'. In *Seduced and Betrayed: Exposing the Contemporary Microfinance Phenomenon*, edited by M. Bateman and K. Maclean, vii–viii. Albuqurque: University of New Mexico Press.

References

Gautam, M., and R. Faruqee. 2016. *Dynamics of Rural Growth in Bangladesh: Sustaining Poverty Reduction. Directions in Development – Agriculture and Rural Development.* Washington, DC: World Bank. © World Bank. https://openknowledge.worldbank.org/handle/10986/24544. Licence: CC BY 3.0 IGO.

Gillies, J. C., S. W. Mercer, A. Lyon, M. Scott and G. C. Watt. 2009. 'Distilling the Essence of General Practice: A Learning Journey in Progress'. *British Journal of General Practice* 59 (562): e167–76. https://doi.org/10.3399/bjgp09X420626.

Goletti, F., R. Ahmed and N. Farid. 1995. 'Structural Determinants of Market Integration: The Case of Rice Markets in Bangladesh'. *Developing Economies* 33 (2): 196–98. https://doi.org/10.1111/j.1746-1049.1995.tb00713.x.

Goodenough, O., and M. G. Cheney. 2008. 'Is Free Enterprise Values in Action'. Preface in *Moral Markets: The Critical Role of Values in the Economy,* edited by P. J. Zak, xxiii–xxx. Princeton; Oxford: Princeton University Press.

Gotur, M. P. 1991. 'Bangladesh: Economic Reform Measures and the Poor'. IMF Working Paper no. 91/39, International Monetary Fund, Washington, DC.

Government of Bangladesh. 1972. *First Five-Year Plan of Bangladesh.* Dhaka: Ministry of Planning, Government of Bangladesh.

———. 1981. *Bangladesh Contraceptive Prevalence Survey Report, 1979.* Dhaka: Ministry of Health and Family Planning, Government of Bangladesh.

———. 1983. *Bangladesh Contraceptive Prevalence Survey Report, 1981.* Dhaka: Ministry of Health and Family Planning, Government of Bangladesh.

———. 1994. *Bangladesh Demographic and Health Survey 1994.* Dhaka: Ministry of Health, Government of Bangladesh.

———. 1997. *Bangladesh Population Census 1991: Urban Area Report.* Dhaka: Ministry of Planning, Government of Bangladesh.

———. 2001a. *Action Programme for the Development Of Bangladesh 2001–2010.* Report presented at the Third United Nations Conference on the Least Developed Countries, Brussels. http://digitallibrary.un.org/record/441561/files/A_CONF.191_CP_37-EN.pdf. Accessed 27 December 2021.

———. 2001b. *Population Census 2001 Preliminary Report.* Dhaka: Ministry of Planning, Government of Bangladesh.

———. 2005. *Bangladesh Economic Review 2005.* Dhaka: Ministry of Finance, Government of Bangladesh. https://mof.gov.bd/. Accessed 27 December 2021.

———. 2007. *Bangladesh Economic Review 2007.* Dhaka: Ministry of Finance, Government of Bangladesh. https://mof.gov.bd/. Accessed 27 December 2021.

———. 2011. *Bangladesh Economic Review 2011.* Dhaka: Ministry of Finance, Government of Bangladesh. https://mof.gov.bd/. Accessed 27 December 2021.

———. 2019. *Bangladesh Economic Review 2019.* Dhaka: Ministry of Finance, Government of Bangladesh. https://mof.gov.bd/. Accessed 27 December 2021.

———. 2020. *Bangladesh Economic Review 2020*. Dhaka: Ministry of Finance, Government of Bangladesh. https://mof.gov.bd/. Accessed 27 December 2021.

Gray, J. 1981. 'Hayek on Liberty, Rights and Justice'. *Ethics* 92 (1): 73–84.

Greenspan, S. I. 1992. *Infancy and Early Childhood: The Practice of Clinical Assessment and Intervention with Emotional and Developmental Challenges*. Dhaka: Book Syndicate, xvi, 814.

Gross, P. H., and M. Selim. 1983. 'Appropriate Technology and Rural Development in Bangladesh: A Directory of Institutions; With Special Reference to Organizations from the USA, UK, and Southeast Asia'.

Haddad, L., H. Alderman, S. Appleton, L. Song and Y. Yohannes. 2003. 'Reducing Child Malnutrition: How Far Does Income Growth Take Us?' *World Bank Economic Review* 17 (1): 107–31.

Haggblade, S., and P. Hazell. 1989. 'Agricultural Technology and Farm–Nonfarm Growth Linkages'. *Agricultural Economics* 3, no. 4 (December): 345–64.

Haggblade, S., P. Hazell and J. Brown. 1989. 'Farm–Nonfarm Linkages in Rural Sub-Saharan Africa'. *World Development* 17 (8): 1173–1201.

Haggblade, S., P. Hazell and T. Reardon. 2010. 'The Rural Non-farm Economy: Prospects for Growth and Poverty Reduction'. *World Development* 38 (10): 1429–41. https://doi.org/10.1016/j.worlddev.2009.06.008.

Haque, M. A., and A. Abdullah. 2019. 'Bangladesh Steel Industry: A Comprehensive Review'. EBL Securities Limited, 26 December 2019. https://www.arx.cfa/-/media/regional/arx/post-pdf/2019/12/29/bangladesh-steel-industry--a-comprehensive-review.ashx. Accessed 4 December 2021.

Haque, W. 1978. *Exploitation and the Rural Poor*. Comilla: Bangladesh Academy of Rural Development.

Haque, W., N. Metha, A. Rahman and P. Wignaraja. 1977. 'Towards a Theory of Rural Development'. *Development Dialogue* 2: 7–137.

Haroon, Jasim Uddin. 2018. 'BoP Hits Negative Territory in Seven Years'. *Financial Express*, 3 September 2018. Accessed 12 November 2021. https://www.thefinancialexpress.com.bd/economy/bangladesh/bop-hits-negative-territory-in-seven-years-1535946104.

Harris, M., and A. Raviv. 1979. 'Optimal Incentive Contracts with Imperfect Information'. *Journal of Economic Theory* 20, no. 2 (April): 231–59.

Harriss, B. 1979. 'There Is Method in My Madness: Or Is It Vice-Versa? Measuring Agricultural Market Performance'. *Food Research Institute Studies* 17 (2): 197–218.

Harriss-White, B. 1997. 'Maps and Landscapes of Grain Markets in South Asia'. In *The New Institutional Economics and Third World Development,* edited by J. Harriss, J. Hunter and C. Lewis, 87–108. London: Routledge.

———. 1999. 'Power in Peasant Markets'. In *Agricultural Markets from Theory to Practice, Field Experience in Developing Countries*, edited by B. Harriss-White, 261–86. London; New York: Macmillan and St. Martin's.

———. 2008. *Rural Commercial Capital: Agricultural Markets in West Bengal*. New Delhi: Oxford University Press.

Hartmann, B., and J. K. Boyce. 1983. *A Quiet Violence: View from a Bangladesh Village*. London: Zed Books.

Hasan, S. 1993. 'Voluntarism and Rural Development in Bangladesh'. *Asian Journal of Public Administration* 15 (1): 82–101. https://doi.org/10.1080/02598272.1993.10800274.

Hashan, M. J. 2020. 'OP-ED: Dhaka University: A Beacon of Inspiration'. *Dhaka Tribune*, 1 July 2020. https://www.dhakatribune.com/opinion/op-ed/2020/07/01/op-ed-dhaka-university-a-beacon-of-inspiration. Accessed 27 December 2021.

Hasell, Joe, and Max Roser. 2017. 'Famines'. Our World in Data, 7 December 2017. https://ourworldindata.org/famines. Accessed 15 December 2021.

Headey, D. D. 2013. 'Developmental Drivers of Nutritional Change: A Cross-Country Analysis'. *World Development* 42 (February): 76–88. https://doi.org/10.1016/j.worlddev.2012.07.002.

Headey, D. D., and J. Hoddinott. 2016. 'Agriculture, Nutrition and the Green Revolution in Bangladesh'. *Agricultural Systems* 149 (November): 122–31. https://doi.org/10.1016/j.agsy.2016.09.001.

Headey, D. D., J. Hoddinott, D. Ali, R. Tesfaye and M. Dereje. 2015. 'The Other Asian Enigma: Explaining the Rapid Reduction of Undernutrition in Bangladesh'. *World Development* 66 (February): 749–61. https://doi.org/10.1016/j.worlddev.2014.09.022.

Heaver, R., and Y. Kachondam. 2002. 'Thailand's National Nutritional Program: Lessons in Management and Capacity Development'. HNP Discussion Paper Series. Washington, DC: World Bank. © World Bank.

Heltberg, R. 2009. 'Malnutrition, Poverty, and Economic Growth'. *Health Economics* 18 (S1): S77–88. https://doi.org/10.1002/hec.1462.

Hickey, S., N. Hossain and OUP (eds.). 2019. *The Politics of Education in Developing Countries: From Schooling to Learning*. 1st ed. London: Oxford University Press.

HIES. 1995. *Household Income–Expenditure Survey, Bangladesh Bureau of Statistics*. Dhaka: Ministry of Planning, Government of Bangladesh.

———. 2000. *Household Income–Expenditure Survey, Bangladesh Bureau of Statistics*. Dhaka: Ministry of Planning, Government of Bangladesh.

———. 2005. *Household Income–Expenditure Survey, Bangladesh Bureau of Statistics*. Dhaka: Ministry of Planning, Government of Bangladesh.

———. 2010. *Household Income–Expenditure Survey, Bangladesh Bureau of Statistics*. Dhaka: Ministry of Planning, Government of Bangladesh.

———. 2019. *Household Income–Expenditure Survey, 2016–17, Bangladesh Bureau of Statistics*. Dhaka: Ministry of Planning, Government of Bangladesh.

Horton, S. 1988. 'Birth Order and Child Nutritional Status: Evidence from the Philippines'. *Economic Development and Cultural Change* 36 (2): 341–54. https://doi.org/10.1086/451655.

Hossain, M. 1988a. *Credit for Alleviation of Rural Poverty: The Grameen Bank in Bangladesh*. Research report. Washington, DC: International Food Policy Research Institute; Dhaka: Bangladesh Institute of Development Studies.

———. 1988b. *Nature and Impact of the Green Revolution in Bangladesh*. Research report. Washington, DC: International Food Policy Research Institute (IFPRI).

———. 2004. 'Rural Non-farm Economy: Evidence from Household Surveys'. *Economic and Political Weekly* 39 (36): 4053–58. Accessed 21 August 2020. http://www.jstor.org/stable/4415506.

Hossain, M., and N. Nargis. 2009. 'Dynamics of Poverty in Rural Bangladesh, 1988–2007: An Analysis of Household Level Panel Data'. Paper presented in the Conference on 'Employment, Growth and Poverty Reduction in Developing Countries' organized by Political Economy Research Institute, University of Massachusetts, Amherst, in honor of Professor Azizur Rahman Khan, 27–28 March 2009.

Hossain, M., H. Z. Rahman and M. H. Khan. 1997. 'Recent Developments in Bangladesh Rural Economy: Implications for Strategies and Policies for Alleviation of Poverty [with Comments]'. *Pakistan Development Review* 36 (4): 811–36.

Hossain, M., and B. Sen. 1992. 'Rural Poverty in Bangladesh: Trends and Determinants'. *Asian Development Review* 10 (1): 1–34.

Hossain, M., B. Sen and H. Z. Rahman. 2000. 'Growth and Distribution of Rural Income in Bangladesh: Analysis Based on Panel Survey Data'. *Economic and Political Weekly* 35 (52/53): 4630–37.

Hossain, Mokerrom, and R. F. Lowy. 1990. 'Migration from Bangladesh to the Middle East: Volume, Trends and Consequences'. *Asian and African Studies* 24 (1): 75–88.

Hossain, Monzur, and M. Ahmed. 2009. 'An Assessment of Exchange Rate Policy under Floating Regime in Bangladesh'. *Bangladesh Development Studies* 32 (4): 35–67.

———. 2020. 'Exchange Rate Management under Floating Regime in Bangladesh: An Assessment'. In *Bangladesh's Macroeconomic Policy*, edited by H. Monzur, 293–321. Singapore: Palgrave Macmillan.

Hossain, Monzur, H. R. Bhuyan, I. Hossain and M. Hossain. 2018. 'An Evaluation of BSCIC Industrial Estates'. Project report, Bangladesh Institute of Development Studies (BIDS).

References

Hossain, M. B., M. A. Noman, J. A. Lipi, A. H. M. Kamal and M. H. Idris. 2020. 'Effects of Ship-Breaking Activities on the Abundance and Diversity of Macrobenthos in Sitakundu Coast, Bangladesh'. *Biodiversitas Journal of Biological Diversity* 21 (11): 5084–93. https://doi.org/10.13057/biodiv/d211113.

Hossain, N. 2004. 'Access to Education for the Poor and Girls: Educational Achievements in Bangladesh'. https://web.worldbank.org/archive/website00819C/WEB/PDF/BANGLADE.PDF. Accessed 28 December 2021.

Hossain, N. 2017. *The Aid Lab: Understanding Bangladesh's Unexpected Success*. Oxford: Oxford University Press.

Hossain, N., and N. Kabeer. 2004. 'Achieving Universal Primary Education and Eliminating Gender Disparity'. *Economic and Political Weekly* 39 (36): 4093–4100.

Hossain, N., M. M. Hassan, M. A. Rahman, K. S. Ali and M. S. Islam. 2019. 'The Politics of Learning Reforms in Bangladesh'. In *The Politics of Education in Developing Countries from Schooling to Learning*, edited by S. Hickey and N. Hossain, 10:64–85. Oxford: Oxford University Press. https://library.oapen.org/bitstream/handle/20.500.12657/37376/9780198835684.pdf?sequence=1#page=89. Accessed 28 December 2021.

Hossain, S. 2008. 'Rapid Urban Growth and Poverty in Dhaka City'. *Bangladesh E-Journal of Sociology* 5 (1): 1–24.

Hossain, S. M. M., A. Duffield and A. Taylor. 2005. 'An Evaluation of the Impact of a US$60 Million Nutrition Programme in Bangladesh'. *Health Policy and Planning* 20 (1): 35–40. https://doi.org/10.1093/heapol/czi004.

Howlader, Md. H. U. 2015. 'Privatization in Bangladesh: An Evaluative Study'. PhD diss., Dhaka University, Department of Management Studies.

Hussain, M. B. 2020. 'Starting of Port of Chalna after Independence of Bangladesh'. https://bdmariners.org/port-of-chalna-capt-m-belayet-hussain-1n/. Accessed 28 December 2021.

Huang, Y., and M. G. Quibria. 2018. 'The Global Partnership on Foreign Aid for Sustainable Development'. In *Aid Effectiveness for Environmental Sustainability*, edited by Y. Huang and U. Pascual, 397–439. Singapore: Palgrave Macmillan. https://doi.org/10.1007/978-981-10-5379-5_12.

Hulme, D. 2000. 'Is Microdebt Good for Poor People? A Note on the Dark Side of Microfinance'. *Small Enterprise Development* 11 (1): 26–28.

Hulme, D., and T. Arun. 2009. *Microfinance: A Reader*. London: Routledge.

Hulme, D., and K. Moore. 2006. 'Why Has Microfinance Been a Policy Success in Bangladesh?' In *Development Success: Statecraft in the South*, edited by A. Bebbington and W. McCourt, 105–39. Basingstoke: Palgrave-Macmillan UK. https://doi.org/10.1057/9780230223073_5.

Hulme, D., and P. Mosley.. 1996a. *Finance against Poverty*. Vol. 1. London: Routledge Publications.

———. 1996b. *Finance against Poverty*. Vol. 2. London: Routledge Publications.

Humphrey, J. H. 2009. 'Child Undernutrition, Tropical Enteropathy, Toilets, and Handwashing'. *Lancet* 374 (9694): 1032–35. https://doi.org/10.1016/S0140-6736(09)60950-8.

Hunter, W. W. 1876. *A Statistical Account of Bengal*. Vol. 6. London: Trubner & Company.

Huq, A. F. M. H. 1978. 'Labour Force Analysis: Bangladesh, 1974'. *Bangladesh Development Studies* 6 (2): 163–90.

Huq, M. A. (ed.). 1976. 'Exploitation and the Rural Poor: A Working Paper on the Rural Power Structure in Bangladesh'. Bangladesh Academy for Rural Development, Comilla.

ILO. 2015. 'Management of Short-Term Labour Migration: A Comprehensive System Review of the Bureau of Manpower Employment and Training of Bangladesh'. International Labour Organization, Dhaka. https://www.ilo.org/dyn/migpractice/migmain.showPractice?p_lang=en&p_practice_id=102. Accessed 28 December 2021.

———. 2020. *Understanding the Gender Composition and Experience of Ready-Made Garment (RMG) Workers in Bangladesh*. Policy Brief, International Labour Organization, Dhaka. https://www.ilo.org/wcmsp5/groups/public/---asia/---ro-bangkok/---ilo-dhaka/documents/publication/wcms_754669.pdf.

———. n.d. 'Labour Force Survey Data 2002–03 (Data Relates to 1999–2000), 2005–06, 2010 and 2016 (Related to 2013 Data)'. https://www.ilo.org/dyn/lfsurvey/lfsurvey.list?p_lang=en&p_country=BD. Accessed 28 December 2021.

Inkeles, A., and D. Smith. 1974. *Becoming Modern*. Cambridge, Mass.: Harvard University Press.

InM and CDF. 2011. *Bangladesh Microfinance Statistics, 2010*. Dhaka: Institute of Microfinance, and Credit and Development Forum.

Iqbal, K. 2019. 'The Rural Non-farm Sector in Bangladesh: A Review'. Special research project for the Government of Bangladesh, Bangladesh Institute of Development Studies (BIDS).

Ireen, S., M. J. Raihan, N. Choudhury, M. M. Islam, M. I. Hossain, Z. Islam, S. M. Rahman and T. Ahmed. 2018. 'Challenges and Opportunities of Integration of Community Based Management of Acute Malnutrition into the Government Health System in Bangladesh: A Qualitative Study'. *BMC Health Services Research* 18 (1): 256.

Islam, A. M. 1999. 'Foreign Assistance and Development in Bangladesh'. In *Foreign Aid: New Perspectives*, edited by K. L. Gupta. Recent Economic Thought Series, vol. 68. Boston, MA: Springer. https://doi.org/10.1007/978-1-4615-5095-2_12.

Islam, K. 1966. 'Economic History of Bengal (c. AD 400–1200)'. PhD diss., SOAS University of London.

References

Islam, M. T. 2011. 'The Advent of Islam in Bengal: An Economic Perspective'. *IIUC Studies* 7: 91–106.

Islam, N. 2003. *Making of a Nation. Bangladesh: An Economist's Tale*. Dhaka: University Press Ltd. http://www.uplbooks.com/book/making-nation-bangladesh-economists-tale. Accessed 28 December 2021.

Islam, Nazrul. 1973. *Need for Urban Research*. Monograph no. 1. Dhaka: Centre for Urban Studies, University of Dhaka.

———. 1976. 'Spacing of Urban Centres in Bangladesh'. *Oriental Geographer* 19–20 (1/2): 68–73.

———. 1996. 'Dhaka: From City to Megacity: Perspectives on People, Places, Planning, and Development Issues'. Urban Studies Programme, Department of Geography, University of Dhaka.

Islam, R. 1978. 'The Bengali Language Movement and the Emergence of Bangladesh'. In *Language and Civilization Change in South Asia*, edited by C. Maloney, 2:142–54. Contributions to Asian Studies. Leiden, Netherlands: Brill Academic Publications.

Islam, R., and A. Rahman. 1985. 'Agrarian Change, Labour Contracts and Interlinked Transactions, in Labour, Land and Credit in Rural Bangladesh: Study with Microlevel Data'. ARTEP Working Paper, ILO, Bangkok.

Islam, R., S. Hossain, F. Bashar, S. M. Khan, A. A. S. Sikder, S. S. Yusuf and A. M. Adams. 2018. 'Contracting-out Urban Primary Health Care in Bangladesh: A Qualitative Exploration of Implementation Processes and Experience'. *International Journal for Equity in Health* 17: 1–16. https://doi.org/10.1186/s12939-018-0805-1.

Islam, S. 2021. 'Remittance Grows by 18.4 pc in 2020'. *Financial Express*, 20 May 2021.

Islam, S. N. 2016. 'Deltaic Floodplains Development and Wetland Ecosystems Management in the Ganges–Brahmaputra–Meghna Rivers Delta in Bangladesh'. *Sustainable Water Resources Management* 2 (3): 237–56. https://doi.org/10.1007/s40899-016-0047-6.

Islam, S. S. 1984. 'The State in Bangladesh under Zia (1975–81)'. *Asian Survey* 24 (5): 556–73. https://doi.org/10.2307/2644413.

Jahan, M. 2019. 'Women Workforce Declining in RMG Sector'. *Daily Prothom Alo*, 4 September 2019. https://en.prothomalo.com/bangladesh/Women-workforce-declining-in-RMG-sector#:~:text=The%20number%20of%20female%20workers,Bureau%20of%20Statistics%20(BBS). Accessed 28 November 2021.

Jahan, R. 1976. 'Bangabandhu and After: Conflict and Change in Bangladesh'. *Round Table* 66 (261): 73–84. https://doi.org/10.1080/00358537608453206.

——— (ed.). 2000. *Bangladesh: Promise and Performance*. Dhaka: The University Press Limited.

———. 2013. 'Genocide in Bangladesh'. In *Centuries of Genocide: Essays and Eyewitness Accounts*, edited by S. Totten and W. S. Parsons, 249–76. New York: Routledge.

Jahangir, B. K. 1979. 'Tribal Peasants in Transition: Chittagong Hill Tracts'. *Economic and Political Weekly* 14 (11): 597–600.

Jalal, A. 1994. *The Sole Spokesman: Jinnah, the Muslim League and the Demand for Pakistan*. Cambridge, UK: Cambridge University Press. https://doi.org/10.1017/CBO9780511558856.

Jansen, E., and T. Bolstad. 1992. *Sailing Against the Wind*. Rugby, UK: Practical Action Publishing.

Janssen, M. A., R. L. Goldstone, F. Menczer and O. Elinor. 2006. 'Effect of Rule Choice in Dynamic Interactive Commons'. CIPEC Working Paper no. CWP-06-04, Indiana University, Bloomington.

Januzzi, F. T., and P. T. Peach. 1980. *The Agrarian Structure of Bangladesh: An Impediment to Development*. Colorado, USA: West View Press.

Jayachandran, S., and R. Pande. 2013. 'Choice Not Genes: Probable Cause for the India–Africa Child Height Gap'. *Economic and Political Weekly* 48 (34): 77–79.

Jensen, R. 2012. 'Another Mouth to Feed? The Effects of (In)Fertility on Malnutrition'. *CESifo Economic Studies* 58 (2): 322–47. https://doi.org/10.1093/cesifo/ifs014.

Jha, R. 2005. *Economic Growth, Economic Performance and Welfare in South Asia*. London: Palgrave; Macmillan Publishers.

Joarder, M. A. M., A. K. M. N. Hossain and M. M. Hakim. 2010. 'Post-MFA Performance of Bangladesh Apparel Sector'. *International Review of Business Research Papers* 6 (4): 134–44.

Johnson, D., T. M. Smeeding and B. Torrey. 2005. 'Economic Inequality through the Prisms of Income and Consumption'. *Monthly Labor Review by U.S. Department of Labor, Bureau of Labor Statistics* 128 (4): 11–24.

Jou, S., and D. S. Chen. 2001. 'Latecomer's Globalization: Taiwan's Experience in FDI and Reproduction of Territorial Production Networks in Southeast Asia'. *Journal of City and Planning* 4: 421–50.

Kabeer, N., and S. Mahmud. 2004. 'Globalization, Gender and Poverty: Bangladeshi Women Workers in Export and Local Markets'. *Journal of International Development* 16 (1): 93–109.

Kabeer, N., S. Mahmud and J. G. I. Castro. 2010. 'NGOs' Strategies and the Challenge of Development and Democracy in Bangladesh'. IDS Working Papers 343, Institute of Development Studies, Sussex, 1–71. https://doi.org/10.1111/j.2040-0209.2010.00343_2.x.

Kabir, M., S. Singh and M. J. Ferrantino. 2019. 'The Textile-Clothing Value Chain in India and Bangladesh How Appropriate Policies Can Promote (or Inhibit) Trade and Investment'. Policy Research Working Paper 8731, World Bank.

Kabir, S. H. 1998. 'The Six Points Movement: A Factor Transforming East Pakistani Regionalism into Bangladeshi Nationalism – ProQuest'. *Journal of the Pakistan Historical Society, Karachi* 46 (1): 51–75.

Kamal, Humayun A. 2014. 'In the Spirit of Brotherly Love'. *Daily Star*, 30 May 2014. https://www.thedailystar.net/in-the-spirit-of-brotherly-love-26052. Accessed 26 December 2021.

Karim, A. 1962. 'Murshid Quli Khan and His Time'. PhD diss., School of African and Asian Studies, University of London, UK. https://www.proquest.com/openview/7ef64590b787a643211e6bacbf8fccb6/1?pq-origsite=gscholar&cbl=2026366&diss=y. Accessed 28 December 2021.

———. 1964. *Dacca: The Mughal Capital*. Dhaka: Asiatic Society of Pakistan.

Karim, L. 2011. *Microfinance and its Discontents: Women in Debt in Bangladesh*. Minneapolis, USA: University of Minnesota Press.

———. 2008. 'Demystifying Micro-Credit: The Grameen Bank, NGOs, and Neoliberalism in Bangladesh'. *Cultural Dynamics* 20 (1): 5–29.

Kasahara, S. 2004. 'The Flying Geese Paradigm: A Critical Study of its Application to East Asian Regional Development'. UNCTAD Discussion Papers.

Kashem, A. 2020. 'Loss-Making Industries Only Waste Govt Funds'. *Business Standard*, 8 August 2020. https://www.tbsnews.net/economy/industry/loss-making-industries-only-waste-govt-funds-116686. Accessed 29 December 2021.

Kaufmann, D., A. Kraay and M. Mastruzzi. 2010. 'The World-Wide Governance Indicators: Methodology and Analytical Issues'. World Bank Policy Research Working Paper no. 5430.

Keynes, J. M. 1920. *The Economic Consequences of the Peace*. New York: Harcourt, Brace and Howe.

Khan, A. R. 2005. 'Measuring Inequality and Poverty in Bangladesh: An Assessment of the Survey Data'. *Bangladesh Development Studies* 31 (3/4): 1–34.

Khan, A. H. 1973. *The Comilla Project: A Personal Accounts*. Box no. 5907, Folder 14, Pakistan Project records, UA-2.9.5.12. University Archives and Historical Collections. https://findingaids.lib.msu.edu//repositories/2/archival_objects/32754. Accessed 29 December 2021.

———. 1974. 'Reflections on the Comilla Rural Development Projects'. Overseas Liaison Committee, American Council on Education, OLC Paper no. 3. https://archive.lib.msu.edu/DMC/African%20Working%20Papers/Round%202/pakistan4/pakistan4.pdf. Accessed 29 December 2021.

Khan H. T., and R. Raeside. 1994. 'Urban and Rural Fertility in Bangladesh: A Causal Approach'. *Social Biology* 41, nos. 3/4 (Fall–Winter): 240–51. DOI: 10.1080/19485565.1994.9988875. PMID: 7761907.

Khan, M. R. 1984. 'Economic Development and Population Policy in Bangladesh'. *Bangladesh Development Studies* 12 (3): 1–18.

Khandker, S. R. 1996. 'Role of Targeted Credit in Rural Non-farm Growth'. *Bangladesh Development Studies* 24, nos. 3/4 (September–December): 181–93.

———. 2005. *Microfinance and Poverty: Evidence Using Panel Data from Bangladesh*. Published by Oxford University Press on behalf of the World Bank. © World Bank.

Khandker, S. R., M. A. B. Khalily and H. A. Samad. 2016a. *Beyond Ending Poverty: The Dynamics of Microfinance in Bangladesh*. Directions in Development—Poverty. Washington, DC: The World Bank.

———. 2016b. 'Rural Nonfarm Growth and Poverty Reduction'. In *Beyond Ending Poverty*, edited by Khandker, Khalily and Samad, 9–16. Washington, DC: The World Bank.

Khandker, S. R., and G. B. Koolwal. 2010. 'How Infrastructure and Financial Institutions Affect Rural Income and Poverty: Evidence from Bangladesh'. *Journal of Development Studies* 46 (6): 1109–37.

———. 2016. 'How Has Microcredit Supported Agriculture? Evidence Using Panel Data from Bangladesh'. *Agricultural Economics* 47 (2): 157–68.

Khandker, S. R., and H. A. Samad. 2014. 'Microfinance Growth and Poverty Reduction in Bangladesh: What Does the Longitudinal Data Say?' *Bangladesh Development Studies* 37 (1/2): 127–57.

Khandker, S. R., H. Samad and Z. Khan. 1998. 'Income and Employment Effects of Micro-Credit Programmes: Village-Level Evidence from Bangladesh'. *Journal of Development Studies* 35 (2): 96–124.

Kharas, H., and G. Gertz. 2010. *The New Global Middle Class: A Cross-Over from West to East*. Wolfensohn Center for Development, Brookings Institution, Washington, DC, 1–14. https://www.brookings.edu/research/the-new-global-middle-class-a-cross-over-from-west-to-east/. Accessed 29 December 2021.

Khondker, B. H., and S. Raihan. 2004. 'Welfare and Poverty Impacts of Policy Reforms in Bangladesh: A General Equilibrium Approach'. Centre on Regulation and Competition (CRC) Working papers no. 30588, University of Manchester, Institute for Development Policy and Management (IDPM). https://ideas.repec.org/p/ags/idpmcr/30588.html. Accessed 29 December 2021.

King, C. C. 2020. 'Income Analysis of Microloan Borrowers'. *International Journal of Business and Social Science* 11 (2): 77–85.

Kochanek, S. A. 1993. *Patron–Client Politics and Business in Bangladesh*. New Delhi: Sage Publications.

Kojima, K. 1960. 'Capital Accumulation and the Course of Industrialisation, With Special Reference to Japan'. *Economic Journal* 70, no. 280: 757–68.

———. 1970. 'Towards a Theory of Agreed Specialization: The Economics of Integration'. In *Induction, Growth and Trade: Essays in Honour of Sir Roy Harrod*, edited by W. A. Eltis, M. F. G. Scott and J. N. Wolfe, 305–24. Oxford: Clarendon Press.

———. 1995. 'Dynamics of Japanese Investment in East Asia'. *Hitotsubashi Journal of Economics* 36 (2): 93–124.

———. 2000. 'The "Flying Geese" Model of Asian Economic Development: Origin, Theoretical Extensions, and Regional Policy Implications'. *Journal of Asian Economics* 11 (4): 375–401. https://doi.org/10.1016/S1049-0078(00)00067-1.

Kopicki, R., Y. Peng, Y. Liu and D. Li. 2004. *The Current State of Supply Chain Development in the Western Provinces*. Report produced for the Western Region Leadership Group by the World Bank. Beijing: World Bank.

Korten, D. C. 1990. *Getting to the 21st Century: Voluntary Action and the Global Agenda*. Boulder, Colorado: Kumarian Press.

———. 2010. 'NGO Strategic Networks: From Community Projects to Global Transformation'. *David Korten*, 15 November 2010. https://davidkorten.org/community-to-global-transformation/. Accessed 29 December 2021.

Krueger, A. 2012. 'The Rise and Consequences of Inequality'. Presentation made to the Center for American Progress, Washington, DC, 12 January 2012.

Kumar, K. B., and J. G. Matsusaka. 2009. 'From Families to Formal Contracts: An Approach to Development'. *Journal of Development Economics* 90, no. 1 (September): 106–19.

Kundu, T. K., and I. Kato. 2002. 'Access and Performance of Groundwater Irrigation in Bangladesh'. 農業経営研究 40 (1): 168–73.

Lanjouw, O. J., and P. Lanjouw. 1999. 'Rural Nonfarm Employment: A Survey'. Policy Working Paper 1463, World Bank, Washington, DC. https://documents1.worldbank.org/curated/en/153261468740697353/pdf/multi-page.pdf. Accessed 29 December 2021.

Lanjouw, P. 1999. 'Rural Nonagricultural Employment and Poverty in Ecuador'. *Economic Development and Cultural Change* 48 (1): 91–122.

———. 2007. 'Does the Rural Nonfarm Economy Contribute to Poverty Reduction?' In *Transforming the Rural Nonfarm Economy: Opportunities and Threats in the Developing World*, edited by S. Haggblade, P. B. R. Hazell and T. Reardon, 55–82. Baltimore: The Johns Hopkins University Press.

Larson, A., and S. N. Mitra. 1992. 'Family Planning in Bangladesh: An Unlikely Success Story'. *International Family Planning Perspectives* 18 (4): 123–29.

Latif, M. 2019. *The State of Handloom Industry in Bangladesh*. Dhaka: Bangladesh Institute of Development Studies. Mimeo.

Levinson, F. J., and J. E. Rohde. 2005. 'Responses to: "An Evaluation of the Impact of a US$60 Million Nutrition Programme in Bangladesh"'. *Health Policy and Planning* 20 (6): 405–6. https://doi.org/10.1093/heapol/czi049.

Levy-Yeyati, E., and F. Sturzenegger. 2005. 'Classifying Exchange Rate Regimes: Deeds vs Words'. *European Economic Review* 49 (6): 1603–35.

Lewis D. J. 1997. 'NGOs, Donors, and the State in Bangladesh'. *ANNALS of the American Academy of Political and Social Science* 554 (1): 33–45. DOI: 10.1177/0002716297554001003.

———. 2011. *Politics, Economy and Civil Society*. New York: Cambridge University Press.

———. 2017. 'Organising and Representing the Poor in a Clientalist Democracy: The Decline of Radical NGOs in Bangladesh'. *Journal of Development Studies* 53 (10): 1545–67.

———. 2019. 'Reflecting on Bangladesh's "Green Revolution"'. Institute of Development Studies, 5 June 2019. https://www.ids.ac.uk/opinions/reflecting-on-bangladeshs-green-revolution/. Accessed 29 December 2021.

Lewis, D. J., and A. Hossain. 2019. 'Local Political Consolidation in Bangladesh: Power, Informality and Patronage'. *Development and Change* 53 (July): 1–20. https://doi.org/10.1111/dech.12534.

LFS. 1985. *Labour Force Survey 1984–85*. Bangladesh Bureau of Statistics, Dhaka: Ministry of Planning Dhaka, Government of Bangladesh.

———. 1996. *Labour Force Survey 1995–96*. Bangladesh Bureau of Statistics, Dhaka: Ministry of Planning Dhaka, Government of Bangladesh.

———. 2002. *Labour Force Survey, 1999–2000*. Bangladesh Bureau of Statistics, Dhaka: Ministry of Planning Dhaka, Government of Bangladesh.

———. 2004. *Labour Force Survey, 2002–2003*. Bangladesh Bureau of Statistics, Dhaka: Ministry of Planning Dhaka, Government of Bangladesh.

———. 2007. *Labour Force Survey, 2005–06*. Bangladesh Bureau of Statistics, Dhaka: Ministry of Planning Dhaka, Government of Bangladesh.

———. 2011. *Labour Force Survey, 2010*. Bangladesh Bureau of Statistics, Dhaka: Ministry of Planning Dhaka, Government of Bangladesh.

———. 2018. *Labour Force Survey, 2016–17*. Bangladesh Bureau of Statistics, Dhaka: Ministry of Planning Dhaka, Government of Bangladesh.

Lightcastle. 2019. 'Industry Insight: Can ICT Become Bangladesh's 3rd Engine?'. https://www.lightcastlebd.com/insights/2019/04/industry-insight-can-ict-become-bangladeshs-3rdengine. Accessed 29 December 2021.

———. 2020. The Ails of Textiles in Bangladesh: Challenges and Possible Amelioration'. 2 April 2020. https://www.lightcastlebd.com/insights/2020/04/02/the-ails-of-textiles-in-bangladesh-challenges-and-possible-amelioration. Accessed 29 December 2021.

Lin, A., B. F. Arnold, S. Afreen, R. Goto, T. M. N. Huda, R. Haque, R. Raqib, L. Unicomb, T. Ahmed, J. M. Colford and S. P. Luby. 2013. 'Household Environmental Conditions Are Associated with Enteropathy and Impaired Growth in Rural Bangladesh'. *American Journal of Tropical Medicine and Hygiene* 89 (1): 130–7. https://doi.org/10.4269/ajtmh.12-0629.

Lin, J. Y. 2012. *New Structural Economics: A Framework for Rethinking Development and Policy*. Washington, DC: World Bank. https://elibrary.worldbank.org/doi/abs/10.1596/978-0-8213-8955-3. Accessed 29 December 2021.

———. 2016. 'Industrial Policy Revisited: A New Structural Economics Perspective'. In *Efficiency, Finance, and Varieties of Industrial Policy*, edited by A. Noman and E. Stiglitz, 225–44. New York: Columbia University Press.

Lipton, M., and R. Longhurst. 1989. *New Seeds and Poor People*. London: Unwin Hyman.

Luard, C. E. 1929. *Travels of Fray Sebastien Manrique, 1629–1643*. Vol. 2, translated. Oxford: Oxford University Press.

Lutz, W. 2017. 'Education Empowers Women to Reach Their Personal Fertility Target Regardless of What the Target Is'. *Vienna Yearbook of Population Research* 15: 2731.

Lyon, F., and G. Porter. 2009. 'Market Institutions, Trust and Norms: Exploring Moral Economies in Nigerian Food Systems'. *Cambridge Journal of Economics* 33 (5): 903–20.

Mahbubullah, M. 1984. *Impact of Coastal Polders on Agricultural Productivity: Evidence from Five Coastal Villages*. Dhaka: Bangladesh Ministry of Agriculture.

Mahmood, R. A. 1991. 'Bangladeshi Returned Migrants from the Middle East: Process, Achievement and Adjustment'. In *Migration to the Arab World: Experience of Returning Migrants*, edited by G. Gunatileke, 238–89. Tokyo: United Nations University Press.

Mahmood, R. A., and T. Siddiqui. 2014. 'Differential Impact of Migration on Poverty and Wellbeing: Evidence Based on Bangladesh Data'. Paper presented at KNOMAD Conference on Internal Migration and Urbanization, Dhaka. https://www.knomad.org/sites/default/files/2017-05/5%20Dr.%20Raisul%20A%20Mahmood%20DIFFERENTIAL%20IMPACT%20OF%20MIGRATION%20ON%20POVERTY%20AND%20WELLBEING_0.pdf. Accessed 29 December 2021.

Mahmud, S. 2004. 'Health and Population: Making Progress under Poverty'. *Economic and Political Weekly* 39 (36): 4081–92.

Mahmud, S., N. M. Shah and S. Becker. 2012. 'Measurement of Women's Empowerment in Rural Bangladesh'. *World Development* 40 (3): 610–9. https://doi.org/10.1016/j.worlddev.2011.08.003.

Mahmud, W. 1996. 'Employment Patterns and Income Formation in Rural Bangladesh: The Role of Rural Non-farm Sector'. *Bangladesh Development Studies* 24, nos. 3/4: 1–27.

———. 1998. 'Agricultural Development Strategy'. In *Bangladesh: Agriculture in the 21st Century*, edited by R. Faruqee, 11–32. Dhaka, Bangladesh: University Press.

Mahmud, W., M. N. Asadullah and A. Savoia. 2013. 'Bangladesh's Achievements in Social Development Indicators: Explaining the Puzzle'. *Economic and Political Weekly* 48 (44): 26–28.

Mahmud, W., and S. R. Osmani. 2016. *The Theory and Practice of Microcredit*. Vol. 130. London: Taylor & Francis.

Mallick, B., and B. Etzold. 2015. 'Migration Policies: Country Profile Bangladesh'. *Bpb*, 30 November 2015. https://www.bpb.de/gesellschaft/migration/laenderprofile/216106/migration-policies. Accessed 29 December 2021.

Mamun, M. Z., and S. S. Andaleeb. 2013. 'Prospects And Problems of Medical Tourism in Bangladesh'. *International Journal of Health Services* 43 (1): 123–41.

Mandal, B., and K. Das. 2010. 'Role of Growth Center: A Rural Development Perspective'. *Journal of Bangladesh Institute of Planners* 3 (December):129–41.

Maniruzzaman, T. 1976. 'Bangladesh in 1975: The Fall of the Mujib Regime and Its Aftermath'. *Asian Survey* 16 (2): 119–29. https://doi.org/10.2307/2643140.

———. 1980. 'Civilianization of Military Regimes: A Comparative Analysis'. *BIISS Journal* 1 (2): 37–81.

Manjur-ul-Alam, M. 1978. 'Rural Structure and Cooperatives in Relation to Modernization of Agriculture: A Comparative Case Study of Five Villages'. In *Exploitation and the Rural Poor*, edited by M. A. Huq, 215–23. Comilla: Bangladesh Academy for Rural Development.

Mann, S. 1987. *Local Merchants and the Chinese Bureaucracy, 1750–1950*. Stanford: Stanford University Press.

Mannan, M. A. 1982. *Selected Information about the Village Child Development and Anti Poverty Development Project*. Bogura: RDA. rda.gov.bd. Accessed 30 December 2021.

Marshall, P. J. 2006. *Bengal: The British Bridgehead: Eastern India 1740–1828*. New York: Cambridge University Press.

Martinek, M. 2014. 'Special Economic Zones in China and WTO: Bleak or Bright Future?' *German Journal of Chinese Law* 21 (1): 41–51.

Mascarenhas, A. 1986. *Bangladesh: A Legacy of Blood*. London: Hodder and Stoughton.

Maswood, M. 2017. 'Patients Flock Abroad.' *New Age*, 18 September 2017. https://www.newagebd.net/article/24306/patients-flock-abroad. Accessed 30 December 2021.

Mathews, J. A., and I. Zander. 2007. 'The International Entrepreneurial Dynamics of Accelerated Internationalisation'. *Journal of International Business Studies* 38 (3): 387–403. https://doi.org/10.1057/palgrave.jibs.8400271.

Mathews, J. A. 2006. 'Catch-Up Strategies and the Latecomer Effect in Industrial Development'. *New Political Economy* 11 (3): 313–35.

Mazid, M. A. 2012. 'Missing Links in the History of Dhaka University'. *Daily Star*, 21 July 2012. https://www.thedailystar.net/news-detail-242879. Accessed 30 December 2021.

McGregor, P. P. L., and V. K. Barooah. 1992. 'Is Low Spending or Low Income a Better Indicator of Whether or Not a Household Is Poor? Some Results from the 1985 Family Expenditure Survey'. *Journal of Social Policy* 21 (1): 53–69.

McKinsey and Company. 2021. 'What's Next for Bangladesh's Garment Industry, After a Decade of Growth?' https://www.mckinsey.com/industries/retail/our-insights/whats-next-for-bangladeshs-garment-industry-after-a-decade-of-growth. Accessed 30 December 2021.

Mears, L. 1957. *Rice Marketing in the Republic of Indonesia*. Institute of Economics and Social Research, University of Indonesia, Jakarta.

Medhekar, A., and M. M. Ali. 2012. 'A Cross-Border Trade in Healthcare Services: Bangladesh to India'. *Business and Management Review* 2 (1): 1–13. https://search.proquest.com/openview/ff4cc5514395e49939dcad7682184e00/1?pq-origsite=gscholar&cbl=2026610. Accessed 30 December 2021.

Mellema, R. L. 1961. 'The Basic Democracies System in Pakistan'. *Asian Survey* 1 (6): 5–12.

Minten, B., K. A. S. Murshid and T. Reardon. 2013. 'Food Quality Changes and Implications: Evidence from the Rice Value Chain of Bangladesh'. *World Development* 42 (February): 100–13. https://doi.org/10.1016/j.worlddev.2012.06.015.

Mitra and Associates. 2003. *Bangladesh Maternal Health Services and Maternal Mortality Survey 2001*. National Institute of Population Research and Training (NIPORT), Dhaka.

Mitra and Associates, and ICF International. 2016. *Bangladesh Demographic and Health Survey 2014*. Dhaka, Bangladesh; Calverton, Maryland, USA: NIPORT, Mitra and Associates and ICF International.

———. 2019. *Bangladesh Demographic and Health Survey 2018*. Dhaka, Bangladesh; Calverton, Maryland, USA: NIPORT, Mitra and Associates and ICF International.

Mitra and Associates, and ORC Macro. 2001. *Bangladesh Demographic and Health Survey 1999–2000*. Dhaka, Bangladesh; Calverton, Maryland, USA: NIPORT, Mitra and Associates and ORC Macro.

Mitra, R. C. 1954. *The Decline of Buddhism in India*. Visva-Bharati Studies 20. Calcutta: Visva-Bharati, v, 164.

Mitra, S. N. 1979. 'Infant and Childhood Mortality in Bangladesh: Levels and Differentials'. Master's thesis, Australian National University. https://openresearch-repository.anu.edu.au/handle/1885/117377. Accessed 30 December 2021.

Mitra, S. N., A. Al-Sabir and R. Anne. 1997. *Bangladesh Demographic and Health Survey 1996–1997*. National Institute of Population Research and Training (NIPORT), Dhaka, Bangladesh.

Mitra, S. N., and G. M. Kamal. 1984. *Bangladesh Contraceptive Prevalence Survey, 1983: Key Results*. Mitra and Associates, Dhaka.

Mollah, Md. A. H. 2020. 'Privatization in Bangladesh'. *Public Administration* 2 (1): 11–23.

Mondal, B., and K. Das. 2010. 'Role of Growth Center: A Rural Development Perspective'. *Undefined* 3 (December): 129–41. https://citeseerx.ist.psu.edu/viewdoc/download?doi=10.1.1.1085.1622&rep=rep1&type=pdf. Accessed 30 December 2021.

Monga, C., and J. Y. Lin. 2019. *The Oxford Handbook of Structural Transformation*. New York: Oxford University Press.

Mookerji, R. 1912. 'A History of Indian Shipping. A History of the Sea-Borne Trade and Maritime Activity of the Indians from the Earliest Times'. Bombay; London: Longmans, Green and Company.

Morduch, J., and D. Roodman. 2011. 'The Impact of Microcredit on the Poor in Bangladesh: Revisiting the Evidence'. NYU Wagner Research Paper no. 2011-04, New York University, New York.

———. 2014. 'The Impact of Microcredit on the Poor in Bangladesh: Revisiting the Evidence'. *Journal of Development Studies* 50 (4): 583–604.

Morshed, A. Z. 2019. 'Understanding Mughal Dhaka'. *Daily Star*, 11 February 2019. https://www.thedailystar.net/in-focus/news/understanding-mughal-dhaka-1700224. Accessed 30 December 2021.

Morshed, N., C. Yorke and Q. Zhang. 2017. 'Urban Expansion Pattern and Land Use Dynamics in Dhaka, 1989–2014'. *Professional Geographer* 69 (3): 396–411.

Mostafa, R., and S. Klepper. 2009. 'Industrial Development through Tacit Knowledge Seeding: Evidence from the Bangladesh Garment Industry'. Research paper, Columbia University Press, New York, November 2009. http://www.columbia.edu/~ev2124/igc/spring_2010/papers/mostafa.pdf. Accessed 28 November 2021.

MRA. 2018. *Annual Report, 2018*. Annual report, Microcredit Regulatory Authority. https://www.mra.gov.bd/images/mra_files/Publications/annualreport18.pdf. Accessed 30 December 2021.

Mridha, R. U. 2020. 'Leather Turning into a Big Draw for Foreign Investors'. *Daily Star*, 13 October 2020.

Mukherjee, R. 1948. 'Economic Structure of Rural Bengal: A Survey of Six Villages'. *American Sociological Review* 13 (6): 660–72. https://doi.org/10.2307/2086819.

Murata, A. 2018. 'International Migration and Remittances for Economic Development in Bangladesh: An Overview'. In *Economic and Social Development of Bangladesh*, edited by Y. Sawada, M. Mahmud and N. Kitano, 93–113. Cham, Switzerland: Palgrave Macmillan. DOI: 10.1007/978-3-319-63838-6.

Murgai, R., and S. Zaidi. 2004. *Food Assistance Programs in Bangladesh*. Washington, DC: PREM, South Asia Region, World Bank.

Murshid, K. A. S. 1985a. 'Instability in Foodgrain Production: Causes, Adjustments, Policies: A Case Study of Bangladesh'. PhD. diss., University of Cambridge. https://ethos.bl.uk/OrderDetails.do?uin=uk.bl.ethos.355035. Accessed 30 December 2021.

———. 1985b. 'Is There a "Structural" Constraint to Capacity Utilisation of Deep Tube-wells?' *Bangladesh Development Studies* 13 (3/4): 147–54.

———. 1997. 'Generalised Morality and the Problem of Transition to an Impersonal Exchange Regime: A Response to Plateau with Insights from the Bangladesh Rice Market'. *Journal of Development Studies* 33 (5): 693–713.

———. 2014. 'Exploring Transition and Change in a Complex Traditional Market: The Case of the Rice Market in Bangladesh'. *Journal of Agrarian Change* 15 (4): 480–98.

———. 2019. 'LDC Graduation of Bangladesh: Moving Towards a Smooth Transition'. *EGov*, 10 October 2019. https://egov.eletsonline.com/2019/10/ldc-graduation-of-bangladesh-moving-towards-a-smooth-transition/. Accessed 11 November 2021.

Murshid, K. A. S., Shahid Khandker, Khandker Shakhawat Ali, Hussain Samad and Monzur Hossain. 2020. *The Impact of Mobile Financial Services: The Case of bKash in Bangladesh*. Monograph, Bangladesh Institute of Development Studies.

Murshid, K. A. S., and N. S. Murshid. 2019. 'Adolescent Exposure to and Attitudes toward Violence: Empirical Evidence from Bangladesh'. *Children and Youth Services Review* 98 (March): 85–95. https://doi.org/10.1016/j.childyouth.2018.12.025.

Murshid, K. A. S., S. Hager and M. Männlein. 2019. *South–South Ideas: Report on the Potential for Monitoring and Evaluation of Special Economic Zones in Bangladesh*. © Bangladesh Institute of Development Studies. http://hdl.handle.net/11540/9974.

Murshid, K. A. S., Y. Mohammad, S. M. Zulfiqar Ali and N. Ahmed. 2013. 'Bangladesh Food Market Performance: Instability, Integration, and Institutions'. Research monograph no. 23, Bangladesh Institute of Development Studies (BIDS), Dhaka.

Murshid, K. A. S., S. C. Zohir, M. Ahmed, I. Zabid and A. Mehdi. 2009. 'The Global Financial Crisis Implications for Bangladesh'. BIDS-PRP Working Paper Series no. 1, Bangladesh Institute of Development Studies.

Murshid, T. 1995. *The Sacred and the Secular: Bengali Muslim Discourses, 1871–1977*. Calcutta: Oxford University Press.

Musacchio, A., S. G. Lazzarini and R. V. Aguilera. 2015. 'New Varieties of State Capitalism: Strategic and Governance Implications'. *Academy of Management Perspectives* 29 (1): 115–31.

Nadkarni, M. V. 1991. 'The Mode of Production Debate: A Review Article'. *Indian Economic Review* 26 (1): 99–104.

Naqvi, S. S. N. 1986. *Role of Muslim League in the Pre-Partition Politics of India 1937–1947*. Doctoral thesis, Aligarh Muslim University. http://ir.amu.ac.in/8530/. Accessed 30 December 2021.

Nath, P. 2014. 'Battles, Boats and Bridges'. In *Cinese and Indian Warfare: From the Classical Age to 1870*, edited by K. Roy, 146–165. London: Routledge.

National Public Radio (NPR). 2013. *How It All Began*. Washington, DC, 2 December 2013.

NBR. 2011. *Bangladesh Economic Survey, 2011*. Dhaka: National Board of Revenue, People's Republic of Bangladesh.

———. n.d. *Annual Report Statistics*. https://nbr.gov.bd/. Accessed 16 March 2021.

Nevelling, P. 2014. 'Structural Contingencies and Untimely Coincidences in the Making of Neoliberal India: The Kandla Free Trade Zone, 1965–91'. *Contributions to Indian Sociology* 48 (1): 17–43.

New Age. 2018. '3 More Banking Licences to Be Granted on Political Ground: Muhith'. 2 November 2018. https://www.newagebd.net/article/54783/3-more-banking-licences-to-be-granted-onpolitical-%20ground-muhith. Accessed 30 December 2021.

New Humanitarian. 2014. 'Minorities Targeted in Bangladesh Political Violence'. 31 January 2014. https://www.thenewhumanitarian.org/analysis/2014/01/31/minorities-targeted-bangladesh-political-violence. Accessed 30 December 2021.

NIPORT, N. I. of P. R. and T., Mitra and Associates and ICF International. 2013. *Bangladesh Demographic and Health Survey 2011*. Dhaka, Bangladesh; Calverton, Maryland, USA: NIPORT, Mitra and Associates and ICF International.

Nisbett, N., P. Davis, S. Yosef and N. Akhtar. 2017. 'Bangladesh's Story of Change in Nutrition: Strong Improvements in Basic and Underlying Determinants with an Unfinished Agenda for Direct Community Level Support'. *Global Food Security* 13 (June): 21–29. https://doi.org/10.1016/j.gfs.2017.01.005.

Nölke, A., T. ten Brink, S. Claar. and C. May. 2015. 'Domestic Structures, Foreign Economic Policies and Global Economic Order: Implications from the Rise of Large Emerging Economies'. *European Journal of International Relations*, 21 (3): 538–67.

North, D. C. 1981. *Structure and Change in Economic Performance*. New York: Norton.

———. 1989. 'A Transaction Cost Approach to the Historical Development of Polities and Economies'. *Journal of Institutional and Theoretical Economics (JITE) / Zeitschrift Für Die Gesamte Staatswissenschaft* 145 (4): 661–68.

———. (1990) 2012. *Institutions, Institutional Change and Economic Performance*. London: Cambridge University Press, online.

———. 1998. 'Economic Performance through Time'. In *The New Institutionalism in Sociology*, edited by M. C. Brinton and V. Nee, 247–57. New York: Russell Sage Foundation.

O' Hara O'Connor, E. A. 2006. 'Trustworthiness and Contract'. In *Moral Markets: The Critical Role of Values in the Economy*, edited by P. J. Zak, 173–203. Princeton:

References

Princeton University Press. SSRN Scholarly Paper ID 929503; Issue ID 929503. https://papers.ssrn.com/abstract=929503. Accessed 30 December 2021.

Olsen, W. 1999. 'Village Level Exchange: Lessons from South India'. In *Agricultural Markets from Theory to Practice: Field Experience in Developing Countries*, edited by B. Harriss-White, 40–86. London: Palgrave Macmillan UK. https://doi.org/10.1007/978-1-349-27273-0_2.

Orr, A. 2012. 'Why Were So Many Social Scientists Wrong about the Green Revolution? Learning from Bangladesh'. *Journal of Development Studies* 48 (11): 1565–86. https://doi.org/10.1080/00220388.2012.663905.

Osman, F. A. 2008. 'Health Policy, Programmes and System in Bangladesh: Achievements and Challenges'. *South Asian Survey* 15 (2): 263–88. DOI: 10.1177/097152310801500206.

Osmani, S. R. 2008. 'Achievements and Challenges of the Bangladesh Economy: An Overview'. In *Emerging Issues in Bangladesh Economy: A Review of Bangladesh's Development 2005–06*, edited by S. R. Osmani, 1–24. Dhaka: Centre for Policy Dialogue (CPD) and The University Press Limited.

———. 2016. 'Models of Microcredit Delivery and Social Norm'. *Bangladesh Development Studies* 39 (3/4): 1–40.

Osmani, S. R., and M. A. Latif. 2013. 'The Pattern and Determinants of Poverty in Rural Bangladesh: 2000–2010'. *Bangladesh Development Studies* 36 (2): 1–41.

Osmani, S. R., and Md. A. Quasem. 1990. *Pricing and Subsidy Policies for Bangladesh Agriculture*. Dhaka: Bangladesh Unnayan Gobeshona Protisthan.

Osmani, S. R., and B. Sen. 2011. 'Inequality in Rural Bangladesh in the 2000s: Trends and Causes'. *Bangladesh Development Studies* 34 (4): 1–36.

Ostrom, E. 1998. 'A Behavioural Approach to the Rationale Choice Theory of Collective Action'. *American Political Science Review* 92 (1): 1–22.

———. 2005. *Understanding Institutional Diversity*. Princeton, NJ: Princeton.

Ostrom, E., and S. E. S. Crawford. 2005. 'Classifying Rules'. In *Understanding Institutional Diversity*, edited by E. Ostrom, 186–216. Princeton, NJ: Princeton University Press.

Ostrom, E., and J. Walker. 2003. *Trust and Reciprocity: Interdisciplinary Lessons for Experimental Research*. New York: Russell Sage Foundation.

Ovi, Ibrahim Hossain. 2020. 'ADB Supports Rural Road Network Expansion in Bangladesh'. *Dhaka Tribune*, 15 June 2020. https://www.dhakatribune.com/business/2020/06/15/adb-supports-rural-road-network-expansion-in-bangladesh. Accessed 25 March 2022.

Owen, J. E. 1972. 'The Emergence of Bangladesh'. *Current History* 63 (375): 206–33.

Ozawa, T. 2001. 'The "Hidden" Side of the "Flying Geese" Catch-Up Model: Japan's Dirigiste Institutional Set-Up and a Deepening Financial Morass'. *Journal of Asian Economics* 12, no. 4 (Winter): 471–91.

———. 2009. *The Rise of Asia: The "Flying-Geese" Theory of Tandem Growth and Regional Agglomeration*. Cheltenham, UK: Edward Elgar.

Pande, R. P. 2003. 'Selective Gender Differences in Childhood Nutrition and Immunization in Rural India: The Role of Siblings'. *Demography* 40 (3): 395–418. https://doi.org/10.1353/dem.2003.0029.

Parvez, S. 2019. 'Chemical Imports Treble'. *Daily Star*, 5 March 2019.

Patnaik, U. 1972. 'On the Mode of Production in Indian Agriculture: A Reply'. *Economic and Political Weekly* 7 (40): A145–51.

———. 1986. 'The Agrarian Question and Development of Capitalism in India'. *Economic and Political Weekly* 21 (18): 781–93.

———. 1990. 'Introduction'. In *Agrarian Relations and Accumulation*, edited by U. Patnaik, 1–9. New Delhi: Oxford University Press.

Paul, B. P. 2010. 'Does Corruption Foster Growth in Bangladesh?' *International Journal of Development Issues* 9 (3): 246–62. https://doi.org/10.1108/14468951011073325.

Paul-Majumder, P., and A. Begum. 2006. *Engendering Garment Industry: The Bangladesh Context*. Dhaka: The University Press Ltd.

Picketty, T. 2017. *Capital in the Twenty-First Century*. Cambridge, MA: Harvard University Press.

Pingali, P. L. 2012. 'Green Revolution: Impacts, Limits, and the Path Ahead'. *Proceedings of the National Academy of Sciences* 109 (31): 12302–08. https://doi.org/10.1073/pnas.0912953109.

Pitt, M. M., and S. R. Khandker. 1998. 'The Impact of Group-Based Credit Programs on Poor Households in Bangladesh: Does the Gender of Participants Matter?' *Journal of Political Economy* 106 (5): 958–96.

———. 2002. 'Credit Programmes for the Poor and Seasonality in Rural Bangladesh'. *Journal of Development Studies* 39 (2): 1–24. DOI: 10.1080/00220380412331322731.

———. 2012. 'Replicating Replication: Due Diligence in Roodman and Morduch's Replication of Pitt and Khandker (1998)'. Policy Research Working Paper no. 6273. World Bank, Washington, DC. © World Bank. https://openknowledge.worldbank.org/handle/10986/12111. Licence: CC BY 3.0 IGO.

Platteau, J. P. 1994a. 'Behind the Market Stage Where Real Societies Exist – Part I: The Role of Public and Private Order Institutions'. *Journal of Development Studies* 30 (3): 533–77.

———. 1994b. 'Behind the Market Stage Where Real Societies Exist – Part II: The Role of Moral Norms'. *Journal of Development Studies* 30 (4): 753–817.

Polanyi, K. 2013. *The Logic of Liberty: Reflections and Rejoinder*. London: Routledge.

Purkait, P., N. Kumar, R. Sahani and S. Mukherjee. 2020. 'Major Famines in India during British Rule: A Referral Map'. Research paper, Department

References

of Anthropology, Panjab University, India. https://www.researchgate.net/publication/340224385_Major_Famines_in_India_during_British_Rule_A_Referral_Map. Accessed 30 December 2021.

Qadir, S. A. 1960. *Village Dhanishwar: Three Generations of Man-Land Adjustment in an East Pakistan Village*. Comilla, Bangladesh: Pakistan Academy for Rural Development.

Qimiao, F., and M. Azad. 2017. 'Towards a Cleaner Bangladesh: Safe Water, Sanitation, and Hygiene for All'. *World Bank Blogs*, 15 September 2017. https://blogs.worldbank.org/endpovertyinsouthasia/towards-cleaner-bangladesh-safe-water-sanitation-and-hygiene-all. Accessed 30 December 2021.

Quah, J. T. 1999. 'Corruption in Asian Countries: Can It be Minimized?' *Public Administrative Review* 59 (6): 483–94.

Quibria, M. G. 2012. 'Microcredit and Poverty Alleviation: Can Microcredit Close the Deal?' WIDER Working Paper no. 2012/78, UNU-WIDER.

———. 2019. *Bangladesh's Road to Long-Term Economic Prosperity: Risks and Challenges*. Cham, Switzerland: Springer.

Rafi, M. 2003. 'Farewell Freire? Conscientisation in Early Twenty-First Century Bangladesh'. *Convergence* 36 (1): 41–62. https://search.proquest.com/openview/ca541f4aa6990e2152969ae08c171cc2/1?pq-origsite=gscholar&cbl=34715.

Rahman, A. 1999. *Women and Microcredit in Rural Bangladesh: An Anthropological Study of Grameen Bank Lending*. Boulder, CO: Westview Press.

———. 2004. 'Microcredit and Poverty Reduction: Trade-Off between Building Institutions and Reaching the Poor'. In *Anthropological and Sociological Perspectives in Savings and Debt*, edited by H. Lont and O. Hospes, 25–42. Delft: Eburon Academic Publishers.

Rahman, A., and R. Islam. 1985. 'Labor Use in Rural Bangladesh: A Study with Micro-Level Data'. Asian Regional Team for Employment Promotion, International Labour Organisation, Bangkok.

Rahman, A., and R. Islam. 1995. 'Labour Use in Rural Bangladesh: A Study with Micro Level Data'. Bangladesh Institute of Development Studies (BIDS), Dhaka, Bangladesh.

Rahman, H. 1992. 'Structural Adjustment and Macroeconomic Performance in Bangladesh in the 1980s'. *Bangladesh Development Studies* 20 (2/3): 89–125.

Rahman, H. Z. 1986. *Landed Property and the Dynamic of Instability. Bengal: State-Formation under Colonialism and Its Contemporary Significance*. UK: The University of Manchester. https://search.proquest.com/openview/8ade39c31cefec5095bb79577ad1d86d/1?pq-origsite=gscholar&cbl=18750&diss=y. Accessed 30 December 2021.

———. 1989. 'Mode of Production Debate Revisited: Conceptual Issues in Bengal's Agrarian Transition'. *Bangladesh Development Studies* 17 (4): 53–70.

Rahman, H. Z., and M. Hossain. 1995. *Rethinking Rural Poverty: Bangladesh as a Case Study*. New Delhi: Sage Publications.

Rahman, K. M. 1976. *Kamlapur Farmers' Co-operative Society: Potato Marketing by the Small Farmers of a Village of Comilla, Bangladesh*. https://agris.fao.org/agris-search/search.do?recordID=XF7700616. Accessed 30 December 2021.

Rahman, M. 1986. *Tradition, Development, and the Individual: A Study of Conflicts and Supports to Family Planning in Rural Bangladesh*. Canberra, Australia: Department of Demography, Australian National University.

Rahman, M. C., V. Pede, J. Balie, I. M. Pabuayon, J. M. Yorobe and S. Mohanty. 2021. 'Assessing the Market Power of Millers and Wholesalers in the Bangladesh Rice Sector'. *Journal of Agribusiness in Developing and Emerging Economies* 11 (3): 280–95. https://doi.org/10.1108/JADEE-04-2018-0053.

Rahman, M. M. 2013. 'Gendering Migrant Remittances: Evidence from Bangladesh and the United Arab Emirates'. *International Migration* 51, supp. 1 (July): e159–78. https://doi.org/10.1111/j.1468-2435.2012.00763.x.

———. 2020. 'Taiwan: A Potential Economic Partner for South Asia'. ISAS Working Paper Series. https://www.isas.nus.edu.sg/papers/taiwan-a-potential-economic-partner-for-south-asia/#:~:text=Bilateral%20Investment%20between%20Bangladesh%20and,year%20(Bangladesh%20Bank%202020). Accessed 28 December 2021.

Rahman, M. M., and W. V. Schendel. 2003. '"I Am Not a Refugee": Rethinking Partition Migration'. *Modern Asian Studies* 37 (3): 551–84. https://doi.org/10.1017/S0026749X03003020.

Rahman, S. 1960. 'A Village of East Pakistan: A Comparative Study'. Bachelor's thesis, Department of Sociology, Dhaka University.

———. 2006. 'Development, Democracy and the NGO Sector: Theory and Evidence from Bangladesh'. *Journal of Developing Societies* 22 (4): 451–73. https://doi.org/10.1177/0169796X06072650.

Rahman, S., I. A. Begum and M. J. Alam. 2014. 'Livestock in Bangladesh: Distribution, Growth, Performance and Potential'. *Livestock Research for Rural Development* 26 (10): 233–38. http://www.lrrd.org/lrrd26/10/rahm26173.html. Accessed 30 December 2021.

Raihan, S. 2008. 'Trade Liberalisation and Poverty in Bangladesh'. Macao Regional Knowledge Hub, Working papers no. 15, UN-ESCAP, Bangkok.

Raihan, S., G. Sugiyarto, H. K. Bazlul and S. Jha. 2009. 'Remittances and Household Welfare: A Case Study of Bangladesh'. Asian Development Bank Economics Working Paper no. 189.

Raisuddin, A., H. Steven and C. Tawfiq-e-Elahi. 2000. *Out of the Shadow of Famine: Evolving Food Markets and Food Policy in Bangladesh*. Washington, DC: International Food Policy Research Institute.

References

Ranis, G. 1974. 'Brief Reflections on the Central Issues of Policy in Bangladesh'. *Bangladesh Development Studies* 2 (4): 839–56.

Ranis, G., and F. Stewart. 1993. 'Rural Non-Agricultural Activities in Development'. *Journal of Development Economics* 49 (1): 75–101.

Raper, A. F. 1970. *Rural Development in Action: The Comprehensive Experiment at Comilla, East Pakistan*. Ithaca: Cornell University Press.

Rashid, S., and X. Zhang. 2019. *The Making of a Blue Revolution in Bangladesh Enablers, Impacts, and the Path Ahead for Aquaculture*. Washington, DC: IFPRI.

Rashid, S., N. Minot and S. Lemma. 2019. 'Does a "Blue Revolution" Help the Poor? Evidence from Bangladesh'. *Agricultural Economics* 50 (2): 139–50. https://doi.org/10.1111/agec.12472.

Rashid, S., M. Sharma and M. Zeller. 2004. 'Micro-Lending for Small Farmers in Bangladesh: Does It Affect Farm Households' Land Allocation Decision?' *Journal of Developing Areas* 37 (2): 13–29.

Rashid, S. F. 2000. 'The Urban Poor in Dhaka City: Their Struggles and Coping Strategies during the Floods of 1998'. *Disasters* 24 (3): 240–53.

Rashiduzzaman, M. 1970. 'The Awami League in the Political Development of Pakistan'. *Asian Survey* 10 (7): 574–87. https://doi.org/10.2307/2642956.

Rasul, M. G. 1986. 'The Advent of Islam in Bengal: Its Socio-Cultural Impact'. In *Society and Culture in Islam*, edited by M. I. Hoque, 100–16. Chittagong, Bangladesh: University of Chittagong.

Ravallion, M. 1982. 'Agricultural Wages in Bangladesh before and after the 1974 Famine'. *Bangladesh Development Studies* 10 (1): 75–89.

———. 1985. 'The Information Efficiency of Traders' Price Expectations in a Bangladesh Rice Market'. *Oxford Bulletin of Economics and Statistics* 47 (2): 171–84. https://doi.org/10.1111/j.1468-0084.1985.mp47002005.x.

———. 1986. 'Testing Market Integration'. *American Journal of Agricultural Economics* 68 (1): 102–09.

———. 1987. *Markets and Famines*. Oxford: Clarendon Press.

Rawls, J. 2009. *A Theory of Justice*. Cambridge: Harvard University Press.

Ray, A. 2010. 'General President's Address: An Approach to the Study of Morphology of Selected Towns and Cities of Medieval Bengal, c. 1500 to c. 1727'. *Proceedings of the Indian History Congress* 71: 1–27.

Reardon, T., and C. P. Timmer. 2005. 'Transformation of Markets for Agricultural Output in Developing Countries since 1950: How Has Thinking Changed?' In *Handbook of Agricultural Economics: Agricultural Development; Farmers, Farm Production and Farm Markets*, edited by R. E. Evenson, P. L. Pingali and T. P. Schultz, 3:2807–855. Amsterdam: North-Holland.

Reardon, T., K. Z. Chen, B. Minten, L. Adriano, T. A. Dao, J. Wang and S. D. Gupta. 2014. 'The Quiet Revolution in Asia's Rice Value Chains'. *Annals of the New York Academy of Sciences* 1331 (1): 106–18.

Reeves, R. V. 2018. *Dream Hoarders: How the American Upper Middle Class Is Leaving Everyone Else in the Dust, Why That Is a Problem, and What to Do about It.* Washington, DC: Brookings Institution Press.

Reeves, R. V., K. Guyot and E. Krause. 2018. 'Defining the Middle Class: Cash, Credentials, or Culture?' *Brookings*, 7 May 2018. https://www.brookings.edu/research/defining-the-middle-class-cash-credentials-or-culture/. Accessed 30 December 2021.

Riaz, A. 1993. 'State, Class and Military Rule in Bangladesh: 1972–1982'. PhD diss., University of Hawaii, Manoa.

———. 2019. *Voting in a Hybrid Regime: Explaining the 2018 Bangladeshi Election.* Politics of South Asia Series. Singapore: Palgrave Macmillan.

———. 2021. 'The Pathway of Democratic Backsliding in Bangladesh'. *Democratization* 28 (1): 179–97.

RMMRU. 2017. *Role of Dalals in Migration System of Bangladesh: Extent of Fraudulence.* Dhaka, Bangladesh: RMMRU.

Robert, K. 2021. *A General History and Collection of Voyages and Travels.* Vol. 7. https://www.e-reading.life/book.php?book=80243. Accessed 1 January 2022.

Robinson, W. C., and J. A. Ross. 2007. *The Global Family Planning Revolution: Three Decades of Population Policies and Programs.* Washington, DC: World Bank. © World Bank. https://openknowledge.worldbank.org/handle/10986/6788. Licence: CC BY 3.0 IGO.

Rodríguez, José J. Romero. 2020. 'Development Aid In Crisis: Donor Fatigue'. *Envio* 229 (August). https://www.envio.org.ni/articulo/1442. Accessed 25 March 2022.

Roodman, D., and J. Morduch. 2009. 'The Impact of Microcredit on the Poor in Bangladesh: Revisiting the Evidence'. Center for Global Development, Working Paper no. 174.

Roome, J., A. Gapihan and H. Lee. 2019. 'An Upper Middle-Income Bangladesh Starts with a Livable Dhaka'. *World Bank Blogs*, 12 December 2019. https://blogs.worldbank.org/endpovertyinsouthasia/upper-middle-income-bangladesh-starts-livable-dhaka. Accessed 1 January 2022.

Roy, D. K. 1993. 'Impact of Incentives on Export Performance of Bangladesh: A Preliminary Assessment'. *Bangladesh Development Studies* 25 (2): 25–44.

Roy, R. 2017. 'The Political Economy of Migration from Bangladesh: Power, Politics and Contestations'. Ph.D. diss., School of Social Sciences, University of Adelaide.

Rudra, A. 1978. 'Class Relations in Indian Agriculture: I'. *Economic and Political Weekly* 13 (22): 916–23.

Rudra, A., A. Majid and B. D. Talib. 1969. 'Big Farmers of Punjab'. *Economic and Political Weekly* 4 (39): A143–A146.

Rutherford, S. 2009. *The Pledge: ASA, Peasant Politics, and Microfinance in the Development of Bangladesh.* New York: Oxford University Press.

References

Rutstein, S. O. 2008. 'Further Evidence of the Effects of Preceding Birth Intervals on Neonatal, Infant, and Under-Five-Years Mortality and Nutritional Status in Developing Countries: Evidence from the Demographic and Health Surveys'. DHS Working Paper no. 41, USAID. https://dhsprogram.com/pubs/pdf/WP41/WP41.pdf. Accessed 1 January 2022.

Salim, M. M. 2013. 'Revealed Objective Functions of Microfinance Institutions: Evidence from Bangladesh'. *Journal of Development Economics* 104 (C): 34–55.

Sally, D. 2002. 'Two Economic Applications of Sympathy'. *Journal of Law, Economics and Organization* 18 (2): 455–87.

Santacreu, A. M., and H. Zhu. 2018. 'How Did South Korea's Economy Develop So Quickly?' *On the Economy Blog*, St Louis Fed, 20 March 2018. https://www.stlouisfed.org/on-the-economy/2018/march/how-south-korea-economy-develop-quickly. Accessed 1 January 2022.

Saqui, Q. Md. H., and K. Akhtar. 1987. *Village Studies in Bangladesh: An Annotated Bibliography*. Dhaka: National Institute of Local Govt. https://trove.nla.gov.au/work/18222601. Accessed 1 January 2022.

Sarao, K. T. S. 2012. *The Decline of Buddhism in India: A Fresh Perspective*. New Delhi: Munshiram Manoharlal Publishers.

Sarkar, G. M. 1927. *Early History of Bengal*. Calcutta: Calcutta University Press. http://14.139.211.59/bitstream/123456789/2375/1/26224.pdf. Accessed 1 January 2022.

Sattar, Z. 2020. *Deemed Exports: Import Substitution par Excellence*. Report, Policy Research Institute (PRI), Dhaka.

Sawada, Y., M. Mahmud and N. Kitano. (eds.). 2018. *Economic and Social Development of Bangladesh*. Cham, Switzerland: Palgrave Macmillan. https://doi.org/10.1007/978-3-319-63838-6.

Schwab, D., and E. Ostrom. 2008. 'The Vital Role of Norms and Rules in Maintaining Open Public and Private Economics'. In *Moral Markets: The Critical Role of Values in the Economy*, edited by P. J. Zak, 204–27. Princeton: Princeton University Press.

Sen, A. 1980. 'Famines'. *World Development* 8 (9): 613–21. https://doi.org/10.1016/0305-750X(80)90053-4.

———. 1982. *Poverty and Famines: An Essay on Entitlement and Deprivation*. New Delhi: Oxford University Press.

———. 1999. *Poverty and Famines: An Essay on Entitlement and Deprivation*. New York: Oxford University Press.

———. 2013. 'What's Happening in Bangladesh?' *Lancet* 382 (9909): 1966–68. https://doi.org/10.1016/S0140-6736(13)62162-5.

Sen, B. 1996. 'Rural Non-farm Sector in Bangladesh: Stagnating and Residual, or Dynamic and Potential?' *Bangladesh Development Studies* 24 (3/4): 143–180.

———. 2010. 'Size and Growth of Middle Class in Bangladesh'. Dhaka: Bangladesh Institute of Development Studies. Mimeo.

Sen, B., and D. Hulme. (eds.). 2004. *Chronic Poverty in Bangladesh: Tales of Ascent, Descent, Marginality and Persistence: The State of the Poorest, 2004–2005*. Bangladesh Institute of Development Studies, Chronic Poverty Research Centre, Institute for Development Policy and Management, University of Manchester, UK.

Sen, B., P. Dorosh, M. Ahmed and J. Van Asselt. 2018. 'Drivers, Trends, and Consequences of Changing Household Employment Patterns in Rural Bangladesh'. IFPRI Discussion Paper 1733. Washington, DC: International Food Policy Research Institute (IFPRI).

Seventh Five-Year Plan of Bangladesh, 2016–20. 2020. Dhaka: Ministry of Planning, Government of Bangladesh.

Shawkat Ali, A. M. M., I. Jahan, A. Ahmed and S. Rashid. 2008. 'Public Food Distribution System in Bangladesh: Successful Reforms and Remaining Challenges'. Chap. 5 in *From Parastatals to Private Trade: Lessons from Asian Agriculture*, edited by S. Rashid, A. Gulati and R. Cummings, Jr. Johns Hopkins University Press, Maryland: International Food Policy Research Institute (IFPRI). https://ideas.repec.org/b/fpr/ifprib/9780801888151.html. Accessed 2 January 2022.

Shilpi, F., and S. Emran. 2016. 'Agricultural Productivity and Non-farm Employment: Evidence from Bangladesh'. Policy Research Working Paper no. 7685, World Bank, Washington, DC. © The World Bank.

Siddiqi, D. M. 1991. 'Discipline and Protect: Women Factory Workers in Bangladesh'. *Grassroots: An Alternative Development Journal* 1 (2): 42–49.

Siddiqui, K. 1982. *Political Economy of Rural Poverty in Bangladesh*. National Institute of Local Government, Dhaka. https://agris.fao.org/agris-search/search.do?recordID=US201300369176. Accessed 1 January 2022.

Siddiqui, K., J. Ahmed, K. Siddique, S. Huq, A. Hossain, S. Nazimud-Doula and N. Rezawana. 2010. *Social Formation in Dhaka, 1985–2005: A Longitudinal Study of Society*. Oxon: Ashgate Publishing; New York: Routledge.

Siddiqui, T. 2001. *Transcending Boundaries: Labour Migration of Women from Bangladesh*. Dhaka: Dhaka University Press.

———. 2006. 'Protection of Bangladeshi Migrants through Good Governance'. In *Merchants of Labour*, edited by C. Kuptsch, 63–90. Geneva: International Institute for Labor Studies, ILO.

———. 2008. 'Migration and Gender in Asia'. Issue UN/POP/EGM-MIG/2008/6, United Nations Economic and Social Commission for Asia and the Pacific (UNESCAP), Bangkok, Thailand, 19 September 2008.

———. 2011. *Recruitment Cost in Bangladesh: Challenges of Governing Migration in the Countries of Origin*. Dhaka: RMMRU.

References

Siddiqui, T., and R. A. Mahmood. 2014. *Impact of Migration on Poverty and Local Development in Bangladesh*. Dhaka: SDC/RMMRU.

Sinkovics, N., S. M. Hoque and R. R. Sinkovics. 2016. 'Rana Plaza Collapse Aftermath: Are CSR Compliance and Auditing Pressures Effective?' *Accounting, Auditing and Accountability Journal* 29 (4): 617–49.

Smith, L. C., and L. J. Haddad. 2000. *Explaining Child Malnutrition in Developing Countries: A Cross-Country Analysis*. Washington, DC: International Food Policy Research Institute.

Sobhan, R. 1991. 'An Industrial Strategy for Industrial Policy: Redirecting the Industrial Development of Bangladesh in the 1990s'. *Bangladesh Development Studies* 19 (1/2): 201–15.

———. 2015. *From Two Economies to Two Nations: My Journey to Bangladesh*. Dhaka: Daily Star Books.

Sobhan, R., and M. Ahmad. 1980. *Public Enterprise in An Intermediate Regime: A Study in the Political Economy of Bangladesh*. Dacca, Bangladesh: Bangladesh Institute of Development Studies.

Sosale, S., T. M. Asaduzzaman and D. Ramachandran. 2019. 'Girls' Education in Bangladesh: A Promising Journey'. *World Bank Blog*, 24 June 2019. https://blogs.worldbank.org/endpovertyinsouthasia/girls-education-bangladesh-promising-journey. Accessed 27 December 2021.

Spears D., A. Ghosh and O. Cumming. 2013. 'Open Defecation and Childhood Stunting in India: An Ecological Analysis of New Data from 112 Districts'. *PLoS ONE* 8 (9): e73784. https://doi.org/10.1371/journal.pone.0073784.

Srinivasan, C. S., G. Zanello and B. Shankar. 2013. 'Rural–Urban Disparities in Child Nutrition in Bangladesh and Nepal'. *BMC Public Health* 13 (1): 1–15.

Stein, G., and A. Charters. 1990. *Three Lives*. New York: Penguin Classics.

Stiglitz, J. 1993. 'Incentives, Organizational Structures and Contractual Choice in the Reform of Socialist Agriculture'. In *The Agricultural Transition in Central and Eastern Europe and the Former USSR*, edited by A. Braverman, K. Brooks and C. Csaki, 27–46. Washington, DC: World Bank.

———. 1994. 'The Role of the State in Financial Markets'. Proceedings of the World Bank Conference on Development 1993, suppl. to the *World Bank Economic Review* and *World Bank Research Observer*. Washington, DC: World Bank.

Sujauddin, M., R. Koide, T. Komatsu, M. M. Hossain, C. Tokoro and S. Murakami. 2015. 'Characterization of Ship Breaking Industry in Bangladesh'. *Journal of Material Cycles and Waste Management* 17 (1): 72–83.

Sultana, M. 2020. 'Japanese Investments in Two SEZs Unlikely in Two Years'. *Financial Express*, 14 October 2020.

Swapan, M. S. H., A. U. Zaman, T. Ahsan and F. Ahmed. 2017. 'Transforming Urban Dichotomies and Challenges of South Asian Megacities: Rethinking Sustainable Growth of Dhaka, Bangladesh'. *Urban Science* 1 (4): 1–20.

Swarna, N., and T. Banik. 2018. 'A Study on Sector-Based Need Assessment of Light Engineering Sector of Bangladesh'. *American Journal of Economics* 8, no. 6: 244–53.

Talukder, R. K. 2005. 'Food Security, Self-Sufficiency and Nutrition Gap in Bangladesh'. *Bangladesh Development Studies* 31, nos. 3/4 (September–December): 35–62.

Tarafdar, M. R. 1965. *Husain Shahi Bengal, AD 1494–1538: A Socio-Political Study*. Dacca: Asiatic Society of Pakistan.

Tarozzi, A., J. Desai and K. Johnson. 2015. 'The Impacts of Microcredit: Evidence from Ethiopia'. *American Economic Journal: Applied Economics* 7 (1): 54–89.

Taylor, A. J. 1979. *Emergency Sanitation for Refugees: Experiences in the Bangladesh Refugee Relief Camps, India, 1971–1972*. Oxford, UK: Pergamon Press Ltd.

Taylor, J. 1840. *Topography and Statistics of Dacca*. Calcutta: Huttman, Military Orphan Press.

Textile Today. 2021. 'Youngone Invested $65 mn in Man-Made Fibre in KEPZ and Planning to Invest $120 mn'. 22 February 2021. https://www.textiletoday.com.bd/youngone-invested-65-mn-man-made-fibre-kepz-planning-invest-120-mn/. Accessed 2 January 2022.

Thomas, D., J. Strauss and M.-H. Henriques 1991. 'How Does Mother's Education Affect Child Height?' *Journal of Human Resources* 26 (2): 183–211.

Thorner, A. 1982. 'Semi-feudalism or Capitalism? Contemporary Debate on Classes and Modes of Production in India'. *Economic and Political Weekly* 17 (49): 1961–68.

Thorp, J. P. 1987. 'Sheikh Mujibur Rahman, A Cyclone and The Emergence of Bangladesh'. *South Asia Research* 7 (2): 143–67.

Toufique, K. A. 2017. 'Bangladesh Experience in Rural Development: The Success and Failure of the Various Models Used'. *Bangladesh Development Studies* 40, nos. 1/2 (March–June): 143–67.

Toufique, K. A., and C. Turton. 2002. *Hands Not Land: How Livelihoods are Changing in Rural Bangladesh*. Dhaka: Bangladesh Institute of Development Studies.

Trading Economics. 2021. 'Bangladesh iIternational Tourism: Number of Arrivals'. 16 March 2021. https://tradingeconomics.com/bangladesh/international-tourism-number-of-arrivals-wb-data.html. Accessed 2 January 2022.

Transparency International. 2019. *Corruption Perceptions Index*. Transparency.org. https://www.transparency.org/files/content/pages/2019_CPI_Report_EN.pdf. Accessed 2 January 2022.

Ullah, M. S., and R. Akhter. 2021. 'Automation of the Readymade Garment Sector in Bangladesh: Who Is Paying the Price?'. *FemLab.co*, Connected2Work, 15 May 2021. https://connected2work.org/blog/automation-of-the-readymade-garment-sector-in-bangladesh-who-is-paying-the-price/. Accessed 29 November 2021.

References

UN Statistical Office. 1955. *Demographic Yearbook of 1955*. New York. https://unstats.un.org/unsd/demographic-social/products/dyb/dybsets/1955%20DYB.pdf. Accessed 2 Janaury 2022.

UNCOMTRADE Data Bank. n.d. https://comtrade.un.org/data/. Accessed 2 January 2022.

UNESCO. n.d. *Bangladesh: Trends in Dropout Rates*. Accessed on 16 March 2021. http://uis.unesco.org/.

UNICEF. 1990. *Strategy for Improved Nutrition of Children and Women in Developing Countries*. New York. http://digitallibrary.un.org/record/132779.

———. 2013a. *Multiple Indicator Cluster Survey 2012–2013*. Bangladesh Bureau of Statistics, Dhaka.

———. 2013b. *Improving Child Nutrition: The Achievable Imperative for Global Progress*. New York. https://reliefweb.int/sites/reliefweb.int/files/resources/Improving%20child%20nutrition%20The%20achievable%20imperative%20for%20global%20progress.pdf. Accessed 2 Janaury 2022.

———. 2019. *Bangladesh Mics 2019 Report*. Dhaka: UNICEF and Bangladesh Bureau of Statistics.

———. 2021. 'Ending Child Marriage'. 14 March 2021. https://www.unicef.org/bangladesh/en/ending-child-marriage. Accessed 2 Janaury 2022.

United Nations Development Programme (UNDP). n.d. 'Human Development Data Center'. Human Development Reports. http://hdr.undp.org/en/data. Accessed 16 March 2021.

———. n.d. 'Gender Development Index (GDI)'. Human Development Reports. http://hdr.undp.org/en/indicators/137906. Accessed 16 March 2021.

USAID. 2018. *USAID: Bangladesh: Nutrition Profile 2018*. Dhaka. https://www.usaid.gov/sites/default/files/documents/tagged_Bangladesh-Nutrition-Profile.pdf. Accessed 2 January 2022.

———. 2019. *Comprehensive Private Sector Assessment*. USAID and Government of Bangladesh. https://www.usaid.gov/angladesh/press-releases/nov-5-2019-usaid-private-sector-study-reveals-potential-industries-enhance. Accessed 2 January 2022.

Van der Laan, H. L. 1975. *The Lebanese Traders in Sierra Leone*. The Hague: Mouton and Co.

Van Schendel, W. 1981. *Peasant Mobility; the Odds of Life in Rural Bangladesh*. Assen: Van Gorcum. https://agris.fao.org/agris-search/search.do?recordID=XF2015012887. Accessed 2 January 2022.

Varma, S., and P. Kumar. 1996. 'Rural Non-farm Employment in Bangladesh'. *Bangladesh Development Studies* 24 (3/4): 75–102.

Von Pischke, J. D. 1991. *Finance at the Frontier: Debt Capacity and the Role of Credit in the Private Economy*. EDI Development Studies, The World Bank, Washington, DC.

Wali, M. A. 1904. 'Ethnographic Notes on the Muhammedan Caste of Bengal'. *Anthropological Society of Bombay: Journal* 7 (2): 98–112.

Wallace, B. J., and M. Harris. 1989. 'Anthropology and Development in Bangladesh'. *Urban Anthropology and Studies of Cultural Systems and World Economic Development* 18 (3/4): 241–64.

Wang, J. H. 2004. 'FGP and the Experience of Japan in East Asia'. *Issues and Studies* 43 (1): 1–31.

Webb, P., and S. Block. 2004. 'Nutrition Information and Formal Schooling as Inputs to Child Nutrition'. *Economic Development and Cultural Change* 52 (4): 801–20.

Weeramantry, C. G. 1997. *Justice without Frontiers, Furthering Human Rights*. Vol. 1. The Hague: Kluwer Law International.

Weinralib, B. 1973. 'Bengalis Held in Pakistan Long for Home'. *New York Times*, 5 April 1973. https://www.nytimes.com/1973/04/05/archives/bengalis-held-in-pakistan-long-for-home-religion-was-link.html. Accessed 2 January 2022.

Wennergren, E. B., C. H. Antholt and M. D. Whitaker. 1984. *Agricultural Development in Bangladesh*. Boulder, Colorado: Westview Press.

Westergaard, K. 1985. *State and Rural Society in Bangladesh: A Study in Relationship*. London: Curzon Press.

Wharton Jr, C. R. 1962. 'Marketing, Merchandising and Money-Lending: A Note on Middleman Monopsony in Malaya'. *Malayan Economic Review* 7 (October): 24–44.

White, H. 2005. 'Comment on Contributions Regarding the Impact of the Bangladesh Integrated Nutrition Project'. *Health Policy and Planning* 20 (6): 408–11.

White, S. C. 1992. 'Arguing with the Crocodile: Gender and Class in Bangladesh'. London: Zed Press.

———. 1999. 'NGOs, Civil Society, and the State in Bangladesh: The Politics of Representing the Poor'. *Development and Change* 30 (2): 307–26.

WHO. 1978. 'Declaration of Alma-Ata'. International Conference on Primary Health Care, Alma-Ata, USSR, 6–12 September 1978. https://www.who.int/publications/almaata_declaration_en.pdf. Accessed 2 Janaury 2022.

Williamson, O. E. 1975. *Markets and Hierarchies: Analysis and Anti-Trust Implications*. New York: Free Press.

Wood, G. D. 1981. 'Rural Class Formation in Bangladesh, 1940–1980'. *Bulletin of Concerned Asian Scholars* 13 (4): 2–17.

World Bank. 1979. *Bangladesh Food Policy Issues*. Report no. 2761-BD, 19 December 1979.

———. 1982. *World Development Report 1982*. New York: Oxford University Press. Published for the World Bank.

———. 1994. *Bangladesh Privatization and Adjustment*. Report no. 12318-BD World Bank Group, Washington, DC.

———. 2006a. *Bangladesh: End of MFA Quotas; Key Issues and Strategic Options for Bangladesh Ready Made Garments*. Report No. 34964-BD, World Bank (South Asia Region).

———. 2006b. 'Repositioning Nutrition as Central to Development'. *Directions in Development - General*. https://doi.org/10.1596/978-0-8213-6399-7.

———. 2007. 'Dhaka: Improving Living Conditions for the Urban Poor'. Bangladesh Development Series Paper no. 17, The World Bank Office, Dhaka.

———. 2008. 'Bangladesh: Poverty Assessment for Bangladesh; Creating Opportunities and Bridging the East–West Divide'. Bangladesh Development Series Paper no. 26, World Bank. © World Bank. https://openknowledge.worldbank.org/handle/10986/7886. Licence: CC BY 3.0 IGO.

———. 2012. *Bangladesh: Towards Accelerated, Inclusive and Sustainable Growth; Opportunities and Challenges*. Vol. 2. Main report, Washington, DC, June 2012.

———. 2013. 'Bangladesh Poverty Assessment: Assessing a Decade of Progress in Reducing Poverty, 2000–2010'. Bangladesh Development Series Paper No. 31, The World Bank Office, Dhaka, June 2013.

———. 2015. 'Bangladesh Public Expenditure Review Update'. Report No. 97067-BD, South Asia Region, The World Bank, Dhaka.

———. 2018a. *Promising Progress: A Diagnostic of Water Supply, Sanitation, Hygiene, and Poverty in Bangladesh*. WASH Poverty Diagnostic; World Bank, Washington, DC. © World Bank.

———. 2018b. *Export Diversification through Bonded Warehouse Reforms*. https://openknowledge.worldbank.org/handle/10986/30551?show=full. Accessed 16 March 2021.

———. 2019a. *Bangladesh Poverty Assessment: Facing Old and New Frontiers in Poverty Reduction*. Vols. 1 and 2. International Bank for Reconstruction and Development (IBRD), The World Bank, Washington, DC.

———. 2019b. 'Bangladesh Development Update, April 2019: Towards Regulatory Predictability'. World Bank, Dhaka. © World Bank. https://openknowledge.worldbank.org/handle/10986/31504. Licence: CC BY 3.0 IGO

———. 2020a. *Demographic Transition: Lessons from Bangladesh's Success Story*. Washington, DC.

———. 2020b. *Thailand Economic Monitor Productivity for Prosperity*. TEM Report, World Bank Group, Bangkok.

———. n.d. *Institutional Assessment of Migration Systems in Bangladesh*. Dhaka: World Bank Group.

World Bank Group. 1980. *World Development Report 1980*. World Bank, Washington, DC.

———. 2019. 'World Bank: Bangladesh Economy Continues Robust Growth with Rising Exports and Remittances'. Press Release, World Bank, Washington, DC, 10 October 2019.

'World Bank Open Data'. n.d. https://data.worldbank.org/. Accessed 16 March 2021.

Woutersen, T., and S. R. Khandker. 2014. 'Estimating the Long Run Impact of Microcredit Programs on Household Income and Net Worth'. World Bank Policy Research Working Paper 7040.

Yeung, Y., J. Lee and G. Kee. 2009. 'China's Special Economic Zones at 30'. *Eurasian Geography and Economics* 50 (2): 222–40.

Yunus, M. 1999. *Banker to the Poor: Micro-Lending and the Battle against World Poverty*. New York: Pacific Affairs.

Yunus, M., and A. H. Mondal. 2018. *Enclave Industrialization: Evidence from Export Processing Zones in Bangladesh*. Dhaka: Bangladesh Institute of Development Studies. Mimeo.

Yusuf, S., and P. Kumar. 1996. 'Developing the Nonfarm Sector in Bangladesh: Lessons from Other Asian Countries'. Discussion paper no. 340, World Bank Publications, Washington, DC.

Zahid, S. H. 2019. 'Departure of Pharmaceutical Companies'. *Financial Express*, 15 September 2019. https://thefinancialexpress.com.bd/views/departing-pharmaceutical-companies-1568563625. Accessed 2 January 2022.

Zamir, M. 2017. 'Reconstruction of Bangladesh in Post-War 1972'. *Financial Express*, 3 April 2017. https://today.thefinancialexpress.com.bd/public/print/reconstruction-of-bangladesh-in-post-war-1972. Accessed 2 January 2022.

Zhang, X., and J. Ruan. 2014. '"Flying Geese" in China: The Textile and Apparel Industry's Pattern of Migration'. *Journal of Asian Economics* 34 (October): 79–91.

Zohir, S. 2004. 'NGO Sector in Bangladesh: An Overview'. *Economic and Political Weekly* 39 (36): 4109–13.

Zohir, S. C. 2001. 'Social Impact of the Growth of Garment Industry in Bangladesh'. *Bangladesh Development Studies* 27 (4): 41–80.

Index

Abdullah, A. A., 159
Abed, Fazle Hassan, 46
access to health services, 25–26
Accord on Fire and Building Safety in Bangladesh (ACCORD), 107
Adamjee Jute Mills, 134
Agreement on International Trade in Cotton and Textiles (1964), 99
agricultural input market reforms, 54–55
agricultural market
  aratdar, 65
  bepari, 64
  faria, 64
  intermediaries, types of, 63
  long-distance circuit, 63
  paddy circuit, 63–64
  paikar, 65
  processors, 65–66
  retailer, 65
  simple, local circuit, 63
  socio-economic profile, traders, 65
Ahmed, J., 187, 193
Ahmed, M., 92, 109
Ahmed, Redwan, 109
Akash, M. M., 187
Akhtar, K., 150, 153
Akhtar, N., 28
Alam, S. M. N., 154
Alavi, H., 154
Alder, S., 130
Ali, Khandker Shakhawat, 94
Alliance for Bangladesh Worker Safety, 107

Alma-Ata Declaration, 160
Amin, S., 158–59
Annual Development Programme (ADP), 132
Arakanese-Portuguese occupation, 172
Arif, F., 153
Armendáriz, B., 155
Asadullah, M. N., 144
Asian Development Bank (ADB), 53
Asian 'super-performers', 100
Awami League (AL), 44, 47
Azad, M., 161

'back-to-back letter of credit' facility, 104–07
'backward' agrarian forms, 154
balance of payments (BOP) data, 13–15
Banerjee, A., 155–56
Bangladesh Agricultural Development Corporation (BADC), 50
Bangladesh and India
  employment shares, 21
  share of industry and services in GDP, 20
Bangladesh Association of International Recruiting Agencies (BAIRA), 81–82
Bangladesh Bank, 104
Bangladesh Bureau of Statistics (BBS), 33
Bangladesh Chemical Industries Corporation (BCIC), 134
Bangladesh Contraceptive Prevalence Survey (BCPS), 43

Bangladesh Demographic and Health Surveys (BDHS), 26
Bangladesh Economic Zones Authority (BEZA), 125
Bangladesh Institute of Development Studies (BIDS), 33
Bangladesh Integrated Household Survey (BIHS), 86
Bangladesh Integrated Nutrition Programme 1995–2004 (BINP), 168
Bangladesh Jute Mills Corporation (BJMC), 132
Bangladesh Nationalist Party (BNP), 46
Bangladesh nutrition data, 27
Bangladesh Overseas Services Limited (BOESL), 81
Bangladesh Power Development Board (BPDB), 132
Bangladesh private sector, 126
Bangladesh Small and Cottage Industries Corporation (BSCIC), 125
Bangladesh Sugar and Food Industries Corporation (BSFIC), 134
Bangladesh Water Development Board (BWDB), 51
Bangladeshi 'NGO model', 152
Basher, S., 38
Bazlul, H. K., 82
Becker, S., 145
Begum, A., 96, 164
Bengali Naval Commandos, 37
Bhattacharya, D., 108
Bhuiya, A., 143, 160
Birdsall, N., 199
'Blue Revolution', 96
Bose, S. R., 38
Boyce, J. K., 153
Bureau of Manpower Export and Training (BMET), 81

'cash assistance scheme', 104
cash-food imports, 49

Chambers, Robert, 154
Chami, R., 82
Chandpur Irrigation Project, 51
Chen, D. S., 141
Chen, L. C., 143, 160
Chen, M. A., 153
Cheng, C. P., 141
China, 129–31
China, People's Republic of China (PRC), 16–17
Chittagong Port, 37
Choudhry, S., 38
Choudhury, Tapan, 191
Chowdhury, A. M. R., 143, 160
Chowdhury, M. E., 143, 160
chronic and transient poverty, 33
chronology, major government interventions, 80–81
Cleland, J., 158–59
colonial Dhaka, 174–75
Comilla Model (CM), 50, 146–49
community-based organization (CBO), 149
compound annual growth rate (CAGR), 97
conditional cash transfer (CCT), 157
conglomerates, 197–99, 211–16
contraceptive prevalence rate (CPR), 160
contraceptive prevalence survey (CPS), 158–59
contracting-out (CO) mechanism, 162
Copestake, J. G., 155
cost of basic needs (CBN), 33
coup and counter coup (1970s), 45–46
'crawling peg' (2010), 110
Crow, B., 58, 61

Daewoo, South Korean firm, 100
Dasgupta, C., 184
Davis, P., 28
deep tube well (DTW), 50–51, 53

Republic of Korea, services and industry in GDP, 19
Development Assistance Committee (DAC), 18
development financial institution (DFI), 132
Dhaka, the capital of Bangladesh
and rise of a business class, 222–23
in the new century, 196–97
'Matsyanyaya'/Law of the Fishes, 182
1970s Dhaka, the beginnings, 183–89
1980s, game changers and new elites, 189–93
1990s, taking off, 193–96
population of, 180–81
satellite data, 181
socio-economic groups, 182
urbanization, 181–82
direct calorie intake (DCI), 33
'dirty float', 110
distribution systems for chemical fertilizers, 50
domestic and foreign investors, 127
Dorosh, P., 92
dropout rates, Bangladesh, 30
'drug policy', role of, 158
Duflo, E., 144
Duvendack, M., 155

Easterly, W., 199
Eaton, R. M., 172
economic and technological development zone (ETDZ), 130
economic inequality, 35
electronics assembly sector, 115
electronic tax identification number (e-TIN), 12
endogenous traditional market institutions, 59
entrepreneurship and RMG, 192–93
entrepreneurship development, 117
Ershad, H. M., 44–45
Escobal, J., 61

'export performance benefit scheme', 104
'export performance licensing scheme', 104
export processing zone (EPZ), 102, 125–26
extreme poverty, 40

Faaland, J., 38
Fafchamps, M., 61
family planning (FP), 44
family welfare centre (FWC), 158
family welfare visitors, 43
Fan, L. Y., 141
farm and non-farm employment, 88
'Female Secondary School Assistance Project' (FSSAP), 166
'Female Secondary School Stipend' programme, 144
feminization of education, 165–67
fertility rate, total (births per woman, ages 15–49), 22
feudal and semi-feudal forms, 154
financial intermediation, 16
First Five-Year Plan of Bangladesh (1973–78), 42
flying geese paradigm (FGP), 139–42
food aid, 49
food and energy imports, 10
food and nutrition, 26–28
food and population, 217–18
food-energy intake (FEI), 33
Food for Education programme (FFE), 144, 165
Food-for-Work (FFW) programme, 76
food markets, 218
'food' security, 26
food self-sufficiency, 49
foreign direct investment (FDI), 12
foreign exchange gap, 10
Fullenkamp, C., 82
Fu, X., 130

Ganges–Kobadak Irrigation Project, 51–52
Gao, Y., 130
Gender Development Index (GDI), 30
Gender Inequality Index (GII), 30
generalized system of preferences (GSP), 109
Gertz, G., 199
Glennerster, R., 144
Global Financial Crisis (2007–09), 83
governance development, 227–28
government-to-government (G2G), 126
Graham, C., 199
Grameen approach, 152
Green Revolution (GR), 26
gross domestic product (GDP), 9–10
gross national income (GNI), 12
growth rates, Bangladesh, 8–9

handlooms of Bangladesh, 94–95
Harriss, B., 61
Hartmann, B., 153
Headey, D. D., 28, 167
'Hecksher–Ohlin industries', 140
higher than market price (HMP), 66
high-yielding seed varieties, 50
Hi-Tech Park Authority, 125
Hoddinott, J., 28
Hooper, L., 155
Hossain, A., 187, 193
Hossain, M., 90, 94, 109
hoteliers, 118
household decision-making power, 159
household expenditure survey (HES), 33
household income–expenditure survey (HIES), 33
Hulme, D., 155
Human Development Index (HDI), 30
Hunter, W. W., 120
Huq, S., 187, 193
Hussain, Z., 143, 160

Indian Civil Service (1945), 146
Indonesia, 138

infant mortality rate (IMR), 23, 44
information and communications technology (ICT), 18
Information Retrieval and Information Technology Enabled Services (IR-ITES) sector, 117–18
input supply-distribution system, 52
Institute of Microfinance (InM), 33
'integrated rural development' approach, 149
international arrivals (1995–2019), 119
International Centre for Diarrhoeal Disease Research, Bangladesh (ICDDRB), 161
International Food Policy Research Institute (IFPRI), 86
international migration, 190–91, 218–19
International Rice Research Institute (IRRI), 50
intrauterine device (IUD), 43
Iqbal, K., 96
irrigation revolution, 51–53

Jahangir, B. K., 154
Jahjah, S., 82
Jha, S., 82
Jou, S., 141

Kamal, G. M., 158–59
Kee, G., 130
key performance indicator (KPI), 109
khadi woven, 95
Khalily, M. A. B., 86
Khan, A. H., 146, 148
Khan, Z., 155, 157
Khandker, S. R., 86, 155–57
Kharas, H., 199
Kinnan, C., 144
Kochanek, S. A., 194
Kojima, K., 141
Kopicki, R., 61
Korea Republic, 139

Index

labour force survey (LFS), 85–86, 88, 202
labour productivity (LP), 109
Latif, M., 95
'Lean Manufacturing System', 109
least developed country (LDC), 8
Lee, J., 130
letter of credit (LC), 104
Li, D., 61
light engineering industry, 118
Lin, J. Y., 135
Liu, Y., 61
Local Government Engineering Department (LGED), 74
Local Government, Rural Development and Cooperatives (LGRDC), 162
Loke, Y., 155
'low cost solutions', role of, 161
low mobility score, 145

Mahbubullah, M., 153
Mahmood, R. A., 164
Mahmud, S., 144–45
Mahmud, W., 144, 155, 157
management information system (MIS), 43
Mannan, M. A., 153
Manriques, Fray Sebastião, 172–73
marital fertility rate, 42
Mascarenhas, A., 38
Maternal and Child Welfare Centres, 43
maternal mortality ratio, 24
Mears, L., 61
Meghna–Dhonagoda Project, 51
Meghna Industrial Economic Zone (MIEZ), 126
micro-credit revolution, 32, 58
micro-credit, role of, 157
microfinance, 58, 155–57
microfinance institution (MFI), 73
middle and affluent class (MAC), 119
middle class
   economic, educational and social dimensions, 199

profile of Dhaka in 2021, 203–07
from South Town to North Town, 201–03
migrant remittances, 78–79
migration rates, 78–79
millers, 62
milling sector, 67
mobile financial services (MFS), 58
mobile phones, 74–75
mobile telephony, 58
Mollah, Md. A. H., 131
Mondal, A. H., 126
Mongla Port, 37
Mookerji, R., 121
Morduch, J., 155–56
mother and child health (MCH), 44
mother and child health and family planning (MCH-FP) units, 43
motka fabrics, 95
Mughal Dhaka, 172–74
Mukherjee, Ramakrishna, 150
Multi-fibre Arrangement (MFA), 99
multinational corporation (MNC), 191
Murshid, K. A. S., 58, 61, 94
Muslim *bhadrolok* class, 200

Nash equilibrium, 60
National Board of Revenue (NBR), 12
National Drug Policy (1982), 188
National Nutritional Programme (NNP), 168
Nazimud-Doula, S., 187, 193
NGO revolution, 149–55
Nisbett, N., 28
non-clinical family planning services, 43
non-RMG sectors, 121–22
North, D. C., 59
nutrition, 167–68
nutritional status, 26

open market sale (OMS), 76
oral rehydration therapy (ORT), 44, 157
Organization of Economic Cooperation and Development (OECD), 18

Osmani, S. R., 155, 157
overseas development assistance (ODA), 12

Pabna Irrigation and Drainage Project, 51
paddy circuit, 63–64, 66
　growers' transactions, 70
　paddy *aratdars*, 70
Palmer-Jones, R., 155
panel data sets, 33
Parkinson, J. R., 38
Peng, Y., 61
Pettinato, S., 199
pharmaceuticals, 191–92
Phillips, J. F., 158–59
Picketty's 'Switch Points', 146
Pitt, M. M., 155–56
policy regime, 223–26
policy support, sector leaders, 104
population and family planning, 42–43
poverty, 32–35
Primary Education Stipend Programme (PESP), 165
'primary healthcare' (PHC) framework, 160
private and public investment, 11
public curative health system, 163–65
Public Food Distribution System (PFDS), 56
public food reserves, 49
public–private partnership (PPP), 126
purchasing power parity (PPP), 33

Qimiao, F., 161
Quader, Noorul, 100

Rahman, H. Z., 90
Rahman, M., 108
Rahman, Sheikh Mujibur, 38–39, 44
Raihan, S., 82
Rana Plaza fallout, 111–13
Rangpur Dinajpur Rural Service (RDRS), 151

Rao, N., 155
Rasheed, S., 143, 160
Ravallion, M., 38
ready-made garment (RMG). *See also* policy support
　export trends, 100–01
　micro-credit delivery, 102
　structure of production, 103
　supportive government policy, 101
　wages, 102
　workers, 102
real effective exchange rate (REER), 109
re-emergence of textiles, 107–10
remittances, 58, 74
Republic of Korea, 18
reputation, trust and reciprocity, 60
research and development (R&D), 117
'revealed preference' frameworks, 115
Rezawana, N., 187, 193
Riaz, A., 187
rice *aratdars*, 71
rice circuit, 67, 71
rice market, 55–56
rice retailers, 72
rice wholesalers, 72
RMG-led industrialization, 219–20
role of services, 16–22
Roodman, D., 155–56
Rooppur Nuclear Power Plant, 13
Roy, D. K., 104
'rules of origin' (ROO), 108
rural employment, agriculture and non-agriculture, 87
rural finance, 73–74
rural non-farm employment (RNFE), 88
rural non-farm (RNF) sector
　'Blue Revolution', 96
　domestic remittances, 85
　employment in, 86–88
　goods and services, 96
　marine fisheries, 97
　public investments and NGOs, 97
　rural incomes, 88–94
rural roads, 58, 74

Index

Samad, H. A., 86, 94, 155, 157
'samitization' process, 152
sampling technique, 63
Saqui, Q. Md. H., 150, 153
Savoia, A., 144
school enrolment, 29–31
Secondary Education Development Programme (SEDP), 166
sectoral growth rates, 42
sectoral shares of GDP, 15, 41
seed and fertilizer distribution, 50
Sen, B., 90, 92, 202
Seventh Five-Year Plan 2020, 74
Seventh Plan period (2016–20), 74
SEZ experience, 125–27
Shahid Khandker, 94
Shah, N. M., 145
shallow tube well (STW), 52–53
Shanghai Pilot Free Trade Zone, 131
Shao, L., 130
Siddique, K., 187, 193
small and medium enterprises (SME) sector, 125
'Snatch' game, 59–60
Sobhan, R., 193
Social Marketing Project, 43
social sectors, 222
South Asian Association for Regional Cooperation (SAARC), 108
special bonded warehouse (SBW), 104–05
special economic zone (SEZ), 12
state-owned enterprise (SOE), 123
　benefits of, 134
　Chinese/Vietnamese models, 135
　nationalization, 131
　privatization, 131
　profits and losses, 133–34
　'state capitalism', 135
state policy reforms, 75–76
'statutory rationing', 42
structural adjustment, 32
structure–conduct–performance literature, 61

student–teacher ratios over time, 31
Sugiyarto, G., 82
'Survey of Damages and Repairs', 38

Taylor, J., 120
tetanus toxoid immunization, 44
textiles and clothing (T&C) sector, 108, 110
Thailand, 138
Thana Central Cooperative Association (TCCA), 147–48
Thana Drainage and Roads Works Programme, 147
thana health complex (THC), 43
Thana Irrigation Programme, 147
Thana Training and Development Centre (TTDC), 147
'The Analysis of Poverty Trends' Project, 90
tied transactions
　dhaner upore rate over time, 69
　risks of, 69
　tying loans, 68
　types of, 68
total fertility rate (TFR), 158
total reserves, months of imports, 13
trade liberalization, 32
Trade-Related Aspects of Intellectual Property Rights (TRIPS), 117
traditional birth attendant (TBA), 44, 157–58
traditional boat builders, 121
Transforming Secondary Education for Results (TSER), 166
trends in rural poverty, 34
trust-enhancing institutions, 59–60

Umbricht, Viktor, 38
unexploded ordnance (UXO), 183
UNICEF framework, 168
United Nations Relief Operations in Dhaka (UNROD), 38
Urban Primary Health Care Project (UPHCP), 162–63

USAID-funded study (USAID 2019)
  healthcare sector, 116
  pharmaceutical sector, 117

value-added tax (VAT), 12
Van Asselt, J., 92
Vietnam, 136–38
Village Agricultural and Industrial Programme (V-AID), 146–47
village/cluster of villages, 150
'Village Organizations' (VO), 151–52
Vulnerable Group Development (VGD), 75

wage earners' scheme (WES), 81
Walton, electronic company, 119–20
Walton Hi-Tech Industries, 120

Wharton, C. R. Jr., 61
white-collar occupations (2016–17), 203
women's empowerment, 31, 165–67
women's mobility, 159
working class, 207–09
work-in-process (WIP) inventory, 109
World Bank, 12, 33, 40, 54, 82–83, 132, 161, 218

Yeung, Y., 130
Yosef, S., 28
Yunus, M., 126

Zilibotti, F., 130
Zuenko, Sergey Pavlovich, 37